Mother's Century
A Survivor, Her People and Her Times

Also by Richard L. Hermann

Encounters: Ten Appointments with History (Persimmon Alley Press)

Manufacturing Business and the Law (American Bar Association—ABA)

Practicing Law in Small-Town America (ABA)

Landing a Federal Legal Job (ABA)

Managing Your Legal Career (ABA)

From Lemons to Lemonade in the New Legal Job Market
(Lawyers Avenue Press)

The Lawyer's Guide to Job Security (Kaplan Publishing)

The Lawyer's Guide to Finding Success in Any Job Market (Kaplan Publishing)

JD Preferred: 600+ Things You Can Do With a Law Degree
(Other Than Practice Law) (Federal Reports Inc.)

The ALJ Handbook: An Insider's Guide to Becoming a Federal Administrative
Law Judge (Federal Reports Inc.)

The 110 Biggest Mistakes Jobhunters Make (And How to Avoid Them)
[co-author: Linda P. Sutherland] (Federal Reports Inc.)

21st Century Legal Career Series (H Watson LLC)

Vol. 1 – Data Protection Practice: The Brave New Legal World
Vol. 2 – Careers in Compliance: JDs Wanted
Vol. 3 – Health Law: Career Opportunities in a Fast-Changing Environment
Vol. 4 – Energy Law: Fueling a Dynamic Legal Career
Vol. 5 – "Soft" Intellectual Property Law: IP Opportunities
    for Non-STEM Attorneys
Vol. 6 – Risk Management: The Indispensable Profession
Vol. 7 – The Administrative Law Revolution: Learning to Litigate
    in a Forgiving Environment
Vol. 8 – Digital Assets Practice: Three New Practice Opportunities in One
Vol. 9 – The Education Sector: Overwhelmed by the Law
Vol. 10 – Law Teaching and Training: Law School and Way Beyond
Vol. 11 – Insurance Careers for Attorneys: Opportunity in Expected-
    and Unexpected-Places
Vol. 12 – JD Advantage Jobs in Corporations: Expanding the Legal Function
Vol. 13 – Tricks of the Trade (and Professional) Associations: A Huge "Hidden" Legal Job
    Market
Vol. 14 – Planes, Trains, and Automobiles: The Transformation of Transportation Law
Vol. 15 – I, Robot Lawyer: Opportunities in Robotics Law and Artificial Intelligence
Vol. 16 – Financial Services: A World of Evolving Opportunities
Vol. 17 – Elder Law: Riding the Age Wave
Vol. 18 – Non-Traditional Family Law: Serving the "New Normal"

Mother's Century
A Survivor, Her People and Her Times

Richard L. Hermann

Persimmon Alley Press
Arlington, VA
www.persimmonalleypress.com

Copyright © 2018 by Richard L. Hermann

All rights reserved. No part of this book may be reproduced in any form or by any electronic or mechanical means, including information storage and retrieval systems, without written permission from the author, except in the case of a reviewer, who may quote brief passages embodied in critical articles or in a review.

Published by Persimmon Alley Press
Cover design by David E. Manuel

All images and cover photographs property of Richard L. Hermann or from Public Domain

Library of Congress Control Number: 2018959377

ISBN: 978-0-9991366-1-4

Acknowledgements

First, to my mother Margarete Sobel Hermann, both the inspiration for and the fulcrum of this book, who deferred until her hundredth year to relate her life story.

My father, Ernest Hermann, whose tales of his youth and young adulthood in Europe were always a source of exotic fascination; and whose wise judgment and decisiveness were traits I greatly admired and hope reside somewhere in my DNA and that of my children and grandchildren.

My grandparents, David and Ernestine Sobel and Solomon Hermann. David would put me to bed every night when I was a child. I fell asleep listening to his tales of growing up in rural Poland (now Ukraine). Ernestine died when I was only five years old. My memories of her are of hugs and kisses. Solomon's surviving 14 bloody World War I battles on the brutal Isonzo Front is a source of wonder.

My great-grandparents, Liber and Julie Lapajowker, who perished at Auschwitz/Birkenau in 1944. I never knew them, but they lived in my mother's heart for the remaining 63 years of her life and she brought them alive for me.

My aunt, Rose Williams, my mother's sister and closest friend, did not quite make it to her hundredth birthday, missing by only 140 days. The fire that took her life was lit when she fell asleep in her favorite reading chair with a lighted cigarette in her hand. The fire occurred almost exactly four years after her sister's death. Rose died a little over three weeks later. Twenty minutes before she died, she regained consciousness for the only time since the fire, opened her eyes, looked at me and squeezed my hand.

My late uncle, Otto Sorel (he changed his name from "Sobel" upon reaching America and after reading Stendhal's *The Red and the Black*, which features Julien Sorel), whose three days of deathbed conversations with me provided a great deal of insight and perspective about the family, especially his sister, my mother. It was the only time this reserved and somewhat repressed man opened himself up to me.

My son, David Hermann, and my daughter, Elizabeth Hermann Smith, who provided "filler" material about their grandmother, sharing stories she told them of which I was unaware.

My cousins Lucy Spector, James Friend, Michael Hirsley, Clare Vlazny, and Lana Hirschl who provided me with some history about the family.

My wife, Anne Hermann, whose indulgence of my writing, and whose advice and wise counsel has nurtured me through eleven books and, hopefully, more to come. She was also privy to some stories my mother told her that I did not know.

My friends Michele Shomaker and David Gilson, who gave many hours during which they could have accomplished useful projects in order to read the manuscript and make hundreds of valuable suggestions that found their way into the final draft.

Finally, the dedicated staffs of the Leo Baeck Institute, Jerusalem's *Yad Vashem* holocaust memorial museum, the United States Holocaust Memorial Museum, the International Tracing Service, and the National Archives of the United States for access to their collections and their staffs' telephonic and email guidance.

To my "bookends:"

My mother Margarete "Grete" Sobel Hermann, the protagonist of this book, who gave me life and shared with me the richness of her life.

My grandson Julian Marcus Hermann, so that he and his generation will know of his great-grandmother and keep her memory and those of her generation, its trials and its ideals, alive . . . and profit from their example. This is my—and her—legacy to him.

Contents

Introduction	1
Part One: Vienna, 1905-1934	
Chapter 1. The Calendar Turns	9
Chapter 2. The World's Magnet	14
Chapter 3. Antecedents	18
Chapter 4. Shrinks	29
Chapter 5. Vindobona and Its Jews	33
Chapter 6. Angst	41
Chapter 7. Sclerosis	46
Chapter 8. Leopoldstadt	49
Chapter 9. The Wienerwald	51
Chapter 10. Sarajevo	54
Chapter 11. The War to End All Wars	61
Chapter 12. Privation	66
Chapter 13. The Spoilage of War	73
Chapter 14. Aftermath	77
Chapter 15. Rump State	84
Chapter 16. Intermezzo: Post-War Austrian Politics	91
Chapter 17. Prosperity Returns (Briefly)	102
Chapter 18. Education	104
Chapter 19. Graduation	107
Chapter 20. Musical Interlude	110
Chapter 21. Rejection	113
Chapter 22. Numerus Clausus	116
Chapter 23. Religion	121
Chapter 24. Medical School	126
Chapter 25. Smitten	141
Chapter 26. Hospitant, Aspirant, Rezident	143
Chapter 27. Crash	149

Chapter 28. Sanatorium   151
Chapter 29. The Practice   154

Part Two: Vienna, 1934-1939

Chapter 30. Setting the Stage   161
Chapter 31. Portents from the North   164
Chapter 32. The Downward Slide   167
Chapter 33. Anschluss   171
Chapter 34. The Taming of the Jews   175
Chapter 35. Ernst Escapes   179
Chapter 36. Closing the Vice   182
Chapter 37. The Noose Tightens   187
Chapter 38. The Summer of '38   192
Chapter 39. Kristallnacht—The Night of Broken Glass   197
Chapter 40. Blood, Not Religion   208
Chapter 41. Implementing Mass Murder   218
Chapter 42. Getting Out   222
Chapter 43. Getting In   233
Chapter 44. War   245
Chapter 45. The Final Solution Hits Home   251
Chapter 46. Mountbatten and Marriage   258
Chapter 47. Endgame   268
Chapter 48. Reckoning   273
Chapter 49. Selective Punishment   276

Part Three: Bi-Coastal, 1939–1948

Chapter 50. In Transit   281
Chapter 51. The New World   284
Chapter 52. Following Her Heart   288
Chapter 53. It Was San Andreas' Fault   290
Chapter 54. Choosing Poorly   295
Chapter 55. Searching for Shangri-La   297

Part Four: Small-Town America, 1948–1978

Chapter 56. Into the Provinces   303
Chapter 57. The Chosen People in the Chosen Place   313

Chapter 58. Friends	315
Chapter 59. Refugee Quest	318
Chapter 60. American Provincial	328
Chapter 61. Making It in America	332
Chapter 62. Going Back	343
Chapter 63. Madly for Adlai	349
Chapter 64. Books	352
Chapter 65. Caring	354
Chapter 66. Suddenly It's 1960!	360
Chapter 67. November 21, 1963	364
Chapter 68. College Unbound	366
Chapter 69. The Sixties	368
Chapter 70. Animal Magnetism	375
Chapter 71. Enemy Territory	379

Part Five: Miami Beach, 1978-1994

Chapter 72. Following the Sun	383
Chapter 73. The Impact of the Florida Phenomenon	391
Chapter 74. Gloom Over Miami	394

Part Six: Arlington, 1994–2007

Chapter 75. Final Relocation	399
Chapter 76. Dad Departs	402
Chapter 77. Decline	404
Chapter 78. Maternal Vignettes	409
Chapter 79. Eulogy	421
Epilogue	427
Illustrations follow pages 70, 88, 194, 292, 341, 389, and 406	
Bibliography	429
About the Author	441

Introduction

"Man-made catastrophes such as wars, revolutions, persecutions, hijackings, etc., not only reveal what is worst in human nature, in some people at least, they also release what is best."
                                         Anna Freud

"The whole of human history is a Holocaust."
                                 Isaac Bashevis Singer
            (April 14, 1987 interview with Mark Kurlansky)

"Science presently placed novel and dangerous facilities in the hands of the most powerful countries. Humanity was informed that it could make machines that would fly through the air and vessels which could swim beneath the surface of the seas. Certainly it was a marvelous and romantic event . . . This vast expansion was unhappily not accompanied by any noticeable advance in the stature of man, either in his mental faculties, or his moral character. His brain got no better, but it buzzed the more . . . Our need was to discipline an array of gigantic and turbulent facts. To this task we have certainly so far proved unequal . . ."
                     Winston Churchill (speech at MIT), 1949

"Freedom's just another word for nothing left to lose."
                                       Kris Kristofferson

"The 'Chosen People?' Chosen for what?"
                           Margarete Sobel Hermann (2005)

The narrative arc of this book, more than ten years in the making, is primarily the story of my mother, Margarete "Grete" Sobel Hermann, and of both the people she loved and the times she lived through during her more than 100 years on Earth. Her story is, in many respects, the story of the 20th century. She was born in 1905, at the end of one era and the beginning of another, and died over 100 years later in 2007, at the end of another era and the beginning of a new century.

When I was a little boy growing up, my parents made me stand in the corner when I misbehaved. I never minded that—although I made a pretense of objecting and putting up a big fuss—because I eagerly sought that punishment. The punishment corner contained a cabinet the top drawer of which was stuffed with family pictures. My parents did not seem to notice that I spent my frequent "time-outs" rummaging through this trove, staring at relatives whom I had never met, many of them frozen in time in the nineteenth and early twentieth centuries.

I spent hours in that corner and many more pondering who these mysterious people were. It did not occur to me until my early teens to inquire. My parents' rather reluctant responses to my questions about the photographs were my earliest exposure to what the world now calls "the Holocaust."

Today my parents are both gone. My father died in 1996 at age 91 after difficult years of increasing dementia that transformed a highly intelligent, vibrant individual into a shell of his former self. My mother, in contrast, was sharp as ever to the very end. Those good genes run in the distaff side of her family. My mother's sister, Rose, celebrated her 99th birthday in 2010 by reading one of the 7-8 books she took out of the library every week. Rose had been a chain smoker since 1926. She never contracted a smoker's cough. Other than an occasional aspirin for arthritis, she was never on any of the usual medications that accompany old age. Absent a fatal fire four years and one day after my mother died, Aunt Rose surely would have outlived even her sister.

All of those pictures in that corner drawer now belong to me. I ponder them periodically, wondering what became of these mysterious people who dressed oddly and looked so unmodern. I know many of them were erased by the Nazis and their East European minions.

My mother lived in America for 68 years, but she was never able to acclimatize herself to the easy way in which Americans spill their guts to each other about the most intimate details of their lives. Tell-all books, magazine articles, and television talk shows where "celebrities" reveal their deepest, darkest, most sordid secrets for their titillated audiences disgusted her. Consequently, squeezing any personal information out of her at all was difficult.

What made this book possible was a series of oral history tapes that I persuaded her to make when she was 99 years old, with me as the interrogator, in order to help my daughter with a college project. Elizabeth prepared a set of questions for me to use to coax Grandma to describe her life and immigrant experiences.

It worked. My mother would do anything for her grandchildren, even suspending her discomfort at talking about herself. What ensued was a riveting, four-month exercise. The transcribed tapes that resulted became the backbone of, and impetus for, this book.

This "mosaic" is the story of an ordinary woman who lived an extraordinary life in the most turbulent of times. The book travels through my mother's century—both her hundred-plus years and the parallel years of her twentieth century, back and forth between her own story and that of her era.

There were certain things my mother would not talk to me about and which, consequently, do not make it into this volume. Her interrogation by Adolf Eichmann upon being arrested by the Gestapo, when he was the director of Vienna's Zentralstelle für Jüdische Auswanderung (Central Office of Jewish Emigration) in 1938, was something she refused to discuss. Eichmann, of course, went on to become the most famous Nazi war criminal of the post-World War II era. While in hiding in Argentina after the war, he was tracked down and captured by the Israeli Mossad, and subsequently tried and executed by Israel in 1962 for crimes against humanity. Years later, I argued with the late professor Hannah Arendt, whose best-selling book, The Banality of Evil, about Eichmann's arrest, trial, and execution contended that it was all a pointless exercise in futility. Mindful of my mother's arrest and three-day incarceration by the Gestapo, the particulars of which she refused to talk about, I maintained otherwise.

She was arrested in summer 1938 for illegally practicing medicine in violation of the Nazi decree prohibiting Jewish doctors, first from treating non-Jews and later from practicing at all. One of her Gentile patients turned her in after she performed an abortion. I knew about this only from overhearing conversations between my parents, as well as from one of her brothers, but did not press her on it during our taping, knowing how uncomfortable it made her. I suspect that some very bad things happened to her during those 72 hours at the mercy of the Gestapo: my mother at age 32 was a striking woman.

This book encompasses Grete's entire life. The focus of the first two-thirds of its pages is on the first one-third of her history, when she lived in Vienna and endured the privations and difficulties that shaped her.

While the Holocaust necessarily occupies a central place in both mother's history and the twentieth century, it was by no means the only existential challenge she had to overcome. Growing up Austrian in the first four decades of the century meant a series of survival tests: World War I, the collapse of a 500-year old empire, starvation, runaway inflation, the Great Depression, political chaos, Socialists and Fascists battling in the streets, domestic terrorism, the Anschluss, the Nuremberg Laws, Kristallnacht, the desperate urgency to escape from certain death, and finally, adjusting to a new life in a new country speaking a new language and doing so without any public assistance. Mother did all of this with exceptional bravery, grit, resourcefulness, and class.

Mother was eight when Gavrilo Princip murdered Archduke Franz Ferdinand, the unloved heir-by-default to the Austro-Hungarian throne, in Sarajevo. She was 12 when Vladimir Ulyanov, a.k.a. Lenin, facilitated by Germany, traveled to St. Petersburg in a sealed train, where he launched the Bolshevik Revolution. She was 14 when the Treaty of Versailles was signed; 21 when Charles Lindbergh landed in Paris and became the third person with The Right Stuff (Alcock and Brown preceded him across the pond, to minimal acclaim), Babe Ruth was swatting home runs, and Bobby Jones was winning Grand Slams. She was 27 when the former postcard painter who was living in Vienna when she was born came to power in Germany and turned the world upside down. She was 32 when Der Führer marched triumphantly into Vienna to the cheers of a delirious multitude. She was 33 when she escaped the noose tightening around Europe and came to the United States. She was 39 when she married, and almost 41 when her only child was born. She was 52 when the 28-lb tiny ball called Sputnik announced the dawn of a new era, and 58 when John Fitzgerald Kennedy's assassination announced the end of post-war innocence. She was 62 when her son graduated from college four days after the assassination of another political leader, Robert Francis Kennedy, whom she expected to give the baccalaureate address at graduation, and 63 when her son left her in tears at a snowed-in airport for the Army and an uncertain destiny.

She was 68 when the Arabs turned off the spigot, and 75 when the Republicans moved hard right and began whittling away at the Liberal hegemony. She was 83 when the father of her son's college lab partner was elected the 41st president of the United States, and 95 when the lab partner himself made it to the pinnacle of American power.

She lived through both the greatest runaway inflation the world has ever seen and the Great Depression. She endured and survived the Holocaust and was a pained observer of many more modeled on the first one. She witnessed more political assassinations than she can count, and stayed around from the administrations of Theodore Roosevelt through George W. Bush and the intervening sixteen men who served as president of the United States during her lifetime.

This book project began as my attempt to tell a "micro" story—my mother's life—woven into the backdrop of her century's "macro" story. I quickly realized that what I was really doing—as I noted earlier—was a cathartic attempt to pay homage to a remarkable person who, to me and to many others who encountered her, exemplified the best that human evolution has achieved; but also to come to grips with my own guilt about my good fortune in avoiding the catastrophes that marked my mother's life.

Part One
Vienna, 1905-1934

"The streets of Vienna are paved with culture, the streets of other cities with asphalt."
Karl Kraus

"The paradox of anti-Semitism is that it is invariably up to the Jews to explain away the charges. The anti-Semite simply has to make them."
Jack Schwartz

"I dream of giving birth to a child who will ask, 'Mother, what was war?'"
Eve Merriam
Kris Kristofferson

Chapter 1
The Calendar Turns

It is still debatable when the twentieth century really began. Most historians have concluded that the chronological commencement was at a time that was still steeped in the nineteenth century, attitudinally and otherwise. Their preferred starting date is 1905, the year of my mother's birth.

Russia Heralds the New Century

In January 1905, three events took place in Russia that demarcated the new century.

1. On January 1, the Trans-Siberian Railway was inaugurated, linking the eleven time zones of the world's largest country from the Polish border in the west to Vladivostok in the far east.
2. The next day, Russian General Anatoly Stoessel surrendered to the Japanese Imperial Army at Port Arthur in China, auguring the end of the Russo-Japanese War and marking the first time that an Asian country had defeated a Western power. The fighting continued for several more months, resulting in massive Russian losses (200,000 casualties in March 1905 alone).
3. The third event signified a portent so ominous that the world would spend the rest of the twentieth century dealing with the Pandora's Box it opened. A week after the Russian surrender at Port Arthur, 80,000 workers went on strike in St.

Petersburg. Their leaders petitioned the Tsar—their revered "Little Father" who could not, in their view, possibly know what his functionaries were committing in his name—for relief from grinding poverty and intolerable working conditions. But Tsar Nicholas II was a weak, pathetic personality, undereducated, easily influenced by corrupt courtiers and relatives, and henpecked by his domineering wife, Alexandra. In short, he was completely unsuited to deal with the earth-shattering events buffeting him and his far-flung realm.

On January 22, a peaceful march to the Tsar's Winter Palace by 140,000 workers and their families to petition for better working conditions ended in horror. The Tsar's Cossacks tried to push back the crowd with whips, but there were too many demonstrators to be handled that "gently." So the Cossacks began using their swords—flats first. This also did not have the desired effect. Next, they sealed the doom of Holy Russia and the Romanov dynasty by opening fire. Over 500 men, women and children were murdered that Bloody Sunday. That fatal mistake drove the survivors away from the palace and, ultimately, into the arms of the extreme radicals who manipulated their rage to come to power and turn Russia and the planet upside down and inside out for most of the remaining years of the century.

The next day, the now militant workers called a general strike. Within a week, 30 more workers were shot and civil unrest spread. Next, the Tsar's police went after dissident intellectuals, imprisoning such luminaries as the writer Maxim Gorky, thus radicalizing them and transforming their powerful pens into implacable foes of the regime.

The Tsar tried to make amends on February 1 when he met with a delegation of workers. However, he only made matters worse by stupidly saying:

"I believe in the honest feelings of the working people and in their unshakable loyalty to me. *Therefore, I forgive them.*" [italics mine]

The situation deteriorated as the year progressed. On February 17, the Tsar's uncle and close advisor, Grand Duke Sergei Aleksandrovich, was assassinated as he rode into the Kremlin in his carriage. The bomb throwers had warned Duke Sergei's wife not to ride with him that morning. She begged off, but neglected to alert her husband to the warning.

On March 3, the Tsar agreed to the establishment of a Duma, an elected parliament. Five days later, a peasant revolt spread to Georgia in the Caucasus. The next day, Parisian bankers stopped loaning money to Russia.

Invariably, the Jews became the convenient scapegoat for the Russian government's ineptitude. Right-wing newspapers were encouraged by the government to incite anti-Semitic agitation in order to divert the workers' anger at the government against the Jews and to depict the revolutionaries as Jews. Pogroms were launched in the Jewish Pale of Settlement (the narrow strip of territory where Jews were permitted to reside), creating a reign of terror throughout the Jewish community. Over 2,000 Jews were killed, many more raped and mutilated, and thousands of Jewish shops, homes and synagogues were looted, destroyed, and burned.

The iniquities visited upon Russia's Jews spurred 1.2 million of them to emigrate, primarily to Palestine and the United States, thus sparing them and their descendants the greater twentieth century horrors to come.

Russia's problems continued to escalate throughout the year. In late June, revolutionary sailors on the battleship *Potemkin* in Odessa harbor on the Black Sea mutinied, massacred the captain and most of the officers, and hoisted the red flag of revolution.

Russia never recovered. What happened to it was a profound delineation, the end of one era and the beginning of another one of great uncertainty and ominous forebodings.

Elsewhere

The rest of the world did not sit idly by in 1905 observing events in Russia. Germany foretold World War I when the Kaiser visited Morocco, a blatant provocation to France, Morocco's European "protector." This "First Moroccan Crisis" would be followed several years later by an even bolder and more reckless German challenge when the German gunboat *Panther* made port in Agadir on the Moroccan coast. The Second Moroccan Crisis pushed Britain and France together against Germany since the Brits viewed the *Panther*'s visit as a challenge to British naval supremacy.

The United States, blissfully isolated from the European and Asian mayhem by two vast oceans, witnessed the marriage of sixth cousins Franklin and Eleanor Roosevelt (the bride was given away by her uncle, President Theodore). Behind the shield of the Monroe Doctrine and its Roosevelt Corollary, which asserted an American right to intervene militarily to keep European nations out of Latin America, the U.S. wrested Panama from Colombia in order to have free rein to build a canal linking the Atlantic and Pacific oceans.

My mother was born on September 24, 1905, 19 days after President Roosevelt mediated the Treaty of Portsmouth that ended the Russo-Japanese War, winning himself a Nobel Peace Prize. The world into which she was born was in the middle of a transformation from the placid, peaceful nineteenth century to the tumultuous maelstrom of the twentieth.

Only 22 months before her birth, the Wright Brothers flew a heavier-than-air craft 40 yards across a North Carolina sand dune. The automobile was just emerging. Four years before her birth, Guglielmo Marconi transmitted the first radio signal across the Atlantic. These three disruptive, transformational technologies would leave their indelible mark on her century.

My mother was born into a century that would take violence to a new level. Russia was not the only place seething as the new baby took her first breath.

In Germany's African territories the natives, tired of being brutalized by their imperial overseers, rebelled. The Germans established concentration camps in their unruly African possessions to try to force the rebel tribesmen to surrender. They learned about the value of such camps from the British, who had invented the concept during the Boer War in South Africa a few short years before.

On India's Northwest Frontier, the natives were fired into frenzy by fanatical Muslim mullahs. Rival claimants to the Moroccan throne battled each other, prompting France to intervene militarily.

In her own Austria, the Habsburg Empire's outlier nations agitated for greater autonomy and even outright independence. Romanians, Hungarians, Poles, Czechs, South Slavs and Italians all wanted out. The Empire, led by its aging, increasingly disconnected Kaiser Franz Josef, a man who by 1905 had lost everyone dear to him to violence, was unable to keep itself together. More than any other place on Earth, Imperial Vienna clung by her fingernails to the waning nineteenth century lifestyle.

September was hardly more peaceful than the first eight months of that tumultuous year. An earthquake in Italy killed several thousand people; Sweden and Norway became separate countries; and Armenians and Tartars battled over jobs and ethnic hostility on the Baku oil fields. On the plus side, Arthur Koestler, one of my mother's favorite writers, and Greta Garbo, her favorite actress (outside of Hedy Lamarr), also entered the world.

Perhaps the most optimistic development of the year was the founding of the Audubon Society. Could there still be hope for a world where someone thinks it is important to protect birds?

Chapter 2
The World's Magnet

In the run-up to the First World War, Vienna had achieved a certain prominence among the world's great cities. It was home to the three giants of the new discipline of psychotherapy—Sigmund Freud, Karl Jung and Alfred Adler. It remained the music capital of the world, home to Gustav Mahler, Arnold Schoenberg, Alben Berg and Anton von Webern among its melodic (or not, depending on how you rate the 12-tone scale) luminaries. It was one of the leading art centers of the planet, featuring the innovative works and experimentation designed to shock society of Gustav Klimt, Egon Schiele, Oskar Kokoschka and Fernand Khnopff, who was in love with his sister and portrayed her as a tigress in a tight-fitting outfit and as a leopard tempting a naked youth. Provocateurs all. Vienna was also the epicenter of architectural ferment, dazzled by the creations of Adolf Loos and Otto Wagner. Karl Kraus, Robert Musil, Arthur Schnitzler and Joseph Roth were among the greatest writers of their era, experimenting on the precipice of societal propriety and even madness.

My mother, like so many Viennese of her generation, found that her attitudes toward life, society, humanity and the new century were heavily influenced by every one of these genres, if not by every exemplar I mentioned above. Freud, for example, gave the world the gift of "hysteria" which, for my parents, became the convenient explanation for an array of psychological maladies that afflicted relatives and friends. Mahler was a god to my father who kept the composer's picture prominently displayed in every one of his residences until the day he died. (In his honor, we still keep Mahler's fading portrait hanging on our wall.) The atonal trio of Schoenberg, Berg and von Webern however, did not impress Grete at all. The "Secessionist" artists—the mavericks Gustav Klimt, Koloman Moser, Josef Hoffmann, Oskar Kokoschka, Egon Schiele and other lesser luminaries—were all the rage in *fin-de siècle* Vienna and favorites of my parents. Grete was also a great fan of Marcel Proust and Thomas Hardy, whose works she returned to many times during her life.

Vienna was also a center of political ferment. One of the oddities of the politically moribund Habsburg Empire was its attraction as a haven for radical political dissidents and malcontents. In 1913 alone, Vienna was simultaneously home to Adolf Hitler, Vladimir Lenin, Josef Stalin, Lev Bronstein (soon to be "reincarnated" as Leon Trotsky) and Josip Broz (a.k.a. "Tito"), all of whom went on to become twentieth century paragons of unimaginable butchery and brutality. In January 1913, they all dined at one time or another at Vienna's Café Central (also a favorite of Sigmund Freud) If you aspired to become a brutal dictator later in life—or to psychoanalyze them—then Vienna was a must stop before the First World War.

Dichotomy and Decline

At the same time, Vienna was hurtling rapidly toward the abyss. The Habsburgs, the oldest continuous dynasty in the world (dating to 1246), whose territorial gains and great power status came principally through shrewd marriages rather than wars of conquest, was nearing the end of its almost 700-year run.

The dichotomy between political decay and decline and aesthetic apex was stark. No other city in the world could claim the intellectual ferment that roiled Vienna in the years leading up to the First World War. No other city could brag about the brainpower and creative fireworks that Vienna produced at the same time it was unraveling politically.

When mother was born, Kaiser Franz Josef had been on the throne for almost sixty years, ever since the revolutionary year of 1848. When he came to the Imperial throne at age 18, his empire was the largest and wealthiest in Europe. When he left the scene in 1916, it was a pale shadow of its past glories. Within three years of his death, his polyglot empire of Germans, Hungarians, Czechs, Slovaks, Ukrainians, Poles, Croatians, Slovenes, Serbs, Kossovars, Bosnians, Romanians and Italians had disappeared from the map. Non-German speakers comprised almost 70 percent of the old Empire. What remained was a pathetic remnant that did not even include all of the German speakers of the former empire.

Franz Josef's life was framed by ultra-conservatism and incredible tragedy. He married young, to his first cousin Elizabeth, a princess of the Bavarian Wittelsbach dynasty. She was universally considered the most beautiful woman in Europe. Elizabeth, however, was nervous, high-strung, and very restless. She bore five children, four daughters (one died in infancy) and a son. However, she had little to do with her children's upbringing, hamstrung by an unforgiving mother-in-law and an overbearing aunt. Consequently, she quickly became bored and increasingly stayed away from Vienna, wandering aimlessly around Europe.

The Kaiser, the very definition of a dour fellow, was made more so by insisting on sleeping every night on an uncomfortable military camp bed and spending most of his waking hours working at his desk. For all his effort, he learned very little about his realm or conditions affecting ordinary people within it.

The incessant personal tragedies he suffered did little to help his attitude or demeanor. His younger brother Maximilian, installed in 1864 as Emperor of Mexico, was deposed by Benito Juarez three years later and executed by a firing squad in 1867. His only son and heir, Crown Prince Rudolf, allegedly killed himself and his mistress, the voluptuous, 17-year old Maria Vetsera, at the royal hunting lodge at Mayerling deep in the Vienna Woods in 1889. To this day, conspiracy theorists wallow in the uncertainty of how and why the Crown Prince met his end. Franz Josef's wife, the Empress Elizabeth, was assassinated by an Italian anarchist on Geneva's lakeside promenade in 1898. Despite their separate lives, he was devastated by her loss. His wife's nephew, King Louis of Bavaria (a.k.a. "Crazy Ludwig"), who built the Disney-like castle of *Neuschwanstein*, killed his handler-psychiatrist and then was found dead in mysterious circumstances floating in Lake Starnberg. Finally, the Kaiser lost his "replacement" heir, his unlikeable nephew Franz Ferdinand, to assassination in Sarajevo in June 1914, the event that triggered World War I.

When he died in 1916 at age 85, this mid-19th century relic had ruled longer than any of his Habsburg forebears and longer than any other European ruler ever outside of Louis XIV.

Sensing that their era could not last, the Viennese partied hard. Vienna was vibrant, gay, joyful, decadent and unheeding of what lay just around the corner.

Chapter 3
Antecedents

Grandpa David

Grandpa David, in contrast to his wife (see below), was resilient like no one I have ever encountered. He had to be.

I was blessed to know him for 15 years during which he became both my best friend and greatest fan. When he lived with us or visited, he always put me to bed and told me stories about growing up in Poland. When I stepped off the school bus a block-and-a-half from home, he would be there. Every day we stopped at the candy store and he bought me a Three Musketeers bar (for a nickel!). As he held my hand for the short walk home, he always said: "Don't tell mama about the candy bar."

David wore his emotions on his sleeve, but they never went particularly deep. He had a remarkable ability to rebound from adversity, something that he had plenty of experience with throughout his life. This kind of superficiality is not a bad thing. On the contrary, it is probably healthy for sorrow not to go too deep. Unfortunately, Grete did not inherit that particular gene. She internalized her sorrows and they ate at her despite her stoic external demeanor.

During his 45 years in Vienna, David immersed himself in work tempered by evening visits to his favorite coffee houses where he played cards with his cronies, exchanged tall stories, and tippled more than a little *schnapps*. He resorted to this kind of therapy whenever life dealt him a bad hand.

David died on my fifteenth birthday when he was 81. He had just undergone a major surgical procedure and was too impatient to remain confined to his hospital bed. The day after the surgery, he leaped out of bed, strained his heart to the breaking point, and expired on the hospital floor. A half-century later, I still miss him terribly.

David was born in 1880 in the Jewish *shtetl* of *Jezierzany* (or *Jezerzianka*) in the Polish province of Galicia (now well within Ukraine), southeast of *Lvov* (now *Lviv*), and lived there the first 13 years of his life. Galicia was the most distant (500+ miles from Vienna) and most backward province of the Austro-Hungarian Empire. It was a violent border land straddling Poland and Ukraine and had spent its history bouncing back-and-forth between Poland, Prussia, Russia, Lithuania and Austria-Hungary. At various times, it was occupied—pillaged is more accurate—by Scythians, Alans, Avars, Huns, Tatars, Bulgars, Ruthenians, Magyars, Ottoman Turks and other nomadic tribes who roamed across Eurasia plundering, raping and killing. All of this to-ing-and-fro-ing made for an impossibly complicated nomenclature history, and Jezierzany, like so many communities in Eastern Europe, has been called by many names and victimized by innumerable spellings over its long history.

When David was born, Polish was the principal language of Galicia with Ukrainian and Ruthenian close behind. David grew up speaking Polish and some Yiddish.

His people were mainly subsistence farmers, but in good years they were able to take their produce to Lvov and sell it at local outdoor markets. It was a hardscrabble existence, but the family always had enough to eat . . . in the good years.

Galicia was, however, largely dirt poor and conditions steadily deteriorated when David was a child. Its impoverished Jewish peasantry began to leave *en masse* in the 1880s, prompted by government-encouraged pogroms that blamed the Jews for bad harvests, with the first wave of Jews heading for Germany. Many also went to the United States and Brazil. A smaller but still significant number went to Vienna, including one of David's older brothers. In all, several hundred thousand Jewish peasants left the region during the decade.

The good years became fewer and were overtaken by a succession of very bad ones in the late 1880s and early 1890s. The pogroms escalated and caused considerable anguish for shtetl inhabitants. David's first beatings came at the hands of frenzied Christian peasants and Cossacks on horseback who periodically marauded the village.

When David turned thirteen, his parents took the ancient Jewish rite of passage to manhood to heart. Immediately following his cursory *Bar Mitzvah*, they sent him off on foot to Vienna, where his older brother had semi-established himself as a peddler. He began the 500-mile journey with one change of clothes and enough food for only several days. His brother agreed to take him in and teach him a trade.

Such a long trek on foot would be daunting for anyone. For a thirteen-year old boy who had to scale mountains and cross rivers, the potential victim of both the elements and millions of anti-Semites along the route, it was monumental. I don't know how he did it or how long it took him. He never talked much about it, other than an occasional allusion sometimes while putting me to bed, referencing bears, wolves, and nights sleeping out in the open. Sometimes he snuck into haylofts to sleep, and when he ran out of food, he stole it.

When David reached Vienna, he did not immediately locate his brother, so he bedded down the first night in a boarding house. He paid for one-third of the bed with money he stole from a sleeping beggar on the side of the *Stephanskirche*, Vienna's iconic cathedral. There was no one else in bed when he lay down to sleep. Dog-tired and luxuriating in a real bed for the first time in months, he fell into a deep sleep. Several hours later, he was awakened by a loud commotion accompanied by a lot of jostling. Two men, one on each side of him, were battling each other with knives. David jumped out of bed and ran out of the boarding house, leaving his meager possessions behind. He spent the rest of the night wandering the streets.

The next day, he managed to find his brother and moved in with him and his family for a brief time. David apprenticed himself to him, observing closely as his brother purchased dry goods in Vienna and sold them in the surrounding villages. He accompanied his brother on his travels around the province of Lower Austria, learning to drive the cart and horse, off-loading sold goods, and learning how to play countless card games every night in the inns where they stayed when on the road.

Two years later, David felt confident enough to move out on his own. He had saved enough from the pittance his brother paid him to buy his own cart and horse, an ancient swaybacked creature that moved at a snail's pace when it deigned to move at all. David said that his German was not yet good enough for the horse to understand his commands. With what little he had left over, he bought a small assortment of dry goods and traveled far beyond the immediate environs of Vienna to some of the smaller towns in Lower Austria, south of the city, that were not on his brother's route.

His business model was to buy city goods and sell them in communities far enough from Vienna that it was unlikely the inhabitants would travel into the city to buy them and even less likely that rival peddlers would be competing with him for business so far away. At night, he slept in or, if it rained, under the cart.

David was a terrific negotiator and, despite having only three years of education, a prodigious natural mathematician. I marveled as a child at how he could tote up big numbers in his head. These abilities, plus the fact that he looked like a typical Slav, blond and blue-eyed, with a pronounced widow's peak, helped him immensely when dealing with the anti-Semitic locals in the provinces. Moreover, despite his protestations to me about communicating with his horse, he picked up the Viennese German dialect—*Wienerisch*—so quickly that he soon spoke like a native.

After several years riding the peddling circuit, he became successful enough to open a clothing store in Vienna's Second

District. By the time he married at age twenty-four, he was a reasonably prosperous merchant with employees.

I know little about David's forebears. He had brothers and sisters from whom he drifted apart. Several came to Vienna, but he had little or no contact with them. All of them were murdered in the Holocaust.

Grandmother Ernestine

David's wife—my grandmother Ernestine Lapajowker ("Grandma Tinny" to me), was born in 1884 in *Kamianka Strumilowa* on the Bug River in Poland, a tributary of the Vistula. In the late nineteenth century, the town numbered just over 5,000 population and was 55 percent Jewish. The Bug was the border between Austro-Hungarian Poland and Ukraine at that time. Kamianka today lies inside Ukraine.

Jews had lived in Kamianka for hundreds of years, with early records dating back to the fifteenth century. In all likelihood, her family probably resided in Kamianka for four centuries.

Their last name, Lapajowker, is the same as a small village just north of Kamianka. Either they took their surname from the village or the village from them.

The family for several generations had been fairly successful eel fishermen, thriving in a relative sense from the Bug's abundance of eels and the enthusiasm for them among the area's Christian population. Grandma's grandfather caught and sold them, live, in the Kamianka central market.

As the nineteenth century advanced, the position of Polish Jews deteriorated. In addition to economic constraints, violent outbursts from the primarily Catholic communities surrounding Kamianka became increasingly frequent. By the early 1890s, the isolated, quiet life that the family had enjoyed for centuries was no more. Ernestine's father, Liber, made the momentous decision to move to Vienna. In this, he was hardly alone. Tens of thousands of Polish Jews, especially those from these borderlands, arrived at the same decision. Vienna was, thus, inundated with Polish—principally Galician—Jews, a development that only intensified Austrian anti-Semitism.

These Galician Jews were unlike Vienna's indigenous, highly assimilated and very sophisticated Jewish population. They dressed differently, were overtly religious and ritualistic, spoke German with heavy Polish and Yiddish accents (the Lapajowkers were fluent in all three), and were viewed by the Viennese as a filthy, alien, peasant rabble.

Much later, Kamianka earned a place in history at 0400 hours on June 22, 1941, when General Fedor von Bock's German Army Group Centre launched *Operation Barbarossa*, the invasion of the Soviet Union, from staging points along the Bug.

In 1943, Kamianka's remaining Jews were rounded up and transported to the Auschwitz/Birkenau and Sobibor concentration camps, where almost all of them were selected for the gas chambers immediately upon arrival. A few became slave laborers, which made for a delayed but still likely death. One of Grandma's younger sisters died in the Auschwitz/Birkenau gas chamber (I discovered that via the Internet), along with several cousins. The sister's two daughters, attractive women in their late 20s, were scooped up by the German *Waffen SS* and forced into sexual slavery for the enjoyment of Nazi troops. They "worked" in mobile brothels that followed the German army into Russia, and were never heard from again.

Ernestine's parents married very young—Liber was 18, his first wife 19. Grandma was the oldest child, 14, when her family moved to Vienna in 1898.

David and Ernestine met and married in 1904, and their first child, my mother, was born a little over a year later. They named her Margarete, but she was familiarly known from the beginning of her life to its end 101 years and three-and-a-half months later as "Grete."

Aunt Stella

My mother's first childhood memory was of standing at the front window of the family's' apartment watching her little sister's lifeless body being taken away for burial. Stella died, probably of scarlet fever, when she was only three and my mother was five. The little boy standing next to her, his teary-eyed face plastered against the window, was her four-year old brother, Benno.

Scarlet fever is caused by the same bacterium that causes strep throat. It is highly infectious and spreads rapidly when children are in close quarters to one another. The disease's gestation period is only 1-2 days. Stella's initial symptoms were a neck rash that quickly spread down her body accompanied by fever, chills, stomach pain, violent shaking, and a sore throat. Once the symptoms took hold, the disease advanced so quickly that, by the time a physician arrived at the second-floor apartment, it was too late. She died within days of the first appearance of the rash.

Scarlet fever can be treated easily today. Not so in the early 1900s before the discovery of antibiotics. Then it was a very grave illness that rapidly sickened and often killed its victims.

Grete's parents watched helplessly as their little girl suffered. There was nothing they could do. Her father was not a particularly religious man, but during Stella's illness he went so far as to don his *tefillin*, the two little boxes with leather straps containing four Bible passages that Jewish men tie on an arm and forehead when they recite their morning prayers, and prayed to a god that he was skeptical existed. Grandpa David, however, always believed in covering all his bases, just in case. God must have been on one of his innumerable sabbaticals because grandfather's prayers went unanswered.

My grandmother Ernestine returned home from the cemetery distraught, her heart permanently broken. According to family lore, it was never whole again for the next thirty-five years, until I was born on her 62nd birthday (I was her only grandchild when she died). After Stella's death, Grete believes her mother suffered the first of several major depressions. Grandmother immediately took to her bed and did not get up for weeks. Grete and Benno had to grow up fast and learn to do household tasks on the fly.

Uncle Benno

My mother and her brother, my Uncle Benno (Ben in America), only a year apart in age, were very close growing up, but drifted apart as adults. Their personalities and interests were just too different. At one stage, there was a rift between my family and Uncle Ben's that lasted seven years, during which we had no contact despite living only three hours apart. I never found out what caused the rift.

Ben was an accomplished violinist as a child and was by far the most "musical" of the siblings, who grew up in the most musical place on Earth. All four Sobel children loved music and were avid listeners all their lives, but Ben also had talent.

He was the only one of the four saddled with the "Vienna disease," being highly nervous, fearful and afflicted by a laundry list of neuroses. He was an exceptional student throughout his school years, including at the University of Vienna Medical School, where he was a classmate of my father's. When he graduated from medical school, he obtained a prestigious position at the city's premier hospital, from which he moved into a private practice where he did quite well until the Nazi takeover of Austria in 1938, thanks to a contract with an insurance company. He left Austria immediately after the Nazi *Anschluss*, managing to slip over the border into Italy before the Germans could secure the frontiers. He obtained the all-important Affidavit of Support required to enter the U.S. from an Irish-American aunt by marriage.

Once in the United States, he quickly became licensed to practice medicine in New York State and joined the U.S. Army.

He served stateside in various posts during the war and met his wife, Mildred, an Army nurse who saw combat in North Africa during Operation Torch in 1942-43.

Unable to have children, Ben and Mildred adopted a baby boy, Bobby, in 1951. Bobby died of a calcified pancreas in 2008, the same extremely rare illness that contributed to his father's death despite their lack of biological kinship.

Financially, Ben became the most successful of the siblings despite spending his entire American existence as a general practitioner, first in Whitney Point, New York, then just down the road in Binghamton. His financial success is attributable to the care he took with every dollar that came into his possession. While in Whitney Point, he did some experimenting with cocaine, but never developed an addiction. Ben lived into his early 80s.

Aunt Rose

There would be two more children: Rose, born in 1911, and the baby of the family and favorite child, Otto, born in 1913. Rose was the only sibling uninterested in education. She was very good-looking and her primary interests, growing up, were dancing, partying, cigarettes and boys.

Despite her attitude toward formal education, Rose was arguably the smartest of the siblings. Wherever she worked—primarily as an executive secretary—she became the indispensable employee. When, late in her career, she and her husband, Ted, fell into the opportunity to run their own business, she was a terrific manager and finally realized the economic success that had escaped her and Ted until their seventh decade. I saw her in action and was in awe of her business acumen, managerial prowess and ability to climb the learning curve quickly. She was a voracious reader, devouring 7-8 books each week, an avid follower of world events, and highly opinionated about everything.

Aunt Rose was also the most stubborn human being I have ever encountered. After her husband died in 1979, I visited Rose in Miami several times a year for the next 32 years, the number of visits increasing after my parents left Miami Beach in 1994. She and I battled constantly over my concerns for her health and safety. I lost the vast majority of those confrontations.

Rose was a few months short of 100 years old when she fell asleep while smoking in her easy chair in her Miami Beach condo and set fire to both the apartment and herself. She slipped immediately into a coma and only came out of it 20 minutes before she died, opening her eyes and holding my hand. Until the fire, she was strong as an ox and mentally sharp. Her hearing was poor and she hobbled around with a walker, but was otherwise healthy. Rose did not believe in doctors, despite all three of her siblings being physicians. The only medication she was on at her death was Tylenol. Following her last physical exam, her physician told me that her lungs were completely clear.

She began smoking in 1926 when Calvin Coolidge was in the White House and continued for 85 years, moving through multiple packs per day. Her apartment was brown all over—brown ceilings, brown walls, brown carpeting, brown furniture, brown curtains, and brown books—thanks to decades of incessant smoking.

Uncle Otto

Otto was not so blessed, genetically speaking. He died at age 70 of stomach cancer after a highly successful career as an obstetrician/gynecologist. Otto was enormously bright and an excellent student. He began his medical education in Vienna, but it was interrupted by the political upheavals that afflicted Austria beginning in 1934, requiring him to complete his studies in Switzerland. Being in Switzerland when the *Anschluss* occurred, he was able to get to the U.S. without having to go through the nightmare that was required of his parents and my mother, which is described in detail later in this book. Like his brother, he received a U.S. Affidavit of Support from his Irish-American aunt in Massachusetts.

Once in the U.S., Otto quickly passed the English and medical licensing exams and moved into an obstetrics residency in Rochester, New York. Following that, he opened a practice in Rochester, married my Aunt Marie (they had no children), and moved to Melbourne, Florida. Several years later, they built a beautiful house on the ocean in Indialantic Beach, Florida. Simultaneously, Otto and Marie's best friends, a wealthy Rochester industrialist and his socialite wife, built a home next door. The two houses were designed and constructed as a compound, and proved very difficult to sell when the friends fell out with each other years later.

When Otto was dying, I flew down to Florida and spent three days listening to this most private of men open up to me about his life and his sibling relations. It was both painful and uplifting. Two weeks later, Uncle Otto was dead.

Chapter 4
Shrinks

Vienna was the psychoanalytic capital of the world when Grete was born. If you were born and grew up in the Vienna of the first third of the 20th century, you inevitably came under the influence of the psychoanalytic movement even if you never were in therapy yourself.

Vienna was the perfect petri dish for nurturing psychoanalysis. The *fin-de-siècle* Viennese, especially the moneyed elite and intellectual classes, never tired of their fascination with themselves. I noted the same obsession when I first visited the city in the late 1960s. No place on the planet was more ready for the new "science" than Vienna, with all of its attendant pathologies. For many years, for example, Vienna was known as the suicide capital of the world.

Grete was never "in analysis" and, in fact, spent her life in contemptuous denial of its salutary effects. Her own mother's experience with depression made a huge impact on her, including the failure of psychoanalysis and some of its more draconian treatment regimens—such as electroshock therapy—to do anything for Ernestine.

Despite growing up in Vienna when psychoanalysis was achieving worldwide fame, Grete thought it was largely a bogus pseudo-science, a conviction that she held to firmly for the rest of her life. Grete believed that a person should be able to overcome depression through will-power. She kept noting that Sigmund Freud developed psychoanalysis on the basis of only six case studies. To her, this constituted an irresponsible leap of faith. She said "Freud" was synonymous with "fraud."

Grete's skepticism concerning psychoanalysis could not even be broken by her contact with her husband's lifelong friend from his earliest school days, Viktor Frankl. Viktor became one of the world's most prominent psychoanalysts and philosophers at mid-century. His epic work, *Man's Search for Meaning*, derived from his years in a Nazi death camp during which he lost his entire first family. More about Viktor later in this book.

Sigmund Freud, Carl Jung, Alfred Adler, and Richard Kraft-Ebbing formed the founding core of psychoanalysis in Vienna, which spread rapidly to the rest of the world. However, the giants of early psychoanalysis suffered from a major psychological problem themselves that self-diagnosis and auto-therapy could not cure; extraordinarily thin skin. All of them eventually broke with each other over what, for the layperson, appeared to be petty, nitpicking nuances reminiscent of the theological battles that divided the early church, and subsequently Catholics from Anglicans, Methodists from Wesleyan Methodists and Sunnis from Shiites. To outsiders, these seemed based upon fuzzy premises. Freud, for example, broke with sexologist Kraft-Ebbing over a critical remark the latter made about male hysteria. Much of early psychoanalytic development was marked by academic arguments that appear quaint and utterly irrelevant today.

Grete's rejection of Carl Jung from serious consideration had less to do with his theses than his Nazi sympathies and his dabbling in alchemy. In addition, it did not help his cause with her that he is credited with establishing the basis for the Myers-Briggs Type Indicator—a non-scientific exercise that almost invariably confirms its adherents' pre-conceived notions about themselves and has a decided "Emperor's New Clothes" acceptance among moderns. For Grete, that was more than enough to consign Jung to the same circle of Hell in which she posited snake oil salesmen and televangelists.

In medical school she took the required course in psychiatry, but was vocally dismissive of it both while attending the lectures and thereafter. Notwithstanding, she received the highest grade in her class.

However, being Viennese, she could not avoid psychoanalysis altogether. The principal indicator of its influence on her was her avid lifetime interest in observing people, a pastime of which she never tired. I never met anyone more intrigued by human behavior than her. We often discussed our impressions of the id, ego and superego of the people we ran across. My father Ernest was a very close second to Grete when it came to interest in others, although his was prompted less by his Vienna origins and more by his consuming interest in gossip. His interest was superficial. Grete, in contrast, wanted to drill down into personalities and determine what made people tick.

Freud spent most of the Vienna phase of his life unappreciated by the locals, who nevertheless took to his theories like ducks to water. They were able to differentiate the man from his ideas because he was Jewish.

Freud was one of those fortunate Jews whose global reputation saved his life once the Nazis absorbed Austria. Unlike the overwhelming majority of his co-religionists, he had little trouble emigrating to escape the Holocaust. His friends began lobbying for him to leave Austria five years before the Anschluss, when he was 77 years old. He deluded himself into believing that the Catholic Church (Austria was 90 percent Catholic) and the Austrian Fascist government would be able to resist Hitler. He also felt that he was too old to adapt to an alien environment elsewhere.

Two days after Austria was annexed to Germany on March 13, 1938, his apartment was searched by Nazi thugs. Shortly thereafter, his daughter Anna was arrested by the Gestapo and detained for several days. Freud was compelled to change his mind. American ambassador to France William C. Bullitt intervened on Freud's behalf and assisted in getting him to England, where his son Ernst had established himself and which, due to the mass emigration of psychoanalysts to London during the 1930s, was the natural safe harbor for Freud. The German authorities let him go once he paid the so-called "refugee tax," a confiscatory theft that was also imposed on my grandfather several months later.

Freud's four sisters were not so lucky. They all perished in the Nazi death camps.

Chapter 5
Vindobona and Its Jews

Even before Roman times, the site where Vienna sits today was a gateway to all four directions. Its favorable location at the place where the Alps finally give way to the broad Central European Plain and its bisecting Danube River permitted the easy transportation of goods and people from one horizontal direction to the other. It was also where the "Amber Road" (stretching north to south from the Baltic Sea to the Adriatic Sea) crossed the Danube. This propitious set of circumstances made it one of the most important trading posts in the ancient world.

Roman Vienna

Vindobona, the Roman name for Vienna, started as a Roman army frontier post in 9 BC. For the next four centuries, the Danube was the northern boundary of the Roman Empire.

During the reshuffling of Roman forces after the annihilation of two legions by the German warlord Arminius (Hermann) in the Teutoburg Forest (September, 9 AD), the Fifteenth Legion was transferred to the Vindobona region.

Late in the first century, the emperor Domitian transferred the Thirteenth Legion to Vindobona to counter a barbarian invasion. The Thirteenth constructed the base that was to become the center of what is modern Vienna. Once peace was established, Vindobona became a permanent Roman garrison for the next 300 years.

In 166 AD, the *Marcommani*, a German tribe, crossed the Alps and conquered Italian territory all the way to the Adriatic Sea. The war lasted 14 years, during which Vindobona was sacked and largely destroyed. Emperor Marcus Aurelius took personal command of the legions, marched north from Rome, successfully defended the Danube frontier and rebuilt Vindobona, making it his campaign headquarters. This most enlightened, literate and tolerant of Roman emperors died there on March 17, 180.

Vindobona was sacked and destroyed again in 395 AD, and subsequently rebuilt on a smaller scale. A decade later, a fire destroyed Vindobona, which by then had become a Christian city. Barbarian tribes gradually moved into the city and, in 433 AD, the Eastern Roman emperor, Theodosius II, allowed the Huns to occupy the city. A possible urban legend has Attila marrying the beautiful Kriemhild in Vindobona.

In the sixth century, Vienna was occupied successively by the *Langobards* and *Avars*, a nomadic tribe from the Caucasus who dominated the town for over 200 years until they were defeated by Charlemagne.

Jewish Vienna

Wherever there was trade, there were Jews. Commerce was one of the handful of occupations allowed them. Jewish merchants began to buy and sell goods in Vindobona in Roman times.

The first actual documentation of Jews in Vienna, however, dates from the tenth century. They came in droves at the beginning of the 1200s, forced East by widespread pogroms in the Rhineland and Bavaria. A synagogue appears in the records in 1204. Several years later, Jews began settling in other Austrian towns, including *Wiener Neustadt*, where my paternal grandmother's family lived. By 1230, Jews were well-established in commerce and began to believe themselves secure in their Austrian communities. As history always demonstrates when it comes to the Jews, this was illusory.

Over the next several centuries, the usual waves of oppression and violence erupted from time-to-time. Much of this was fomented by the Catholic Church which, frustrated by its failure to convert them, did not miss many opportunities to demonize Jews. Among the traditional scurrilous accusations against the Jews—Christ-killers, kidnappers, ritual murderers of Christian children at Passover so that their blood could be used to bake *matzoh* (many European churches still harbor shrines to these allegedly martyred children)—a new, rather creative one emerged: theft of the Eucharist and stabbing it until it bled. Consecrated wafers did on occasion "bleed," due to metabolic activity of the bacterium *Serratia marcescens.*

By the late Middle Ages, the Jewish population of Vienna had grown rapidly. The first major pogrom took place in 1421, officially endorsed by the government at the urging of the Church. Conveniently, a plague and war were blamed on the Jews and served as the justification for what followed. Two hundred seventy Jews were burned at the stake in Vienna and their children forcibly converted. Children who refused conversion were sold into slavery.

Expropriation of Jewish property was widespread, and debts owed by Christians to Jews were cancelled. Many Jews were forcibly converted and baptized on pain of death, and many more were expelled from the country. By the time the pogrom was over, the entire Jewish population of Vienna had disappeared.

As the crossroads of two major trade routes, the city was especially vulnerable to flea-carrying rats. The plagues were viewed as God's punishment for some reason, generally fixing on the Jews. Recurring plagues were often followed by pogroms and expulsions.

The situation quieted down by 1440 and the Jews were invited back, due to economic necessity. One of the few benefits of living in an eternal diaspora is that one makes contacts all over the world who become valuable for things like facilitating commerce and money exchanges. This proved a big advantage to emperors who were constantly spending themselves into dire straits. They needed the Jews' contacts, money, and financial acumen.

If you study European economic history, you will see a pattern emerge. Banishing the Jews was invariably followed by national economic decline. Spain discovered this in 1492 when it expelled a million Jews, much to the delight of Rome and Turkey, which welcomed them and their economic prowess.

Having nowhere else to live that was any more secure, many Jews took up the invitation and returned to Vienna. They had to pay a "Jews' Tax" in gold and their lives were heavily regulated by the authorities.

Less than two generations after their return, Emperor Maximilian I issued another Edict of Expulsion in 1496. As was always the case when Jews were sent packing, they were not allowed to take any property or valuables with them.

A handful of Jews began drifting back after a century-and-a-half. However, in 1670, the Jews were again expelled from the city by Emperor Leopold I. This expulsion was based on economics. Christian Viennese merchants were angry that their Jewish counterparts were more successful than they were, so they lobbied the Emperor to get rid of the competition. He hesitated at first, but his Spanish wife, a Catholic zealot in the mold of her ancestor Isabella, the mother of the Inquisition, convinced him to go ahead with the expulsion.

Somehow, a Jewish financier named Samuel Oppenheimer was able to remain. In 1683, his money saved Vienna by financing the defense forces that stopped the Turkish advance at the gates of the city. This was not necessarily in Oppenheimer's countrymen's best interest, since the Turks always treated Jews far better than did Europeans.

Jews continued to finance Austria's wars well into the eighteenth century. Following the devastation of the Thirty Years War, Jews were the only Viennese able to maintain an international credit network. This worked to the advantage of the Habsburg state.

Next up in the unending pantheon of Austrian Jew-haters was Empress Maria Theresa (1740 – 1780). She was a virulent anti-Semite from childhood. An urban legend claims that, on excursions from the palace as a child, she was frightened by the odd clothing and beards of the Jewish men she observed on her way to church.

Her repugnance did not, however, extend to financial matters. Most of the construction funds for *Schönbrunn* palace came from a Portuguese Jew. Whenever the need arose to replenish the Imperial treasury, she extracted "voluntary gifts" from the Jewish community. Nevertheless, in 1744 she expelled the Jews from Prague and the rest of Bohemia for "treason." Four years later, after coercing them to pay a fine of 300,000 florins, she permitted them to return for a ten-year period.

In 1772, the Austro-Hungarian Empire participated in the first partition of Poland, which brought 2.6 million Jews into the Habsburg fold. This did nothing to increase Maria Theresa's fondness for the race.

In 1777, she had this to say about the Jews:

> "I know of no greater plague than this race, which on account of its deceit, usury and hoarding of money is driving my subjects to beggary."

The Empress was not alone. Her subjects, especially the poor and those who lived in the countryside, were even more anti-Semitic.

There were certain common refrains in this sad history. Whenever Church and State colluded against the Jews, the scenario went something like this:

1. An accusation of desecration of the host or ritual murder of a child.
2. Incarceration of the entire Jewish community.
3. Torture of the Jewish leadership.
4. Forced conversions.
5. Expropriation of property.
6. Killing of Jews who refused baptism.
7. Expulsion of the rest.

Maria Theresa's son Joseph II was different from his mother. He was an Enlightenment advocate and, for the time, considered a liberal. He did not hate or despise Jews. Rather, he understood that their intelligence, hard work and penchant for finance and trade could benefit Austria economically. He admitted Jews to public educational institutions and allowed them to engage in industry and agriculture. He also lifted many restrictions, including the Jew's Tax, the wearing of the yellow star (something the historically attuned Nazis revived), and many occupational constraints. Certain residence restrictions, however, remained intact, except for very wealthy Jews such as the Rothschild family, who could be relied upon to finance state ventures. His proposals became law in 1782. Joseph's detractors gave him the pejorative title "Emperor of the Jews."

Napoleon, one of the greatest mass murderers in history, was remarkably tolerant of Jews. When he conquered Austria, liberation and a measure of equality quickly followed. Even after his defeat at Waterloo and exile to St. Helena, many of his reforms remained in place

In 1848, the Austrian parliament went so far as to grant the Jews limited civil rights. This caused Jewish communities throughout the country to grow and prosper. In 1860, Vienna's Jewish population was 6,000. By the time of Grete's birth in 1905, it had exploded, reaching 175,000. In 1938, at the time of the Anschluss, Jews numbered just under 200,000, over ten percent of the city's population.

Jewish entrepreneurs played a key role in Austria's economic expansion during the nineteenth century. A large portion of the capital financing for the growth of the Austrian economy during this period came from Jewish investment. Jewish money was instrumental in the great physical transformation of Vienna that revitalized and beautified the city during this era.

Emperor Franz Josef, who ascended to the throne in 1848 at age 18, came to power with the usual Habsburg anti-Semitic baggage. One of his first acts as emperor was to deny his Jewish subjects total emancipation, i.e., the right to unfettered participation in civil society. However, by 1860, he found himself and his government totally beholden to Jewish bankers, so much so that he was compelled to grant a constitution to Austria that gave the Jews equality. Anselm Rothschild, the leading banker of his time, stated the case for the constitution thusly:

"No constitution, no money"

Under the constitution, Jews received the right to own land and the freedom to change domiciles. That did not mean that everything came up roses for them. Synagogues, for example, were still not permitted to have street frontage.

In 1866, Prussia's chief minister Otto von Bismarck achieved his long-sought goal of Prussian supremacy over the German states through Prussia's victory over Austria at the Battle of *Sadowa* in Bohemia. The battle marked the end of any significant Austrian influence in German affairs.

Meanwhile, life in Vienna went on much as before, consoled by Strauss waltzes, Sunday *spazieren* (walks) in the beautiful *Wienerwald* (the Vienna Woods) and good coffee, sublime confections, and conversation in Vienna's innumerable coffee houses, for many Viennese their home away from home.

Despite more than one hundred years of positive reform, Austria's Jews hardly experienced anything resembling an era of good feeling. The deeply ingrained prejudices of the majority population were not going to be legislated out of existence. Moreover, the last half of the nineteenth century witnessed the rise of a dark philosophy of pan-German nationalism and racial purity that foretold bad tidings for Jews, reaching its apotheosis in Adolf Hitler a few decades hence.

Around the turn of the century, an overt anti-Semite, Karl Lueger, was elected mayor of Vienna and shrewdly manipulated the visceral anti-Jewish biases of the voters to advance himself. He launched several attempts to curtail Jewish rights (he declaimed that he "yearned for the day when the trees lining the city's boulevards would be decorated with hanging Jews"), but was stymied by Emperor Franz Josef who, whether through a change of heart or creeping dementia combined with memory loss, decided to protect the Jews.

Following Sadowa, the Empire's decline into comfortable decadence and its eventual disappearance took only 50 years. For most of this period, the old Austria of myth and legend was only hanging on by its painted fingernails. With his typical malevolence and biting satire, Karl Kraus, Vienna's answer to our H.L. Mencken (and a Jew), called Austria-Hungary "a proving ground for the world's destruction."

Chapter 6
Angst

Our era is not the first age in which humanity has confronted massive and increasingly rapid technological change, disruptive upheavals with huge social and economic consequences. People have short memories. Everything that happens today, we are often told, is "new," "unprecedented," or "never happened before." In fact, little that happens is really new. It has all transpired, in one guise or another, before. The roots of our own frenetic, often dystopian civilization go back over 100 years to when my mother was born.

The world Grete was born into was undergoing radical change, among the most profound in history. Moreover, the pace of change was accelerating to such an extent that thousands of people—in Vienna naturally—sought professional help in dealing with it. Change and the anxiety it caused found the perfect storm in *fin-de siècle* Vienna. Psychoanalysis, that peculiar profession that originated in Vienna, emerged in large part because of societal disruption and its accompanying neuroses. Its practitioners reaped a bonanza.

Around the transition from the nineteenth to the twentieth century, technology achieved a tipping point unprecedented in all of recorded history. In short order, the automobile and air travel revolutionized transportation. By 1905, internal combustion engine technology was 20 years old (Karl Benz built a motorized tricycle in 1885). Henry Ford began producing the Model A in 1904. Cars were still a novelty and Vienna was still largely a horse-and-buggy city for a few more years. But the city was on the cusp of being overwhelmed by new car companies—Mercedes (named after the daughter of the first Benz car purchaser), Renault, Ford, Porsche, Audi, Fiat (the acronym for *Fabbrica Italiana Automobili Torino*) and Rolls Royce—and their wondrous products.

The world land speed record had already reached 65 miles per hour when Grete first opened her eyes. Within a year, it would almost double.

Flight technology was also speeding ahead. The Wright Flyer III stayed airborne for a record 18 minutes two days after Grete's birth (it would have stayed up longer, but Wilbur ran out of gas). Within two weeks, the Flyer III stayed aloft for just under 40 minutes and 24 miles. Orville and Wilbur confirmed for themselves that they were onto something, and tried that same month to interest the U.S. War Department. The Secretary of War was skeptical, so the brothers turned to Britain and France. Again, they were turned down.

Within two years, the War Department changed its mind and the Wrights were on their way. Progress in aviation accelerated at breathtaking speed. By September 1908, Orville was able to fly for over an hour. Unfortunately, one of his first passengers, Army Lieutenant Thomas E. Selfridge, became the first air passenger fatality when the propeller split and Orville crashed.

Advances in flight technology were rapid. In late 1908, Wilbur flew for over two hours, giving the civil side of aviation its launch. Air freight delivery began in 1910. A hydroplane company began carrying passengers in California in 1913. By the end of the first month of World War I (August, 1914), a German aircraft dropped five bombs on Paris.

Railroad and steamship travel were also progressing rapidly. Speed and more speed was the order of the day and the societal mantra. It proved much too fast for Vienna.

The big scientific event of 1905 might well have been the biggest such event ever. An insignificant 26-year old patent clerk who could not find a teaching job after two years of rejection, and who only wound up in the Swiss Federal Office for Intellectual Property in Bern thanks to the intervention of a former classmate's father, and who had been passed over for promotion, published a paper entitled "*On the Electrodynamics of Moving Bodies.*" Albert Einstein's Special Theory of Relativity revolutionized Newtonian physics and served as the platform for virtually everything in physics that has followed up to the present day. This was Einstein's third paper of the year. The first two, obscured by the ferment over Special Relativity, were startling breakthroughs in their own right: the first explained how light quanta (photons) cause the photoelectric effect; the second explained Brownian motion, the seemingly random movement of particles suspended in a fluid.

The communications revolution had already been in place for sixty years by 1905, triggered by Samuel F.B. Morse in 1844 via a telegraph message sent from Baltimore to Washington, DC. By 1870, it took only four minutes for a message to get from London to Bombay and back. By then, the world was encircled by 650,000 miles of telegraph wire and 30,000 miles of submarine cable.

The expansion of human interconnectivity still wows us today. The profound impact of first the telegraph, then the telephone in the 1880s, was life-changing.

Vienna was largely electrified by 1905. The wireless and the radio followed shortly.

The aggregate impact of these massive technological changes gave new meaning to time and space. The young, as they always do, took to the new world seamlessly and with enthusiasm. For their elders, it was a difficult transformation.

The substance and pace of societal change impacted every other area of human endeavor: the arts, morals, the lives of the body and the mind, politics, and the military. Vienna was uniquely positioned to experiment with and experience all of this.

Vienna, being both geographically well-positioned and inclined to introspection, became a pot-boiler of innovation in art, architecture, music, city planning, crafts, and even local politics; all of this while mired in the middle of the most dated, sclerotic and backward-looking national government of its era. The first decade of the new century found the following individuals living in Vienna: Freud, Jung, Alfred Adler, Gustav Mahler, Franz Werfel, Hugo Gropius, Arnold Schoenberg, Alben Berg, and Max Weber, to name just a handful of the giants of medicine, music, literature, architecture and economics.

Adolf Hitler, age 19, left Linz for Vienna in 1907. He went there to seek his fortune and what he perceived to be his destiny—to become a great artist and architect. Armed with a decent monthly legacy from his late father's pension, he had enough money to live comfortably for a time, at least until he found a job. But he never sought gainful employment, believing he was too good for the menial work for which he was qualified.

The Vienna that greeted him was living a lie—the delusion that it was still the grand capital of a great empire instead of a neurotic metropolis that barely governed a cacophony of peoples aching for independence from an ossified central bureaucracy manned by old men long past their prime. Music filled the air and the intoxicating odor of strong Turkish coffee and delectable pastries wafted out of hundreds of cafes that served as the center of the city's social existence. The sweet smells were, in reality, a deodorant temporarily covering up the stench of civic decay.

Imperial grandeur was ostentatiously on display—vast numbers of petty officials, bedecked in over-the-top uniforms that made them look like bell captains at five-star hotels; Kaiser Franz Josef with his glitzy uniform, feathered headgear, and gaudy horse-drawn carriage a familiar sight as it clomped through the streets of the city. These were illusions whose time was almost up. Everyone else in Europe except the Austrians knew that the Empire was moribund.

Grete's parents were evening regulars at the coffee houses where they would meet friends, play cards and read the many papers that the proprietors made available to patrons. They left her and Benno home with the Christian maid who would become a virtual member of the family, their loyal and well-treated house servant, off-and-on, for years to come.

Kaiser Franz Josef was emblematic of his realm. By 1907, he was a doddering relic who had been on the throne for 59 years, a troglodytic throwback to a romantic era that probably never really existed except in the selective memories of the Austrian aristocracy. By this time, he had been thoroughly beaten down by multiple personal tragedies as well as by the crumbling of his empire and the Habsburg dynasty that had ruled the area between the Alps, the Carpathians and the Adriatic, and at times much more, for 500 years.

Like his subjects, he was unaware that his days and those of his dynasty and empire were numbered. Every morning, his gilded carriage (he refused to travel in automobiles) transported him from the Palace at *Schönbrunn* into the city center to the *Hofburg*, where he worked tirelessly reading exaggerated reports and signing innumerable, irrelevant documents. The horses were pure white and were ridden by courtiers in uniforms that would make the Vatican's Swiss Guard blush. Hungarian guardsmen strode next to each side of the carriage. They wore yellow and black panther furs over their shoulders.

The timeless pageantry was just about all that was left of the Imperium. The Kaiser's daily journey into town was a sight to behold, one that dazzled Grete and her siblings. Both of my parents spoke to me about the pride they felt at seeing the Kaiser in all his finery. As children, they were proud of their emperor and his empire, believing it to be the center of the universe and as enduring and changeless as the oceans.

Adolf Hitler, in contrast, was repelled by the same sights. He raged constantly to his friend and roommate, August ("Gustl") Kubitzek, about the decadence of the Imperium. He understood little of the real world, but he was spot on in this respect.

Chapter 7
Sclerosis

Vienna in the first decade of the twentieth century was an illusion. The pomp and circumstance surrounding the Kaiser, his Lippizaner horses stepping in unison and wearing tassels on their heads, protected by coachmen in foppish costumes, camouflaged the dramatic upheavals going on all around the city and the Empire.

Vienna resisted acknowledging the many changes that made the future uncertain and ominous. People went about their lives as if time had stopped. Despite the air of *gemütlichkeit* (easygoing, lighthearted unconcern) and traditional Viennese *schlamperei* (sloppiness probably comes closest in English), an outside observer would have been struck by how gray and dilapidated the buildings looked, as well as how gray and dilapidated the population appeared.

Beneath the façade of leisurely trips to the *Kaffeehaus*, Sunday walks in the Vienna Woods, trips to the suburb of Grinzing's *Heurigen* to drink the year's new wines, their singular obsession with music (Vienna was, of course, the home of Mozart, Beethoven, the Strausses, Schubert, Mahler and Lehar, among others) and their external "what-me-worry?" demeanor, the people's mood was gray and melancholy. What-me-worry is not so far from "what's the point?"

There was considerable poverty present, with immigrants flocking into the city from all corners of the Empire adding to the bottom socioeconomic stratum. While the native Viennese resented and looked down upon the gaggle of nationalities that descended on them from Bohemia, Moravia, Slovakia, Hungary, the Balkans and Poland, with their alien ways and incomprehensible gibberish, the immigrants they resented most were the provincial Jews who arrived in Vienna in greater numbers than any other ethnic or linguistic group.

The Jews, attracted to Vienna because of economic distress, social discrimination and escalating pogroms, were more alien than other immigrants. Their strange dress, religious practices, and Yiddish language (to Viennese ears a shocking corruption of good German) provided the platform for a surge in Viennese anti-Semitism, never far from the surface under any circumstances in any era (Austria outside of Vienna was even more virulently anti-Semitic despite the fact that so few Jews lived in the provinces that most Austrians had never seen one.). Exacerbating the situation was the fact that many immigrant Jews pulled themselves up by their bootstraps so quickly through hard work, discipline, and innate intelligence.

Their *shtetl shul* experience inculcated almost every Jewish family with a reverence for education. To an extent unknown among their Viennese "hosts," Jewish families pushed their children to a love of learning and exploited education to pursue a better life. What was particularly striking about it was that even uneducated, lower middle-class Jews felt the same way.

Grete's family was no exception. Her father David, whose education stopped in the third grade because his labor was needed on the family's subsistence farm, was, along with his wife, a taskmaster when it came to studying. Three of his four children who made it to adulthood became physicians. This kind of academic achievement was not at all unusual among similarly situated, lower class Jewish families.

Grete's future husband Ernst also became a physician. His father, Solomon, was a cobbler with even less education than David. Nevertheless, he pushed his son toward his goal and encouraged and supported his aspiration wholeheartedly.

Consequently, Jews occupied a disproportionate number of positions at the apex of society and the economy. At one point, Jews accounted for 75 percent of Austrian Nobel Prize winners in Medicine, more than half of Austria's physicians and dentists, more than 60 percent of its lawyers, and a majority of its university professors.

All of this visible success bred deep resentments in the majority Viennese population. Making the problem worse was the fact that many Jews were publicly atheistic or agnostic. The final straw stimulating Austrian anti-Semitism was the fact that many Social Democratic Party leaders were Jewish, this in an overwhelmingly Catholic country whose national politics were dominated by rightist clerics.

Christian Vienna watched and stewed as the Jews advanced up the economic ladder. It made them realize that Vienna had changed and, from their point of view, decidedly not for the better. Gemütlichkeit and schlamperei no longer sufficed. In time, this was to prove deadly for the Jews. Anomie and social and economic alienation consumed the Viennese and contributed to the rise of intolerance.

Chapter 8
Leopoldstadt

Leopoldstadt is the popular name of Vienna's Second District. The city is divided into 23 administrative districts (*bezirke*). The districts are mini-cities in themselves, with their own councils and administrative heads who report to the mayor. Leopoldstadt gets its name from Leopold I, a Habsburg ruler who was also Holy Roman Emperor.

When Grete lived there, Leopoldstadt was home to the largest Jewish concentration in Vienna, with a Jewish population of more than 100,000, earning it the nickname *Mazzesinsel* (Matzoh Island).

The Second District is located in the heart of the city. Together with the Twentieth District, it forms a large island surrounded on three sides by the Danube Canal and, on its northern end, the Danube River.

Leopoldstadt is also home to the *Prater*, until 1766 the imperial hunting ground closed to the public. By 1905, the Prater was a large amusement park frequently visited by Grete and her family. It was—and still is—famous for one of the largest Ferris wheels in the world, the *Riesenrad*, a ride that terrified Grete as a child. A smaller Leopoldstadt park, the *Augarten*, filled with topiary, was also a favorite haunt for Grete and her friends.

Leopoldstadt had such a high Jewish population because, in 1625, the Chief Rabbi of Vienna was granted the right to establish a central Jewish community there. Jews relocated from all over the city and lived in ghetto-like isolation for more than a generation. That ended abruptly with the accession of Leopold I to the throne. His virulent hatred of Jews led to their forceful expulsion and the destruction of their community. The Christian inhabitants, in gratitude for Leopold's *Judenrein* (Jew-free) policy, named the area Leopoldstadt.

When restrictions on Jewish habitation were lifted by Leopold II in the late eighteenth century, Jews from the eastern part of the empire began moving into Leopoldstadt. This was not because they remembered that Leopoldstadt had been where Vienna's Jews had previously congregated. Instead, it was because the *Nordbahnhof* railway station, the arrival terminal for Jews from the east, was there.

Leopoldstadt was, of course, once more "cleansed" of its Jewish inhabitants during the Holocaust. However today, the vast majority of the 7,000 Jews in Vienna, principally immigrants from the former Soviet Union, live there again. A small Orthodox Jewish grocery now occupies the first floor of my mother's *Hollandstrasse* apartment building.

During its heyday, Leopoldstadt was home to Sigmund Freud (he later relocated to the more elite First District), Theodor Herzl (the founder of Zionism), Viktor Frankl, Lise Meitner (the co-discoverer of nuclear fission), Johann Nestroy (the "Austrian Shakespeare"), Arthur Schnitzler (novelist), Arnold Schönberg (composer), both Johann Strausses, Billy Wilder, and Carl Djerassi (who developed the first oral contraceptive).

Leopoldstadt was peppered with Jewish businesses, butchers, bakers, shoemakers, haberdashers, bookshops, pawn shops, etc. It was a Jewish cocoon.

Its proximity to the Viennese epicenter in the First District, just across the *Donaukanal*, made Leopoldstadt a very convenient place to live. Grete and her family and friends could go on foot almost everywhere. Grete and her friends often walked on the *Ringstrasse*, the ring road that circled the inner city. Walking was their primary mode of transportation. And walk they did, a recreation Grete continued well into her 90's.

Chapter 9
The Wienerwald

Eight-year old Grete had no conception of the power politics playing out all around her during the bright, sunny, leisurely summer of 1914. She was focused on having a good time, wandering around her beautiful city, hiking in the Wienerwald, visiting the Prater, and playing outside with friends from dawn to dusk. I once asked her how her parents could allow a small child to wander so far from home, unsupervised. She said that it was a different era and that all Viennese children were allowed that same degree of independence.

The Wienerwald is a magical landscape that wraps around the western and southern precincts of Vienna. It is a land of firs, beeches, oak, birches, vineyards, rolling hills and verdant valleys. The giants of Viennese music roamed through the Wienerwald and some of their most famous works were inspired by it. Beethoven's Ninth Symphony, for example, was composed there. Both Johann Strausses, Elder and Younger, composed some of their famous waltzes there. Strauss the Younger was inspired to write his *Tales of the Vienna Woods* by his excursions into the Wienerwald. Mozart and Franz Schubert composed a number of dances and songs there. Poets and writers like Hugo von Hofmannstal and W.H. Auden spent time living in the Wienerwald and extolled its charms in their works. (A sidebar on Auden. I met him when he was on a one-week fellowship at my residential college at Yale. He was an unfriendly curmudgeon who quickly alienated us to the point that his student rotations at mealtimes in our dining hall found him sitting mostly by himself.)

Sigmund Freud was prompted to write his breakthrough work, *The Interpretation of Dreams*, thanks to the solitude he found during his Wienerwald walks.

Young Egon Shiele, one of the great Art Nouveau artists of "end-times" Vienna, painted in the Wienerwald and did time in a local prison for alleged underage sex offenses (not an uncommon offense in hedonistic Vienna). During his 3-week incarceration, he painted thirteen watercolors of his prison cell. Schiele was drafted during World War I and spent most his service time billeted in comfort on the home front before dying of the Spanish Flu three days after his wife succumbed to the pandemic.

The Vienna Woods are best known to outsiders because of *Mayerling*, the castle where in 1889 Crown Prince Rudolf and his mistress, buxom teenage Maria Vetsera, were found shot to death in bed. Mayerling today evokes the great romantic tragedy and historical mystery of these deaths, made unforgettable by numerous books and movies. What happened there is still the stuff of incessant speculation and legend, a lively discussion topic today a century-and-a-quarter after the event.

Rudolf was a fascinating character. He wrote the Wienerwald chapter of a Habsburg encyclopedia, a project he initiated and edited, in which he advocated freedom of religion and equal rights for all subjects of the Imperium, radical notions for his era. He also advocated a pro-French foreign policy and wanted Austria-Hungary to move away from the German orbit. He wrote an anonymous column for the *Neues Wiener Tagblatt*, the liberal newspaper published by his good Jewish friend, Moritz Szeps.

Mayerling was his favorite haunt away from the claustrophobic confinement of the royal household. He had many mistresses and affairs and used Mayerling for numerous trysts. He married at age 22 in 1881 to Princess Stephanie, the 17-year old daughter of King Leopold II of Belgium, the conqueror—many would say butcher—of the Congo. It was an arranged marriage and Rudolf had little love or respect for his wife, largely ignoring her.

Frustrated by his marriage, his contrarian views, and his father's keeping him from any say in affairs of state, he was depressed. Seeking solace in the arms of his mistresses was not a sufficient distraction. He drank prodigiously and was probably a morphine addict.

On January 28, 1889, Rudolf retreated to Mayerling for an assignation with Vetsera. The next morning, two of Rudolf's friends arrived at the castle for a hunt. They breakfasted with him and went out for the shoot. One of the friends, Hoyos, had an early dinner with Rudolph, then retired for the night. The next morning, he was awakened by the prince's valet, who reported that he was having trouble waking the crown prince. Hoyos went to the castle, knocked on the bedroom door, then hammered on it, and finally asked the valet to break it down. Rudolf and Maria were both dead of gunshot wounds. Hoyos left for Vienna and informed Empress Elizabeth (one of the rare occasions she was present in Vienna). Tearfully, she then told her husband the news.

The assumption was that Rudolph killed Vetsera and then himself. The inability to confirm that still suggests intrigue 130 years after the tragic event.

By the time of Mayerling, the Viennese propensity for, and fascination with, suicide was well-established. Even today, Austria has one of the highest suicide rates in the world. Many such instances of self-destruction take place in the serenity of the Wienerwald.

My mother often walked in and around Mayerling with her friends, fascinated and titillated by the tragedy that took place there.

Chapter 10

Sarajevo

The summer of 1914 was only one week old when one of the great inflection points of the twentieth century occurred. It happened in Sarajevo, the capital of Bosnia, a polyglot South Slav city where East literally meets West, church spires competing for air space with minarets.

Neighboring Serbia to the north was a hotbed of resistance to Habsburg rule. What began as mild protest demonstrations in the late nineteenth century had escalated into sporadic outbursts of terrorist violence by 1914. The failure of moderates to squeeze any concessions out of Vienna led to the rise of extremists and numerous secret societies, foremost among them a sinister Serbian cabal known as the "Black Hand."

The Black Hand was intent on uniting all of the South Slavs—Serbians, Croatians, Bosnians, Herzegovinians, Albanians, Kossovars, Slovenes, and Macedonians—and doing so by force. Austria was adamant about holding on to these troublesome provinces. The issue came to a head when Archduke Franz Ferdinand announced that he would be making a military inspection tour of Bosnia accompanied by his wife, Sophie.

By the time Franz Ferdinand decided to visit Bosnia in June, 1914, South Slav xenophobia was full to overflowing, primed for the spark that would launch a conflagration.

Franz Ferdinand was, ironically, the best friend Serbia and the South Slavs had among the Austrian leadership. He empathized with their desire for autonomy, much to the annoyance of both his uncle the Kaiser and the rest of the Austrian government. He advocated replacing the "Dual

Monarchy" (Austria and Hungary) with a Triple Monarchy in which the South Slavs would have equal status with Austrians and Magyars.

Annoying his own government was only one of the ways in which Franz Ferdinand was an irritant. He greatly vexed Uncle Franz Josef with his insufferable arrogance, but more so by his choice of life partner.

Countess Sophie Chotek came from the minor Bohemian nobility and was serving as a lady-in-waiting to Archduchess Isabella in Pressburg (now Bratislava, Slovakia) when she won the heart of Franz Ferdinand. Being only a countess, she was deemed unsuitable to marry Franz Ferdinand by his Habsburg relations. For Franz Josef, it was the final blow, the last disappointment. "Was I not to be spared even this?" lamented the Emperor on hearing that his nephew was determined to marry Sophie.

After much venting, Franz Josef relented and permitted the marriage to go forward provided that none of her children could ever succeed to the throne. Franz Ferdinand was forced to sign an Oath of Renunciation documenting this. Neither Franz Josef nor any other members of the royal family attended the wedding.

Conspiracy

The story of what happened during Franz Ferdinand's visit to Sarajevo is well-known, but the drama is just as poignant today, a century later. Accounts differ as to the facts surrounding the events of June 28, 1914. I base the following rendition on the only primary source I was able to uncover: an account written years later by Borijove Jevtic, one of the Black Hand conspirators directly involved in the plot to murder the Habsburg heir.

The plan was initially conceived thanks to a newspaper clipping that appeared in *Srobroban*, an obscure Croatian newspaper, mailed by a terrorist band in Zagreb to their colleagues in Belgrade in late April, 1914. The article said that Franz Ferdinand would visit Sarajevo on June 28 as part of an inspection tour of Imperial army maneuvers in the neighboring mountains. The Belgrade conspirators sat around a small table in a café in the Serbian capital and read the article beneath a flickering gaslight.

The terrorists were outraged that the Austrian heir would visit the Balkans at all, much less on the most sacred day in the Serbian calendar, a day imprinted in the DNA of every Serb. The Serbs call June 28 *Vidovnan*, St. Vitus Day, the day on which in 1389 the Turks conquered Serbia at the battle of *Amselfelde*, and also the date on which, during the Second Balkan War of the previous year (1913), the Serbs had their revenge on the Turks. This was no day for a Habsburg to visit. It was an insult. The terrorists decided on the spot to kill the Archduke.

Franz Ferdinand, despite warnings of possible danger from the Serbian ambassador to Vienna and many briefings about the dark doings of the Black Hand, left Vienna by train on June 24. Sophie met him in *Ilidze* on June 27 when the maneuvers ended, and the couple went on to Sarajevo where they hosted a dinner for local luminaries. At the dinner, Sophie said to her husband: "You were wrong after all . . . We have been received with friendliness and sincere warmth by everybody, including the Serbian population." (Sidebar: Sophie's comment was eerily similar to one uttered by Nellie Connally, the first lady of Texas, at 12:29 PM on November 22, 1963 as President John F. Kennedy's limousine turned onto Elm Street in Dallas. She turned to the President and said, "Mr. President, you certainly cannot say that Dallas does not love you." He smiled at her when, suddenly, three shots rang out . . .)

The Habsburg heir's official schedule for the next day was widely publicized. There would be an official procession by open motor coach through the city, an inspection of military installations, followed by lunch and a visit to City Hall and a new museum.

The Motorcade

Franz Ferdinand had been advised by the Austrian intelligence service to avoid Sarajevo on that Sunday, counsel he brushed aside. In fact, the local security officials were very anxious about the visit. Sarajevo police chief Edmund Gerde recommended that a police cordon line the streets over which the Archduke would travel, but this was rejected by Oskar Potiorek, the Austrian military governor. Instead, the procession began with only minimal protection by a handful of soldiers.

Twenty-two conspirators, armed with bombs and pistols, fanned out 500 meters apart from one another along the entire motorcade route.

The six-vehicle motorcade entered downtown Sarajevo at 10:00 AM with the Archduke and Sophie occupying the second open car. He was in full uniform, topped off by a heavy feathered helmet. Sophie was dressed all in white. It was brutally hot that morning. The middle seat was occupied by the military governor. Franz Ferdinand's aide-de-camp sat next to the driver. As they rode along the *Miljacka* River embankment at 10:10 AM, a young man in the crowd on the sidewalk made a bowling motion with his hand. A black ball rolled toward the car, ricocheted off and wound up underneath a trailing vehicle, causing its front tire to blow. The car swerved and its occupants, a group of military officers, were thrown into the street. The bomber, 19-year old Nedjelko Cabrinovic, jumped down from the embankment to the river and swallowed a cyanide capsule that induced him to vomit. The police immediately apprehended him and began beating him. Aside from its fuse cap grazing Sophie's neck and a lieutenant who suffered cuts to his face, the crude bomb caused no other injuries. The remaining five cars in the motorcade proceeded on to City Hall at a slightly greater speed than before the attack.

Upon arriving at City Hall, Franz Ferdinand was livid with rage: "What is the meaning of this? We come here on a peaceful mission and we get bombs thrown at us." Potiorek assured him it was an isolated incident, the act of a lunatic. The scheduled speeches went on, and afterwards, the Archduke said he wanted to visit the injured lieutenant at the hospital. As the Austrian party left, he turned to Potiorek and asked: "Do you think there will be any more bombs?" The military governor's response has been variously reported, but the gist was something like this: "You may continue without worrying. I accept the entire responsibility." He did, however, recommend that, following the hospital visit, the rest of the official program be cancelled, just to be safe. Franz Ferdinand agreed.

The caravan resumed at 11:15 AM. When Cabrinovic's attempt failed, most of the other terrorists panicked and fled, blending into the crowd and giving up the assassination attempt.

This is where the series of events leading up to the "shot heard 'round the world" became a tragicomedy of errors. No one had bothered to inform the driver of the lead car of the change of plans. Consequently, he assumed that the official schedule was still in place and proceeded accordingly. The original itinerary had him turning right onto *Franz Josef* street, and this he did. The second car, containing the Archduke, Sophie, and Potiorek followed. Noticing this, Potiorek shouted out to the lead car driver: "Not that way, you idiot! Go straight!" Whereupon both drivers stopped their cars in order to back up.

Nineteen-year old Gavrilo Princip, one of the handful of terrorists who remained determined to carry out the plot, watched from the corner. Princip was something of a mystic, and believed himself to be a man of destiny who would perform a great deed in the name of freedom. He had a loaded Browning M1910 pistol in his pocket, never thinking he would have occasion to use it since the plan called for the assassination to be carried out by one of the bomb throwers.

But now, ten feet in front of him, were Franz Ferdinand and pregnant Sophie in a stopped, open vehicle.

Princip saw his destiny unfold. He pulled out his gun, took careful aim, and fired two shots. The first one hit Franz Ferdinand in the chest; the second hit Sophie in her abdomen. After a few seconds, Sophie slumped, unconscious, against her husband, who remained upright. Bystanders jumped on Princip as he put the gun to his head. He was nearly clubbed to death when the police rescued him.

Blood spewing from his mouth, the Archduke gasped: "Sopherl, Sopherl, don't die! Live for our children!" She was unresponsive and died seconds later.

Harrach, the aide-de-camp standing on the running board, asked Franz Ferdinand how badly he was wounded. "It's nothing," he said, repeating himself six times in an ever weakening voice. Then he died.

Post-Mortem

The Viennese were not particularly upset by the death of the heir to their throne. The Habsburg clan was actually relieved, their dislike of Franz Ferdinand and his commoner wife being intense. Otherwise, life went on in Vienna as before.

The bodies arrived back in Vienna on July 2 at night accompanied by no public ceremony. The coffins were placed in the Hofburg Palace chapel, the Archduke's a level above his wife's. The royal regalia was placed on his coffin; Sophie's supported just a fan and a pair of white gloves, a reminder that she had once been an insignificant lady-in-waiting. The coffins were on public display for four hours the next morning and, at 4:00 PM, a brief, private service took place attended by the Kaiser and a few royals. The pair was quietly buried at Franz Ferdinand's castle in *Artstetten*.

Grete heard the news from her parents the day after the assassination when her father picked up a newspaper at his favorite coffee shop. She says that it did not affect her emotionally at all. Habsburg royalty might have been distant galaxies as far as Leopoldstadt's Jewish population was concerned.

The consequences of that murderous act would, however, soon affect her greatly.

Chapter 11
The War to End All Wars

Assassination Aftermath

A month passed between the events of Sarajevo and any military response. In fact, it appeared at first as if nothing very dramatic would happen at all. July 1914 was one of the balmiest, most beautiful summer months Europe had experienced in many years. To the general public, it seemed as if nothing important was afoot.

Even the politicians seemed unaffected. The leaders of the great European powers continued about their business as usual and took their annual vacations. The same was true of Grete and her family. Little did they realize that everything was about to change.

Three weeks after the Archduke's death, things began to churn in the capitals of the Central Powers. By then, Austria-Hungary and Germany began to see Sarajevo in a different light, one they viewed as advantageous to their interests. The assassination gave Austria the excuse she needed, combined with a big push from her equally reckless German ally, to settle her long-standing score with Serbia. In mid-July, she confronted the small Balkan nation with a preposterous ultimatum that the Serbs could not possibly accept.

Suddenly, there was a frenzy of back-and-forth within the complex web of European power politics. Representatives of the powers traveled between their capitals and communicated by telephone and telegraph, attempting to avoid war, but not making all that much of an effort to keep the peace. To a large extent, this was because they almost all suffered under the delusion that, if there was a war, it would be a short affair, fought like the nineteenth century conflicts which they had all either studied or participated in, and that the world would quickly return to normal after their glorious victories.

What they failed to incorporate into their calculations were the huge advances in military technology that would cause stalemate, devastating losses, and incomprehensible horror. The advent of the Dreadnought (the new type of battleship first launched in 1906) with its steam turbine propulsion system and huge guns; the airplane, with its military implications; the tank, which the British were just developing; the machine gun, which killed millions due in large part to the thickheaded continuation of the nineteenth century infantry charge; and soon-to-be-developed poison gas, perhaps the most dreaded weapon of all, silent, deadly, and able to be employed against soldiers in their trenches even during lulls in the fighting. Moreover, the ability of these new technologies to inflict mass casualties not only on opposing forces, but on civilians as well, and the willingness of the combatants to do so, was a new factor injected into the equation.

Ultimatum

The Austrian ultimatum assumed that the Serbian government was implicated in the Archduke's assassination. It was presented to Belgrade on the evening of July 23, 1914, and demanded a response within 48 hours. In addition to demanding that the Serbian government publicly condemn both the assassination and anti-Austrian propaganda, it contained a series of demands that Austria and Germany assumed could not possibly be accepted, and which would thus give Austria the excuse for military action.

Serbia, to the amazement and disappointment of both the Austrians and their German advisors, accepted virtually the entire ultimatum, rejecting only the demand that Austria-Hungary take over an internal Serbian investigation into the assassination. After receiving assurances that Germany would support Austria militarily if Russia (Serbia's ally) mobilized against the Dual Monarchy, Austria on July 28 declared war on Serbia.

Mobilization

Earlier that week, Grete's 34-year old father David was ordered to report for a military draft physical. The family was shocked since, up to this point, no one realized that the events roiling Europe had reached this stage. David reported for his physical and feigned a severe and chronic stomach illness. His ruse worked and he was excused from the general conscription. He spent the entire war years continuing to run his haberdashery store on the first floor of the family's apartment building.

My father's family was much more directly affected. My grandfather, Solomon, was drafted and absorbed rapidly into the utterly unprepared and anachronistic Austro-Hungarian Army. He left by rail for a training site south of Vienna to the frenzied cheers of a delirious nation that was convinced that the Serbs would quickly capitulate without much bloodshed and that their loved ones would be home by Christmas.

My grandmother Theresa, Solomon's wife, was not so sure. Although the Hermanns (my father's family) were poor, living in much more distressed circumstances than the Sobels, the sudden loss of Solomon's livelihood and family income was not a catastrophe. Theresa was very close to her family in her hometown of Wiener Neustadt, and immediately took her two young children—Ernst, age 9 and Hedwig, age 5—to her relatives' four-house compound where they lived out the four years of the war in comfort and security, fed by her extended family's abundant farm produce and relative prosperity.

While the death of Franz Ferdinand and Sophie had not meant very much to the Sobel family, they were deeply affected by a second assassination that summer, one that took place on

July 31, 1914, the eve of total war. The family's political leanings were Socialist. Every May Day, David marched in solidarity with his Socialist compatriots through the streets of Vienna, a red armband on his sleeve.

The victim of the second assassination was the foremost international Socialist leader of his era, Jean Jaurès, head of the French Socialist party and founder of the great Paris Socialist newspaper, *L'Humanité*, which is still publishing today. Jaurès was the champion of the working classes and the foremost anti-war activist on the planet; a giant astride the world stage. He had spent much of July talking to the politicians about how to avoid war. To his dying breath, he did what he could to deter the nations of Europe from the coming conflict.

Jaurès was eating his evening meal in a Montmartre café when he was shot by a 29-year old French nationalist, the aptly surnamed Raoul Villain. Villain was tried and acquitted after the war. He was subsequently killed by Spanish Republicans in 1936 in that country's civil war.

The Sobels heard the news of Jaurès' death cried out by paperboys on the streets below their apartment. When David and Ernestine returned home from their regular evening excursion to their favorite café, they came in looking strained and unhappy. Grete knew something was up but thought it had something to do with the building war fever. As she aged and became more "politically" aware, Jaurès also became one of her heroes.

The Austrian declaration of war was the trigger that began the devastation that ensued. Now the intricate matrix of European defense treaties began to unravel the peace. Russia, Serbia's treaty partner and "soul mate," mobilized on July 29. Germany, having committed itself to defend Austria, mobilized in response. France, fearing a German mobilization, moved hundreds of thousands of troops to the Belgian frontier. Germany, fearing being pincered by a two-front war, automatically unrolled the Schlieffen Plan which had been developed and refined for the past 20 years by the German General Staff. It called for the German army to traverse neutral Belgium, invade France, quickly defeat it, and then turn its attention to the East and Russia. Britain, committed to defend Belgium, warned Germany what a Belgian incursion would mean. When the German army crossed into Belgium, Britain declared war. Sir Edward Grey, Britain's Foreign Minister, said it best: "The lamps are going out all over Europe, we shall not see them lit again in our life-time."

Austria's most prominent anti-war activist was probably Sigmund Freud, whose attacks on his government for fomenting the war were unreserved and did not stand him in good stead within the University of Vienna where he taught.

It was more difficult to be anti-war in Austria than anywhere else. Austria had suffered the outrage of the assassination of its Imperial heir, the triggering event for everything that followed. Moreover, unlike Britain and France, Austria lacked a system of conscientious objection.

Chapter 12
Privation

Austria, like all of the nations that went to war with such enthusiasm, did not bother to plan for adversity, believing that the war would not last very long. When, as 1914 drew to a close, it became evident that this was going to be a long-term affair, Austria still put blinders on, relying heavily on Hungarian agriculture to feed both its army and civilian population.

The Hungarian harvest dropped by one-third in 1914, rose modestly in 1915, and plummeted thereafter. There were no longer any foreign suppliers to whom Austria could turn, thanks to the highly effective allied blockade of the Central Powers. Austria's lack of planning proved a grievous oversight, one that its German ally shared.

Pre-war Austria-Hungary produced over 1,375 metric tons of wheat. By 1917, that figure had dropped 88 percent to 163 metric tons. One of the biggest problems was the lack of fertilizer, which generated a chain reaction up the food chain and engendered great hardship in Vienna. Limited supply and desperate demand drove food prices sky high, and the government responded by imposing price controls. Price controls rarely succeed, and this time was no exception. Worse, the Hungarian half of the Dual Monarchy hoarded its limited grain supplies and refused to "export" to Austria. By 1916, the situation was so grave that Hungary supplied only 5 percent of the grain and flour to Austria that it had before the war. Other food supplies were similarly tight.

Rationing was imposed in 1916. By mid-1917, the British naval blockade began to hit home very hard. Fish and egg consumption fell 50 percent and other foodstuffs such as vegetables, sugar, coffee, potatoes and butter disappeared from store shelves. Soap and fuel for stoves also began being rationed.

For a child, war at first seems exciting, a welcome interruption to the daily routine. Grete was no different. She enjoyed watching the jaunty Hussars and troops march confidently off to what they believed would be a walk in the park. The Imperial juggernaut would teach those Serbs and Russians a lesson and that would be that. That was not to be.

Grete's family was able to survive without much sacrifice for the first year of the war, but thereafter their situation deteriorated and quickly became acute. The family was starving.

Grete and Benno had to grow up fast. Their parents sent them out to the countryside several times a week to glean, beg and even steal what they could—eggs, butter, potatoes, etc.—from farms. They did this mainly in the Vienna Woods. They also came back with sacks full of mushrooms and, with the assistance of their mother, soon became adept at distinguishing the edible ones from those that were poisonous.

Grete and Benno became accomplished food thieves and fortunately were never caught. On several occasions, they were able to steal a chicken, break its neck, and bring it home for Ernestine to pluck and cook.

Thoughts of food crowded out everything else. Meatless days, which previously followed the dominant Catholic population's Friday and Lenten proscriptions, became everyday routines. Potatoes, impossible for most Austrians to come by, were available intermittently, thanks to Ernestine's parents, who made periodic trips to Vienna from Kamianka, bringing potatoes with them. The potato became such a prized delicacy that David's favorite meal the rest of his life was a heaping plate of them, boiled, steamed, *au gratin*, mashed or smashed. Grandpa could do more with a potato than any Food Channel talent could possibly imagine today. It rose to the level of "food aristocrat" in the family whenever starvation threatened.

Instead of the harsh German term for this humble starch—*"Kartoffel"*—in *Wienerisch*, the peculiar German dialect spoken in Vienna and nowhere else, the potato was referred to as *Erdäpfel*, "apple of the earth," a more poetic and justifiably exalted label.

The Sobel family's lifestyle was deeply affected by the shrinking food supply. Instead of coffee and tea, they gathered a variety of plants from the Wienerwald, dipping whatever was palatable into a kettle of hot water to make *ersatz* tea. Turnips began showing up in their meals. After a meal, they experienced a constant, nagging hunger, slept in an apartment that could not be heated quite enough, and got used to sleeping under heavy featherbeds, sometimes wearing their winter clothes, dreaming every night of food.

Grete remembered what desperate hunger felt like for the rest of her long life. Well into their 90s, Grete and her sister Rose would often speculate whether having been nutritionally deprived as growing children might affect their longevity!

Desperation

The blockade of Germany and Austria continued for almost two years after the armistice, keeping both countries in desperate straits. The victors wanted revenge and they took it out on millions of innocent children. By 1920, the infant mortality rate in Austria rose to an unprecedented 90 percent.

Vienna's workers suffered severe wage declines (50 percent in 1916 and another 50 percent in 1917), which had a major impact on David's haberdashery business. Customers dried up and the family's income, which pre-war had been steadily climbing, nose-dived. David had to give credit to most of his customers, the majority of whom never made good on their debts.

The general inflation caused by the Austrian government's expansion of the money supply (currency in circulation skyrocketed by 1,000 percent between 1913 and 1918) exacerbated Vienna's struggles. Austria was not alone in taking this path. All the combatants either formally or informally suspended gold convertibility, printed "new" money without any backing, and undertook general financial sorcery. Money supplies were detached from their pre-war relationship to central bank reserves. Much more money was in circulation than ever before. Inflation was the inevitable result and was far worse in wartime Austria than anywhere else. Consumer prices rose more than 1,000 percent, compared to 105 percent in Germany, 127 percent in Britain, 233 percent in France, and 326 percent in Italy.

Austrian morale, already rock bottom, plunged further when Emperor Franz Josef died in November 1916. He had been on the throne since 1848 and it was unimaginable that he was now gone. Even the Sobels, despite their Socialist leanings, nevertheless viewed the Emperor with a certain reverence and awe. This last remaining symbol of the *ancien régime* was gone, and the country's sense of hopelessness, already acute, bottomed.

The bulk of the Habsburg's imperial possessions had been won not by conquest, but rather through strategic marriages. A famous Latin couplet says it all: *Bella gerant ali–Tu felix Austria nube.* "Let others wage war–you, happy Austria, marry." By 1916, *felix* Austria was not so *felix* anymore.

Grete came out of the Great War weighing less than when it began despite having aged four years. At the conclusion of the war, more than 80 percent of Austrian children suffered from malnourishment. The percentage rose following the end of hostilities. For the rest of her life, Grete would remain on the thin side of the ledger.

Town dwellers suffered the most as the bulk of the supplies went to landed estates as feedstock for animals. Austrian pigs ate better than humans.

Food was not the only commodity in short supply. Wood, the primary energy source for home heating, was difficult to get. Although cutting wood there was illegal, the Wienerwald was seriously denuded of trees as the conflict wore on. Grete and Benno, although much too young to chop down trees, went on expeditions under cover of darkness to retrieve tree limbs and branches for their family's wood stove, which stood in the kitchen and served as the center of family life.

The absence of heat led fathers and mothers to leave their homes in the evening and go to the coffee houses, staying there until well into the night. There the warmth emanating from other human bodies and hot coffee and tea substituted for what was lacking at home. The children stayed home and huddled beneath blankets.

Censorship was imposed early in the war when it became apparent that Austria was in the midst of a war of attrition. Austria-Hungary set up a War Supervision Office (*Kriegsüberwachungsamt*) which, among other restrictions, forbade the publication of casualty statistics.

I asked Grete, a paragon of honesty and integrity, whether she and her brother ever felt remorse about stealing food and wood. Her response: "Not at all. We needed to survive." Oddly, Grete said she never thought of her family as suffering during the Great War. She went about her "childish business," as she put it, as if nothing was happening. Hunger, cold and general privation became routine. "We adapted," she said. "You can get used to almost anything." That was a viewpoint that would be tested, many times over, during the next quarter century of her life.

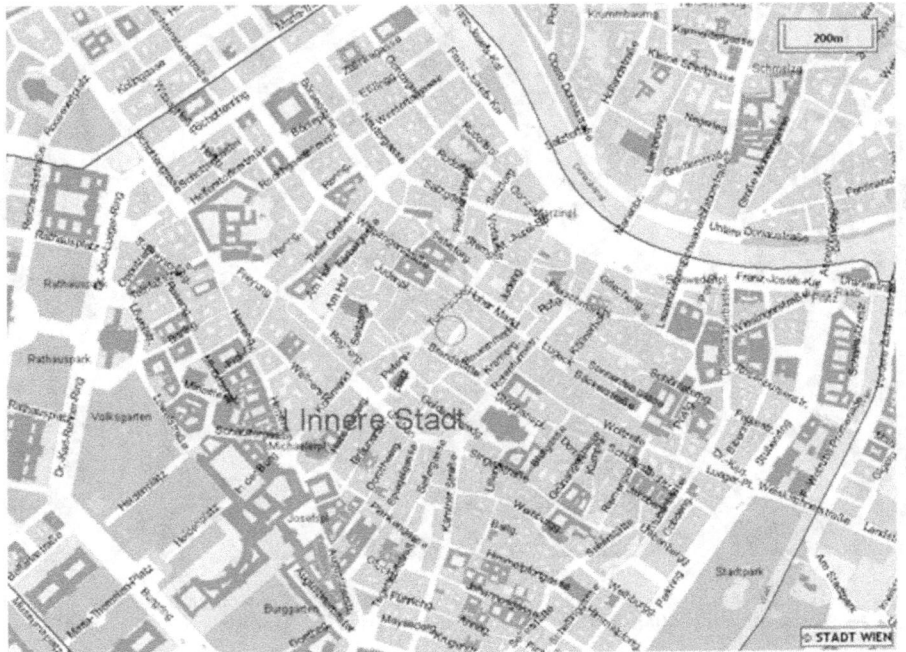

Central Vienna. Grete was born in the second building on the right side of Hollandstrasse, just over the Salztor bridge spanning the Donaukanal (upper right).
(*Source: www.hotel-amadeus.at*)

Vienna street scene ça 1905, the year of Grete's birth. The building is the Opera House.
(*Source: www.burtonholmes.org*)

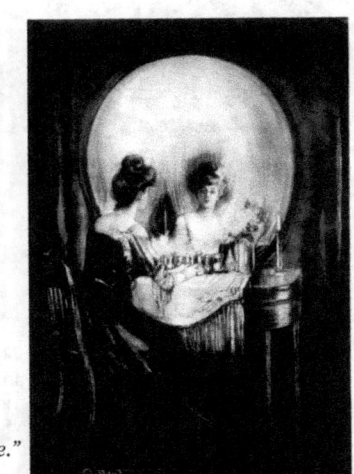

This painting captured the anxiety about the future that obsessed Vienna at the "fin-de-siècle."
"All is Vanity" C. Allan Gilbert Weird Optics

Kaiser Franz Josef toward the end of his 68-year reign.
(*Source: www.cityofart.net*)

Empress Elisabeth of Austria, reputedly the most beautiful woman in Europe.
(*Source: arrayedingold.blogspot.com*)

Austrian Archduke Franz Ferdinand and his wife, Sophie, in Sarajevo moments before the June 1914 assassination that launched World War I.

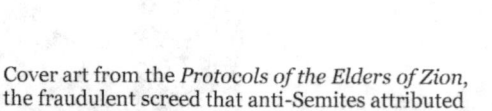

Cover art from the *Protocols of the Elders of Zion*, the fraudulent screed that anti-Semites attributed to the non-existent International Jewish Conspiracy.

Chapter 13
The Spoilage of War

Carnage

As the Eleventh Hour of the Eleventh Day of the Eleventh Month approached and the agreement imposed on Germany by the Entente powers was about to be signed in a railroad car in the forest of **Compiègne** in Northern France, the streets of the cities of the Old World were in turmoil. In Berlin, Bolshevists led by the rabble-rousing Karl Liebknecht attempted to establish a Marxist republic. In Munich and other cities throughout Germany, similar agitation seemed headed for success.

Corporal Adolf Hitler recuperated at a military hospital at *Pasewalk* in northern Germany from temporary blindness brought on by either a gas attack on the Western Front or what some of his physicians diagnosed as extreme hysteria. His confinement gave him plenty of time to buy into the delusion that Germany's surrender had nothing to do with the armies in the field, but rather was the result of a "stab in the back" by the Jewish speculators and war profiteers who were supposedly making hay on the home front while millions suffered and died in Flanders' fields. He decided that, upon recovery, he would go into politics to point out what had happened and correct it.

Mons, Belgium was the site of the first British army action in August, 1914 and the poster child for the tragic absurdity of the war. For the next 51 months the front barely moved. On November 11, 1918, Canadian troops took Mons just before 11:00 AM, the moment when hostilities ceased on all sides in all locations. It was the last major action of the Great War. Tens of thousands of young men on both sides lost their lives at Mons during what essentially amounted to a battle that endured for the entire war . . . for absolutely nothing.

But the futility and stupidity of Mons was not the most glaring example of how badly the crowned heads and military marshals of Europe had misjudged the situation and plunged their nations into misery and themselves onto the trash heap of history. That dubious honor was reserved for the now forgotten *Isonzo* Front.

The Isonzo

In Spring 1915, Austro-Hungarian Army Private Solomon Hermann was sent with his infantry unit to the Italian front on the banks of the Isonzo River in extreme northeast Italy, not far from Trieste and Venice. Armed with his standard issue *Mannlicher-Schönauer* rotary bolt-action rifle, he would spend the next three-and-a-half years in this inhospitable region, easily the most challenging military terrain in Europe. The Isonzo is a mountainous region, but not the kind of mountains that you see on Alpine promotional travel brochures. Instead, the Isonzo is all sharp crags, spurs, points and collines, as well as atrocious winter weather. The front was only 60 miles long from north to south. That small space witnessed human agonies that rank with the worst in the history of warfare.

Solomon was involved in all 12 inconclusive Battles of the Isonzo that raged from early 1915 through the next three-and-a-half years, as well as in Austria's unsuccessful attempt to push west into the more accommodating landscape of the *Trentino* above Lake *Garda.*

Fortunately for Austria's woefully inept generals, Italy countered with, hands down, the most incompetent wartime leadership of any of the combatants, and that is quite an assertion given the level of maladroit clumsiness displayed by virtually all of the political leaders and generals of the era. The worst Italian military debacle, attributable to the misguided ambitions of the consensus sorriest general of the First World War, the Italian commander Luigi Cadorna, took place on the Isonzo. After more than 40 months, the aforementioned 12 battles, hundreds of thousands of casualties on both sides, and hardships matching the worst suffered by any armies in the Great War, the front, like its Western counterpart, had barely budged an inch.

The horrors suffered by the combatants are unimaginable. Both sides were criminally ill-equipped for what they faced. Almost as many soldiers froze to death and lost limbs to frostbite as died or were maimed in combat. It is nothing short of a miracle that Solomon survived this ordeal intact. In 42 months of constant fighting, during which he was subjected to gunfire and artillery barrages (the most feared and most devastating weapon in every war), Solomon was never wounded. Of course, Post Traumatic Stress Disorder was unknown until very recently, and it is hard to imagine that he came home completely normal, mentally, psychologically, or emotionally.

Overall, almost 9 million men were killed in action or died from wounds in the Great War. Austria-Hungary lost 922,000 men, many of them on the Isonzo front. To put that into perspective, the much larger population of Britain lost 650,000 men, almost all in the much more highly publicized trench battles on the Western front.

My wife's great uncle, "Zio" Vitalone, was across the river from Solomon the entire time fighting for the Italian side. His standard weapon was the *Mannlicher-Carcano*, the joint Italian-Austrian design that Lee Harvey Oswald left behind on the sixth floor of the Texas School Book Depository in 1963.

Exhaustion

As the antagonists staggered, completely spent, to the finish line, the autocrats of Central and Eastern Europe who had so confidently and recklessly pushed Europe into an unnecessary and indescribably brutal war ignominiously exited the scene. With the glaring exception of Russia and, to a lesser extent Hungary, they were replaced by democratic regimes. The Tsar and his family were dead, shot by the Bolsheviks. German Kaiser Wilhelm abdicated and hastened by train to Holland for a humiliating exile, reviled along the way by crowds on both sides of the railroad tracks. Thirty-one year old Kaiser Karl I Franz Joseph Ludwig Hubert Georg Maria of Austria-Hungary, who ascended to the throne on the death of his great uncle Franz Josef in 1916, abdicated and left Vienna for his country hunting lodge. Thus quietly and ignominiously ended the reign of the House of Habsburg.

When the church bells of Europe marked the hour of the Armistice, the last soldier to die in the First World War was still alive. More than 2,000 battle deaths were recorded that day, *after* the war officially ended.

Chapter 14
Aftermath

World War I devastated Europe like nothing had since the Thirty Year's War three hundred years before. The summer and fall of 1916, when both the Battles of the Somme and Verdun were fought, 950,000 soldiers died and over a million more were grievously wounded, all for nothing. Virtually no ground changed hands as a consequence of these two slaughterhouses. Another 15.5 million soldiers in total were wounded, many of them suffering permanent physical disabilities.

Austria-Hungary's war deaths were the equivalent of the contemporary United States losing 7.5 million men today. An entire generation of men was lost.

What did all of this bloodshed achieve? Germany, Austria-Hungary, Russia and Turkey saw their rulers disappear into the mists of history, their governments transformed, their territories diminished. Serbia realized its goal of independence, becoming the dominant entity in the new Yugoslav state. Czechoslovakia, Finland, Poland and the three Baltic states (Estonia, Latvia and Lithuania) achieved their independence. Italy acquired the South Tyrol (which is still being disputed today by the great-grandsons of the original *Irredentist* rebels who even now blow up the occasional border post), Istria and part of Dalmatia. France got back Alsace and Lorraine, which it had lost to Germany in 1871 and would lose again in 1940. Germany relinquished its African and Oceanic colonies to France, Britain, Australia and New Zealand. Belgium and Portugal received snippets of Africa. Large chunks of the Middle East became part of the British and French orbits through League of Nations mandates. Armenia was divided between Russia and Turkey. Mapmakers the world over had a field day.

Austria's demise was total. The former empire that stretched throughout central and southern Europe was now a minimalist state, a geopolitical irrelevancy about the size of South Carolina.

The Great War was also the first time that modern weaponry, with its vast buffet of efficient killing technology, came into play. German aerial bombing of England, beginning in early 1915, added a new element to the horror of war. Almost 6,000 bombs were dropped on English cities, including London, killing more than 500 people and injuring many more. The Germans also bombed Paris. Submarines and tanks, explosive ordnance that could be hurled at seagoing targets barely visible to the shooters, and exotic chemicals that killed, paralyzed and maimed silently, added to the ability of man to destroy himself and all that is positive about human civilization. Both aerial bombing and the use of submarines had been outlawed a few years before by international treaties signed by all of the World War I belligerents. No matter.

It did not take long for the Great War combatants to label it "the war to end all wars." Horrors worse than the carnage and brutality of 1914-1918 were beyond the imaginations and nightmares of the participating countries and their traumatized warriors and citizens. The natural offshoot of that assumption was an optimistic view of the future. The world that emerged from the blood and grime of Verdun and the Isonzo River/*Alto Adige* region of South Tyrol had to be an improvement over the one that led to the conflict. Didn't U.S. President Woodrow Wilson proclaim that the war had been fought to "make the world safe for democracy"?

The successor states that arose out of the rubble were, initially, vibrant and dynamic, bursting with hope for the future. Freedom and justice for all were watchwords that swept through the continent. It looked to be the dawn of a new, more humane era.

Europe's Jewish communities involuntarily assumed the role of the canary in the coal mine. If this was really to be a new world of promise and optimism, the Jews would be the immediate beneficiaries, the first to know. Consequently, they hurled themselves into the new era—its politics, economies, culture and societies—with unbridled enthusiasm. They joined the Communist and Socialist parties in droves; they pressed for social reform; they became utopians. They rushed to join their Christian fellow citizens in building new societies.

To a limited extent, the Jews had called it right. The early post-war years were heady ones for virtually every European power, even Germany. Only one country did not join in the general enthusiasm: Austria.

Austria-Lite

Austria was now a mere footnote, home to less than 10 percent of its pre-war population. No longer would Vienna be the capital of a great power.

Vienna's post-war population of two million accounted for a full third of the entire Austrian population. Despite its sudden transformation, Austria's capital still retained its leading position in many fields. Three, in addition to the ones described in previous chapters, merit mention:

- Philosophy, led by Ludwig Wittgenstein, whose originally Jewish family were now Catholic converts, and his *Tractatus Philosophico Mathematicus*, following the writing of which this very bizarre character taught elementary school and worked for a time as a gardener in a monastery.
- Medicine, the centerpiece of which was the University of Vienna Medical School, the greatest medical school in the world at that time. People came from all over for treatment and consultation

with the luminaries who taught there. Fearing throat cancer, Adolf Hitler sought the advice of Professor von Neumann, the world's foremost ear, nose and throat specialist, who also happened to be Jewish. The diagnosis, unfortunately, was negative. The hysterical hypochondriac was sent on his way reassured by the eminent physician that he was suffering from nothing more than a mild sore throat.
- Social Services were pioneered in Vienna, where low-cost housing projects for workers went up in many sections of the city.

The wartime suffering of the Austrian people did not end on November 11, 1918 or the next year with the signing of the Versailles Treaty, nor with the Entente's specific peace treaties with Austria, the Treaties of *Trianon* and *St. Germain*. Living conditions immediately after the war actually deteriorated. The immediate impact of the break-up of the empire was that Austria was left without any of its previous ties to foodstuffs and other essential commodities. As indicated previously, Austria during the Imperial era got most of its foodstuffs from Hungary. The new administration in Budapest stopped all food shipments. The newly independent Czech regime stopped Bohemian coal shipments.

The winter of 1918-1919 was harsh and starvation killed many Viennese. One year after the war ended, 96% of Austrian children were officially classified as "undernourished." Grete and her siblings were part of the suffering and lack of sustenance. She and her siblings lost considerable weight and had to scrounge for food to an even greater extent and even more creatively than during the war.

My mother attributed her thin physique to the privations of the Great War and its aftermath. For the rest of her life, she worshipped food and viewed a hearty meal as something approaching a miracle. When a piece of bread fell to the floor, she picked it up and kissed it before putting it back on her plate.

Hunger in Vienna was a bonanza for farmers in the countryside. Extortionate price gouging predominated. Grete and Benno, now teenagers, continued their wartime modus *operandi* and went out to the country to beg and, if necessary, steal food from farmer's fields.

When farmers came to town to buy tools and equipment, they found that the merchants had doubled, tripled and quadrupled their prices in order to pay for overpriced food. A dangerous price spiral emerged that soon escalated out of control. A barter economy arose as money became less valuable. People, Grete's family included, traded antiques, rare books, jewelry and artworks for food. Combined with the reckless fiscal policies of the wartime government, hyperinflation loomed.

Grete and Benno were not the only thieves in Vienna. Petty crime exploded during and immediately after the war. Leaving a milk bottle on a doorstep was a guarantee that the family inside would never see the milk.

Herbert Hoover's American Relief Administration (ARA) successfully lobbied the victorious nations for permission to feed the Austrians and Germans. Once the ARA program got going, it delivered over 4 million tons of food to 23 European nations; 500,000 tons went to Austria. Like certain elements of the post-World War II Marshall Plan, one of the ARA's aims was to stop the spread of Communism to Central Europe. It succeeded.

Grete and her family were among the beneficiaries of ARA relief. She said that the best thing about it was that she and her brother no longer had to steal food. Another lasting vestige of the effort was her admiration for Herbert Hoover. Her respect for him survived his failure to deal effectively with the 1929 stock market crash and the ensuing Great Depression.

"Herbert Hoover saved our lives."

All in all, the Sobels were lucky. They survived the war without appreciable damage to themselves or their health, and David's haberdashery, which carried many of life's clothing necessities, began doing well again soon after hostilities ended. Returning veterans needed civilian clothes, and the store was well-stocked.

Pandemic

As if the war were not enough. The Spanish Flu, which took more than 20 million European lives (an estimated 50 million worldwide), reached Vienna in October 1918, a month before the end of the war. It was probably brought home by soldiers who were either mustering out at the end of their tours of duty or were injured or sick and medically discharged. The high concentration of troops in close quarters at the end of the war and for months thereafter, as well as the huge troop movements during the post-war demobilization, contributed to the high death toll.

It is estimated that fully one-third of the planet's population was infected. My mother and her three siblings contracted the flu and caused their parents enormous worry because this particular brand of infection was more dangerous to adolescents and young adults than the annual flus that typically threaten infants and the elderly. Fortunately, all four children survived. Not everyone was so lucky.

In its last stage, a flu victim's face turned blue, he or she coughed up blood, and then quickly drowned when the lungs became swamped with bodily fluids.

Where did it come from? Epidemiologists to this day cannot pinpoint its origins. Several theories vie for consideration. The first cases were documented in the United States at Fort Riley, Kansas in June 1918. At Fort Riley, it is believed, the virus jumped species from poultry and/or swine raised at the fort for food. Another theory is that the flu originated at a British staging camp in France.

The flu arrived in Europe, most likely carried by American Expeditionary Force troops as the U.S. escalated its participation in the war. The pandemic lasted until December 1920 and spread to every corner of the world.

While Spain was hardly the country most affected, the name Spanish Flu stuck because of widespread news reporting of the contracting of the disease by Spanish King Alfonso XIII (he survived).

Ten to twenty percent of those infected died, compared to the average annual flu mortality rate of one-tenth of one percent. There was no vaccine. A blood transfusion from a diseased survivor was the best cure. However, public health was an afterthought in war-torn Europe.

The Spanish Flu was the greatest medical holocaust in history, exceeding even the ravages of the Black Death in the Middle Ages. It was the first holocaust that Grete had to endure and survive, but not the last.

Chapter 15
Rump State

The end of the war was both a relief to the Jews of Vienna and a jarring shock at the same time. Politically, the empire was gone. In its place was a tiny rump state with a geographic presence that looked like a European afterthought.

It took considerable getting used-to for the citizens of Austria. The pomp of the Hofburg and Schönbrunn palaces instantly became museum pieces, relics of a fantastical bygone era. When the new Kaiser, Karl I, retired to his hunting lodge, the monarchy was replaced by an elected government. Karl died in 1921, poverty stricken, a virtual prisoner on a small Portuguese island.

The Versailles Treaty with Germany paralleled the victorious Allies' Treaty of *St. Germain-en-laye* with Austria, which was signed in September, 1919. The treaty dissolved the Austro-Hungarian Empire and, in its (partial) place, created the Republic of Austria, which consisted of all of the German-speaking Habsburg lands except the *Sudetenland*, which became part of the new state of Czechoslovakia, and the South Tyrol, awarded to Italy as a pay-off for switching sides during the war (a "180" that Italy was to repeat in 1943 during World War II). To this day, nationalist Austrians still mourn these losses.

Vienna at the end of the war was a city in shock. From its inhabitants' comforting delusion that they lived in the center of the universe, it had become a beaten down shell of its former self. Vienna lost everything: the war, the emperor, the imperium, most of its territory, and its relative prosperity. The entire nation suffered from depression.

Runaway Inflation

During the twenty years between the two world wars, Europe confronted a series of unimaginable man-made disasters: epidemics, revolutions, the breakup of states, currency collapses, severe unemployment and underemployment. These caused budding Western democracies like Germany and Italy to fall into the Fascist totalitarian trap which in turn led to the most devastating war in history.

The Versailles Treaty quickly became a rallying point for all Germans, and the French did more to fan the flames of reaction and resentment than anyone. When Germany defaulted on reparations payments toward the end of 1922, France jumped at the opportunity to teach its enemy a lesson and marched troops into the Ruhr, Germany's only remaining industrial pocket. To rub it in, the French invasion purposely consisted of African troops from the French colonial empire, mindful of Germany's deeply racist psyche. A general strike of German workers ensued and it was not long before the currency collapsed.

Following the First World War, aggregate European gross domestic product (GDP) did not reach 1913 levels again until the late 1950s. But that was only the beginning of the economic devastation that befell Germany and Austria.

Everyone who knows the history of the post-war era has heard about the German hyperinflation of 1922-23, when prices daily went through the roof. But Germany was not the only defeated nation to suffer from this economic scourge. By the end of the war, the value of the Austrian krone had fallen to 1/16 of its pre-war value due to indiscriminate government printing of banknotes to pay its war bills. By August 1922, the currency had collapsed and paper money was close to being worthless. Consumer prices rose to a level *14,000 times higher* than their pre-war level.

Germany and Austria financed their Great War by borrowing and printing money. The natural result was inflation. The unnatural consequence was the worst runaway inflation the world had ever seen. At the beginning of the war, currency in circulation in Austria totaled 3.4 billion kroner. By the end of the war four years later, the money supply had grown to just under 34 billion kroner, a 1,000 percent increase. The cost-of-living index had increased by 1,640 percent. And that was just the beginning.

The new successor states of Eastern Europe imposed heavy tariffs on Austrian goods, and even provinces within the new, much smaller Austria imposed trade barriers on each other. The country was out of control.

The inflationary numbers are almost impossible to grasp. Over the next five years, the cost of living index went up to *1,183,000 percent* of the pre-war figure. The foreign exchange rate went up from 16.1 kroner to the dollar in 1919 to 70,800 kroner to the dollar in May 1923.

It was even worse in Germany. In early 1922, the mark had stabilized at an awful 320 to one U.S. dollar. By the end of the year, it reached 8,000 marks to the dollar. Eleven months later, the exchange rate was *4.2 trillion* marks to the dollar. No one could afford to buy anything.

Strangely, the Austrians did not think that they had it so bad. Relative to what was happening in neighboring Germany, they didn't. The political weakness and resulting gridlock of Germany's Weimar government, combined with monstrous reparations payments due the victorious nations, and a refusal to accept the fact that Germany had lost the war, plus the reckless spending and monetary policies of the war years, caused the German currency and economy to go into free-fall. At its peak toward the end of 1923, there were 49,700,000,000,000,000,000,000 (almost 50 *sextillion*) marks in circulation. The annual inflation rate reached *182 billion* percent. Prices were 1.26 *trillion* times their 1913 levels. Industrial production fell to 50 percent of its pre-war level, and unemployment peaked at 25 percent, with another 25 percent in part-time jobs.

By late 1923, the economies of both Germany and Austria could no longer even be called economies. Nothing was available for purchase. No one could afford to manufacture anything. Workers who were paid at noon on Friday found that, by the time they carted their wheelbarrows and baby carriages full of bank notes to the grocery store, the prices had again skyrocketed beyond their ability to pay. Women and girls took to the streets by the thousands, hoping to sell their bodies in return for food for their families. Few would-be takers, however, could afford their fleshly delights.

Grete's *gymnasium* (high school) graduation trip to Bavaria at around this time made her an eyewitness to the German hyperinflation. She and her classmates watched from their bus slack-jawed as factory workers paid with mountains of paper currency raced to the factory gates where their wives waited with wheelbarrows. The wives then raced off to buy food before prices escalated again. On her return home, she told her family of foreigners who were buying luxury apartments in Munich for the equivalent of two U.S. dollars!

In November 1923, Adolf Hitler, flying ace Hermann Göring and 2,000 Nazis, along with World War I hero General Erich Ludendorff, staged an amateurish attempt at a *coup d'état* against the Bavarian government in Munich. After one of his increasingly frequent, hysterical harangues at the *Burgerbraukeller*, the liquored-up group (led by the tee-totaling Hitler) took off down the street toward the seat of government. As they neared the War Ministry, someone among the Nazi rabble fired his weapon and all hell broke loose. The Bavarian police shot back and Hitler dove for the ground. The melee was over after only thirty seconds and eighteen deaths—fourteen Nazis and four policemen. Typical of Nazi hagiography, this tragi-comic event was elevated in later years to a position at the apex of the Nazi pantheon of revisionist lies.

Hitler was arrested and briefly imprisoned. He used his incarceration to dictate *Mein Kampf* to his devoted acolyte, Rudolf Hess. His trial, which he dominated, made him a national figure. Grete and her friends believed that Hitler was a ludicrous figure, a clown. They quickly dismissed him as a serious player in German politics.

In Austria, tethered as it was to the German economy, hoarding became the norm and food and fuel again became scarce. They were available to some extent on the black market, and Grete often went out with some of her father's savings to buy necessities. She became quite an accomplished price negotiator, a talent that I witnessed several times when she and I went shopping and she actually negotiated down prices in stores like Pier One and Macy's. Her post-war experiences gave her a totally different perspective on posted prices in conventional shops. She viewed them as the opening gambit in a protracted negotiation.

The term "inflation" does a disservice to what happened in Germany and Austria following World War I. "Hyperinflation," "runaway inflation," call it what you will, there is no term that can adequately describe what happened.

The Hermann family, Vienna, 1909 (Therese, Hedwig, my father Ernst, Solomon)

The Isonzo Front, World War 1, where Solomon Hermann fought from 1915-1918.
(*Source: Axis History Forum - forum.axishistory.com*)

German 1 Mark (25 U.S. cents) postage stamp revalued to 1 billion marks ($1 trillion U.S.) to keep up with the post-World War I hyperinflation.
Author's stamp collection

David Sobel's haberdashery on Hollandstrasse in 1926, the peak year of the Sobel family's prosperity. David is second from left, with his staff and his 13-year old son, Otto (far right). *Author's collection*

A *Graf und Stift* automobile like the one David Sobel purchased in the late 1920s.

Chapter 16
Intermezzo: Post-War Austrian Politics

This chapter diverges from the otherwise chronological sequence of this book because the political evolution of Austrian politics during the inter-war period needs to be viewed as an organic whole in order to understand its impact on Grete, her family, and the Viennese Jewish community.

The Setting

Austrian Socialism traced its origins back to the mid-nineteenth century, but it took its founders the first 30 of those years to develop a viable political movement. When the Austrian Socialist Party formally organized in 1888, it was both internationalist and revolutionary, much more so than its German counterpart, due to two factors: (1) the supra-national character of the Habsburg Empire, and (2) the dismal conditions of the working class when compared to German laborers.

The Austrian Right found its principal political home in the Christian Social Party, which developed contemporaneously with the Socialists and dominated the Viennese government from the turn of the century to the beginning of World War I. By 1919, the two parties were the principal contenders for power in the new republic that succeeded the Habsburgs. Until 1930, they hotly contested five successive national elections that always resulted in a conservative national government.

The biggest obstacle facing the new republic was the deep division between Vienna and the rest of Austria that emerged from the dissolution of the Empire. The Kaiser had been the only glue that bound the fractious national entities together. When Kaiser Karl abdicated in 1918, Austria lost any common bond.

The Socialists consistently dominated in urban Vienna while the overwhelmingly Roman Catholic, agrarian provinces were deeply conservative. The rift became so wide in 1918-19 that the provinces became reluctant to send their food products to Vienna. Several provinces seriously discussed secession. Westernmost Vorarlberg voted in May 1919 to begin negotiations to leave Austria and unite with Switzerland. Eighty percent of Vorarlberg voters opted in favor of becoming a Swiss canton. However, the campaign never gained traction because the power to decide the future frontiers of Austria rested with the Paris peace conference. The conference deemed this a minor issue and decided against Vorarlberg. Further efforts by the province to persuade the League of Nations to agree to union with Switzerland did not succeed. The province of Tyrol also discussed secession, but never got very far with its agitation.

The Democratic Experiment

Despite this internal turmoil, it appeared that Austria, above all of the other new nations that emerged from the war, had the best chance of becoming a democratic bastion. Its parliamentary tradition dated back further than any of the other new states in the region. Moreover, it was suddenly the most homogeneous of all the emerging democracies. Having lost all of the other nationalities that comprised the Empire, what was left was an overwhelmingly Catholic, German-speaking nation. National minority problems were gone. Austria also boasted a highly trained and experienced professional civil service.

Tragically, the war victors failed to consider what would happen once the proud Empire became a tiny rump state shorn of its past glory. It was inevitable that Austria would yearn for union with Germany. However, union was forbidden by the Treaty of St. Germain between Austria and the World War I victors.

No party during the republican era was ever able to win a majority in Parliamentary elections. Consequently, the right-wing Christian Socials always had to forge governing coalitions with smaller, radical Fascist parties. As the 1920s advanced, the enormous socio-economic disruptions of the war, the dissolution of the Empire, post-war starvation, runaway inflation, banking system corruption (a disproportionate number of Jews were in banking, so it was easy to blame them for this), and the Great Depression devastated the middle classes and encouraged extremism. This benefited the Right much more than the Left and gave the Fascist parties a choke-hold on forming governments. The Socialists consistently came out on top, but never with enough votes to govern. As late as the 1930 election, the Socialists won 72 seats to the Christian Socials 66. Nevertheless, it was the latter in coalition with the Pan-Germans and *Heimwehr* (27 seats between them) who formed the government. Even more ominous, by this time the National Socialists (Nazis) had made considerable inroads into Austrian politics.

Anti-Semitism, never far below the surface *gemütlichkeit* so ingrained in the Viennese character, exploded and expanded, fueled further by the fact that many of the Social Democrats who governed in Vienna were Jewish. Despite the fact that the opposition Christian Social Party initially shared the democratic tendencies of the Socialists, it was the latter who were invariably blamed for Austria's troubles.

Social Democracy's Mistakes

The Social Democrats deserve considerable blame for the inability of democracy to gain traction in Austria. When they first had the opportunity at the end of the war, they hesitated to impose their program. By the time they were ready to go forward with their "social revolution" in the 1930s, they were long out of government.

When the Danube monarchy collapsed in 1918, its bureaucracy and military were absorbed into the new, democratic Austrian state, but not in the same positions they held under the Kaiser. Instead, almost all were demoted several grades. Resentment with their reduced circumstances was enormous. This was the Social Democrats' first major mistake. The next 15 years was nowhere near enough time for these imperial military officers and civil servants to become committed democrats. Their hearts still belonged to the old regime. When opportunity presented itself, they permitted their frustrations to go public, shed their false skins, and proudly displayed their colors as enemies of democracy.

Adding to this dismal mix was the fact that their savings were wiped out by the post-war inflation. They were ripe for right-wing, extremist appeals. Many joined the Heimwehr, which aligned itself with Chancellor Engelbert Dollfuss in the *Vaterländische Front*—the Fatherland Front—which mimicked the German Nazis in its adoption of the *Sieg Heil* salute and the *Hakenkreuz* (Swastika) symbol.

Proportional representation, the basis of the new republican electoral system, inevitably meant coalition governments that added to the instability of the country. By 1920, the Christian Socials were led by Dr. Ignaz Seipel, a Catholic priest who believed that the Socialists were not the loyal opposition, but rather enemies of the state. Seipel was additionally aroused by the constant Socialist drumbeat of anti-Catholic propaganda.

Another factor was the traditional antipathy of the country to the city, exacerbated in Austria's case by the fact that Vienna was bursting with leftists and Jews. The country, in contrast, was conservative, Catholic and reactionary. The Christian Socials appealed to the countryside and received virtually universal support from that quarter.

The Militias

The final nail in the democratic coffin—and the key factor that differentiates both Weimar Germany's and democratic Austria's politics from present day America's political polarization—was the existence of powerful, ideologically-based militias, the Social Democrats' *Schutzbund* and the Right's *Heimwehr*. While the Schutzbund got its money from workers and labor unions, the Heimwehr was financed by the former imperial aristocracy and numerous industrialists and was publicly endorsed by Chancellor Seipel. As the 1920s advanced, any possibility of support for democratic government from the Right evaporated.

The Rightist private armies consisted mainly of unemployed men. In addition to the Heimwehr, they included the *Frontkämpfer* (Battle Front Veterans) and the surging Nazis in their brown shirts.

These reactionary militias clashed frequently and violently with the Schutzbund. Blood flowed freely in the streets of Vienna while the police and authorities usually looked on, restrained by the hope that these warring political militias would cancel each other out.

The summer of 1927 foreshadowed much of what was to come during the next decade. In January, a man and boy were killed in a fight between the Schutzbund and the Frontkämpfer. When the responsible Frontkämpfer fighters were acquitted of the murders on July 15, the Socialists called a general strike. Thousands of workers left their jobs to demonstrate against the verdict, marching on parliament. Chancellor Seipel called out the mounted police and violence erupted. The protestors scavenged materials from construction sites and constructed barricades.

The workers then broke through the police cordon and entered the Ministry of Justice, destroying property and setting fires. Seipel called in militia troops and the violence escalated.

The final toll of the riots was more than 100 deaths and 600 injuries.

That evening, Socialist leaders called another general strike and told workers to remain in their homes for one day in order to prevent the demonstrations from evolving into a civil war. The next day, it appeared that the strike was a success. However, six young communists were killed, allegedly by the police, although there is evidence that the Schutzbund could have had a hand in the killings.

While the general strike might have prevented a revolution, its short-term success was overcome by its long-term implications for Austrian democracy. *Die Schreckentage*, the "Days of Horror," marked the beginning of the end of the republic and the prodigious rise of the Fascist parties that were determined to bring down democratic Austria.

Grete and her family remained indoors during the riots. Her father closed the store and put boards over the windows. This proved a good idea given that $35 million worth of Viennese property was destroyed and numerous Jewish-owned businesses were looted. From their apartment, they heard the sounds of gunshots, explosions and the sirens of fire trucks and police vehicles that went on for more than 24 hours.

The direction in which the government was going was of great concern to the Sobels, Socialist supporters despite David being a small, intermittently successful shopkeeper, an occupation whose sympathies were generally not inclined to the Left. His relative business success notwithstanding, David could not forget the poverty from which he emerged and admired the good works the Socialists had accomplished for the working classes. His contributions to the Socialists amounted to small monetary donations and marching in their annual May Day parade.

The 1930s

By 1932-33, Austria was surrounded on almost all sides by totalitarian regimes. Its own days as a democracy were clearly numbered.

The year 1932 was the turning point. Dr. Engelbert Dollfuss, the illegitimate son of a farmer's daughter, became chancellor and, despite his lack of height (under five feet tall), became Austria's first and last "strong man." Dollfuss spent his youth dreaming of becoming a priest, and he came to power closely allied with and influenced by the corporate conservatism of Austria's reactionary Catholic hierarchy. Moreover, he believed in Aryan superiority, although not quite to the extreme degree as his northern counterpart, Adolf Hitler.

Dollfuss' drive toward authoritarianism was given a big boost by the Kreditanstalt bank collapse (discussed in greater detail later in this book), the trigger for the Great Depression's spread to Europe. The Depression caused fence-sitters to abandon democratic capitalism and seek an alternative economic and political model. More ominously, Dollfuss' efforts to form a majority coalition government with either the Pan-Germans or even the Social Democrats came to naught. He was compelled to seek out the Heimwehr and put its leader, Major Emil Fey, in charge of the powerful Interior Ministry. This gave the militant Right authority over the entire security service. The Fascists now attained their long-sought wedge into power.

Dollfuss initially governed by emergency decree and thus avoided having to seek parliamentary approval of his policies. The failure of the Socialists to protest this illegal abandonment of democratic norms encouraged him to go after the Schutzbund next. He arrested its leaders and attempted to dissolve the organization. This brought things to a head.

The Final Conflict

By 1934, the divide between Left and Right reached canyon-like proportions. Dollfuss had few options politically and, despite a personal distaste for the right-wing militias, knuckled under to them and began a campaign to suppress Austrian socialism. The tyranny of the minority, which had already manifested itself the year before in Germany with Adolf Hitler's accession to the chancellorship, now arrived in Austria. The triumph of extremist ideology was about to bring the country to the breaking point.

In early 1934, the Heimwehr, in league with both the government and Fatherland Front, decided that the time had come to eliminate the Socialists. Despite their ban by Dollfuss a year earlier, Nazi cells were still active and, on February 12, 1934, precipitated the ensuing chaos, blood, and death by searching a Social Democratic-owned hotel in Linz. No one knows who began shooting, but soon both the police and Army became involved.

What began in Linz alarmed Vienna's Social Democrats. Schutzbund fighters barricaded themselves into council houses—the workers' residence blocks the Social Democrats had constructed after the war. They had only small arms. Dollfuss ordered that artillery be used against them.

The most famous barricaded residence was Vienna's half-mile long *Karl Marx Hof*, which came under heavy artillery fire from government troops, police, and the Heimwehr. A day later, the Socialists surrendered. Several hundred Socialists died. Austrian democracy died with them. The Social Democratic party was declared illegal and dissolved. The Schutzbund was crushed. More than 1,500 Socialists were arrested and nine were executed.

That Monday, February 12, Grete heard the artillery bombarding the Karl Marx Hof about a mile away from her apartment. The artillery barrage was followed by the distinctive sound of machine gun fire. She looked out her window and saw soldiers with machine guns in the streets and armored vehicles at the intersections at either end of her block. Otherwise, the streets were deserted. She closed her medical office for the duration of the crisis and stayed upstairs in the Sobel apartment.

The carnage was over in a few days, followed by a somber ceremony at the *Rathausplatz* populated by the flag-draped coffins of soldiers, police, and Heimwehr who had died fighting the Socialists. Grete walked by the coffins and what she saw woke up her until-then largely dormant political persona.

Although Socialism was no longer a factor in Austrian politics, Socialists could not all be eliminated. Her sympathies had always been vaguely with the Socialists, but now she became an activist and marched in May Day parades with her father, contributed what little she could spare to the cause, and attended the occasional underground party meeting. During her walks with friends around the Ringstrasse and in the Wienerwald, the talk was now of politics and the Fascist threats closing in on Austria from north and south (Mussolini's Italy). Although she was approached several times, she did not join one of the Socialist cells that engaged in activities that the Austrian government had declared illegal. Her hesitation was due to her parents' need for her financial contribution to the family that would be jeopardized should she be arrested and imprisoned.

Later in the decade, the Spanish Civil War (1936-1939) became an obsession for Socialists worldwide. Vienna's Socialists were no exception. Grete contributed money to the Spanish Republican cause.

Dictatorship and Assassination

Following the "revolution," Dollfuss established what amounted to a dictatorship, but not for long. On June 30, 1934, Hitler staged his "night of the long knives" coup against Ernst

Röhm and his powerful *Sturmabteilung* (SA), the Nazis' 3-million strong paramilitary arm. Röhm had ambitious aspirations, including the radical goal of merging the German Army into the SA. This was something the *Wehrmacht* generals could not tolerate. In return for their pledges of support, Hitler agreed to get rid of Röhm and his followers. Röhm and several hundred SA leaders who had convened in the Bavarian Alps for a meeting and homosexual tryst were purged and executed that day, and the SA was relegated to subordinate status within the *Schutzstaffel* (SS). Hitler's rise to absolute power was now almost complete.

Encouraged by Hitler's triumph, the Austrian Nazis sensed that their time had also come. On July 25, 1934, Dollfuss was assassinated by ten Austrian Nazis who entered the Chancellery in Vienna and gunned him down in an attempted, but unsuccessful *putsch*. When Hitler, who was attending the annual Wagner Festival at *Bayreuth* watching a performance of *Das Rheingold*, received news of the assassination, he was unable to restrain himself and jumped for joy.

Mussolini mobilized the Italian army and sent troops to the Brenner Pass on the Austrian border, threatening Hitler with war if Germany invaded Austria. He sent Italian troops into the Austrian province of Carinthia to subdue Nazis who were attempting to seize power. In a widely publicized announcement, the *Duce* proclaimed: "The independence of Austria, for which he [Dollfuss] has fallen, is a principle that has been defended and will be defended by Italy even more strenuously." In an accompanying symbolic gesture, he had the statue of Walther von der Vogelweide, the German troubadour who was the inspiration for Wagner's opera, *Die Meistersinger von Nürnberg*, replaced with one of Drusus, the great Roman general who conquered part of Germany almost 2,000 years before and wanted to restore the Roman Republic. The symbolism of the statue was obvious, albeit an odd choice for a ruthless dictator who had overthrown a republican government.

Dollfuss' assassination led to violent uprisings throughout Austria. The Nazis attempted Vienna *putsch* was quickly put down by the army. The Nazi conspirators were subsequently tried and executed.

The young Minister of Education, Kurt von Schuschnigg, was named the new chancellor. He too was a fascist, but a milder version of his predecessor. We will return to Schuschnigg and his fate in a later chapter.

Chapter 17
Prosperity Returns (Briefly)

Despite the post-war hyperinflation, the mid-to-late 1920s economy roared just as loudly in Austria as in the United States. Remarkably, the Austrian economy quickly recovered, thanks to a currency reform where the *Schilling* replaced the *Krone* at a ratio of 1:10,000. The ravages of inflation soon dissipated and Austria began its climb to recovery.

What saved Grete's family from utter ruination during the inflationary period was inventory. Much of her father's money had been tied up in his store's inventory. While he did not sell much during the years of runaway inflation, once people returned to work and the economy began to recover, they needed clothing. The store prospered.

By the late 1920s, David was even able to buy a car and hire a chauffeur; he himself never learned to drive. The car was a glossy brown *Graf und Stift* convertible, the product of an Austrian carmaker that was still in business into the twenty-first century (the company went out of business in 2001 after 99 years). Archduke Franz Ferdinand and Sophie were riding in a Graf und Stift Double Phaeton when they were assassinated in Sarajevo.

Graf und Stift was primarily a luxury automobile manufacturer. However, in 1928, it began to build a car designed for the middle classes, and the 2-litre *Typ VK* model was the one David purchased.

The family had the car for ten years. Two weeks after the Anschluss in March 1938, however, the car was commandeered (translation: stolen) without compensation by the local Nazis.

For the first time since the beginning of the Great War, the family did not have to worry about where its next meal was coming from. The store provided a good income, so much so that David and Ernestine were able to support not only their family of six, but also pay for the chauffeur and a full-time maid as well as a constant stream of newly-arrived relatives who would stay for months at a time until they were able to go out on their own. In addition, several of Ernestine's relatives worked in the store, an arrangement that sadly proved the time-tested admonition that one should never hire a relative or friend. One of Ernestine's siblings, who had a gambling problem, systematically stole from David.

What Grete remembered more than the car, in which she rarely rode, preferring to walk whenever she could, was the acquisition of a radio. By the mid-1920s, the family had one and listened to it often. Grete and her siblings liked to listen to the BBC from London, especially as political conditions worsened in Austria. It also proved a good way to improve their school-taught English.

Radio took the world by storm. The numbers for the United States are representative: five thousand radios sold in 1920; by 1924, the number was 2.5 million. From 1922 to 1929, the number of U.S. radio stations grew from 30 to 606.

The good times for the Sobel family continued for almost a decade despite rising anti-Semitism and the growing influence of right-wing extremists and National Socialists in the Austrian government. However, an ever-sharpening sword of Damocles hung over the family's prosperity.

Chapter 18
Education

The modern Austrian education system traces its history to 1775 when Empress Maria Theresa mandated seven years of primary education for both boys and girls. By the time Grete was ready for school at age six, the system had expanded ever so slightly: eight years were now mandatory. The standard routine for middle and working-class families was four years in a *Volksschule*, an elementary school, followed either by eight years in a *Real Gymnasium* (high school) for students preparing for college, or four years in a *Hauptschule* (middle school) in a vocational course of study.

The divide between gymnasium and hauptschule was a major determinant of future economic success, as was the first day of hauptschule when students were divided into two tracks based on their volksschule performance. Group A went on to two or four-year vocational-technical training schools after hauptschule. A handful—less than 10 percent—of Group A graduates were able to finish their education at a gymnasium. Group B received one year of compulsory education, then went into apprenticeship programs or directly into the labor force.

Once children were thus differentiated, it was virtually impossible to switch. That these critical, life-altering educational decisions were made when a student was 10 years old was monumentally unfair. Grete and I often discussed the injustice of such an arbitrary system that did not countenance the concept of the late bloomer, a term that defined many of her and my friends.

Not surprisingly, a child's socioeconomic background was almost always determinative of whether they attended a gymnasium or a hauptschule. Children from lower middle-class and working-class backgrounds typically wound up in hauptschule, while others born into more fortunate circumstances went into gymnasium. Grete and her siblings were somewhat unusual in that respect, although by the time she was ready for gymnasium in 1916, her family had gone a long way toward clawing its way out of the working class. That Grete's future husband, Ernst, was able to go to gymnasium was even more unusual given that his father was a cobbler, albeit with his own shoemaking shop.

Although I have been unable to unearth any confirming statistics, anecdotal evidence points to a disproportionate number of Jewish children attending gymnasium.

Gymnasium studies concentrated on languages, sciences, humanities and mathematics. The capstone at the end of gymnasium was a series of written and oral examinations and the conferring upon graduates of a diploma called the *Matura*, required in order to enter university.

Each of the four Matura examinations was five hours in length. Grades were either 1 *(sehr gut)* - excellent; 2 *(gut)* - good; 3 *(befriedigend)* - satisfactory; 4 *(genügend)* – sufficient; and 5 *(nicht genügend)* - failed. Students who scored very high in their Matura exams graduated with honors. Grete received scores of 1 on all of her written and oral exams and graduated with distinction, first in her class. Somehow, her gymnasium report cards survived the political chaos and life-threatening times she endured in Austria and made it with her to the United States.

Gymnasium was rigorous and, by graduation at age 19, graduates were the beneficiaries of a very solid education, likely the equivalent of two years at a selective American university. This system has not changed very much in the ensuing 100 years and is not much different today anywhere else in Europe.

Grete's gymnasium was around the corner from her Hollandstrasse apartment, on *Grosse Sperlgasse*. One of her language teachers was Frau Ilse Kraus. Grete considered her an inspiration and mentor. At the same time, in another nearby gymnasium, Grete's future husband Ernst developed an equally close relationship with one of his language teachers, Herr Kraus, the husband of Frau Kraus. Years later in San Francisco, when Grete and Ernst got married, the Krauses were their witnesses.

All Vienna gymnasiums were single-sex. That meant that the natural inclinations of hormonal teenagers were elevated by segregation. There was a great deal of discussion of boys and sex among the girls, and a certain shock, awe, and admiration accorded those who claimed they were no longer virgins.

There was also a great deal of political talk. Grete's high school years coincided with the advent of the Bolshevik Revolution in Russia, and Marxism, Socialism, and Social Democracy captured the imaginations of many of the girls. Later on, once Stalin consolidated his dictatorship and his regime's human rights abuses began to surface, Grete's early interest in leftist politics waned.

Not so, however, for many of her friends. Following graduation, a number of her classmates left Vienna for life in the Soviet "workers' paradise." One close friend, Genia Quittner, married an engineer and immediately left with him for the Soviet Union to help build the workers' paradise. They soon found conditions much different than advertised. Life was a daily struggle for survival. One night in 1938, the second year of the Great Terror during which Stalin eliminated virtually all of his real and fictitious enemies, there was a sharp rap on Genia's apartment door. Several NKVD (precursor of the KGB) operatives burst in and dragged Genia's husband away. That was the last time she and her children ever saw or heard of him.

Devastated and disillusioned, she plotted her family's escape and eventually pulled it off after what amounted to an agonizing journey. Much later, she wrote a book about her experiences, *Weiter Weg Nach Krasnogorsk* (*A Long Way to Krasnogorsk*), which became a best seller in Europe.

Chapter 19
Graduation

Grete's gymnasium graduating class was rewarded with a train trip to Munich. This was a source of great excitement for the girls, most of whom had never been more than a few miles from home.

It was late fall 1924, a tumultuous time to visit the Bavarian capital. By the time the class arrived in Munich, Hitler had only just been released from his incarceration in Landsberg Prison for having staged the November 1923 "Beer Hall Putsch," a ludicrous attempt to overthrow the Bavarian government. He was back in Munich agitating once more against the Versailles Treaty and the fictitious "stab in the back" that he claimed lost the war for Germany. He occupied himself in jail dictating *Mein Kampf* ("My Battle") to his fellow inmate, Rudolph Hess. *Mein Kampf* would become both the Nazi bible and the roadmap to the horrors that manifested themselves in the Holocaust and World War II.

In Munich, the class was provided with a bus and tour guide, a handsome young man who immediately captured the hearts of most of the girls. One evening, as the bus was delivering the girls to a restaurant, the guide requested that the bus stop in front of the *Burgerbraukeller* for a few minutes so that he could go inside and listen to Hitler speak. He told the girls that he was skeptical of the Nazis. When he came out after half-an-hour, however, he was gushing with enthusiasm for Hitler. Grete, who had heard tangentially of Hitler during the past several years, thought he was an irrelevant buffoon who would never amount to much because no one could possibly take seriously such a ridiculous figure. This was not her best prediction.

Politics aside—not easy in a city that was a hotbed of political demonstrations, protests, and often violent counter-protests—the girls enjoyed a wonderful week visiting its great museums, theaters, parks, and eateries. Munich, like Vienna, was (and is) one of the world's great walking cities and the girls took full advantage.

After Munich, the class went by train to Passau, a pretty little Bavarian city close to both the Austrian and Czech borders, lying at the confluence of three rivers, the *Inn*, the *Ilz*, and the Danube. The joining of the three rivers gives the city its nickname, *Dreiflüssestadt* ("City of the Three Rivers"). There the similarity to Pittsburgh ends.

Grete concluded that the rivers were misnamed. At Passau, the Inn is by far the major torrent while the Danube appears as a modest tributary flowing into the Inn. Nevertheless, the continuation, all the way through Austria, Hungary, the Balkans, Bulgaria and Romania for more than 700 miles to the Black Sea, is called . . . the Danube. My wife and I had the same impression when we visited Passau many decades later.

Her other impression of Passau was its unusual way of coping with the Inn's annual floods. Riverfront houses have two garages, one on top of the other. Residents use their automobiles when the river is at its normal level and their boats in the upper garages during flood times. The lower garages are tightly sealed against the water.

Passau's physical beauty hides a dark side that the city fathers attempted to cover up following the Second World War. The city tried to hide its sordid Holocaust history, but thanks to a local high school girl, Anna Rosmus (who became well-known by the local pejorative, "The Nasty Girl"), the city's dark past was revealed. During World War II, Passau housed three sub-camps of the *Mauthausen* concentration camp where 320,000 men, women, and children were killed, most of them Jews. Passau also had several camps where pregnant Polish women were forced to have abortions or watch their newborns being killed by the SS. Also, thousands of Russian POW's were murdered here in the final hours of the war. Anna Rosmus would not let Passau forget its past and finally had to leave town due to death threats. Today, this brave woman lives in the United States.

Hitler was a big fan of Passau, which was not far from where he was born and grew up in Austria. It was from Passau that the German forces invaded the Czech *Sudetenland* in late 1938.

Another strong impression left on Grete by the class trip was the visible indicators of the aftermath of the runaway German hyperinflation that had only just been brought under control a few months before. She saw people dressed in shabby clothing and rags, beggars all over the city surrounding tourists, pleading their cases in quiet desperation. Houses and apartment buildings were boarded up. Despite Vienna's own hyperinflation experience, what had gone on in Munich was worse.

Grete loved the trip, the camaraderie with her classmates, and the experience of being on her own away from home for the first time. On arriving back at Vienna's *Westbahnhof* railroad station, reality re-emerged. Grete knew that she needed to decide what she wanted to do next.

Chapter 20
Musical Interlude

Vienna and Music

No Viennese goes through life without intense exposure to music. Music's arteries and veins ran deep in Vienna, embedded in the city's DNA and soul. Grete was no exception.

Adding to the intensity of Vienna's musical saturation was the poignancy of the lives of the great musicians. Mozart died at age 35 in 1791 and was buried in an unknown pauper's grave, largely unappreciated in his own time despite having made the most sublime music that ever excited a human ear and despite a precocious and prodigious talent that defies comprehension. Franz Schubert died even younger of syphilis. Each composed more than 600 works in their short lives. Beethoven suffered tragically from early deafness, yet was able to compose some of the most powerful and emotionally moving works in the history of music.

Gustav Mahler also died relatively young (age 50), after being appreciated for his day-to-day vocation—conducting—but not very much for his musical compositions. Like Mozart, it was only after his death that his genius as a composer was recognized. During his life, he suffered from a steady drumbeat of anti-Semitic diatribes despite having converted to Catholicism in order to advance his career.

Practical Music

While a lifetime dreamer, Grete was also practical, very much grounded in reality. She knew that the time was soon coming when she would need to earn an independent living and decided that music might be her best bet for a temporary solution. Her decision to pursue a musical vocation was strategic. While earning a living in music, she would allow herself the time and flexibility to pursue her dream (see below).

Becoming a concert virtuoso was not her aim. She had far more modest goals, intending to earn her keep as a piano teacher. Consequently, a week after coming home from the graduation trip, she enrolled in the *Hochschule für Musik*, the Vienna Academy of Music. This storied Vienna institution was founded in 1819 when Mozart's supposed nemesis, Antonio Salieri (despite the rivalry so brilliantly depicted in the movie *Amadeus*, they were in fact professional colleagues, not enemies), was appointed its first director. After nine months of intensive training in piano and music theory, Grete became certified as a piano teacher.

Teaching piano in Vienna had a glorious history. Mozart taught piano for years while struggling to make ends meet and churning out perfection in the form of his compositions.

One of Mozart's piano students was the teenage Beethoven, but their association lasted less than a full afternoon because a messenger arrived at the Mozart house and summoned the young man home to Bonn where his mother had suddenly become gravely ill from consumption (tuberculosis). When he rushed out in the middle of his audition, Mozart turned to his wife Constanze and said: "Some day that boy will make some noise." By the time Beethoven was able to return to Vienna, Mozart was dead.

Grete, however, never actually taught piano because, while completing her music education, she suffered a crisis of confidence about her abilities. Her innate shyness had something to do with this. It always took her a long time to become comfortable with any new acquaintance or scenario. All her life in America, she was wary of social gatherings and deferred reluctantly to her very social husband when attending get-togethers. This was in sharp contrast to her ability to step up to the plate when survival demanded courage and boldness. This irrational anxiety was not her only one. If she thought a mouse was loose in the house, she would grab a broom and leap up on a piece of furniture poised to do the critter in if it ventured within broom handle distance.

Much later, my mother tried for a vicarious music career through me. When I was eight years old, she insisted on piano lessons. She engaged a piano instructor who was what, in those days, we called a "maiden lady" or "spinster," an unmarried elderly woman who lived among similar colleagues in Canandaigua's most prominent residence, the Granger Homestead, a stately mansion a block from our house that urban legend attributed to an architectural design by Thomas Jefferson.

Edith Honeyman was a superb professional piano teacher, but was unfortunately saddled with a monumentally untalented student. She was very proud of two things: (1) being the direct descendant of John Honeyman, a Revolutionary War spy who reported directly to General Washington; and (2) that one of her first piano students was a fellow resident of her home town of Whittier, California named Richard Milhous Nixon. She often contrasted my lack of skill and diligence to his musical prowess and eagerness to learn. I concede his superior keyboard abilities, but I am not a crook.

> Sidebar: my family had another tie to Nixon (and Watergate). My second-hand, red *Radio Flyer* wagon was a gift to me from my Uncle Ben (Grete's brother) when I was six years old. He bought it for a dollar from the parents of one of his patients in his Binghamton, New York medical practice: John Dean.

Our house came with a baby grand piano, which Grete would often play. She was wistful whenever she was at the keyboard. Occasionally, the hint of a tear coursed down her cheek, this from a woman who almost never cried about anything. I believe she harbored regrets that she had never done more with her music. Music's loss, however, was humanity's gain.

Chapter 21
Rejection

Grete's anxiety about actually having to teach someone how to play the piano meant that she needed a new career strategy. Having interrupted her journey down the path toward a practical economic platform via the piano, she turned to another creative endeavor that she loved and hoped might provide some remuneration: art, drawing in particular. Grete loved to draw. And she was quite good at it. Well into her centennial decade, she was still composing amusing drawings for her grandchildren's birthday cards. Combined with her poetic instincts, I always thought she missed her opportunity to go to work for Hallmark Cards.

Her attempt to nurture her creative side in drawing to some extent mimicked Adolf Hitler's exactly, ending before it began.

She applied for admission to the *Akademie der bildenden Künste Wien*—the Vienna Fine Arts Academy—specifically to its Drawing School. The Akademie was and still is a public institution dating all the way back to 1692. Among its more prominent graduates was Egon Schiele, the great early twentieth century Expressionist artist.

When Hitler moved to Vienna in 1907, it was with the intention of gaining admission to the same Drawing School. The Akademie was located on the Ringstrasse, situated on the *Schillerplatz* in the *Innere Stadt*—the Inner City—surrounded by other imposing public buildings of over-the-top design.

Like the young dreamer Hitler, my mother and her friends loved to wander around the Ringstrasse admiring its architectural wonders. Every time she passed the Akademie, its neo-Renaissance design, Doric columns, and grand front stone stairwell entrance guarded by two centaurs excited her and fueled the notion of someday enrolling as a student.

Hitler's portfolio of drawings consisted primarily of architectural sketches he had done while living in Linz. They were not bad technically, but they lacked authenticity. Each one was done in a grandiose, overblown style reminiscent of Imperial Rome. He took them with him to the Akademie entrance examination, convinced that his portfolio would dazzle the examiners and that he would soon begin his artistic career and eventually amaze the world with his creative style. He did amaze the world, but not quite as he originally intended.

The future *Führer* was rejected twice by the Akademie, which left him even more frustrated and bitter than his natural state of elevated rage. According to his biographers and his roommate at the time, being turned down contributed directly to his overweening hatred of authority and deep-seated anger at the world. Whether it was a Jewish administrator or professor who rejected him for admission is unknown.

Dejected and having frittered away his quite handsome sum of money from his father's legacy, it never occurred to him to look for a real job like other young men his age. His delusional self-image would not allow that kind of mundane career path. Instead, he idled away his time in coffee houses reading the free newspapers, thinking "deep thoughts," and arguing violently about politics with other patrons who found him bizarre in the extreme. Eventually, desperate for money, he began drawing postcards of Viennese scenes and buildings and selling them outside the *Stefanskirche*, Vienna's great cathedral, for enough of a pittance to barely get by.

By 1913, he had had it with Vienna, gave up his artistic dreams and left town. Vienna thereafter became for him an object of derision and, for the next 25 years, he never lost sight of his revenge fantasy toward the city that did not appreciate him. His youthful fascination with the city turned into something dark and evil. When he returned for the first time in March 1938 at the head of the conquering Wehrmacht, he was like the bullied high school boy who returns to his reunion after making good in the wider world, the head cheerleader on his arm, the envy of his less successful classmates. By then, his vengeance on this town without pity was going to be to build up Linz and make it the capital of Austria.

Grete was similarly rejected by the Akademie's Drawing School, but for a different reason. She misinterpreted the instructions on the drawing test and turned in a piece that, while demonstrating talent, was rejected for "inability to follow instructions."

While disappointed, she, unlike Hitler, picked herself up and moved on. Her practical, healthy reaction to rejection was, mercifully for the world, a stark contrast to Hitler's. As Grete herself put it: *"Instead of reacting to rejection by conquering the world and killing millions, I decided to enroll in medical school . . ."*

Chapter 22
Numerus Clausus

Grete had been interested in her science courses during grammar school and gymnasium and had done exceptionally well in them. She concluded that it would be both practical and interesting to pursue a medical degree as an alternative to teaching piano or earning a living as an artist.

It was too late for her in 1924, when she decided to apply, to matriculate in the Class of 1930 (medical school in Vienna was a 6-year program). She would have to wait one year. In the meantime, she worked in her father's haberdashery store. She had helped out in the store many times while growing up, so she required no training.

In Spring 1925, she applied for admission to the *Medizinische Universitat Wien*—the University of Vienna Medical School. By then, the school was almost 600 years old and was widely considered the finest medical school in the world.

The Medical School was the bargain of the century. Tuition was only 100 Schillings a semester. In 1925, that was the equivalent of five U.S. dollars. Grete's six-year medical education cost her $60 dollars! Since she was able to live at home, she had virtually no expenses. It was more expensive for foreign students: $270 for the six years.

Admission was hardly a given, although the school's policy at the time was for the most part to admit anyone who wished to study medicine. The notion was that everyone should have the opportunity to attend and prove themselves. The unworthy would quickly weed themselves out. Surprisingly, the failure rate was quite low.

However, that open admission policy was somewhat illusory. Two unofficial exceptions that were not on the books were brought to bear. They intervened when the candidate was either a woman, a Jew, or both.

The school scrutinized women more carefully than men. In the 1920s, it was still unusual for women to study medicine in Austria. Women were first permitted to enroll in the medical school in the early 1900s, thanks to the intervention of the Emperor. The push had come from Emil Zuckerhandl, one of the school's most prominent anatomy professors. He, in turn, was urged to advocate for the admission of women by his remarkable wife, Berta, the daughter of newspaper publisher Moritz Szeps, the close Jewish friend of the late Crown Prince Rudolf. Berta was one of Vienna's first female journalists. Her sister married the brother of future French Premier Georges Clemenceau.

The dean at the time summarily rejected Professor Zuckerhandl's plea, commenting: "You, as an anatomist, should know perfectly well that women's brains are less developed than those of men." Emil shrewdly appealed to the Emperor by citing the need for women doctors to treat Muslim women in the Balkan regions of the Empire.

Despite two decades of experience with a handful of female medical students, the men who ran the school in the 1920s were still skeptical of women as physicians. The school's admission officers subjected women's application documents to additional scrutiny. Because of her consistent top grades and superb performance in her science and mathematics classes, Grete easily survived this analysis. In fact, only a handful of women bothered to apply and only five matriculated in the Class of 1931 out of more than 100 medical students.

The Jewish quota (a.k.a. *Numerus Clausus*—"closed number") was another matter altogether. The numerus clausus concept originated in Roman law as a means of limiting certain classes, races, and nationalities' participation in Roman society.

The unwritten quota was the result of the ingrained anti-Semitism that informed almost every facet of Austrian society. By 1925, it was deeply entrenched throughout Austria, infusing every societal layer, and was all-pervasive.

The way that the numerus clausus was applied by Vienna Medical School was very ad hoc. The dilemma for the school authorities was this: a hugely disproportionate number of Jews versus Christians sought admission every year. While Austria's Jewish population was just under 3 percent, the proportion of Jewish doctors was over 50 percent and even higher in Vienna. This caused a great deal of hand-wringing among medical school administrators. The other factor in play was that Austrians *preferred* Jewish doctors. That compelled the school to apply the Jewish quota somewhat lightly.

Anti-Semitic discrimination was hardly a uniquely Austrian phenomenon. A more rigorously enforced Jewish quota also applied to American medical schools at that time and even much later. Every Ivy League medical school limited the number of Jews they admitted until quite recently. In 1935, for example, Yale Medical School accepted 76 out of 501 applicants (15 percent). Only five of the approximately 200 Jewish applicants were admitted (2.5 percent).

Yale and the other Ivies were not ashamed to be transparent about their discriminatory tactics. The Yale dean's instructions to the medical school administrators that year (1935) read as follows:

> *"Never admit more than five Jews, take only two Italian Catholics, and take no blacks at all."*

Pre-numerus clausus, Cornell Medical School had a Jewish student population of more than 40 percent in the early 1920s. By the 1940s, the number of Jews declined to just over 3 percent. Dr. Jonas Salk, the hero of polio vaccine fame, was rejected by Yale, Columbia, Cornell and the University of Pennsylvania Medical Schools. He wound up at New York University instead.

The numerus clausus in the U.S. was at varying times employed by more than 90 percent of colleges and universities and also applied to women, Catholics, and Eastern and Southern Europeans. Blacks were the most severely affected, often being completely excluded (known as the numerus null). The way in which these restrictions were most commonly imposed was through identifying the most "desirable" candidates—native-born, white, Anglo-Saxon Protestants—through college application form questions about religious preference, race, and nationality. Limiting scholarships was another way the elite institutions controlled the admission of "undesirables."

The concept of the "legacy applicant"—preference accorded the child of an alumnus—originated because of a fear of too many Jewish applicants. Yale invented legacy preference in 1925, alarmed by the growing rate at which Jews were being admitted. This permitted the admissions officers to pass over Jews in favor of admitting "Yale sons of good character and reasonably good record" [1929 dean's memo]. Harvard and many other schools quickly adopted the same policy. For the next four decades, Jewish Ivy League students comprised about 10 percent of the Ivy student population. It was not until the 1960s that these restrictions were completely eliminated. Legacy preference still remains on the books.

The first year in which the Jewish quota was relaxed even a little at Yale was with respect to the Class of 1968 (the author's class) due to an enlightened admissions dean, R. Inslee ("Inky") Clark, who was hired in 1963. It took him three more years to get rid of it completely.

Jewish educational quotas were a global phenomenon and, to some extent, still exist in a few countries. They only disappeared in Austria with the almost total disappearance of that country's Jewish population.

In many countries, the numerus clausus was a matter of law. While that should come as no surprise in places like Germany under the Nazis, Hungary, Latvia, Poland and Romania, it was also the case in Canada through the 1940s.

The numerus clausus was not exclusive to education. In many countries, it was all-encompassing, covering employment, admission to labor unions, entry into golf and other clubs, etc.

In any event, the numerus clausus, while not much of an issue for Grete, would once again rise up and present a significant roadblock once she graduated.

Had Grete been able to apply in the ordinary educational sequence a year earlier, she would have found herself in the same class (1930) as her future husband, Ernst. Instead, their getting together was postponed for more than a decade-and-a-half.

Chapter 23
Religion

The Sobels and Hermanns thought of themselves as Austrians first and patriotic ones at that. Their Jewish affiliation came second, as it did for most Austrian Jews. Just as most of us, even we who are first generation, believe ourselves to be 100 percent American, loyal to our country, its flag, and its heritage, so did my Austrian forebears. When Ernst as a boy watched the Kaiser's carriage pass by on the Ringstrasse, he doffed his cap and cheered.

Religion, at least its rituals, was more important to Ernst's family than to Grete's secular parents and siblings. The Hermanns kept a kosher table, lit candles on Friday nights, and attended synagogue, not only on the high holidays, but all year round. Listening to my father's stories of his childhood, I suspect that the family did these things largely because their forebears had done them, not out of any strong religious fervor.

The Hermanns' religiosity derived from Ernst's mother's family, the Jauls (pronounced "yowls") of Wiener Neustadt. Ernst's paternal grandfather, Edward Hermann of Bratislava in Slovakia, was a lawyer and not much of a believer, although he went to synagogue on Rosh Hashanah and Yom Kippur.

The Jauls and their Wiener Neustadt Blum cousins, with whom they were in business, hailed from the *Burgenland*, the easternmost province of post-World War I Austria (the Burgenland was part of Hungary until 1921). Most of them came from *Kobersdorf*, one of the Jewish *Siebengemeinden*, the "Seven Communities" as they came to be known in Jewish lore. These small communities had rich Jewish traditions that went back centuries. Like the much larger Wiener Neustadt just over the Burgenland border in Lower Austria, strong Jewish communities provoked even stronger anti-Semitism. Today you won't find a Jew in the seven towns and only a handful in the entire Burgenland. Virtually all perished in the Holocaust.

An amazing development occurred in the Burgenland in the late seventeenth century. The provincial ruler, Count Esterhazy, granted the Jews communal autonomy and protection from violence. They were even allowed to move into fortresses in time of war or pogroms. Despite the usual heavy "Jews' Tax" that the Count levied, his reforms attracted a significant number of Jews primarily from Bohemia and Moravia (the present-day Czech Republic). These very likely included the ancestors of Ernst's mother, Therese Jaul.

When the Jauls, Blums, and Hirschls (also cousins—Pauline Jaul, my grandmother Therese's sister, married Ahron Hirschl of Kobersdorf) escaped to Wiener Neustadt to avoid pogroms and escalating discrimination, they brought their Jewish orthodoxy with them. When she married, Therese brought that along to her new husband in Vienna.

The irony was that, if one of the two families—the Hermanns and the Sobels—was more likely to be religious, any betting man would have put his money on the Sobels. The East European Jews who converged on Vienna in the late nineteenth century were far more religious and ritualistic than the German Jews who had lived in Vienna for generations or came there from German-speaking lands like Bohemia, Moravia, Slovakia and Lower Austrian towns like Wiener Neustadt. This cohort was much more secular than the East Europeans, whom they looked down upon due in large part to their clinging to their religious beliefs, dress, grooming and rituals. In the case of the two families, the reverse was true.

After Therese died of pancreatic cancer at only age 50 in 1930, the family shed its religiosity. Ernst, his sister Hedwig (Hedy), and their father Solomon did not miss it. Their anguish, which to some degree they never got over, was over the premature death of their beloved wife and mother who, by all accounts, was a gem in every respect.

Solomon's family, in contrast to the Jauls, was more cosmopolitan. My great-grandfather Edward fathered two large families with two successive wives and, like so many such scenarios, deferred to the second wife in favoring the younger set of children. Solomon, unfortunately, was from the first set and was able to take little in the way of a stake from Bratislava when, as a young man, he set out for Vienna. He had to make his own way.

Being Jewish, even in sophisticated Vienna, meant being discriminated against. While the numerus clausus did not keep Ernst or Grete from pursuing a medical degree, that did not mean that discrimination at the university was non-existent. Once, while visiting Vienna, Ernst took me to the Medical School and pointed out the spot where he witnessed a Jewish medical student being thrown to his death from the ramparts by anti-Semitic classmates, a scene that repeated itself more than once in those years.

Grete's family's distancing itself from religion was to some extent the result of both her parents' origins in the Polish-Ukraine border region. In overwhelmingly Catholic Kamianka Strumilova and Jezerzianka, Jews had learned to keep a low profile from years of pogroms and harsh discrimination. Moreover, David and Ernestine arrived in Vienna in the mid-1890s, when the impetus was to assimilate as quickly as possible.

The Sobels had large family gatherings for Passover, but David had no patience for the length of time it took to read through the *Haggadah* (the story of the Jewish Exodus from captivity in Egypt and the significance of the seder) before being allowed to dig into the meal. The traditional Sobel *seder* centered around carp, an edible fish in Europe. I suspect that this unusual choice of entrée (lamb or chicken are the more standard fare) derived from the Lapajowkers' multi-generational livelihood as fishermen on the Bug River.

My mother remembered one particular Passover when her mother bought a large carp and kept it in the bathtub until it was time for it to be sacrificed for the seder. The children became attached to the fish and protested vigorously when its date of execution arrived. Undeterred, Ernestine killed the carp and served it, but the children refused to eat it.

The Sobels did not light Hanukah candles. Grete was never exposed to many Jewish rituals until she got married, and then only casually and intermittently. Only one of her three siblings, Ben, was a believer, but I always had the sense that his belief was prompted more by "taking no chances" than any leap of faith. He tried to cover all contingencies, and I suspect religion qualified as one of those. Neither Grete, her brother Otto, nor sister Rose had any place in their lives for a god who consistently bailed on his so-called Chosen People.

The absence of religion was unusual for Leopoldstadt, which was home to no fewer than 50 synagogues within walking distance of the Sobels' Hollandstrasse apartment.

When Grete and Ernst got married in San Francisco in 1945, it was not in a temple. They opted instead for a quiet civil ceremony before a local judge.

One remaining religious matter that needs addressing is Zionism, the urge to "return" to the Promised Land. The first emergence of the term Zionism occurred 27 years before Vienna's Theodor Herzl was credited with launching the Zionist movement in 1897. In 1870, an organization called *Hovevei Zion* (Lovers of Zion) began to construct Jewish settlements in Palestine. By the time Herzl came along, there were 20 such settlements.

Neither the Sobels nor Hermanns had any interest in Zionism. Even when the coming of the Nazis spurred such interest and found a big following among Vienna's younger Jews, the two families remained unaffected, with one exception.

Ernst's adored younger sister (the siblings were lifelong members of an intense mutual admiration society), Hedy, was courted by and married big, handsome Julius Freund. The Freund siblings may not have been fervent Zionists. Nevertheless, each of the five children ended up in Palestine, three of them permanently. Julius' sister, Erna, was the first to emigrate when she married a *Sabra* (native Israeli) manufacturer who purposely traveled to Vienna to find a wife. He returned to Jerusalem with her and she lived there the rest of her life. Tilda, the second sister, a successful theater owner in Vienna, soon followed, as did brothers Yoshi and Henry. Henry later emigrated to the U.S. where he got a position as an apartment building superintendent in the Bronx.

Shortly after Julius and Hedy married following the Anschluss, Julius slipped over the Italian border and boarded a ship for Palestine. Hedy followed him via a more conventional emigration after assuring that her father, Solomon, would be able to join Ernst in New York.

Julius and Hedy remained in Israel for little more than a year, during which Julius worked for his brother-in-law in his manufacturing plant. His brother-in-law, however, proved a difficult boss, prompting Julius to reconsider his decision to settle in Palestine. In 1940, he and Hedy obtained U.S. Affidavits of Support from one of Ernst's contacts and boarded a ship for the U.S.

Chapter 24
Medical School

The Best Medical School in the World

Grete entered the University of Vienna Medical School in the Fall of 1925, a few weeks short of her 20th birthday. The school's reputation as the best on the planet was due in part to Sigmund Freud who, while teaching there (he never made full professor), suffered severe discrimination. A global giant, but diminished in his own city and university.

The University of Vienna in the 1920s and early 1930s was one of the world's great academic institutions. Its scholars included many Nobel Laureates in addition to names that became household words across a vast variety of disciplines. Among its distinguished graduates are some of the leading figures in physics, philosophy, psychoanalysis (of course), music, literature, politics, biology, religion, entertainment, economics, and medicine.

The medical school was home to an illustrious collection of eminent professors, including quite a few Nobel Prize winners. Grete studied under several of them, including:

- Julius Wagner-Jauregg, who discovered that tertiary syphilis—a scourge of early 20th century Europe—could be cured by high fevers caused by an injection of live malaria virus, a radical treatment for any era. Wagner-Jauregg, who retired after Grete's third year, was so respected that Austria put his image on a postage stamp. His name is also on numerous Austrian roads,

hospitals and schools despite his virulent and very vocal anti-Semitism. His first wife was Jewish, but he became a fervent Nazi supporter in 1938 and a firm advocate of sterilization of mental "defectives." Not a nice man, but a great teacher and one whom Grete liked (at the time, she was unaware of his racist tendencies and he was unaware that she was Jewish).
- Konrad Lorenz, recipient of the Nobel Prize for his animal studies. Lorenz was an Assistant Professor of Anatomy. He later joined the Nazis and spent a number of years in occupied Poland studying the bogus science of racial hygiene as a Wehrmacht military psychologist. His book *On Aggression* was a global best-seller in the 1960s.
- Josef Herzig, who taught organic chemistry and was co-discoverer of the "Herzig-Meyer Alkimide Group Determination," a chemical reaction so complex it is best left unexplained.

The Medical School in 1925 was already 560 years old. In 1365, Duke Rudolf IV of Austria was given permission by Pope Clement VI to establish a university in Vienna. The School of St. Stephen's was, by papal charter, converted "into a university according to the ordinances and customs observed first at Athens, then at Rome, and after that at Paris." From day one, the new university had a medical faculty.

Medical school in the fourteenth century was dramatically different from what it became 500 years later. "Teaching" consisted of professors reading to students from Galen, the second century AD Greco-Roman physician, the *Canon* of Avicenna, a tenth century Arab physician, and the *Liber Medicinalis* of Avicenna's contemporary, the Persian-Arabian physician Rhazes. All three looked for much of their medical knowledge all the way back to Hippocrates. No deviation from or questioning of the teachings of these masters was permitted.

Students received the equivalent of a Bachelor's degree after two years of study that basically consisted of memorizing the writings of the three masters. Patient contact began in the third year and took the form of "Grand Rounds," observing the conduct of a practicing physician. At the end of three years, the student was awarded a medical degree after giving a dissertation on Hippocrates.

For 400 years, the medical school lagged far behind others in Europe. The faculty considered surgical procedures beneath the dignity of a physician and left them to migrant healers who wandered around Europe doing hernia and cataract operations without benefit of anesthesia. Elsewhere, surgery was beginning to be deemed a very prestigious profession and a subject worthy of inclusion in medical education.

When the Renaissance dragged Europe out of the Dark Ages, Vienna Medical School fell even further behind. There was no Vesalius (Padua), Paracelsus (Basel), or Harvey (London) in Vienna.

The entire seventeenth century saw the school's quality plummet even lower. In 1629, Emperor Ferdinand II, a particularly reactionary ruler (and that is saying something!), put the university under the authority of the College of Jesuits, a uniquely oppressive regime at that time that kept the medical faculty from making any progress. The bottom was reached in 1703 when the medical school was suspended by imperial order because teacher and teaching quality was so abysmal.

Empress Maria Theresa (1740-1780) revived the medical school and appointed the talented Gerhard Van Swieten, her personal physician, to the position of *Protomedicus*, director of the medical school. Van Swieten was a great innovator. Under his leadership, the medical school established the first teaching hospital, added obstetrics and eye diseases to the curriculum, began the process of taking a complete medical history of patients, and introduced the maintenance of detailed case records.

However, Van Swieten was not always that enlightened. He dismissed the notion of vaccination against smallpox and the diagnosis of chest disorders via percussion, going so far as to have the latter officially banned from the school!

Maria Theresa's son, Joseph II (1780-1790), the patron of both Mozart and something of a champion of the Jews, gave Austrian medical education its biggest boost. He established the *Allgemeines Krankenhaus* (Vienna General Hospital), where both my father and Uncle Benno later worked, and the *Act of Tolerance* which, for the first time, allowed the admission of Jewish students to the university and eventually to the faculty. Jewish physicians came to dominate the medical faculty, peaking in 1938 when 75 percent of the faculty was fired because of either their Jewish origins or marriage to Jews.

Joseph's death in 1790 and the commencement of the long era during which the arch-conservative Prince Klemens von Metternicht (of 1815 Congress of Vienna fame) rose to power marked another decline in the fortunes and prestige of Vienna Medical School. He placed the school under the authority of a like-minded arch-reactionary who proceeded to get rid of all of the eminent physicians on the faculty, replacing them with politically malleable non-entities.

It was not until almost the mid-nineteenth century that the school achieved first rank, rising from the Metternichian ashes to house some of the greatest physicians and researchers in the world, and making Vienna the world capital of medical science and scholarship. Men like Carl Rokitansky, co-founder of pathologic anatomy; Joseph Skoda—who employed percussion and auscultation verified by autopsies to develop a new clinical system of the pathology of the heart and lungs; surgeon Franz Schuh, who elevated surgical standards by insisting on pathologic evaluation of operative findings; Ferdinand von Hebra, the father of modern dermatology (someone greatly admired by Grete, who seriously considered a dermatological career); Joseph Hyrtl, whose anatomy textbook evolved through no fewer than 22 editions and became the global bible of the discipline; Ernst von Brücke, who made physiology an essential component of medical education; Theodor Billroth, who made Vienna the mecca of surgical training in the world; Hans Horst Mayer, whose *Experimental Pharmacology* became the standard textbook in virtually every medical school in the world; and Richard von Krafft-Ebing, the first psychiatrist to venture into the problems of the psychology of sex and its deviations. This list only scratches the surface of the nineteenth century luminaries on the faculty.

Vienna was for many years in the late nineteenth and early twentieth centuries the epicenter of world medical science. The litany of Austrian and German Jews who studied or taught there and won Nobel and other prizes for their medical breakthroughs is much too long for this book.

One of Grete's inspirations, whom she spoke about often, was Dr. Ignaz Philipp Semmelweis. He was a deeply troubled Hungarian physician who served as the 1846 equivalent of chief resident in the First Obstetrical Clinic at the Allgemeines Krankenhaus, at the time and for much of the next hundred years widely considered the finest hospital in the world. Key to his breakthrough innovation, he also observed at an obstetrical clinic where only midwives performed deliveries.

Semmelweis perceived that the incidence of childbed fever (the variant of septicemia afflicting expectant mothers), a scourge responsible for the deaths of tens of thousands of young women, was *more than ten times higher* when deliveries were performed by physicians rather than midwives. While the doctors were clueless, the difference in mortality rate was well-known outside the hospital, and pregnant women begged to be admitted to the midwives' clinic instead of the hospital.

After eliminating every variable between the two alternative settings, Semmelweis was left with only one difference: Physicians and medical students often came directly to the delivery room immediately after performing an autopsy. He concluded that they must have been carrying what he called a "cadaverous agent" with which they contaminated birthing mothers. This prompted Semmelweis to suggest something that proves the maxim that the simple solution is often the best one.

He recommended that physicians *wash their hands* between procedures.

Semmelweis formally announced his findings and recommendations to the Society of Physicians in Vienna in 1847 and again in a monograph 14 years later. He found himself vigorously opposed by the entire cohort of obstetricians on the medical school faculty.

Semmelweis' brilliant suggestion eventually preserved the lives of millions of women and made medical history, but he himself was never able to bask in the glory of his achievement. In 1848, he was forced out of his position, ostensibly for political reasons, accused of being sympathetic to the revolutions that convulsed much of Europe that year. The greater tragedy was that thousands of women continued to die, deaths that could have been prevented.

Semmelweis remained in Vienna until 1850 in hopes of being appointed a docent of obstetrics, which would have permitted him to lecture medical students privately. He never received the appointment.

In 1850, he left Vienna for Budapest and a year later received an unpaid appointment to the obstetrics ward of a small hospital. During his six-year tenure there, mortality from childbed fever plummeted from epidemic proportions to under one percent. In 1857, his hand-washing advocacy virtually eliminated obstetrical deaths from sepsis at the University of Pest maternity clinic. That was as far as his reforms were permitted to spread.

Semmelweis finally wrote about his findings in an essay and later in a book. That same year, he began suffering from what today might be diagnosed as Early Onset Alzheimer's. In 1865, he was committed to Vienna's State Lunatic Asylum, not far from the Allgemeines Krankenhaus. He was severely beaten, straitjacketed, doused with ice water, involuntarily administered laxatives, and confined in a dark room. He died after only two weeks in the institution, possibly (ironically) from septicemia contracted via a surgically infected finger. He was only 47 years old.

Hand-washing between medical procedures only gained universal acceptance years after Semmelweis' death, principally boosted by Louis Pasteur's confirmation of the germ theory of disease. Once universally accepted, childbed fever deaths fell to under one percent of deliveries.

U.S. physicians were even slower to adopt hand-washing than their European counterparts. That was most graphically illustrated by the events following President James A. Garfield's shooting in 1881. Garfield might have survived had his physicians not caused an infection despite being well-informed about Semmelweis' procedures. Upon the President's return to the White House following the shooting (it did not occur to anyone to take him to a hospital!), a dozen doctors probed his wound with either an uncovered finger or an unsterilized metal rod, plunging deep inside his body to find a channel. None of the doctors had washed their hands first. This kind of abuse went on for all of the 79 days Garfield lingered after the shooting. Sepsis was the predictable result, and it killed him.

His physicians' recklessness did have a positive impact on American healthcare, resulting in the establishment of the predecessor to the National Institutes of Health.

Grete always said that Semmelweis' innovation was the greatest advance in medical history, and moreover, it cost next to nothing, basically just soap, water and towels. Sadly, hand washing is still a problem in many healthcare settings today. According to a recent study by the National Academy of Sciences' Institute of Medicine, up to 50 percent of healthcare professionals do not wash their hands before beginning a medical procedure.

Sidebar: When Grete was 87, she contracted septicemia and almost died. Twenty-three years later, the author did the same.

The Women in the Class

The first day Grete climbed the grand, curved staircase to the medical school's main entrance, her heart beat excitedly and left her a bit giddy. She entered the imposing building consumed by a blend of excitement, curiosity and trepidation.

Until the end of the nineteenth century, medical education was a "men only" preserve. In fact, college education of any sort for a woman was virtually unheard of until the 1860s, when women were grudgingly allowed into the University of Zürich. Between 1870 and 1894, women in almost all European countries were granted access to universities. Prussia and Austria were exceptions: the two German-speaking countries created a legal barrier to admission by not allowing women to obtain the Matura degree from secondary schools, without which university admission was impossible. This only changed in Austria in 1896. In 1900, the first woman was admitted to the Vienna Medical School. However, the number of women remained miniscule for the next 30+ years.

Grete was one of only five women in her class. One dropped out in the first week upon "meeting" her dissection class cadaver, who happened to have been her just-deceased music teacher. The shock of seeing her teacher lying on a slab was too much and she ran out of the building, never to return.

As the year went on, dissection training was divided into teams of six students working together on three cadavers. The four remaining women in the class made up one complete team because it was considered unseemly for men and women to work together on naked bodies. Grete's team learned more about anatomy than their male counterparts because they had only four participants.

No one ever accused Grete of being sentimental. She described for me in clinical detail how she approached her first cadaver. A white sheet covered the corpse. The room smelled of formaldehyde and other noxious odors that, combined, made for an effluvium of corruption. The air in the windowless, basement dissection chamber was stifling. None of these atmospherics particularly bothered her. What got to Grete more than anything else was that the professor who made the first cuts in the body and instructed the girls on dissecting techniques sipped from a teacup while taking them through the procedures! All of this would have been too much information for me had I not spent four weeks one summer during college working in a hospital morgue cleaning up after autopsies.

One of Grete's female colleagues was Anya Rand (not to be confused with the author and right-wing icon Ayn Rand), whom she said was the most sophisticated woman she had ever met up to that time (she defined "sophistication" as having slept with an impressive number of both boys and girls). Another was Edith Reti, a Jewish girl from *Daruvar*, a small resort town in central Croatia home to many of Croatia's Czech population. Edith became Grete's best friend, someone with whom she stayed in contact for the next 40 years. Grete could not remember the name of the other female classmate.

Edith

The first summer between medical school semesters, Grete was invited to Daruvar. She became smitten with Edith's older brother Vladimir, who fell in love with her as well. Their summer romance ended abruptly with her return to Vienna (just like in the popular songs). Vladimir was murdered in 1942 by the *Ustache*, the Croatian version of the German Nazis. The Ustache came in the middle of the night and took him away. After torturing him, they bound his arms behind his back and threw him off a cliff.

I met Edith in 1966 when I traveled to Yugoslavia with my parents and Aunt Rose. We entered Yugoslavia from Austria after traversing the treacherous, 4,500-foot *Loibl* Pass, a switchback, snow-and-ice covered route even in August. Much to Grete's annoyance, my father opted for the road rather than the mile-long Loibl Tunnel which had been constructed by 1,600 slave laborers from the *Mauthausen* concentration camp during the war, many of whom died in the effort. Rather than sending injured and sick workers back to the camp, their SS overseers injected them with oil, an inexpensive means of efficient execution. Kurt Waldheim, the United Nations Secretary-General and later President of Austria, was among the Waffen-SS troops in that region of Yugoslavia. The pass closed a few months after our traverse, being deemed too dangerous.

At the border, we changed dollars into Yugoslav dinars at a rate of 20,000 to 1. The dinar was essentially worthless thanks to Marshal Tito's command economy, which he had run into the ground in his 20-plus years as dictator.

Even so, we went to Yugoslavia with warm fuzzy feelings about the country and its leaders who had dared to defy Stalin and whose economy looked pretty good relative to the rest of the Eastern bloc. The currency transaction was our first indication that things might not be quite that rosy, but not our last.

Driving to the Slovenian capital, *Ljubljana*, we passed a series of pathetic looking farms marked by wilted wheat and emaciated cows, sheep and goats. With few exceptions, every farm laborer we passed either shook a fist at us or menacingly waved a pitchfork or other farm implement. We finally figured out that our rented Opel with its German sticker and license plate was not being received enthusiastically by a people who, only two-plus decades before, had not been treated very well by their German overlords.

By the time we arrived in Ljubljana, we were feeling a bit uneasy about the country. We enjoyed a meager lunch at an outdoor café just off the main square. At the end of the meal, the waiter asked me if I had any Kennedy half-dollars I could give him in return for another bushel of dinars. I had two and gave him both, refusing any consideration. He bowed, expressing his admiration for JFK and all things American in heavily accented German, every Slovene's reluctant second language. After lunch, we went into what passed for a department store. Its shelves were virtually empty, another indicator of Titoism's "success."

Edith, her Czech husband, and son Vladimir ("Vlado" after her deceased brother) joined us in Lubljana. Watching Grete and Edith greet each other after 35 years was very emotional. I was stunned by how much Edith resembled my mother. They could have been sisters.

From there we drove in two cars to *Bled*, a breathtaking mountain resort in Slovenia's Julian Alps not far from the border with Italy and the Isonzo, where my grandfather Solomon fought in World War I. Vlado and Aunt Rose were in one car, the rest of us in the Opel. It was impossible to keep up with Vlado, who drove like a man possessed.

Arriving in Bled, we had to register with the police, where we were assigned a Yugoslav Intourist guide, more of a spy actually than a guide. She was an immensely attractive young woman with luxuriant red hair who filled out her uniform exceptionally well. The hotels were full due to the World Rowing Championships taking place on Lake Bled, so we were put up in a farm house for the *Dinar* equivalent of $2.00 a night for all four of us. The farmer took my father into the bathroom, turned up the volume of the bathtub tap to camouflage his voice, and begged to be paid in U.S. dollars. The rooms were comfortable and breakfast was fabulous, but we felt very awkward having been forced on these innocent people.

Edith and her family took us to see a famous nearby waterfall. Behind the waterfall was a stone walkway. Edith's purpose was not our scenic enjoyment, but rather the opportunity to talk freely about her life without fear of the authorities eavesdropping. The cataract's din impeded the ability of anyone to listen in, including the Intourist guide.

At that time, Edith was 60 years old. She had been a physician in Daruvar until age 55, when the government forced her to retire to make room for newly graduated doctors. Her husband had just retired from his profession (law) at age 60, also forced out by the government. They lived on a miniscule pension that provided barely enough to eat and rent a tiny, two-room apartment. Vlado was an engineering student and had joined the Communist Party for the advantages it brought him; a higher priority to buy a car and a seat at the University of Zagreb Engineering College. He was also saving in order to marry. Vlado had his own apartment in Zagreb.

Edith was spared by the Ustache and the Nazis during the war despite being Jewish, thanks to marriage to a non-Jew and her Slavic looks. Life was very hard for her family during the war. Foraging for food was her daily focus.

Grete and Edith cried together over how fate had dealt so differently with each of them. The pain in Edith's voice touched us deeply.

Later, we had a delicious dinner at a rustic, hilltop "restaurant" that Vlado recommended. We sat on hard wooden benches and were entertained by local farmers far gone on the local *rakija*, a near-toxic brew that is 50-60% alcohol, belting out folk songs at the top of their lungs. My parents and Aunt Rose were not big drinkers, so seeing them tipsy was a real shock. Afterwards, we said our tearful goodbyes to Edith and her family. They drove off to Zagreb and our Intourist guide took us back to the farmhouse in Bled.

Edith and Grete never saw each other again. Edith stopped writing to Grete in the mid-1970s. I wrote to Vlado asking about his mother and sent it to his last known address in Zagreb. The letter did not come back and neither did any response. One of my colleagues at the Pentagon in the late 1970s traveled to Zagreb on vacation and attempted to find out Edith's fate, to no avail. Grete grieved over the loss of her great friend until the day she died.

Trials of the Women Students

Vienna Medical School was located in the *Alsergrund*—the fashionable Ninth District—within walking distance of the Sobels' Hollandstrasse apartment. Grete trudged to and from school every day hauling weighty tomes. Some lectures were held in the main University building in the First District, adjacent to Leopoldstadt, also an easy walk from her home. Since Edith often stayed overnight with the family, she was Grete's constant companion on these walks.

Women medical students were, for the most part, treated just like the men. Although they never amounted to more than a handful, their male counterparts had become used to their presence. Not so the faculty. One of Grete's professors refused to allow women inside his classroom, so they sat outside on the floor in a hallway and took notes. Despite that, Grete and Edith received the highest grades in his class. Fortunately for them, grading was anonymous.

Over the two decades since women had first been admitted, there had been several incidents resulting in the dismissal of obdurate professors (the faculty was exclusively male) who refused to countenance women students. Episodes of forcible ejections from classrooms marked the first decade of co-education, resulting in formal complaints to the dean, of which the palace got wind. The Kaiser, despite his rigidity regarding change and modern ideas in virtually every other facet of life, was not pleased. For whatever reason, Franz-Josef was enthusiastic about the notion of female physicians.

Gender discrimination was insignificant compared to the anti-Semitism that infected the school and the entire university. Despite the fact that the majority of professors were Jewish, anti-Semitism was so virulent that there were two distinct Anatomy divisions teaching exactly the same material, taught in two wings of the Anatomy Building, as far apart from each other as possible. One section was attended by Jews (and Socialists), the other by anti-Semites and Christian Socialists. A majority of the latter had, by 1930, become avowed Nazis. Both Ernst and Grete witnessed several violent assaults by the Nazi Anatomy students against the Jewish/Socialist section.

In her sixth and last year in medical school, Grete and her classmates were required to do an *Internat* in obstetrics, several times spending a week in the Allgemeines Krankenhaus observing deliveries. The four women students were housed in one dormitory; the men in another. A bell announced an impending delivery, whereupon the students donned their white smocks and raced to the labor room to observe.

This being Vienna, psychiatry classes were also mandatory. Unlike the majority of her colleagues, Grete was skeptical of them. She was the only one of the women students who did not sign up for free analysis.

To graduate, it was necessary to pass a series of oral examinations in each major medical subject. Grete feared the orals, especially Anatomy. If a student failed an exam, s/he had to repeat it, which one could do up to four times. However, it was necessary to repeat all of the other oral exams that had been given prior to the one the student failed, even if the student had previously passed all of the others.

The Anatomy interrogators were three distinguished, bearded professors notorious for asking brutally difficult questions about the most obscure musculo-skeletal structures. What concerned Grete the most was that Anatomy was comprised of thousands of stationary and moving human parts, all of which were supposed to be memorized by the students in preparation for the exam. The night before the exam, Grete's last-minute cramming included the bones of the hand and how they relate to one another. When it came time for the Anatomy question, kismet triumphed (one could also say that fortune favors the prepared). Grete was asked to name the bones of the hand and how they related to one another! Having just "boned" up on that precise topic, she aced her orals and was awarded her medical degree. Despite all of the obstacles, she finished first in her class. Dr. Margarete Sobel was now ready to practice.

> Sidebar: Class rank was something I had to pull out of my mother by brute force and intimidation. She was the humblest of individuals in every respect. It was not until I discovered her gymnasium report cards that I had an inkling of her brilliance. However, it took several years of brow-beating to squeeze her other remarkable academic achievements out of her.

Chapter 25
Smitten

It is more than just a little awkward to talk about one's mother's love life prior to her marriage. Nevertheless, it is an important part of the tapestry of Grete's life. It also says a great deal about her impulses, motives and character that inform her story.

Much of what follows in this chapter did not come directly from Grete. I relied heavily on her sister Rose, with whom I had literally hundreds of hours of conversation about Grete, and on her brother Otto, whom I visited and spent several days with as he was dying of stomach cancer. Otto, who spent a lifetime keeping everything close to his vest, knew what was in store for him and was suddenly eager to tell me all he remembered about his sister and the family's life in Vienna. He died at age 70 two weeks after my visit.

Although she never for a moment considered herself good looking, photographs from her youth and maturity tell a decidedly different story. Her formal wedding photo, taken when she was just shy of 40 years old, is that of a stunning woman.

By the time she arrived in medical school, she was beginning to blossom into a very good looking young lady; male eyes noticed. I previously mentioned her first serious flame, her summer infatuation with Edith Reti's brother, Valdimir, in Daruvar. "Infatuation" underplays the effect of someone whom she reminisced about years later, calling him her "first love."

She went through several relationships during medical school, some of the fling variety, but others where she might have contemplated a future. Two of her colleagues proposed to her. She rejected both, one because he seemed too "undisciplined;" the other, a charismatic, tall, handsome Christian who swept her off her feet at first, but with whom she found fault later. Rose could not understand why she did not accept this Adonis, who was "everything a woman could want and a doctor besides." Nevertheless, she did, and he threatened to kill himself (a standard Viennese reaction to bad news). Grete dismissed his threat, telling Rose and Otto that he was "over-dramatizing" and had "read too much German '*herz-schmerz*'" ("heartache" is the best translation, although it does not do justice to the German term) literature.

Fortunately, he did not kill himself. Forty years later, on a visit to Vienna, Grete learned that he had married, served in the Wehrmacht during the war, and was declared missing in action on the Russian front.

Once in practice and having to establish herself in her profession, Grete did not have much time for socializing and did very little of it. What little she did was done in groups with friends of both sexes. The Austrian economy went south once again after the 1931 crash of the Kreditanstalt Bank, a month before Grete graduated from medical school, and the ensuing Great Depression. The men in whom she might have been interested no longer contemplated marriage because they had no hope of supporting a wife and family.

As the 1930s went on and the Fascist parties ascended to power, the country was thrown into further turmoil, and the economy became even worse. Following the Anschluss in early 1938, romance was the last thing on a Jewish girl's mind, superseded by the fight for survival.

Chapter 26
Hospitant, Aspirant, Rezident

Following graduation, Grete was assigned to the tuberculosis ward in one of Vienna's public hospitals, the decidedly non-prestigious *Wiener Krankenhaus*. This was not a choice assignment and was disproportionately reserved for women and Jews. Finishing at the top of her medical school class had no bearing on her assignment.

Such positions were neither internships nor residencies, the common progression out of American medical schools. Instead, in the Austrian system, novices came in as *Hospitants*. After a year of satisfactory service, they were promoted to *Aspirant*; another year of not screwing up and they could expect an appointment as a *Rezident*. The next step was the highest echelon, a *Secondararzt*. Rezidents and Secondararzts were entitled to a salary and many of the latter became permanent hospital employees.

As a Hospitant, Grete was the low person in the physician hierarchy and had no say in her assignment. Thus the hazardous tuberculosis ward.

Grete was terrified of going into the ward every day, but was afraid to decline the offer. By 1931, Austria had become officially anti-Semitic and Jewish physicians were being targeted. Turning down any opportunity could mean the end of her career before it even began. So she accepted the assignment and assumed she would inevitably contract tuberculosis and eventually die from it.

It is impossible today to comprehend the mindset of 1931, when tuberculosis was feared at least as much as AIDs, Ebola, Marburg, MRSA, Avian Flu, Anthrax, bioterrorism and other health scares that strike terror in twenty-first century hearts.

An even better analogy is to the dread and panic conjured by polio in every American parent during the 1940s and early 1950s until the Salk and Sabin vaccines appeared.

By 1931, that TB was caused by an airborne bacillus had been known for 50 years, since its discovery by Robert Koch. It was the overriding preoccupation of every healthcare provider in the world. It obsessed every single practitioner if, for no other reason, his or her own potential risk of exposure. All one had to do to contract TB was . . . breathe.

TB can invade and consume every single organ, bone and tissue in the human body. In the early 1930s, it was ubiquitous. For most of the eighteenth, nineteenth, and twentieth centuries, at least 50 percent of the people alive carried the TB bacterium around somewhere in their systems. Even today, the incidence of carriers is estimated by public health officials to be one-third of humanity, or approximately 2.5 billion people.

Approximately ten percent of TB carriers contract the disease. However, until almost the mid-twentieth century, there was no cure and over one-third of its victims died.

With all that to occupy a new physician's mind, the popular saying locally was that TB was the "Viennese illness." By 1875, every fourth resident of Vienna died of TB, including a large number of prominent people: Antonin Dvorak, Napoleon's son the Duke of Reichstadt, Emperor Franz Josef's daughter Sophie, quantum physicist Erwin Schrodinger, Franz Kafka, novelist Robert Musil, and quite likely Wolfgang Mozart and Frederic Chopin. This list only scratches the surface. Worldwide, thousands of famous men and women were struck down by TB, including: Alexander Pope, Anders Celsius, Andrew Jackson, Anton Chekhov, Cardinal Richelieu, Christy Mathewson, D.H. Lawrence, Doc Holliday, Dred Scott, Eleanor Roosevelt, Emily Bronte, Frederic Bartholdi, Gavrilo Princip, George Orwell, Henry David Thoreau, Henry VII of England, James Monroe, Jane Austen, Jay Gould, Friedrich von Schiller, John C. Calhoun, John Keats, Khalil Gibran, Laurence Sterne,

Louis Braille, Mohammed Ali Jinnah, Pocahontas, Ring Lardner, Simon Bolivar, Stephen Crane, Thomas Wolfe, Vivien Leigh, and Alexis de Tocqueville, to name just a few.

Grete worked in the TB ward off-and-on for two years. At that time, doctors did not wear masks because it was felt that seeing caregivers in them would undermine patient morale.

After a time, Grete became accustomed to her daily routine and stopped worrying about the danger. She listened to patients' chests, often without a stethoscope (they were in short supply), instead placing her ear directly on the patient's body.

Despite being coughed on, sneezed on, spit on, and bled on thousands of times, she never contracted active TB. To my knowledge, she never had a Tine test or any other of the common TB tests or even a chest X-ray, so we cannot know if the bacillus was latent inside her. She lived to be 101 and did not die of tuberculosis.

She called not having contracted TB a miracle. Part of that "miracle" might have been that Tay-Sachs disease carriers may have a natural, genetic protection against TB. How this actually works is not known. Up to 11 percent of the Ashkenazi Jewish population are Tay-Sachs carriers. "Ashkenazi," roughly translated, means the Jews of Germany, a population that traces its origins all the way back to the Israelite tribes of the Middle East who migrated to Europe in two waves: first, during the Jewish Wars with Rome in the first century AD; second, in the seventh century AD when Muslim conquests drove many Jews out of their homeland. They settled in the Rhineland during the early Middle Ages, then migrated East during the mass Jewish expulsions several hundred years later.

In many Eastern European villages with Jewish populations, TB ran riot among Christians while sparing Jewish residents. Healthy relatives of children with Tay-Sachs disease did not contract TB even under repeated exposure. This relative immunity to TB did not sit well with the Christian population and even prompted pogroms.

Tay-Sachs protection against TB did not move into the Christian population because Jews were forced to live in ghettos and generally forbidden from inter-marrying.

What a difference a year made. Grete's future husband, Ernst, who graduated in 1930, received one of the choice assignments—which eventually led to a residency at the *Allgemeines Krankenhaus*, one of the most prestigious hospitals in the world. It was then—and continues to be today—the largest health facility in Europe (second largest in the world), treating more than 400,000 patients per year in addition to 3.5 million outplacement visits. He landed a decent-paying position right away, which was virtually unheard of, and at the same time was able to open his own practice and garner a steady flow of patients, thanks to being engaged by an insurance company to examine applicants for policies.

Since 1903, the hospital had a synagogue, a place for Jewish patients to pray. This was amazing because it was constructed during the mayoralty of Karl Lueger (1897-1910), who based much of his popularity and policies on vocal anti-Semitism. The synagogue was all but destroyed during *Kristallnacht* in November, 1938 (see below). The synagogue was turned into an electric transformer station in 1953.

Grete's brother Benno, who graduated the same year as Ernst, also had little trouble landing a paid position at the Allgemeines Krankenhaus. Benno and Ernst did not know each other in medical school, but became acquainted at the hospital. Just a year later, however, it was almost impossible for a Jewish medical school graduate to replicate Ernst and Benno's good fortune. It was also impossible for a woman to be appointed to the hospital staff.

Hospitants were expected to rotate through different hospital wards, so Grete was theoretically able to move on from the TB ward after three months. However, the constant epidemic conditions in the TB ward necessitated that she be called back in frequently. In between stints there, she rotated through Internal Medicine, Dermatology, Obstetrics, Anesthesiology, and finally Surgery.

Hospitants learned the basics: how to perform simple surgeries, make incisions, and tie ligatures. They were prohibited from performing deliveries, but were able to observe any procedure. Grete learned how to diagnose, a skill she was exceptionally good at to the end of her life. She often pinpointed what was wrong with one of her family members just by observation, asking good questions, and performing a cursory, hands-on examination.

By the time she was promoted to Aspirant, she had narrowed where she wanted to focus. She had become fascinated with dermatology and anesthesiology. She hoped that, should she be fortunate enough to become a Rezident, it would be in one of these two areas.

When she was appointed a Rezident, she requested Dermatology, but was turned down. Although there had never been a female anesthesia Rezident in the hospital, she secured a position in anesthesiology, thanks to the intervention of a young doctor at the hospital who was sweet on her. He persuaded the chief of anesthesiology that she was a worthy candidate. For the next year, she formally studied the subject, making rounds with anesthesiologists and participating in administering a great many anesthesias.

When she completed Rezident training, she was presented with a document (*diplomate*) certifying that she was a trained anesthesiologist. She did not realize at the time that her unique status went far beyond the Wiener Krankenhaus. She became the first officially certified female anesthesiologist in Austria.

Today, considerably more training would be required. Many anesthesias are performed not by physicians, but rather by nurse anesthetists. The training received by nurse anesthetists is superior to what my mother received. Today's certified nurse anesthetist must have a bachelor's degree in nursing and at least a year of professional nursing experience in an acute care setting—preferably surgery or critical care, followed by 2,500 hours of clinical training and the administration of approximately 850 anesthesias. Anesthesiologists must serve a 4-year residency to qualify for board certification.

After Grete opened her general practice, however, there were no opportunities to practice her specialty. Despite her diplomate, no male surgeons wanted a woman administering anesthesias in their operating theaters. She would not administer another anesthesia for almost 15 years.

Chapter 27
Crash

The Great Depression was triggered by the crash of the U.S. stock market on "Black Tuesday," October 29, 1929. In Europe, however, it actually began 19 months later with the bankruptcy of Austria's *Kreditanstalt* bank. Founded by the (Jewish) Rothschilds in 1855, Kreditanstalt was the largest bank in the old empire and was still the largest bank in Central and Eastern Europe after the empire disappeared. Seventy percent of Austrian trade and industry depended on the bank.

In 1931, Kreditanstalt was forced to merge with the *Oesterreichische–Kredit–Anstalt* after rescue attempts of the latter by both the Austrian government and other banks failed. Austria also declared a customs union with Germany in early 1931 that sent the French government into a tizzy and prompted a number of French banks to demand the accelerated redemption of their debts from both Germany and Austria. In addition to being stretched thin by the forced merger, Kreditanstalt was a huge French bank debtor. The bank quickly collapsed.

The situation quickly became so bad that Austria was forced to declare national bankruptcy by abandoning the gold standard. In a chain reaction, most other European countries renounced their obligations and also went off the gold standard.

Panicked Kreditanstalt customers rushed to the bank to withdraw their funds, which in turn prompted customers of other Austrian banks to do the same. The panic quickly spread to Germany and caused a comparable bank crisis in that country. Within two months, Germany's huge *Danat-Bank* collapsed, followed quickly by other German banks. The German government declared a two-day bank "holiday" in an attempt to prevent further customer runs on the banks. Most of the banks remained closed for weeks during which millions of German citizens lost their life savings for the second time in less than a decade (the first was during the runaway inflation of 1922-23).

Kreditanstalt's collapse caused much more than a financial panic. It led many Germans and Austrians to join the nascent Nazi party, attracted by the promise of simple solutions and a return to full employment and economic prosperity.

Despite the tumult, Viennese life somehow continued on its *gemütlich* path, unhurried, comfortable, pleasant and relaxed.

Grete herself was not much affected by the economic collapse. Economic downturns have a direct impact on people's health (witness the rise in physical and mental illnesses during our recent Great Recession). Physicians were in great demand.

The same was not true of her father's business. David's store suffered just like any retail business does in bad times. Sales plummeted. Customers could not afford to buy clothing. Fortunately, my grandmother Ernestine was a saving lady and had amassed a sufficient nest egg so that the family was able to survive for some time. Once she returned from the sanatorium (see the next chapter), she even took in several relatives who were having a tough time feeding and housing themselves.

Meanwhile, David, always generous to a fault, kept giving credit to the few customers who came into the store. Despite his own personal history, he sustained a life-long optimistic view of humanity. When he finally had to abandon his business in 1938 after the Nazi takeover of Austria, he was owed what amounted to a small fortune, one that he never realized.

A collateral benefit to Grete was that, given the lack of customers, she was no longer needed in the store. She could concentrate all of her attention on her studies and, eventually, on her work.

Chapter 28
Sanatorium

Grete was on the cusp of beginning her career when tragedy struck the Sobel family. Ernestine, whose life was turned inside out a quarter century earlier by little Stella's death, fell into a deep, clinical depression. She was prone to depression in any event, due to a genetic predisposition (numerous Lapajowker family members had been depressives). David, never a patient man, was too impulsive and distraught to manage the situation. Consequently, as would be the case in many other circumstances that life threw at the family, Grete was the designated responsible adult tasked with handling her mother's illness.

Deferring the launch of her practice, Grete took her mother to a sanatorium in the Alpine foothills of Lower Austria. She accompanied her and stayed with her day and night for four months until Ernestine was released and sent home, her depression having moderated sufficiently to put her back into her family and society.

For the first two months of Ernestine's confinement, she did not want to get out of bed, but lay curled up in a fetal position, crying off-and-on. Grete's role was largely that of a suicide watch. Rehabilitation manifested itself in the form of the patient being willing to get out of bed and walk with her daughter in the lush gardens surrounding the sanatorium, where the breathtaking mountain scenery was supposed to be uplifting.

The cost of the sanatorium was steep, and even higher because Grete was also staying there. The economic impact on the family was significant and came at the same time as the decline in David's retail business. The Great Depression battered the Sobel family's finances back into the desperate straits familiar from their World War I experience. David sold his car and let the chauffeur go. The family maid was also no longer affordable. Getting enough food to eat became, once again, the primary family focus.

This being Austria, some attempt was made at psychoanalysis. However, Ernestine's depression was sufficiently severe that professionals could make no dent in it. During the sessions, her affect was slumping over, never making eye contact with the therapist, and never uttering a word.

Electroconvulsive treatment (electric shock therapy) was just then emerging, and Ernestine was one of the early patients on whom it was tried. Whether this had any effect is debatable. Time, including time away from the daily stresses of family life, may have been the best therapy. Antidepressant drugs did not yet exist.

My grandmother came back home not quite the same as she had been before her breakdown and spent years teetering on the edge. She no longer spoke much and seemed uninterested in most topics. When David went out to the coffee houses, she stayed home. The family respected her delicate condition, fearing that the slightest life disruption could once again send her over the edge. She did relatively well for a time until the aftermath of the economic collapse forced the family to attempt to move to a smaller apartment in the nearby *Grosse Schiffgasse*.

Although Ernestine was hardly back to normal, Grete could no longer hold her hand 24 hours a day, seven days a week. It was time for her to spread her wings and launch her medical career. Moreover, with the Great Depression staring the family in the face, Grete needed to become a breadwinning contributor to family finances as soon as possible.

The move to the new apartment, however, was so traumatic for Ernestine that she developed what Grete labeled an "hysterical aversion to it." She insisted on giving it up and moving back to the former apartment. Despite that, she suffered a second breakdown. Once again, Grete postponed her career and went away with her mother to a sanatorium, this time for five months.

This new sanatorium (the former facility did not have an available bed), *Mauer bei Amstetten* (the Wall near Amstetten), was in the *Dunkelsteinerwald* 50 miles west of Vienna. The facility was enormous, able to accommodate 1,000 patients at a time. The institution was a famous clinic and had royal backing, having been opened in 1902 by Emperor Franz Josef who, admiring its amenities, proclaimed: "It must be nice being an idiot in Mauer."

While at Mauer, Grete ran into a world-famous actress (she refused to tell me her name, mother having an overdeveloped sense of privacy) as well as a number of other celebrities from the creative world. The Mauer still exists and is even bigger today.

Grete's experiences with her mother's illness left its mark. It reinforced her skepticism about psychoanalysis in particular and psychiatry in general. It strengthened her resolve never to permit herself to become depressed, something she feared because of the family history. She never had much patience with people whom she believed allowed themselves to wallow in self-pity and depression. For a very bright woman, she had little understanding that sometimes will power is not enough.

Chapter 29
The Practice

Grete began her private general medical practice by having a shingle painted and getting permission to hang it outside over the front entrance to the apartment house. It was a simple sign that said (translated): "Doctor Margarete Sobel, Second Floor." Her medical office consisted of two rooms in the family apartment. The sitting room became the waiting room while a smaller room adjacent to it served as the examining room.

Grete's marketing strategy consisted of (1) the sign and (2) word of mouth. Within a few months, the practice, which had been limping along, suddenly received an injection of energy and good fortune. Grete managed to secure two small contracts to perform medical services: one from a labor union through which she served union members; the other from a commercial company for its employees. These arrangements, similar to legal services benefits in the United States today, were quite common in Austria. Without them, few doctors would have been able to make a reasonable living.

Just before the Anschluss in 1938, Grete " . . . was supposed to get a permanent position with one of the big insurance companies, which would have given me a very good position and an excellent practice." Needless to say, that did not happen.

The years between when she began her private practice and its abrupt termination in 1938 were consumed with work interspersed with many slow periods. Medicine was not the key to the mint that it became in America in the 1960s, due in large part to the introduction of Medicare, employer-provided health insurance, and the fee-for service concept that both developments encouraged. Medicare was vigorously resisted by the American Medical Association, which screamed "socialized medicine" when the landmark legislation was first introduced by President Truman in 1948. Eighteen years later, when Medicare became law, the screaming stopped when physicians found themselves enriched by government largesse.

These sorts of disputes were not an issue in Austria or anywhere else in Europe when Grete began practicing medicine. Otto von Bismarck, the legendary German Chancellor who forged a unified and powerful Germany out of a gaggle of small states, is not as well known for his other, perhaps greater triumph—social insurance programs, including national health insurance.

A statesman whom historians have labeled a reactionary was actually far ahead of his time and way out on a left-leaning limb when it came to social welfare. As early as the 1880s, militaristic Germany became the world's first welfare state. Bismarck's shrewd vision was hardly idealistic. Instead, it was deftly designed to trump the Socialists and neutralize their rising political support. His thinking was that a social safety net would dissipate a good deal of Socialist support. It worked. Before any other people, Germans enjoyed health insurance, accident insurance, disability insurance, and old age pensions.

Following Austria's defeat and break-up in 1918, elections were held and the Social Democrats came to power in Vienna, securing the mayoralty and an absolute parliamentary majority. This was the first Austrian election in which women were allowed to vote. Vienna, with one-third of the new nation's entire population, immediately experienced social reforms.

Despite food shortages, hyperinflation, Spanish Flu and raging syphilis, the Social Democrats began to institute radical reforms. An 8-hour workday was quickly established. Unemployment benefits soon followed. The Social Democrats' greatest accomplishment was its extensive public housing program. Between 1925 and 1934, more than 60,000 units were built. These were attractive flats consisting of large apartment blocks built around expansive green courtyards. Rental rates were very modest.

"Clothes packages" for babies were distributed at birth. The city government established kindergartens and an extensive afternoon day-care system to free mothers to go to work and keep children off the streets. Worker vacation resorts were built. Holidays and vacation days were mandated by law. Sports facilities, spas and public baths were constructed and opened to all citizens.

Most significantly, healthcare was made free of charge for all, with physician and hospital reimbursements financed by employer taxes, general tax levies, and some employee contributions.

Grete's practice fell under this regime which, once Austria recovered from the war and its difficult aftermath, dramatically improved the health of its citizens. Infant mortality declined. TB cases plummeted by 50 percent.

By the time the Social Democrats lost power to the Catholic parties of the Right, the Viennese social welfare system was so ingrained and popular that the right-wing parties did not dare repeal it.

Julius Tandler, the Social Democratic Vienna City Councilor for Social and Health Services, neatly summed up the enlightened attitude underpinning these cutting-edge policies:

> *"What we spend for youth homes we will save on prisons. What we spend for the care of pregnant women and babies we will save in hospitals for mental illnesses."*

While Tandler was a visionary when it came to social services, he also favored euthanasia and sterilization for what he called "unworthy life," a chilling portent of the Nazi philosophy. What made this more unsettling was that Tandler was Jewish and was Grete's distant cousin.

Grete's Hollandstrasse office was in the building adjacent to Ernst's office. They had also been born in these neighboring buildings. They knew each other only by sight, although they actually met once while living in Austria. "... *once I met him on the street and he helped me. I had injured my kneecap and I couldn't step off the curb. Ernst saw me and he helped me. And I liked him right away. But he was very firmly attached to someone else at the time.*" They would not meet again until they were both refugees in New York City in the 1940s.

Despite universal healthcare for workers, individuals who were self-employed or were not factory workers were not covered. Although there were plenty of private patients who had to pay for medical services out of their own pocket, and they constituted the vast majority of Grete's patients, she could not charge them very much because competition among physicians was intense, especially in Leopoldstadt. As she put it, she made "just enough to pay her telephone bill every month." That was not exactly accurate as she was able to contribute to the family coffers.

When she did not have patients, she sat and waited for them, biding her time by reading extensively. Advertising was considered unethical for doctors, so she had little choice. Her situation was hardly unique. Most of her medical colleagues also lived with their parents, had an office in their apartment, and sat and waited for patients to ring the doorbell.

Part Two
Vienna, 1934-1939

"The Teutons have been singing the swan song ever since they entered the ranks of history. They have always confounded truth with death."
Henry Miller

"What luck for the rulers that men do not think."
Adolf Hitler

"Who has inflicted this upon us? Who has made us Jews different from all other people? Who has allowed us to suffer so terribly up till now?"
Anne Frank

"When his life was ruined, his family killed, his farm destroyed, Job knelt down on the ground and yelled up to the heavens, 'Why god? Why me?' and the thundering voice of God answered, 'There's just something about you that pisses me off.'"
Stephen King,
Storm of the Century: An Original Screenplay

Chapter 30
Setting the Stage

How did what ended in the extermination of most of European Jewry get started?

The first evidence of the term "anti-Semitism" only goes back to 1879, where it appeared in a book by one Wilhelm Marr entitled *Der Weg zum Siege des Germanismus über des Judentums* (*The Road to Victory of Germanism over Judaism*). The highly agitated and über-paranoid Herr Marr subsequently backed up his *magnum opus* by founding the *League of Antisemites*.

While Marr was a crackpot and not taken very seriously, his notion soon became elevated to respectability through the attentions of a more mainstream historian, Heinrich von Treitschke. Treitschke began publishing his own anti-Jewish screeds a year after Marr's book came out. Anti-Semitism quickly gained traction in Germany. Treitschke was also a member of the Reichstag where he often rose to inveigh against Jews regardless of the issue before the legislature. While what follows may be just an "urban legend" that I heard from a late German Jewish friend (Henry Buxbaum [see below]), German Jews might possibly have achieved some small measure of *schadenfreude* when, in 1896, it is alleged that the stone deaf Treitschke was crossing a street, neglected to look both ways, and was run over and killed by the only milk cart in Berlin owned and operated by a Jew.

The composer Richard Wagner, whose ultra-nationalistic compositions had so much influence on Adolf Hitler, was also a public anti-Semite despite having Jewish friends and engaging in an affair with a half-Jewish woman (the daughter of the

French poet Theophile Gauthier). Wagner's brand of anti-Semitism first became public knowledge when, in 1850, he wrote that Jewish music was ". . . entirely bereft of all expression, characterized by coldness and indifference, triviality and nonsense." Wagner also spoke of the "harmful influence of Jewry on the morality of the nation," contrasting Jewish subversive power with the more honest German variety.

Wagner was a great influence on his son-in-law, the Englishman Houston Stewart Chamberlain, who wrote extensive screeds in German vilifying Jews. Chamberlain was one of Hitler's guiding lights as he formulated his own brand of anti-Semitism.

Notwithstanding, my father Ernst was an admirer of Wagner. When I was stationed in Bamberg, Germany, he insisted I attend the annual Wagner Festival in nearby Bayreuth. I admit to enjoying Wagner overtures, but have never been able to overcome my antipathy to the rest of his overblown music and their ridiculous accompanying librettos.

While all of this and more were the intellectual and philosophical underpinnings of the Nazi ideology, the major cause of the rise of popular animosity toward the Jews was their nineteenth-century success in every field in which they were, often for the first time in history, allowed to participate. Their success, especially in Germany and Austria, was greatly disproportional to their numbers, and gave rise to resentment among their peers.

Another contributing factor was the rise of Europe-wide nationalism. The more nationalistic a people became, the more pogroms there were, often state-sponsored. Scapegoating the Jews, a tactic that governments under pressure have resorted to since time immemorial, escalated as the century wore on.

The murder of Tsar Alexander II of Russia in 1881 precipitated a wave of violence resulting in the murder of several thousand Jews and the flight of hundreds of thousands more. More than two million Jews, mainly from Russia, emigrated to the United States in the last 15 years of the nineteenth century; an additional 300,000 found refuge in Canada, Great Britain, and Argentina. (Note: Alexander's assassins were not Jewish; they belonged to a revolutionary socialist organization named *Narodnaya Volya*—People's Will. Jews were, however, convenient scapegoats.)

The other Jewish reaction to this wave of violence was Zionism, the yearning for a Jewish escape to an ancestral homeland in Palestine. As Zionists became more active and vocal in Europe, anti-Semitism intensified, something of a Newtonian reaction, except that unlike his Third Law of Motion, it was hardly an equal and opposite one.

As the calendar turned over into the twentieth century, the situation became worse. In 1919 in Ukraine, for example, 60,000 Jews were murdered. In Germany, the Jewish "stab-in-the-back" libel about the German defeat in World War I underpinned the rise of the Nazi Party and Adolf Hitler.

Chapter 31
Portents from the North

Adolf Hitler was appointed Chancellor of Germany by the senile octogenarian President Paul von Hindenburg, one of the heroes of World War I, on January 20, 1933. By the time Franklin D. Roosevelt was sworn in as President of the United States 43 days later, anti-Semitism had become official German state policy. The persecution of Germany's tiny Jewish population (525,000) began in earnest.

The Jewish "threat" to Germany came in the form of less than one percent of its population. However, a hugely disproportionate percentage of professionals in banking and finance, real estate, medicine, law, and the arts and cultural institutions consisted of Jews who rose to these positions by dint of raw intelligence and hard work. Germany's Jewish population in 1933 was highly assimilated and only casually religious, if that. It did not matter. They were Jewish and that was enough for Hitler and the Nazis.

The first major action was a Nazi-organized boycott of Jewish businesses called for April 1, 1933. Overnight, signs went up all over the country directing Germans not to buy from Jews. By the end of April, all Jews were purged from the German civil service and an "Aryan clause" was applied to all professional associations and many other organizations. Simultaneously, a *Law to Prevent the Overcrowding of German Schools and Tertiary Institutions* was enacted by the Reichstag which, in effect, imposed a strict Jewish quota on students at all educational levels.

The German Jewish community was shocked. There had never been such a successful, secular Jewish community anywhere at any time in history. Many considered themselves good, loyal Germans. Tens of thousands were World War I veterans who had fought courageously and been awarded numerous decorations for valor. Twelve thousand Jewish soldiers died for Germany in World War I.

On May 10, 1933, the new German government staged its own "Bonfire of the Vanities." Propaganda Minister Joseph Goebbels masterminded a book burning in Berlin's *Opernplatz*, fronted on three sides by the Opera House, National Library, and University, all three the symbols of German culture which, up to then, was considered the most elevated, refined, and sophisticated in the world.

The dwarfish, club-footed Goebbels, not exactly a paragon of Aryan manhood, launched the occasion with a rabble-rousing speech vilifying Jews and Bolsheviks. This was followed by the lighting of a gigantic pyre into which enthusiastic students and frenzied storm troopers flung the works of Thomas Mann, Stefan Zweig, Erich Maria Remarque, Sigmund Freud, Albert Einstein, Heinrich Heine, and even Felix Salten's *Bambi* (go figure) among many others. More than 20,000 books met a fiery death amid the feverish cheers of participants and thousands of excited onlookers.

Reading about the bonfire the next day in the Vienna papers, Grete for the first time realized that these Nazis were different and probably dangerous. She remembered an early nineteenth century quotation of Heinrich Heine from her gymnasium days: *"Whenever they burn books, sooner or later they will burn human beings, too."*

In October, 1933, all Jews were removed from German media jobs. By May 1935, Jews were purged from the army; in September at the annual Nazi Nuremberg rally, the infamous "Nuremberg Laws" were promulgated, which denied Jews German citizenship, forbade marriage and sexual relations between Jews and non-Jews, prohibited Jews from employing German servants, and effectively marginalized Jews from German society. Several thousand Christian men and women were forced to divorce their Jewish spouses. Those who tried to meet secretly thereafter and were discovered were incarcerated in concentration camps. By 1938, Jews were forbidden from practicing any professions.

Societal integration, abandonment of Jewish religious ritual, and even conversion to Christianity meant nothing to Hitler and the Nazis. Only blood counted; "tainted" blood presumably threatened Aryan racial purity.

In all, more than 400 laws were enacted between 1933 and 1939 directed at German Jews. Eventually, Jews could not participate at all in German life. A number of laws deprived them of their possessions and left them prisoners in their homes.

Chapter 32
The Downward Slide

Austria fell under the fascist yoke one year before Germany. In 1932, Engelbert Dollfuss—known to his followers as *"Millimetternich"* because of his four feet, ten inch stature—became chancellor. His powerful personality belied his size. He came into office in a time of great domestic turmoil and also had to cope with a Great Depression economy stubbornly resistant to anything governments could devise to deal with it.

Dollfuss' greatest foreign challenge came from neighboring Germany. The absorption of Austria into the German Reich was an obsession of Hitler's that he harbored long before he came to power. Starting in 1933 when he was appointed German chancellor, Hitler began pressuring Austria, gradually tightening the vise as the years went by.

Despite Dollfuss' fascist leanings and intense domestic pressure from local Nazis—both verbal and violent—Dollfuss resisted. Realistically, he had nowhere to turn for foreign support, but hoped he could count on Italy's dictator, Mussolini, as a counterweight to Hitler. That proved a pipe dream. Germany gambled correctly that Mussolini would remain aloof and began tightening the screws on Austria by incessant demands that Nazis be taken into the government. Secretly, Austrian Nazis went to Bavaria to train militarily in preparation for a possible *coup d'etat*. At the same time, the Austrian Nazis, with the hidden support of Germany, staged a series of terrorist attacks, bombing railroad lines and tourist centers, the aim being to deter German tourists from vacationing in Austria, thus squeezing the already strained Austrian economy.

In addition to battling the Nazis on the Right, Dollfuss had to fight the Socialists on the Left. In 1934, Dollfuss declared a state of emergency, abolished the republic, suspended parliament and essentially became a dictator. The outraged Nazis attempted a coup that same year and Dollfuss was assassinated. Despite Dollfuss' reactionary politics, the Sobel family was horrified at what happened.

Kurt von Schuschnigg succeeded Dollfuss. Unlike his predecessor, he was a genteel man, cultured, but too weak a character to stave off the Nazi onslaught. At the same time, the wily German diplomat and political survivor extraordinaire, Franz von Papen, who had briefly served as German Chancellor in 1932, was sent as Ambassador to Vienna with the purpose of undermining the Schuschnigg government and bolstering the local Nazis.

Schuschnigg's policy emulated Neville Chamberlain's: appeasement of the Germans with piecemeal concessions in hopes that these incremental yieldings would satisfy Hitler's lusts. They did not. After Hitler successfully marched into the Rhineland in 1936, a huge gamble and blatant violation of the Versailles Treaty (opposed by the Wehrmacht chiefs who believed, incorrectly, that the much more powerful French army would resist), everything changed. Schuschnigg now realized that no one was going to intervene to preserve Austrian independence. His panicked response was to step up his appeasement campaign. This put him on a direct bee-line into the belly of the beast.

His first concession was to sign a treaty demanded by Germany in which Hitler acknowledged Austrian sovereignty in return for Austria declaring itself a "German state." That was the public face of the treaty. Its secret protocols called for an amnesty for Nazi political prisoners and Nazi appointments to important government positions.

Now it was 1937, and both the political pressure and the internal Nazi terror campaign escalated. Hitler ordered the German General Staff to draw up invasion plans.

On February 11, 1938, Hitler "invited" Schuschnigg to Berchtesgaden, his Alpine retreat on the German-Austrian border, for talks about future relations between the two countries. Hat in hand and tail firmly between his legs, Schuschnigg arrived to find himself received by a bevy of high-ranking generals in addition to Hitler, a show of force too obvious to miss. Hitler raved hysterically, shouting and waving his arms, at Austria's "intransigence." He demanded that the Austrian government incorporate local Nazis and insisted that Austrian Nazi Artur Seyss-Inquart, a dark figure similar to the traitorous Norwegian Vidkun Quisling, be appointed Minister of the Interior, which would give the Nazis authority over the police and internal security.

This was more ultimatum than demand. The alternative being an immediate German invasion, Schuschnigg succumbed. The die was cast. The only out the Austrian Chancellor saw was his statement to Hitler that the Constitution mandated that only the Austrian President could sign off on the terms of the ultimatum. President Wilhelm Miklas balked for a while, but eventually the pressure became overwhelming and he gave in. The Nazis now controlled Austria's internal security and that meant that the final outcome was inevitable. Huge Nazi demonstrations now erupted all over Austria demanding unification with Germany. The police stood aside.

It was now early March. Schuschnigg's last gasp attempt at staving off a German takeover was to call for a March 13th plebiscite in which Austrians would vote *"Ja"* or *"Nein"* regarding whether they wanted a "free, independent, social, Christian, and united Austria." When Hitler learned of the pending plebiscite, he went ballistic, his fury evolving into a frenzy of hate, hysteria and screaming as he paced about his office like a madman (and, according to some accounts, flung himself down and chewed on the carpet, earning him the pejorative moniker *teppichfresser*–"rug eater"). He ordered an immediate military takeover of Austria. The terrified

Schuschnigg called off the plebiscite and resigned on March 11. He was replaced by Seyss-Inquart who quickly sent out a plea to Germany to help "establish peace and order in Austria."

Chapter 33
Anschluss

The Flower War

Adolf Hitler had a love-hate relationship with his native land. Born in Austria in the hamlet of *Braunau-am-Inn*, he was raised there and in nearby Linz. He lived in Vienna from 1907 to 1913 when he left for Munich to avoid being drafted into the Austrian Army. His Viennese sojourn was not a happy time for this indolent youth whose imagination refused to countenance reality. Despite his self-induced straitened circumstances deriving from extreme torpor and lethargy (he blew through a sizable inheritance in no time at all), he clung to his grandiose opinion of himself and his overblown schemes for redesigning Linz and Vienna after his own image.

A decade later, he wrote in *Mein Kampf*: "Reunion [of Austria to Germany] must be regarded as the supreme task of our lives, and one to be achieved by any means possible. People of one blood should belong to one Reich."

Just before daybreak on March 12, 1938, the 300,000 strong German Eighth Army was poised on the Austrian border, waiting for "Operation Otto" to begin. The German generals expected considerable resistance. To their surprise, the Austrian border guards abandoned their posts and were nowhere to be found. They had even taken down all of the border barriers. To their amazement, the German soldiers were welcomed with open arms. Swastika banners emerged everywhere, suddenly unfurled from hiding places in tens of thousands of Austrian homes and businesses. Enthusiasm on the part of the supposed victims was at a fever pitch. Not a single shot was fired during the entire operation. The action was bloodless and so welcomed by the country whose independent existence was liquidated that it came to be known as the *Blumenkriege*—the "flower war."

Wild Enthusiasm

So much for Austria's post-World War II claim that it, too, was a victim of Nazism. This Big Lie was at the center of Austrian policy for more than 55 years following the end of World War II. It was a convenient excuse for not paying reparations to the former Jewish population of Austria (the fewer than one-third of the country's Jewish citizens not murdered by the Nazis). It also was used to justify the election of former United Nations Secretary-General Kurt Waldheim as Austrian President despite his well-documented Nazi past during which he was probably involved in carrying out crimes against humanity in Yugoslavia.

Cheers, smiles, and wildly enthusiastic "Heil Hitlers!" greeted the invaders all the way to Vienna. At every town along the way, the Germans were greeted with rousing refrains of the *Horst Wessel Lied*, the Nazi anthem penned by the young *Sturmabteiling* (SA) leader who was murdered, either by the Communists, his landlady over a rent dispute, or a jilted homosexual lover . . . the case remains a mystery to this day. Wessel made a convenient martyr to the cause and inspiration for the Nazi marching song, *Wenn Judenblut vom Messer Spritzt* (*When Jewish blood Spurts From Our Knives*).

Meanwhile, in Vienna that day, there was a huge Nazi demonstration on the Ringstrasse. Grete watched as hundreds of thousands of Viennese took part, delirious with joy. She was amazed at the multitudes who had obviously stashed SA and SS uniforms and swastika armbands in their homes and were able to pull them out now that the great day they had so long yearned for was here. The next morning, a Viennese radio announcer proclaimed rapturously: *"Der Führer ist hier!"*

Within minutes, thousands of *Hitlerjugend*—Hitler Youth—and *Bund Deutscher Mädel*—League of German Girls—took to the streets, celebrating joyously.

For the first time in her life, Grete felt visceral fear. She quickly made her way home and stayed inside the rest of the day, listening to the radio with her family as it reported on the German Wehrmacht and Adolf Hitler's grand entrance into and progress through Austria toward Vienna.

At 3:50 PM on March 12, Hitler crossed the Austrian border at Braunau-am-Inn. His 30 minutes in Braunau were highlighted by a visit to the small house where he was born, the very same house that, more than a century before, served as Napoleon's headquarters in 1806 during his preparations for the Battle of Austerlitz. Later, Braunau was the site of the formal transfer from the Austrians to the French of Napoleon's new bride, Marie Louise. In 1813, Napoleon officially declared the village to be the precise geographic center of Europe.

Hitler was next greeted with hysterical enthusiasm in nearby Linz, where he had moved from Braunau and attended—but never graduated from—high school.

Cardinal Theodor Innitzer, the head of the Austrian Catholic church, sent a telegram expressing warmest greetings to Hitler and ordered all of the country's churches draped with swastika flags and all the bells to toll. No one knew where the Catholic church had stored the thousands of swastika flags that suddenly emerged to be hung from churches throughout Austria. The following day, Innitzer received Hitler at his Vienna residence.

When Hitler arrived in Vienna, he spoke to a rally of at least 200,000 ecstatic Austrians in the *Heldenplatz* ("Heroes' Square") in the center of town. Grete's future husband, Ernst, was in the street-side crowd when Hitler's open car passed by not 20 feet from him. For the rest of his life, he often expressed his regret that he did not have a pistol with him. Had he had one, he likely would have missed the target, Ernst never having handled a weapon in his life. Grete was walking home across the bridge into Leopoldstadt when she heard the thunderous roars coming from the Heldenplatz.

There was no resistance whatsoever to the German incursion and complete silence from the so-called Great Powers. Mussolini, who had sent Italian troops to the Brenner Pass border with Austria during the failed 1934 Nazi putsch, now said that he had no interest in Austria. Neither did any other nation.

The historical consensus is that Neville Chamberlain's foolish and disastrous attempt at appeasing Adolf Hitler in Munich in Fall 1938 was the triggering event that encouraged the Nazi dictator to launch World War II. I think that is mistaken. The actual inflection point occurred when Hitler was able to absorb Austria without shedding a single drop of blood or worrying about the reaction of the Western powers to his naked aggression against a sovereign state. After the Anschluss, there would be no holding the monster back.

Chapter 34
The Taming of the Jews

The Nazi war against Austria's Jews began immediately following the Anschluss. Mob action on the streets commenced the day of the invasion with the acquiescence of the new Nazi authorities. Beatings and humiliations became commonplace within hours of the Anschluss. Jews were put to humiliating work cleaning gutters and scrubbing streets and public toilets. Religious Jews were forced to clean out SA and SS barracks' latrines using their prayer shawls. Thousands of Jews were imprisoned, their possessions confiscated. Several thousand were sent to the Dachau concentration camp. Most of them never returned. The speed with which well-to-do Viennese Jews were identified and arrested was the result of tabulations made possible by IBM's *Hollerith* machines (the company made a fortune from its collaboration with the Nazis during the 1930s and 1940s, assisting the efficient functioning of the Holocaust and the German war effort).

Jewish suicides—four in February—skyrocketed to 680 the day after the Anschluss. There were an additional 311 in Vienna in April. A couple that were close friends of Grete's parents were among them. First, the parents threw their children out of their fifth floor apartment window, then they jumped themselves.

Austria's Christian population either joined in the anti-Jewish riots and abuses with great gusto or almost universally approved of what their co-religionists were doing. Elderly Jewish men were stripped naked and forced to crawl along the streets on all fours. Torah scrolls were ripped from their arks in synagogues and thrown to the ground where Orthodox Jewish women were made to dance on them. Storm troopers urinated into the faces of Jews while they were held down by thugs. Grete witnessed hundreds of Jews forced down on their hands and knees, her father among them, and ordered to wash the city streets while onlookers jeered.

She herself was never degraded in this manner. One reason: she did not "look" at all Jewish. Until old age, she had light brown hair, a pale, Slavic face with high cheekbones, and a virtually aquiline nose to go with hazel eyes. Her father, who could have been the poster child for the Slavic race, was a pure blond with greenish-blue eyes. My less-than-scientific assessment of how their looks evolved points to the many pogroms Eastern European Jews endured throughout their 800-year residence in that part of the world. Likely some Cossack horseman raped an ancestor and the resulting offspring injected Russo-Ukrainian blood into the family gene pool.

Within days, random and then systematic looting of Jewish property commenced. Vienna's Great Synagogue was occupied by Nazi troops. Art works, books, jewelry, carpets, furniture, nothing was sacred. Thousands of priceless objects belonging to Jewish families were picked over by the country's museums. Most are still there to this day despite the efforts of the rightful owners to get them back. One Rothschild baron was divested of 3,444 significant works of art. Some Jewish collectors tried to sell off their paintings at bargain-basement prices to circumvent the looting.

If you examine the official, documented provenance of many works of art formerly owned by Jews and now in the possession of either public or private collections, you will see references to prior owners like *Reichsmarshall* Hermann Göring and Hitler's private secretary, Martin Bormann, but not the rightful owners from whom the works were stolen. This kind of blatant, illegal laundering and sanitizing goes on to this day and is often the basis for the refusal of the beneficiaries of these thefts to give them up to the heirs of the true owners.

Jewish shop windows were smashed and their inventories stolen or destroyed. Jewish businesses, including David's haberdashery, were placed under "Aryan" overseers. The Nazis decreed that every Jewish business had to have a *Treuhandler*, an Aryan whose job it was to make sure that all of these "improperly" acquired Jewish assets were applied toward German aims. A total of 9,000 Treuhandlers served in such trustee roles, some handling multiple businesses. David's Treuhandler was a man who, given his mission, was at least semi-respectful and even somewhat deferential to him, at least at first.

The Germans quickly established a central office for the confiscation of Jewish property, the *Vermögensverkehrsstelle*. More than 26,000 Jewish businesses were "Aryanized" through this office. Within a week of the Anschluss, owners were pressured into selling their businesses to Aryans for bargain basement prices. German bankers and businessmen flocked to Vienna to pick over the loot, buying up Jewish businesses for a song.

David's store was vandalized in broad daylight several times in the first two weeks post-Anschluss before he, too, was forced to sell it for a pittance. I filed an official Austrian reparations application on behalf of my mother in 2000, complete with photographs of the storefront with my grandfather standing proudly beneath his sign. The application was denied with no explanation and no opportunity for appeal.

It took 71 years to get any reparations at all for anyone out of the Austrian government, which denied, delayed and dawdled sufficiently long that almost all of the claimants were dead. Grete received a check for $6,500, worth about $500 in Austria in 1938, compensation for the loss of her medical practice.

In the Prater, a mixed civilian/SA mob forced any Jews they encountered down on their hands and knees and made them eat grass. Others were forced to lick the streets. Synagogues were turned into Nazi torture chambers.

Seventy-six thousand men and women—Jews and Gentiles—were arrested in Vienna immediately following the Anschluss. Six thousand were sacked from the now-defunct Schuschnigg government. The former chancellor was arrested. Three years later he was given a job as a death transport officer at the *Sachsenhausen* concentration camp where his principal duty involved burying the bodies of thousands of Soviet prisoners of war murdered by the SS.

Famous Jews were also badly treated. The Rothschilds suffered, although nowhere near as much as middle- and working-class Jews. Franz Rothenberg, Chairman of Kreditanstalt, recently revived after its collapse earlier in the decade, was kidnapped by the SA and killed, thrown from a rapidly moving car. Not even Sigmund Freud was inviolate. Storm troopers invaded his home and stole $12,000 in cash. Days later, his daughter Anna was arrested by the Gestapo.

Official Nazi anti-Semitic policies were imposed much more rapidly and comprehensively in Austria than they had been in Germany. Within a month, Austria's Jews were deprived of their citizenship and all 635 official Jewish organizations were disbanded. In short order, Jews were driven out of the Austrian economy. They lost their jobs in droves. They were no longer allowed to enjoy Vienna's public parks and spaces. Thousands of Christian shop owners put signs in their windows announcing that they would not sell to Jews.

Despite these abuses, many Jews continued to hold out hope that this nightmare could only be temporary.

Chapter 35
Ernst Escapes

At first, Jews were encouraged to emigrate, but only after they were stripped of their livelihoods and assets. A Central Office for Jewish Emigration (*Zentralamt Jüdischer Auswanderung*) headed by a low-ranking functionary, a young SS *Obersturmführer* (equivalent to a First Lieutenant) Adolf Eichmann, was established in Vienna to expedite the process. Sixty-thousand Jews left Austria in 1938, quite an achievement given the Herculean obstacles placed in their way.

Grete's sister Rose and her new husband Ted, as well as Grete's future husband Ernst, were among those who successfully emigrated very early from the Ostmark (the name "Austria" ceased to exist after the Anschluss—*Ostmark* was the new name of this now German province). Some left legally. Ted got out almost immediately following the Anschluss, one day after he and Rose were married. After several months, Rose trailed him to Buenos Aires, where he had a friend who provided the necessary Argentinian immigration papers.

Many others left illegally. In early August, Ernst hopped a train to *Vorarlberg*, the Austrian province bordering on Switzerland, and slipped over the Swiss border after midnight. His attempt failed an hour after he crossed over when he was captured by the Swiss *Grenzwachtkorps*—border guards—less than a mile into the country. The Swiss stepped up their border patrols immediately following the Anschluss.

The Swiss put Ernst on a train under guard and shipped him back to Vienna. Several weeks later, he tried again, and this time succeeded. He took a train from Vienna to *Feldkirch*, one of the larger Vorarlberg towns, about four miles from the Swiss border. He spent much of the rail journey across Austria in one restroom or another in order to avoid the Nazi officials on the train who were on the lookout for Jews trying to escape.

In Feldkirch, he put on his *bergschuhe*—mountain hiking boots—and went overland toward the border, which at that juncture was heavily forested. He avoided roads and went cross country instead. However, he altered his route from before and first crossed into Liechtenstein, one of the smallest countries in Europe, nestled snugly between Vorarlberg and Switzerland.

Although Liechtenstein had also closed its borders with Austria, it took a much more casual approach to sealing its mountainous frontier and had nowhere near the number of border guards that the Swiss deployed. At the place where Ernst crossed into the postage-stamp country (the term has a double meaning, Liechtenstein being both tiny and heavily reliant on the sale of its very colorful and exotic postage stamps for foreign exchange revenues), he only needed to traverse a three-mile stretch of Liechtenstein to arrive at the Swiss frontier.

His tactical plan was well-thought out, which was typical of Ernst when major decisions loomed. As a boy, I often watched him sitting on his *Wiener Werkstätte* chair in his den thinking through the pros and cons of a decision. The intense look on his face as he weighed options was something I have never encountered in anyone else. While I was annoyed at the time because my mother made me be quiet and stay away from him while he sorted things out in his mind, now I admire both his ability to concentrate and the fact that the tough calls he had to make in his life were almost always the right ones.

The logic of proceeding through Liechtenstein was brilliant. Not only were the Liechtensteiners far less vigilant than the Swiss, but the Swiss border with Liechtenstein was porous. Very few *Grenzwachtkorps* patrolled this sector. While Ernst had no facts on which to base his plan, he correctly surmised that this would be a much easier escape route. The fact that so few desperate Austrian Jews figured this out is a further testament to his ability to make good decisions under pressure.

Once in Switzerland, he avoided capture and walked through the forest and over the relatively low Alpine terrain to the tiny village of *Rüthi*, whence he traveled to Zurich by bus. The total distance he walked from Feldkirch to Rüthi was ten miles. Ernst, age 33 when he left Austria, was an accomplished mountain climber and skier and in very good physical condition. A ten-mile trek through three countries over low mountains and through dense forests was not difficult for him.

Walking was something he and Grete kept up throughout their lives. They were religious about it, one of the few things they were religious about. Every day, they took a long walk, often up to 3-4 miles, even into very old age.

Within 6 months of the Anschluss, 45,000 Jews had managed to leave Austria. By September 1938, all of Grete's three siblings were gone—Rose and husband Ted to Argentina; Otto to medical school in Switzerland; and Benno in transit to the United States where he was able to join the Army as soon as he passed his New York State medical boards and English examination. Eventually, Otto also made it to America and became an Army doctor as well.

Only Grete, her parents, and maternal grandparents were left in Vienna.

Chapter 36
Closing the Vice

The Nuremberg Laws

Hitler wasted no time going after the Jews of Austria. The day after he marched triumphantly into Vienna, the Germans imposed the 1935 Nuremberg Laws on Austria. Overnight, Nazi leaders became worried about the random destruction of Jewish businesses and personal wealth and property that local Nazi enthusiasts had wreaked the day of the Anschluss. They viewed with alarm the rapid diminution of Jewish value which could, if regulated, be legally diverted to the state. As happened in Germany in 1935, a ministerial conference quickly enacted legislation to stop the chaos and replace it with a scheme by which Jews could be systematically deprived of their property. The *Gesetz zum Schutze des Deutschen Blutes und der Deutschen Ehre* (*Law for the Protection of German Blood and German Honor*) and the *Reichsburgergesetz* (*Reich Citizenship Law*)—the "Nuremberg Laws"—were the result.

The Nuremberg Laws were unprecedented. For the first time in history, legal acts dehumanized an entire people. They also formalized the unofficial measures that had been taken against Jews since Hitler became Chancellor of Germany in 1933. But their most ominous paragraphs were those that, for the first time, defined who was a Jew.

The Impact on the Family

The immediate impact of the imposition of the Nuremberg Laws on the Sobel family was that their Catholic maid lost her job. It was now illegal for Christians to work for Jews. She had

had to leave before during bad economic times, but always returned. There were many tears at her parting, both on her part and especially on the part of Ernestine. The family feared that this was going to be another triggering event plunging my grandmother once again into a deep, clinical, suicidal depression. That it did not surprised Grete and her siblings.

In 1938, Austria was still mired in the Great Depression and jobs of any kind were hard to find. The unemployment rate exceeded 30 percent. Inflation was running at 25 percent, and banks charged 25 percent interest for loans. I do not know whether the Sobel family maid found another job, but Grete knew of many similar situations where former Gentile maids to Jewish families joined the ranks of the unemployed. At least temporarily, until the German war machine cranked up to maximum output 18 months later, almost all of these former employees, who also now had to find shelter, remained unemployed. The Nuremberg laws, thus, had the unintended effect of disadvantaging a large segment of the non-Jewish population that the Nazis wished to cultivate.

The Pressure Builds

While Austrian Nazis and opportunistic thugs roamed the streets of Leopoldstadt beating up and humiliating Jews and desecrating their property, Grete kept going, seeing occasional patients, keeping a generally low profile, and noting the handwriting on the wall that told her there was no future in Austria. This interregnum would not last long.

The more formal Nazi intention—the complete annihilation of Austrian Jewry—now emerged. The goal was to eliminate Jews from the country's economic life, deprive them of all of their property and financial resources, and compel them either to leave the country or starve to death.

A month after the Anschluss, Hitler held a plebiscite in Austria where voters had to publicly, in front of Nazi poll watchers, mark a ballot either *"Ja"* or *"Nein"* regarding the absorption of their country into the German Reich. The vote, unsurprisingly, was 99.7 percent in favor of the Anschluss. The fate of the handful of "Nein" voters, while not formally documented, was, anecdotally, not a pleasant one. Jews, of course, having been deprived of their citizenship by the Nuremberg Laws, were not allowed to vote.

On April 22, a decree required the declaration of all Jewish property greater than 5,000 Reichsmarks (approximately $1,190). The declaration had to be made in writing to the authorities. The Nazi's official organ, *Der Angriff* (*The Attack*) stated: "all Jewish assets are assumed to have been improperly acquired." This declaration said to both Grete and Ernst, independently, that it was high time to think about how to get out of Austria. Both saw right away that the Germans intended, at a minimum, to confiscate all Jewish wealth.

Two months later, the Germans began making lists of what they called "wealthy Jews." While David had a modestly successful clothing business at this point, he would hardly be deemed wealthy by any contemporary measure—except by the Nazis whose definition was sufficiently broad to include him on the list. Ernst's father, Solomon, on the other hand, did not qualify.

In June, the Germans also rounded up all "previously convicted" Viennese Jews—including those cited for traffic violations—and shipped them off to the Dachau concentration camp. A number of Sobel and Hermann family friends were victims of this charade.

The noose was tightening. On July 21, Jews began receiving identity cards denoting them as Jewish. One week later, disaster struck both Grete and Ernst. A decree was issued cancelling the medical licenses of all Jewish physicians, effective September 30, 1938. Thereafter, Jewish physicians would only be allowed to serve as nurses for Jewish patients.

For Ernst, the decree was the trigger that made it imperative to escape. Grete, in contrast, while she knew she had to get out, felt she could not just up and leave (not easy in any event) without finding a way out for her parents and grandparents.

On September 30, Grete closed her office. She put up a sign to that effect on the apartment building entrance door. A 20-minute walk away, at Berggasse 19, Professor Sigmund Freud did the same.

Meanwhile, the jaws of the German vise became more constricting. On August 17, all Jews were required to add either "Israel" for men or "Sarah" for women following their first names. To the end of her life, Grete could not abide—and was very critical of—any Jewish parents who named their daughters Sarah. This woman who did not hold grudges and rarely disparaged anyone made an exception for "such ignorant people," as she referred to them. When my daughter invited a little Jewish girl named Sarah over to our house to play, my mother exclaimed: "How could they do such a terrible thing? Don't they *know*?" The likely answer was that Sarah's parents did not know. They were "American Jews" without any Holocaust history. Grete looked askance at American Jews, wondering how they could continue to go to synagogues and worship a God who had turned his back on the supposedly Chosen People. "Chosen for what?" she would ask.

On September 12, Jews were prohibited from attending cultural events. A fortnight later, Jewish lawyers were denied their professional status, the only exceptions being service as "Jewish consultants for other Jews."

A few days later, Adolf Hitler and British Prime Minister Neville Chamberlain signed the Munich Agreement ceding the Sudetenland, the German-speaking region of Czechoslovakia, to Germany. This was accomplished without consulting the Czechs, thus adding the word "appeasement" to the geopolitical vocabulary of infamy. Chamberlain arrived back at Northolt Royal Air Force Base in London in the rain, deplaned carrying an umbrella, and proclaimed "peace for our time." He believed he had scored a triumph.

The umbrella became the symbol of appeasement. When the United States entered the war against Germany in December, 1941, the U.S. Army decreed that servicemen were prohibited from carrying umbrellas regardless of the weather. That decree was still in effect when I was in the Army 30 years later, as I discovered one morning when I opened an umbrella during a downpour and was sentenced to KP.

Arrested

The endgame for Grete's European medical career happened shortly after the medical license revocation decree was issued, but before it went into effect. She reluctantly succumbed to the desperate pleading of a young Catholic woman, pregnant by her boyfriend, and performed an abortion. Immediately thereafter, the woman reported Grete to the Gestapo, which did not look kindly on Jewish doctors who aborted Aryan fetuses. She was arrested and taken to Gestapo headquarters at the Hotel *Metropole* across the Danube Canal in the First District, the *Innere Stadt*—Inner City. She was detained there for three days and would never talk to me or anyone else about what happened during those 72 hours. Typically, Jews taken to the Metropole were interrogated, tortured and killed.

After her ordeal, she was released, but her medical career was over. She did not resume it for the next six years.

David and Ernestine were not at home when the Gestapo came to arrest Grete. When they got home that evening and did not see her, they began to worry. After two more days, they became frantic. However, they could not go to the police, by then completely under Nazi control. Ernestine's chronic heart condition worsened. Her daughter's disappearance, I am convinced, ultimately shortened her life. David paced, Ernestine cried and occupied herself making tea and cleaning up, while Grete's grandparents, Liber and Julie, sat quietly, staring into a void.

The plight of Vienna's Jews was about to get much worse.

Chapter 37
The Noose Tightens

Many Viennese Jews still believed that they could ride out the storm, albeit under less than optimal conditions. Jews worldwide and especially in Europe had a 2,000-year history of living under highly discriminatory restrictions among majority populations who barely tolerated them. They had always managed to accommodate themselves, provided that they were allowed to live.

Grete had no such illusions. For her, hope never triumphed over experience. She had a bad feeling about what might be in store for her, her family and the Viennese Jewish community. Despite a lifetime of consistently doubting her own decision-making abilities, this time when it mattered most, she made all the right decisions and began to research where in the world her family might go.

She sensed that it was not just a question of not being wanted. She believed the Nazis had the potential for much worse than expulsion. She had come a long way from her high school graduation class trip to Munich when she concluded that Hitler was a sideshow clown. The buffoon had transformed himself into one of the most dangerous men in the history of the world.

Grete began to make daily trips to the Austrian National Library, housed in the Hofburg Palace, the former city home of the emperor, in order to examine maps and any other useful information she could uncover about countries that might accept Jewish refugees. Oddly, the Nazis had not yet closed off access to the library to Jews. Since she could no longer work legally, Grete had ample time for research. But doing it was not easy.

Library research in post-Anschluss Vienna was a different undertaking than walking into a public library today, especially for Jews. Two large Nazi flags adorned each side of the steps up to the building. The library staff now all wore swastika armbands and put up an ostentatious show of "Heil Hitlers."

Patrons were no longer free to wander in the book stacks. Now, if Grete wanted a particular book that she identified in the card catalog, she had to request it in writing, sign her name, and submit the request to the staff. She was then questioned about why she wanted the book. When the staff saw her Jewish name on the request form and heard her explanation, they were eager to retrieve books for her since it was apparent that she was seeking a way out of the country. Making Austria *Judenrein*—cleansed of Jews—was now official state policy. Other than isolated incidents and special circumstances, such as the mass roundups immediately after the Nazi takeover, the Third Reich had not yet devised its alternative means of ridding the planet of what it called the "Jewish vermin." That would come later.

Grete's extensive research produced only four places that would permanently accept Jews, although not without a lot of planning, sweat equity and plain dumb luck: Palestine, China (more precisely Shanghai), Bolivia, and the United States.

Even in the four lands that would consider taking in Jews, the obstacles to actually getting there were huge. Grete quickly rejected Palestine because its British overlords did everything they could to keep Jews out. Shanghai was tempting because it was the only place in the world that would admit Jews without documentation beyond a passport. The Chinese authorities had an appreciation for traditional Jewish business acumen and initiative and believed that Jews could make an important economic contribution. However, getting there was very expensive. Moreover, she considered China too alien, too distant, and too volatile. The country was in the middle of both a civil war between Mao Tse-tung's Communists and Chiang Kai-shek's *Kuomintang* as well as a war for survival against the invading Japanese since 1931. Add in a number of regional warlords and China looked like much too chaotic a scene for Grete.

Bolivia was possible. The scenic photographs Grete viewed were very enticing. Jews had lived in Bolivia since the early sixteenth century when Spanish *Marranos* (forced converts to Christianity) first arrived in the country, which was then part of Peru. For the next 400 years, few if any Jews entered the country. Immigration picked up again in 1905 when Russians fleeing the pogroms came, followed soon by co-religionists from Argentina, Turkey and the Middle East. In 1938, however, Bolivia's liberal immigration policy (agricultural visas were relatively easy to obtain) attracted a further 7,000 Jews escaping from Nazi Europe, especially from Germany and Austria. They settled primarily in the larger communities like *La Paz, Sucre, Potosi* and *Cochabamba*. Cochabamba was Grete's first choice because an aunt and her family had previously emigrated there. However, although at a lower altitude than the other Bolivian cities, it was still more than 8,000 feet above sea level, which was unacceptable given Ernestine's heart condition.

That left the United States.

Later, after running into what appeared to be serious obstacles to moving her parents into the U.S. (more on that below), Grete in desperation secured passage for them to Shanghai despite her concerns about China. For the moment, however, she rejected Shanghai, although several relatives had already gone there.

Uncle Shulman, the husband of Ernestine's sister Clara, went to Shanghai in summer 1938, temporarily leaving his family behind in Vienna. The Sobels gave him a large portion of their jewelry to take with him for safekeeping, as it was still possible to sneak it out of Austria without undue risk. He sewed them into the lining of his overcoat. They never saw these assets again. Once Uncle Shulman settled in China, he sent for his wife and one of his two sons, a man who later became a U.S.

Army sergeant and made the military his career. Shulman died in Shanghai, and Clara and her son eventually wound up in the Bronx near where Ernestine and David lived in a tiny, basement apartment.

The Shulman's second son, Rudi, was mentally retarded and the family left him behind, a very risky proposition at a time when Hitler and the Nazis were about to embark on a broad-based euthanasia program (a.k.a., the "T-4" program) designed to rid the Reich of "useless, non-productive" people just like Rudi. Miraculously, Rudi survived the euthanasia program, the Final Solution, the Holocaust and the war, and continued to live in Vienna for the rest of his life (see Chapter 74).

Another uncle, Ernestine's brother Willy, who worked for David in his clothing store, also made it to Shanghai, leaving his beautiful wife, Giza, and even more gorgeous daughter, Lucy, behind. He dropped dead of a heart attack on a Shanghai street soon after arriving. He was 50 years old.

Ernst's cousin Erwin Hirschl, also a Vienna-educated physician, made it to Shanghai, a way station for him before coming to America. He was a brilliant man, an amazingly quick study, and a deft survivor. He was also the cousin to whom Ernst was the closest, a brother-like intimacy that lasted all of their lives until Erwin died, much too young, and likely of a broken heart shortly after his wife passed away. Ernst outlived his beloved cousin by more than 20 years and was never able to speak about Erwin without tearing up.

In all, only 20,000 Jews made it all the way to Shanghai from Germany, Austria and the rest of Europe. In 1943, the Germans' Japanese ally captured Shanghai and herded its Jews into a cramped district of the city. Despite intense pressure from the Germans to exterminate them, the Japanese resisted. Those Jewish emigrés who remained in China until the Communist takeover in 1949 left then for either Israel or the United States.

Of the four possibilities, the United States was, by far, the most difficult country to enter. After much argument, Grete persuaded her family that the time had come to sever its half-century tie to its adopted country, Austria, and find a new place—preferably the United States—in which to settle down. It took a lot of coaxing and, at first, she made little headway. Determined, she forged ahead anyway, turning her attention to the steps necessary to get them all out of Austria and over the Atlantic before the lights went out in Europe for the second time in the first half of the twentieth century.

Chapter 38
The Summer of '38

By summer, conditions for Austria's Jews in general and the Sobels in particular had become very bad. There were even more ominous portents in the air shortly to be realized.

Almost 70 percent of Austria's Jews were eventually murdered by the Nazis and their local henchmen. Before they died, they and the other 30 percent who escaped were systematically robbed of their property, their livelihoods, their homes and apartments, their incomes, their assets, their security, their hope, their aspirations and their self-confidence.

Most of this naked theft was carried out by Austrians, both Nazis and neighbors. For the next two-plus generations following the end of World War II, Austria lived a lie, corrupting and revising history to make it appear that it was the "first victim" of the Nazis and not the eager, enthusiastic collaborator it actually was. Go to YouTube and see the newsreel footage from the Anschluss for yourself; you will come away without any sense of Austrian victimhood, to put it mildly. Instead, you will see a level of enthusiasm bordering on orgasmic hysteria among the millions who gathered to welcome Adolf Hitler as if he were the Second Coming and this was the Rapture. This was not a rape at all, but rather lusty, vigorous, consensual mating.

Worse, the United States, Britain and, unsurprisingly, the Soviet Union participated in perpetuating this scurrilous lie regarding Austria's innocence. Any compensation for Austria's Jews was not forthcoming for six decades and then only represented a pittance of what was actually stolen. The Austrians purposely made the application process impossibly complex and denied most applications, even those supported by detailed documentation, photographs, etc. The few who did receive compensation—and in many cases these were heirs because the actual victims had long since died—were fortunate if they received pennies on the dollar.

On August 2, 1938, an art exhibit opened in Vienna after a highly successful 9-month run in Munich. It was entitled *Der Ewige Jude*—The Wandering Jew or The Eternal Jew—a concept dating from the thirteenth century when a Jew who supposedly mocked Jesus was condemned to wander the Earth until Judgment Day. The exhibit was the brainchild of Josef Goebbels, the Nazi Propaganda Minister, one of the more loathsome creatures who emerged out of the Nazi ooze. It was intended to be a "degenerate art" exhibition and represented the visual apotheosis of Nazi anti-Semitism. It broke all Vienna museum attendance records.

The theme was the Jew as parasite feeding on a healthy host. Numerous depictions of Jews as foreigners, dark-complexioned, hook-nosed, filthy, slovenly, and bearded presences teeming through Europe dominated the exhibit. Their supposed crimes were also made visual—not paying taxes, stealing, haggling with decent Germans over prices, and practicing secret, evil rituals. A "documentary" depicting Jews as scum of the Earth accompanied the exhibit.

Grete did not get to see the exhibit or the documentary. By Summer, 1938, Jews were no longer permitted to visit museums.

The exhibit was the stimulus a year later for another Goebbels project, *Jud Süss*, a virulently anti-Semitic film that professed to depict Jews in their "natural state" in Polish ghettos, looking like every Nazi caricature imaginable. The film was also an enormous success. More than 20 million Germans and Austrians saw it.

When Goebbels himself first viewed the film, he proclaimed: *"These Jews must be exterminated."*

As summer drew to a close, the cascade of laws and regulations barring Jews from society had become an everyday obsession for Vienna's Jews. It was dangerous to walk the streets. Individual Jews were harassed, both verbally and physically, often by neighbors next to whom they had lived and peacefully interacted with for decades. They could be pulled aside on a whim and made to do the most degrading tasks, such as cleaning the sidewalk and streets with a toothbrush. Worse humiliations were commonplace. Grete witnessed an elderly Jewish woman who was forced to urinate on a Torah recently removed from a synagogue and flung into the street.

Few Jews ventured out of their apartments. Other than foraging for increasingly scarce food, there was nowhere to go. No jobs. No schools still open to Jews—high-school age and university Jewish students had been expelled in June and permanently barred from any further formal education. Many of Grete's and Ernst's friends were profoundly affected by this particular decree: cousin Herbert, who was in medical school, spent his years in the U.S. as a medical technician, his dreams destroyed and replaced by a deep bitterness that manifested itself in him becoming an avowed Communist. Karl Drechsler, a promising medical student, was never able to go back to medical school, became an attorney in the U.S., and spent his career synopsizing labor law decisions for a legal publisher.

Teenagers, easily bored and infused by their sense of immortality, continued to congregate in groups in public parks like the Prater, where they would try to divert themselves until a Hitler Youth cohort or SS troop came by and ordered them out, accompanied by clubbing and kicking.

Vienna was rife with rumors relating to opportunities for emigration and what might happen if Jews could not get out of Austria. If the Jews of Germany, Austria and the Sudetenland needed any additional motivation to leave their homelands, it was about to arrive, in the form of the worst pogrom of the twentieth century.

The diminutive Austrian Chancellor, Engelbert Dollfuss, (with Mussolini) who brought Fascism into power in the early 1930s, and who was assassinated by the Nazis in a failed 1934 coup.
(*Source: germanhistorydocs.ghi-dc.org*)

Vienna greets Adolf Hitler with wild enthusiasm as he enters the city in March, 1938. The Anschluss—the consensual rape of Austria—is complete.
(*Source: withfriendship.com*)

Hitler addresses 300,000 cheering Austrians in Vienna's *Heldenplatz*, announcing that Austria is now part of the Third Reich.
(*Source: www.democratic-republicans.us*)

Kristallnacht the morning after . . . inside a burned synagogue.

Poster advertising Joseph Goebbels hugely successful anti-Jewish propaganda film, seen and applauded by tens of millions of Germans and Austrians. (*Source: filmaffinity.com*)

Chapter 39
Kristallnacht – The Night of Broken Glass

The Trigger

In early November, everything changed, literally overnight.

Among the thousands of displaced German Jews forcibly deported to Poland by the Nazis in October 1938 was the Grynszpan family of Hannover. Their oldest son, Herschel, age seventeen, was living in Paris at the time, and thus escaped deportation. He knew about it, however, from a postcard sent by his mother.

Herschel was incensed by his mother's description of the family's trials and decided upon revenge. Early in the morning of November 7, he went into a sporting goods store in Paris and purchased a handgun. An hour later, he walked into the German Embassy and asked to speak to the ambassador. Told the ambassador was out, he asked to speak to someone else, claiming he had to deliver an important document. Persisting, he finally was led to the office of Third Secretary Ernst vom Rath who was, ironically, an "anti-anti-Semite." In fact, the Gestapo was investigating vom Rath for his sympathetic views toward Jews.

When vom Rath asked Herschel for the document, he shouted: "You are a filthy Kraut and here, in the name of 12 thousand persecuted Jews, is your document!" Herschel pulled out his handgun and fired five shots at vom Rath at close range. Two bullets hit home and vom Rath collapsed, gravely wounded. He lingered for almost three days before he died in the early evening of November 9, the fifteenth anniversary of the Munich "Beer Hall Putsch," the holiest day in the Nazi calendar.

Once again, an assassin targeted the wrong man, with major repercussions for humanity. In 1914, it was Archduke Franz Ferdinand, the only friend to the Serbs in the upper echelon of the Austro-Hungarian Imperial government. Now it was vom Rath, the closest thing in the Paris embassy to a friend of the Jews.

The news of the assassination reached Joseph Goebbels, Hitler's propaganda minister, at the beginning of a three-day celebration of the anniversary of the Beer Hall Putsch. Goebbels, always attuned to any opportunity for a propaganda coup, immediately ordered all Third Reich newspapers to print a front page story about the attack on vom Rath by a Jew. The accompanying editorial, which was required to be run in all the newspapers, blamed the entire Jewish community for the incident:

> *"We shall no longer tolerate a situation where hundreds of thousands of Jews within our territory control entire streets of shops, throng places of public entertainment, and pocket the wealth of German lease-holders as 'foreign' landlords while their racial brothers incite war against Germany and shoot down German officials..."*

The papers demanded immediate action against the Jews.

The Plan

On the evening of November 9, Hitler and the Nazi principals sat down to a celebratory dinner in Munich when, around 9:00 PM, he was informed that vom Rath had died. He summoned Goebbels and ordered him to launch the most widespread pogrom against the Jews in history. After Hitler left the dinner, Goebbels stood up and incited the party faithful with an incendiary diatribe, first announcing that a Jew had murdered a "loyal servant of the Reich," then following with:

> *"Our people must be told, and their answer must be ruthless, forthright, salutary! I ask you to listen to me, and together we must plan what is to be our answer to Jewish murder and the threat of international Jewry to our glorious German Reich!"*

Goebbels' diary records that the crowd responded with "stormy applause" and that the assemblage immediately ran to find telephones in order to call their local Nazi officials and order them to fan the flames of anti-Semitic riots.

What began as an uncoordinated action against the Jews of Germany and its conquered territories soon—with typical German efficiency—became quite organized. Reichsführer Heinrich Himmler, the SS and Gestapo chief, learned of the "plan" directly from Hitler just before midnight, whereupon he instructed the Gestapo to arrest wealthy Jews and send them to concentration camps. Thousands of Jewish men were rounded up and incarcerated in Dachau, Sachsenhausen, and other camps.

The Gestapo also sent a directive to all police precincts ordering the arrest of 20,000-30,000 wealthy Jews and directing the police and fire departments not to interfere with the burnings of synagogues, but to loot them first for valuable material. Three primary roles were assigned to fire departments:

1. To prevent damage to German (non-Jewish) buildings.
2. To prevent any attempts to put out the fires.
3. To burn confiscated books and documents.

Later that night, SS *Obergruppenführer* Reinhard Heydrich, the young Nazi security chief, expanded the arrest order beyond just rich Jews to healthy Jewish males. In addition, the order directed the destruction of Jewish businesses and homes.

Overnight, the German press put out special editions for early morning consumption in which bold headlines whipped up a public frenzy against the Jews.

Executing the Plan

The violence began just before midnight in Munich, where a Jewish textile shop was set afire, followed immediately by one of the city's synagogues. Within hours, the Munich experience was replicated throughout Germany, Austria and the Sudentenland.

Kristallnacht—the "Night of Broken Glass"—derives its name from the widespread destruction of windows that left the streets covered in broken glass. But that trivializes the damage, both physical and psychological. Broken glass was the least of it. Broken lives are more to the point. Kristallnacht pointed the way to Hell for the European Jewish community.

The next morning, Grete sensed that something bad was about to happen. The tension was palpable. When she looked out the window, the usual bustle of people and traffic was missing. The streets were empty. The stores were all closed. Fear permeated the air.

Grete's father David went downstairs to check on his store. He was gone an unusually long time, so Grete went down to check on him. She found him lying in the middle of the street, bloodied. As he was about to open the store, he was attacked by a gang of young Nazis, beaten up and thrown down on the ground. The result was permanent hearing loss in one ear and both hands full of broken fingers.

Later that day, Uncle Holman suddenly appeared at the apartment door. He lived in a neighboring street, but asked for entry so he could hide from the Nazis. Grete asked him why he did not hide at home? He was hysterical, irrational, and had run away from home in a panic. He begged Grete to go and tell his wife that he was safe in her parents' apartment. Grete was terrified of going out again, but she did. On the way to her aunt's, she passed a temple besieged by a howling mob armed with clubs and stones (the temple was burned to the ground later that day). She ran into a side street and detoured several times until she arrived at her aunt's apartment. After delivering her uncle's message, she took a different, circuitous route back home, hugging the walls of buildings as she made her way.

That was just the beginning. Grete watched out the window as mobs of Nazi youths and private citizens roamed the streets desecrating Jewish shops and looking for individual Jews to beat up.

That evening was unusually balmy for November in Vienna. The streets had been quiet for several hours, so Grete foolishly ventured out to meet some friends at a café that still served Jews. Just after midnight, she was walking home when she heard shouting coming from the side streets. In the distance, she saw smoke and flames through the narrow spaces between buildings. As she crossed the *Donaukanal* bridge and entered Hollandstrasse, she saw an elderly man scrubbing the street with a toothbrush while being taunted with loud, anti-Semitic remarks by five or six young Nazis in SA and SS uniforms. They were yelling "*zal Jude*," dirty Jew, at him.

She passed a grocery store. A truck pulled up in front of it. She watched a number of Nazi youths coming out of the store loaded down with provisions. The store's protective iron gate had been ripped out of its moorings.

Grete hugged the building walls again as she carefully made her way home. The Nazis ignored her as she passed by. She attributed this, as well as many of her other encounters with Nazis from which she emerged intact, to "not looking Jewish."

Once inside the front door of her apartment building, she bounded up the stairs to her family's second floor flat. She was surprised to find her parents wide awake.

"What's happening?" she asked her parents, who sat in the kitchen huddled over their illegal radio.

"We heard on the BBC that a Jewish teenager in Paris killed a German embassy official. And now the Nazis are seeking retribution against all Jews."

Listening to the BBC was a crime after the Anschluss, but until all Jewish radios were confiscated three days after Kristallnacht, it was the only broadcast to which the Jews of Nazi Europe listened.

Uncle Holman was still at the apartment. Now, he begged Grete to take him home. Although she was extremely reluctant to risk going back out on the streets, Grete and her uncle left the apartment at about 1:00 AM and made their way through back streets to his apartment. Grete did not want to go upstairs and delay getting home, so she left immediately and maneuvered her way home through dark back streets, the sky a bright red from the fires all over the city. She arrived home after 3:00 AM.

The Damage

The final Kristallnacht tally was somewhere between 49 and 95 synagogues in Vienna alone burned to the ground, depending on the source. The morning after, the Jews of Leopoldstadt saw Torah scrolls floating down the Donaukanal.

Vienna suffered more from Kristallnacht than any other city. The brown-shirted Austrian storm troopers apparently felt that they had to play catch-up to their German counterparts who had enjoyed harassing Jews since 1933. More than anywhere else, spectators enthusiastically joined in abusing their Jewish fellow citizens. Onlookers who did not actively participate entered the fray later, like jackals, and eagerly looted the destroyed shops taking what they could carry. Grete noted that a large number of the looters were women.

After a sleepless night, the Jews woke to even more destruction. The Gestapo, the *Sicherheitsdienst* (SD), the Hitler

Youth, random youth gangs, assorted thugs and even common citizens who had lived in harmony with their Jewish neighbors for decades, joined in the ruination of Jewish businesses and the beatings administered to any Jews found outside their homes.

David's shop windows were destroyed, his inventory all gone. Going out on Hollandstrasse, he was subjected to another severe beating. The splints Grete had put on his fingers were ripped off and his fingers broken in new places. Grete set new splints, but despite her best efforts, he was never able to straighten his fingers out for the rest of his life. When I knew him, his hands suffered from painful arthritis and were permanently gnarled into misshapen half-fists.

By the evening of November 10, the violence subsided, but Jewish lives had been changed forever. Until Kristallnacht, nothing Grete said could convince her parents of the necessity of escaping Austria. By the time night fell that day, however, David announced that he was ready to depart and move across the world if necessary. Ernestine was still hesitant, primarily because her own father and stepmother, Liber and Julie Lapajowker, adamantly refused to go.

Assessment

The carnage from Kristallnacht is all over the map when it comes to hard numbers. Jewish deaths probably numbered several thousand, including women and children. Thousands of injuries were reported, many like David's, permanent. Treatment for those injuries was close to non-existent. Over 2,000 synagogues were burned to the ground in Germany, Austria and Czechoslovakia. The sole synagogue in Bamberg in Bavaria, where I served in the U.S. Army 30 years later, was torched. At least 7,500 Jewish businesses were destroyed. Thousands of Jewish schools were vandalized, their books and desks thrown out onto the street and burned. Jewish cemeteries were desecrated. There were tens of thousands of thefts from Jewish homes. Over 30,000 men were arrested for the "crime" of being Jewish and sent to concentration camps (5,000 Viennese Jews wound up at Dachau), where many died.

One of those sent to Dachau was the husband and father of a family that were close friends of Grete's family. In the middle of the night of November 9, a bunch of Brownshirts banged on the family's apartment door, broke it down and dragged him away. His wife tried unsuccessfully over the next several weeks to find out where they had taken him. Three weeks after Kristallnacht, she received a package in the mail containing his ashes and the clothes he wore when he was taken. An accompanying note informed her that he had died of "natural causes." The truth was that he had been murdered at Dachau and then cremated.

Another family close to Grete's—the husband and wife used to meet Grete's parents every night at a café—came to a different conclusion than emigration after being victimized by Kristallnacht. After smothering their two children with pillows while they slept, the husband shot his wife, then himself. Grete's family was devastated when they heard the news. Family suicides were common in the aftermath of Kristallnacht. Hundreds of Austrian and German families took their own lives following the pogrom.

Why do you think, I asked Grete, the Nazis spared your apartment that night? The answer was a very brave Christian building concierge, a rare instance of great character in the face of great danger. Brownshirts knocked on the concierge's door at 2:00 AM and asked for the apartment numbers of any Jews living in the building. At enormous risk to himself, he replied that there were no Jews in the building. The Brownshirts believed him and moved on to the next building.

World Reaction

The aftermath of Kristallnacht was worldwide apathy. Only a tiny handful of Germans spoke out, mainly a few clerics. They were immediately sent to concentration camps.

Vatican Secretary of State Cardinal Eugenio Pacelli, soon-to-be Pope Pius XII, received a detailed report on Kristallnacht from the papal nuncio in Berlin. He shelved the report, not wanting to offend the Third Reich. There was only silence from the Vatican.

The Holy See had signed a *concordat* with Nazi Germany in July, 1933, six months after Hitler became Chancellor (the signatories were Pacelli for the Vatican and Vice Chancellor Franz von Papen for Germany). The concordat preserved the Church's right to operate freely and safeguarded its German properties. Implicit was the *quid pro quo* that the Church would not criticize the regime.

Western political leaders publicly condemned the pogrom but took no punitive actions against Germany. British Prime Minister Chamberlain, himself an often overt anti-Semite, inexplicably blamed both Germans—*and Jews*—for the violence. U.S. President Franklin Roosevelt was at least a little more sympathetic and proactive. He recalled the U.S. Ambassador to Germany, publicly protested the Nazi pogrom, and extended indefinitely the visas of 12,000 - 15,000 German and Austrian Jews recently admitted into the U.S. on temporary visitors' visas.

Many Jews suddenly found themselves utterly destitute, their businesses destroyed, their husbands and fathers taken away, their homes ransacked. Many were left homeless, their survival threatened. Signs proclaiming "Jews Not Admitted" suddenly appeared in the windows of virtually every food store, restaurant, café, and farmer's market, as well as banks and most other establishments. The question of survival from one day to the next became all-consuming.

Survival threats prompt people to creative, desperate measures. Grete secured food for her family by visiting neighborhood Christian shopkeepers she had treated in her medical practice and obtaining groceries from the rear of their shops, after dark. Since her practice largely disappeared (she still secretly treated a handful of loyal patients—including non-

Jews—willing to risk personal danger in order to visit her office), the family was forced to sell jewelry and other valuables to Christians on the black market at a deep discount in order to have enough money for food.

Many people I have spoken to about Kristallnacht think it was the take-off point for the inhuman violence that followed over the next seven years. It was not. Widespread physical attacks against Jews and their property was nothing new, and had been going on since the Nazi takeover of Germany in 1933. Grassroots violence was encouraged by the national and local authorities, albeit unorganized for the most part and by no means as widespread or coherent as Kristallnacht. The Anchluss unleashed the worst wave of violence yet with particular emphasis on Vienna, the city Hitler believed had done him so very wrong.

The Sudetenland and Czech crises of fall 1938 and spring 1939, respectively, unleashed more violence against Jews. Frustrated by the gradualism of the resolution of the Czech "problem," Reich citizens once again took out their exasperation on the Jews. October, the month before Kristallnacht, was a particularly violent month in Vienna. Anti-Jewish riots erupted all over the city, with particular virulence in Leopoldstadt.

Kristallnacht was of another order, something of a dress rehearsal for the Final Solution. The actors did very well and decided that the show had great promise and would go on. Within days of Kristallnacht, Hitler, in a speech to the German Reichstag, announced the impending "destruction of the Jews of Europe." The demonization of the Jews had attained a new level.

By the end of November, Jews could not walk into hotels, bars, *gasthäuser*, bakeries, etc. They were not allowed to sit on park benches, which were now plastered with signs that said "Only for Aryans." Grete, who loved to swim, was no longer permitted to go to the *Schwimmbad* just down the street at the Donaukanal.

The perverse capstone on Kristallnacht was that the Jewish community was forced to accept liability for all of the damage caused, including collateral damage to Aryan property from marauding Nazi and citizen bands!

Chapter 40
Blood, Not Religion

Hitler's Grand Design

Religion was never the issue with Adolf Hitler. Instead, it was blood. A family could have converted to Christianity hundreds of years ago, but conversion did not cleanse their blood of the Jewish stain. The Viennese philosopher and polymath, Ludwig von Wittgenstein, whose family had converted to Catholicism two generations before his birth, was proof of that. He was persecuted for being Jewish because three of his grandparents were born Jewish.

Where did Hitler come up with the idea of exterminating human beings solely on the basis of the accident of their birth? Many historians conclude, incorrectly, that the Wannsee Conference of January 20, 1942, which I discuss below, gave birth to the Holocaust. While Wannsee might have, for the first time, formally documented the notion of mass extermination, the idea of mass murder began in 1939, nine days before Germany invaded Poland.

On August 22, 1939, Hitler met with his generals and told them:

> "Our strength lies in our speed and our brutality. Genghis Khan hunted millions of women and children to their deaths, consciously and with a joyous heart. History sees in him only the great founder of a state.
>
> I have issued a command—and I will have everyone who utters even a single word of

criticism shot—that the aim of the war lies not in reaching particular lines but in the physical annihilation of the enemy. Thus, so far only in the east, I have put my Death's Head formation at the ready with the command to send man, woman and child of Polish descent and language to their deaths, pitilessly and remorselessly."

The consequence of this harangue was two-fold:

First, it licensed the Wehrmacht to throw aside any pretense of adhering to the laws of war, the three Geneva Conventions (first negotiated in 1864) to which Germany was a signatory, and international law, providing the army with cover for such abuses, absolving the troops in advance for any human rights violations they might commit.

Second, it led to the creation of five *Einsatzgruppen* ("task forces")—later increased to seven—to follow the Wehrmacht into Poland in order to carry out the intentional murder of selected civilians. The Einsatzgruppen were organized by SS Obergruppenfuhrer Reinhard Heydrich, chief of the Gestapo, the Sicherheitsdienst (SD) and the Kripo (police agency), and also the chair of the Wannsee Conference where the "Final Solution to the Jewish Problem" was worked out several years later. Heydrich was the ideal Aryan Nazi on many levels. He looked the part—tall, spare, blond, poker-faced (his looks made him an early Hitler favorite)—and acted the part perfectly. He was both brutal and brutally efficient.

He appointed the most extremist, reactionary and anti-Semitic underlings he could muster to head the Einsatzgruppen and their subordinate *Einsatzkommando* units and tasked them with eliminating the leading members of the Polish intelligentsia and governing class, resisters, partisans and especially Jews. In effect, this meant that Poland was being occupied by two German armies: first, the Wehrmacht, the regular army fighting a more-or-less traditional war; second, the Einstazgruppen, sent in after the Wehrmacht to fight a racial war and serve as mobile killing squads.

There has been a 70-year myth that Hitler himself was not involved in deciding upon this unprecedented extermination policy; that somehow it was his henchmen—principally Heinrich Himmler and Heydrich—who came up with this monstrous policy. Some Holocaust apologists and revisionist pseudo-historians even claim that Hitler was unaware of what was going on in the East. Not true. Hitler was privy to a very early report from General Johannes Blaskowitz—himself an avid anti-Semite—but one who was nevertheless not in favor of brutal annihilation policies. In his report, Blaskowitz criticized and condemned what he witnessed in Poland. After reading the report, Hitler said, "You can't fight a war with the Salvation Army."

It is natural to think of the Einsatzgruppen troops as thugs, denizens of the "lower classes." That would be inaccurate. Many of them were intellectuals and professionals—doctors, lawyers, even opera singers and a Protestant minister. Their brutality was unmatched despite their "refined" backgrounds and higher education. The 2,700 members of the Einsatzgruppen were very thorough. They killed tens of thousands of Poles and Jews, principally by rounding them up, marching them to a wooded area, forcing them to dig ditches, lining them up on the edge of the ditches, and machine-gunning them to death.

It was not long before the Einsatzgruppen began complaining about the inefficiency of their murder tactics. There were so many Poles, Russians and Jews . . . and so little time. Shooting was inefficient and traumatic for the shooters who had to get up-close-and-personal to do their dirty work. This was the major impetus behind the convening of the Wannsee conference.

How the Einsatzgruppen actually carried out their function is addressed in detail later in this book. But first, let's skip ahead a bit chronologically and examine the Wannsee meeting.

Wannsee

The Wannsee conference was convened in early 1942 by Reinhard Heydrich in order to discuss the "Jewish question." The meeting had been originally scheduled for December 9, 1941 but had to be postponed because of the Japanese bombing of Pearl Harbor on December 7th, Hitler's massive blunder of declaring war on the United States on December 11th, and the U.S.'s immediate reciprocal war declaration against Germany. It was prompted by a directive to Heydrich from Reichsmarschall Hermann Goering, Hitler's number two, six months earlier to pursue what he labeled the "Final Solution." Refreshments were served.

Wannsee is a lovely little lake just outside Berlin. Tourists call it "idyllic." The meeting took place at *Am Grossen Wannsee Nos. 56-58*. Fifteen people attended; eight of them held the German equivalent of a Ph.D.

The principal issue before the conferees was sorting out the various killing methods in place up to this point and developing a coordinated approach to ridding the European continent—and eventually the world—of the Jewish "cancer."

Adolf Eichmann, who by this time had risen rapidly in the Nazi pantheon and was now considered Heydrich's expert on Jews and Judaism, served as conference secretary. His written record of the meeting is a detailed account of the chronology (see Bibliography, below).

Prior to the conference, Eichmann put together a list of the number of Jews in each European country and their "disposition" to date, the idea being that, when Germany had finally conquered all of Europe, it would have to "deal" with the following numbers (English translation mine):

List A – The Reich Plus the Conquered Countries

Germany:	131,800
Austria:	43,700
Polish areas annexed by Germany:	420,000
General Government [occupied Poland]:	2,284,000
Bialystok District under German administration:	400,000
Bohemia and Moravia:	74,200
Estonia:	Free of Jews [all have been murdered]
Latvia:	3,500
Lithuania:	34,000
Belgium:	43,000
Denmark:	5,600
Occupied France:	165,000
Unoccupied France [Vichy]:	700,000
Greece:	69,600
Netherlands:	160,800
Norway:	1,300
Subtotal:	4,527,500

List B – Unconquered Countries

Bulgaria:	48,000
England:	330,000
Finland:	2,300
Ireland:	4,000
Italy:	58,000
Albania:	200
Croatia:	40,000
Portugal:	3,000
Romania and Bessarabia:	342,000
Sweden:	8,000
Switzerland:	18,000
Serbia:	10,000
Slovakia:	88,000

Spain:	6,000
European Turkey:	55,500
Hungary:	742,800
USSR:	5,000,000
Subtotal:	6,755,800
TOTAL:	**11,283,300**

Note: If the number of Jews in some countries (e.g., the Baltic States) seem low, it is because by the time of the Wannsee conference, the Einsatzgruppen had "cleansed" them of the vast majority of their Jews.

Ridding Europe of this 11,000,000-plus "contagion" was going to be a very big job. But somebody had to do it and Heydrich pinned his future elevation in the Nazi hierarchy to doing it well.

Heydrich opened the conference by announcing a formal change in Nazi policy: instead of emigration, i.e., expelling the Jews out of Europe, the new policy called for "evacuation" of the Jewish population of the German-controlled areas to the East. Heydrich said that the policy would apply to all of Europe's 11 million Jews.

Upon arrival in the East, evacuees would first be separated by gender and those deemed fit and healthy would become slave laborers, principally in building roads and railways from Germany to the East. The rest would be killed immediately. The slave laborers would receive only a temporary reprieve from their ultimate fate which would be accomplished by working them to death. None of the attendees questioned the new policy.

After Heydrich's opening remarks, the conference focused on the question of defining who is a Jew. Here, it is important to mention the tremendous effort expended by IBM's wholly-owned German subsidiary company—*Dehomag*. Dehomag was engaged by the Nazis only a few months after Hitler came to power and had been enthusiastically cooperating with the Nazi regime ever since, using its proprietary punch-card Hollerith system to identify Jews and provide incredibly detailed information about their locations, origins, professions, occupations, marital status, and much, much more. These contracts were very lucrative and contributed enormously to IBMs' bottom line.

There was some discussion at Wannsee about what to do with people who were not 100 percent Jewish, with no immediate resolution. The discussion then moved to a consideration of the problem of what to do with the Jews resident in the "General Government," the portion of Poland that had not been incorporated into the Reich but remained under German rule, as well as the Jews now under Nazi control in the Soviet Union. Although, by the time of Wannsee, almost 1.5 million Soviet Jews had already been murdered, millions more were still alive. The number was simply too much for the inefficient shooting methodology. Various alternative extermination methods were discussed, although Eichmann was careful in his notes not to be too specific.

What Wannsee articulated for perhaps the first time were two new ideas:

- First, the Nazi intention of eliminating every single European Jew. The attendees agreed enthusiastically, according to Eichmann's recollections twenty years later at his Jerusalem trial.
- Second, that the killing methods needed to change because face-to-face, one-on-one shootings were "too hard" on the killers. Thus was adopted the idea of the *gaswagen*, a truck in which 60 people could be crammed in at one time and, after a short ride, gassed to death by the introduction of carbon monoxide exhaust piped

from the truck into its closed compartment. It took about thirty minutes of agony for victims to die.

The Chelmno death camp near Lodz, Poland, the first to be built, was also the first one to experiment with the gaswagen method. It began operations on December 8, 1941 with two trucks and quickly expanded its fleet. By the end of 1942, 145,301 people, mostly Jews, died there according to SS records. By the end of the war, 225,000 people had been murdered by this method at Chelmno.

Three other death camps—Belzec, Sobibor, and Treblinka (all in Poland)—also used carbon monoxide, their refinement being stationary gas chambers. By mid-1942, the annihilation of Europe's Jewish population was formally given the name *Operation Reinhard* in honor of Reinhard Heydrich following his May 1942 assassination (he died of his wounds on June 4th) in Prague by Czech partisans directed by Britain's Special Operations Executive. All three camps used captured Soviet tank engines to produce the carbon monoxide. The numbers: Belzec—between 434,000 and 600,000; Sobibor—between 167,000 and 200,000; and Treblinka—925,000.

While this was an excruciatingly painful death, it was much easier on the murderers than *mano-à-mano* shooting. Although one truck logged 30,000 deaths all by itself over a six-month period, the gaswagen approach was eventually deemed too inefficient. Something other than carbon monoxide was needed if the objective of a *Judenrein* ("Jew-free") Europe was to be achieved.

Zyklon B

The "something else" was *Zyklon Blausure* ("Cyclone Blue-acid"). Zyklon B's active toxic agent was hydrogen cyanide (a.k.a. hydrocyanic acid or prussic acid), an insecticide and rat poison that came in blue-green pellets. It had been used first in the *Aktion T-4* euthanasia program ("T-4" derived from the address of the main Euthanasia Action office at Berlin's Tiergartenstrasse No. 4) directed from the early days of the Nazi seizure of power toward eliminating the disabled and other "undesirables" and what the Nazis termed "useless eaters." The T-4 program was accelerated in August 1939, fueled by a decree that hospitals must report all births of deformed, paralyzed, and mentally deficient children to the Nazi government. At the same time, Hitler ordered his staff to consult with physicians and professors to devise a procedure for extending euthanasia to disabled adults, ostensibly to free up hospital beds for military casualties. Not a single one of the doctors or educators consulted questioned the directive.

The methodology of mass murder was perfected at six T-4 facilities spread around Germany. Initially, the Hippocratic oath takers relied on medication overdoses, followed by starvation, direct injection of poison into the heart, or herding victims into small gas chambers. These initially used carbon monoxide (provided by the BASF division of IG Farben [BASF continues to thrive today]) and ultimately Zyklon B.

Zyklon B's expansion beyond the T-4 program was first tested at a new, immense death camp in Poland that the Germans called "Auschwitz." In the pilot, two Polish prisoners wearing gas masks filled a room with filthy clothing riddled with lice. They then threw Zyklon B crystals onto the lice and watched them die quickly. What worked on lice would work on what the Nazis deemed human lice—Jews.

A second experiment was conducted in the infamous Building 11 at Auschwitz, the basement torture chamber from which very few prisoners ever emerged alive. Soil was brought in to insulate the building's windows. Then, prisoners in the camp hospital with severe illnesses were taken down into a basement room along with captured Soviet military commissars. This experiment did not work very well because several victims survived. However, once the proper dosage of Zyklon B was confirmed, the Nazis had found their means to activate the Final Solution.

It took only seconds for most victims to die, but they were horrible seconds. Death was from suffocation. Once larger gassing facilities were constructed at nearby Birkenau, which could house up to 3,000 victims at one time, the large number of victims prolonged death agonies to several minutes. Zyklon B quickly became the murder mechanism of choice throughout the camp system.

Fritz Haber, a German Jew, invented Zyklon B for use as an insecticide. By the time of the Holocaust, he was dead. Members of his family died from being gassed with Zyklon B in the death camps.

The 6 million Jews murdered during the Holocaust is a hard number to grasp, so here's another number that might be easier to comprehend: from mid-1941 to early 1943, the Nazis and their Eastern European followers killed 225,000 Jews a month; and 325,000 per month (more than 10,000 a day) in 1943-1944.

Chapter 41
Implementing Mass Murder

My great-grandfather (Ernst's grandfather), Edward Hermann, was a respected attorney in Bratislava (*Pressburg* to the Germans; *Pozsony* to the Hungarians), the capital of Slovakia, in the late nineteenth century. He and his two families (his first wife died young and he remarried) lived quietly among the overwhelmingly Catholic population and many of Edward's clients and friends were Gentiles. That kind of communal amity—rare even in Edward's time—disappeared completely in 1942, long after Edward had died and most of the rest of his family had moved on to Vienna and Budapest. Only a few relatives still remained in Slovakia. They were doomed.

The first trains to transport Jews from outside the Polish General Government area to Auschwitz followed the Wannsee conference by only two months and came from nearby Slovakia, whose Polish border was only 50 miles from the death camp.

Slovakia was a Nazi creation dating back three years to spring 1939 when the Germans absorbed Czechoslovakia and annexed its two Western provinces, Bohemia and Moravia. The atheistic Nazis then installed Father Josef Tiso, a Catholic priest, as president of Slovakia, which had been part of Czechoslovakia. Tiso was the leader of the right-wing Slovak People's Party, and once in office immediately instituted harsh anti-Semitic policies against the country's 90,000 Jews. Following the Nazi precedent in Germany, Austria, the Sudetenland, Bohemia and Moravia, Jewish businesses were closed, emigration was encouraged, Jews were ousted from the professions, thrown out of the schools, no longer allowed to own property and were made to wear a yellow star. Signs were put up in public places that read: "No Jews or dogs allowed."

As was the case in so many Nazi-occupied countries, the locals enthusiastically participated in the brutality and vicious discrimination. The Slovak People's Party's *Hlinka* Guards, named after its co-founder and long-time leader Andrej Hlinka, tried their utmost to outdo their SS and SD role models when it came to abusing Jews.

When Tiso got wind of Wannsee and the change in Nazi policy toward the Jews, he saw an opportunity to curry favor with his overlords. He eagerly stepped forward and offered up Slovakia's Jews to Adolf Eichmann's Bratislava deputy, SS Major Dieter Wisliceny. Tiso even agreed to pay Berlin 500 Reichsmarks per Jewish deportee, in consideration of the Germans agreeing never to return them to Slovakia and permitting Slovakia to take over all of the deportees' wealth and property.

The Slovakian deportations began with the herding of the country's Jews into a holding camp in a town called *Poprad*, with Hlinka guards in charge. The Jews were starved and regularly beaten by the guards.

At the same time that Camp Commandant Rudolf Höss was embarked on his campaign to make more efficient the killing methods at Auschwitz, the first trainloads of Slovakian Jews arrived. Before then (March, 1942), the only death transports were of Polish Jews. The arrival of the Slovakian Jews put great pressure on the Auschwitz administration to become more efficient. This they managed through an interim arrangement by transforming their "Little Red House"—Bunker 1—into a gas chamber that could accommodate 800 victims at a time as long as they were crammed in like sardines. Meanwhile, work on the much larger, purposely designed crematoria at Birkenau, a few kilometers from the main camp, was accelerated in anticipation of an influx of new business.

The first Slovakian Jews to arrive were not killed immediately. Instead, they were forced to sprint from the trains into the camp in groups of five while being harassed and beaten by SS guards and camp *Kapos*. The elderly, infirm, and those burdened by young children were killed on the spot.

The temporary survivors stayed overnight, were denied food and water, and in the morning were forced to run from the main camp to Birkenau. Approximately 1,000 men comprised this group, and eyewitnesses say that 70-80 were shot en route. The remainder were put to work building the gas chamber and crematoria infrastructure. Meanwhile, the women remained at the main camp where they were stripped, had their heads shaved and examined to see if they were virgins. They were then put to work.

These Slovakian deportees were the first Jews to be "selected" upon arrival at Auschwitz. The selections began intermittently, but became routine by July 1942. Selection meant that Jews fit to work were directed to one side of the tracks while those deemed unfit were immediately sent to the gas chamber. While Birkenau was under construction, the Little Red House was becoming oversubscribed, so a complementary "Little White House" that could accommodate 1,200 victims was also hastily converted into a gas chamber.

The selections were done by physicians who had taken the Hippocratic Oath, which they perverted into something that was the exact opposite of their pledge. At Auschwitz, they went well beyond selecting between slave laborers and dead men (and women and children) walking, even injecting phenol (carbolic acid) into those slave laborers whose health deteriorated to the point where they could no longer work. Phenol was inexpensive, easy to manufacture and so highly toxic that it caused death almost instantly when injected. Thousands of victims were killed by phenol injection. At first the injections were administered intravenously, but for efficiency's sake, it was discovered that injecting the toxin directly into the heart caused instant death. Nothing like German efficiency.

The most notorious physician involved in the selections was the infamous Dr. Josef Mengele, who stood on the siding at Auschwitz when transports arrived in order to make the selections. He also was the principal Nazi medical researcher—but hardly the only one; hundreds of German physicians took part—conducting the vilest, most reprehensible experiments on human beings in history, including vivisections, injecting dye into victims' eyes, freezing people to determine how long they could survive drastic lowering of their body temperature, and so forth.

Gassing initially took place at night in order to keep the rest of the inmates in the dark.

After exterminating Slovakian Jewry, the killings took off, escalating to such an extent that 1942 became the year during which more Jews were killed than any other. The machinery of death was quickly perfected and it was not long before the killing machine expanded throughout the Nazi empire.

One Western European country began sending its first transports to Auschwitz only days after the Slovakian initiative was launched. It came from that beacon of *Liberté, Egalité, Fraternité*—France. The Vichy government enthusiastically participated in the Final Solution.

Chapter 42
Getting Out

While there is language in Hitler's *Mein Kampf* manifesto that could lead a reader to conclude that Hitler intended to annihilate the Jews from the time of his earliest, semi-literate ravings on the subject, the Nazi solution for the Jews did not start out that way. Sure, the Jews had to go, but initially that meant out of Germany, then Austria, then the other conquered territories. Until World War II, Germany's Jewish policy was primarily emigration.

Yet Nazi emigration policy was extraordinarily restrictive, harassing, complicated, confusing, ever-changing, inscrutable to most, and totally inconsistent. The obstacles to successful emigration were immense. Major obstructions appeared at every turn. I cannot fathom how my mother managed it.

The Nazi authorities in Vienna did not stop with imposing the Nuremberg Laws on the local Jewish population. As summer 1938 moved forward, they became even more creative. Among the new restrictions were confiscatory taxes that deprived the Jews of what few remaining assets they possessed. David and Grete were earmarked for these taxes because they both had businesses. Payment was impossible because they had so little left after the earlier confiscations of store assets and the closure of Grete's medical practice. When David went to the bank where he kept both a business and a personal account, he was informed that Jews were now officially forbidden from making withdrawals. The family's inability to pay the new taxes would come back to haunt them a few months later when Grete went through the tortuous process of securing the necessary documents and approvals to leave the country.

The Nazi bureaucracy consisted of countless agencies whose duties and responsibilities overlapped. This was by design. Hitler's paranoia caused him to devise a governing system where power was dispersed among so many organs that it would have been very difficult for any one of them to challenge him. Thus, the Nazis established six police/militia organizations: the *Sturmabteilung* (*SA*), *Schutzstaffel* (*SS*), *Sicherheitsdienst* (SD), *Ordnungspolizei* (*Orpo*), *Sicherheitspolizei* (*Sipo*), and the Gestapo, each capable of wreaking terrible havoc on its victims. Bureaucratic competition meant that multiple agencies converged on the same targets. Those targets were, primarily, the Jews.

Perhaps the most perverse regulation of Jewish life in Austria—and that is saying something—was a matter of *deregulation*. A Nazi directive exempted Jews from speed limits on the most dangerous Alpine highways in the hope that they would kill themselves and save the Germans the trouble of disposing of them.

By the time Grete left Austria in 1939, Jews were the subjects of more than 400 decrees and regulations that restricted every aspect of their public and private lives. While many of these edicts were national laws affecting all Austrian Jews, they were supplemented by provincial and municipal exclusionary and other regulations. No facet of Jewish life was left unaffected.

The initial issue for most aspiring emigrants was where to go. Neighboring countries seemed the most logical places. Czechoslovakia was briefly attractive until the German takeover, first of the Sudetenland in fall 1938, then six months later of the rest of the country. Switzerland was hostile to Jewish immigration from the outset. Italy looked promising until Mussolini introduced his own version of the Nuremberg Laws under pressure from his Nazi ally.

The most attractive destinations were Palestine and the United States, but gaining entry to either was extremely difficult. Palestine was under a British League of Nations Mandate and only a small number of Jews were allowed in,

Britain not wanting to offend the Arabs. Only 18,000 Jews were able to enter Palestine legally between 1937 and 1941. Illegal emigration, romanticized in so many post-war novels, accounted for an additional dribble of refugees.

The United States' restrictive immigration quotas were not filled until 1939. By the end of the war, only 130,000 German and Austrian Jews out of well over half-a-million who desperately wanted to come here made it to America.

Coming to America, however, was not the goal of every Viennese. Sigmund Freud, for example, had no interest in resettling here. He said the U.S. was "a gigantic mistake." "Tobacco," said Freud to Max Eastman for the latter's book, *Heroes I Have Known*, "was the only excuse I know for Columbus's misdeed." (Eastman grew up in Canandaigua, New York, where Grete and Ernst settled, and graduated from the author's high school). Instead, Freud went to Britain. Due to his contacts with powerful world figures, he had little trouble escaping Austria. His egotism was so pronounced that he did not lift a finger to attempt to save his sisters, which would have only required him to request assistance from his wide circle of influential friends and acquaintances. All four died at the hands of the Nazis.

In 1939, the peak year for Jews fleeing the Nazis and the year Grete was able to escape, only 75-80,000 Jews made it out of Europe. By 1940, the number plummeted to 15,000, and then went down further to 8,000 in 1941. On October 23, 1941, all Jewish emigration stopped, prohibited by the Germans who had decided on a different solution to their Jewish "problem."

The ordeal of obtaining the necessary documents to leave Austria had two purposes:

1. To plunder the Jews of all of their money and other assets; and
2. To harass them to the full extent as they made their way out of the country.

Both purposes were famously achieved. The emigration process was harsh beyond imagination. By the end of it, an Austrian Jew was left with nothing.

The Fleecing

Assume for the sake of argument that an Austrian Jew actually found a country in which to settle. That was only the beginning of the nightmare. The Nazis saw Jewish emigration as a golden opportunity to deprive the escapees of everything they owned—businesses, residences, vehicles, jewelry, clothing. Nothing was sacrosanct. Any emigrant who had negotiated his or her way through the myriad of requirements described below could only take 10 Reichmarks (the Austrian Schilling was replaced by the German currency on April 25, 1938) if going to a neighboring country; 20 if going elsewhere. The conversion rate in 1939 was 2.49 Reichmarks to the dollar. Translated, an emigrant could leave with either $4 or $8, along with $400 worth of goods and personal belongings, provided the emigrant had submitted a list for prior approval. This grand theft has never been made right by Austria.

Negotiating the Labyrinth

Step One: The Certificate of Fiscal Harmlessness

Assume further that the would-be emigrant had enough money to buy a one-way ticket for some other country (not everyone did). Now the process gets interesting.

When considering Grete's ordeal (below), keep in mind that she was doing all of this not only for herself, but also for her parents and maternal grandparents. That meant that she needed to get past every tribulation and setback and overcome every obstacle *times five*.

The initial required document was the *Steuerunbedenklichkeitsbescheinigung* (German nouns make the reader yearn for Welsh or Gaelic), roughly translated as a "Certificate of Fiscal Harmlessness." This essential document was proof that all taxes had been paid. Obtaining it was a Herculean feat, involving multiple visits and payments to the *Bezirkshauptmannschaft*, the directorate of the district in which the emigrant resided, in order to obtain a *Kleiner Meldenachweis* ("Certificate of Domicile"). Grete said she went to this directorate every day for several weeks before she was granted the certificates. Next came a trip to the *Magistratsabteilung*, the office of the District Commissioner in the city hall where, after multiple attempts, a Nazi official finally signed off on the certificates.

A huge impediment was Grete's initial inability to demonstrate that her father had, in fact, paid all the taxes he had been charged for annual renewals of his business license. He had paid them, but that did not matter. The Nazis applied the concept of "joint and several liability" to this component of the emigration process, which meant that if one nuclear family member was remiss in paying taxes—or could not produce evidence of payment— then all family members were (1) liable for the payment, and (2) unable to leave Austria until either proof of payment was submitted or payment was made.

The problem was that, since David had been forced to sell his store to a Gentile for pfennigs on the shilling and now had no access to his tax filings (which he kept in the store's back office), neither he nor Grete could produce the requisite documents proving that the taxes had been paid.

When Grete was initially denied the Steuerunbedenklichkeitsbescheinigungen, she returned home and, the next morning, went into the store to request the documents. The new owner shoved her out the door, shouting that he could be prosecuted for permitting a Jew to enter his establishment. That evening, Grete attempted to break into the store after closing time in order to retrieve the documents, but was defeated by double locks and a chain. There was no other recourse than to cobble together the amount her father had already paid in order to present the money to the authorities and secure the Steuerunbedenklichkeitsbescheinigung. It took her a precious week to do this (she sold some jewelry and other artifacts on the black market), enabling her to take the next steps toward climbing the Everest at the summit of which stood the Certificate of Fiscal Harmlessness.

Her success to this point was, as Churchill so succinctly put it, "not the beginning of the end, but only the end of the beginning." Grete then had to go to the Accountancy Department, the Central Tax Office, and the District Tax Office in Leopoldstadt. At each bureaucratic location, she had to complete several forms. Once she filled in all of the myriad forms correctly (which she did not always do the first time she encountered them) and paid the fees required to obtain each approval document, she was issued the Steuerunbedenklichkeitsbescheinigung. Only then could she proceed to the next step.

Each visit to a government office required standing in line for hours while being taunted, insulted, sexually harassed, and occasionally hit with truncheons by various Nazi militiamen (primarily the SA) and flying objects (eggs and rotten tomatoes were popular) by members of the *Hitler Jugend* (Hitler Youth). Sometimes, the lines were shortened when Jewish men who resembled Josef Goebbels' *Jud Süss* caricature (see above) were beaten up so badly that they had to leave the line.

Step Two: The Certificate of Unblemished Good Citizenship

The second hurdle was obtaining the "Certificate of Unblemished Good Citizenship," available only from the local police. It was helpful if you could "prove" your good citizenship by a large donation of cash or jewelry to the Nazis' various funds established for the purpose of divesting Jews of their personal property. Before the Gestapo took over local police functions some months after the Anschluss, Austrian police officials were often fairly easygoing about granting this Certificate. But that was then.

For all her insistence that she was very naïve, Grete understood these sordid facts of life very well and managed to persuade her mother to part with some of the jewelry she had secreted under floorboards in order to pay the bribe necessary to obtain the certificates. Her mother wept for days after giving Grete the jewelry, wracked by the thought that she had to give up family heirlooms that had been in her stewardship and that she hoped to pass on to future generations.

Step Three: The Reich's Flight Tax

The process did not suddenly become easier. Grete also had to have enough money to pay the *Reichsfluchtsteuer*—"Reich's Flight Tax." By the time she had advanced this far in the process, virtually all of her family's possessions had been either confiscated or sold at a deep discount. This meant borrowing the necessary sums from relatives, many of whom were in similar straightened circumstances. Fortunately, she was able to do so.

The Reichsfluchtsteuer was one of the biggest steps in the Nazi's well-designed program of systematically stripping away Jewish property and assets. It was equal to 25 percent of all Jewish family assets, measured against the April 1938 ordinance requiring the registration of assets by Jews. Since, in the intervening months virtually all of those assets were gone, this presented a huge and often insurmountable problem. However, Grete sold a few additional pieces of jewelry and other items her mother had hidden, and raised enough money to pay this tax, again times five. She sold some to an uncle and the rest illegally to Gentile Austrians on the black market at huge discounts from their actual market value.

Step Four: The Certificate of Good Conduct

Next was a visit to the *Devisenstelle* (Foreign Currency Transactions Office) to obtain a "Certificate of Good Conduct." The lines here were even longer than those in Steps 1-3. Grete stood and slept in line for days, fearing that if she left, she would have to begin all over again the next day. She did not want to run the risk of running out of what she quite correctly perceived as the closing window on Jews being allowed to leave Austria. Family members brought her food and drink.

Here, the Nazis elevated harassment and shakedowns of queuing applicants to a high art, including issuing passes to get inside the office for a price.

When Grete finally arrived at the front of the line, she was told that she had filled out the application forms incorrectly. Devastated, she went to the back of the line and began her wait all over again. While waiting, she carefully reviewed the applications and could not see where she had erred (she had not). She decided that she had simply been harassed. Consequently, she changed nothing on the application forms.

Her second attempt also failed. As she neared the front of the line, several Hitler Youths dragged her out of line, gave her a broom, and ordered her to clean a neighboring street. When she completed her assigned task to their satisfaction, she once more went to the back of the line. The third time was the charm. After several more days in line, she secured the certificates.

Step Five: Passports

It was now time to obtain passports from the *Zentralstelle für die jüdische Auswanderung* (Central Office for Jewish Emigration), headed by Adolf Eichmann and operated by the Gestapo. The Zentralstelle opened for business in the former Rothschild Palace in August 1938, about the time Grete began her quest to get her family out of Austria.

Before appearing there, she had to go to the police precinct in the Second District and respond to questions about what kind of passports she was applying for, whether they were new or reissues, and so forth. Answering these questions satisfactorily was the first step in the passport process. Next it was off to the Zentralstelle to obtain preliminary documents that authorized her to obtain passports. She secured these authorizations without much ado.

Her next stop was the Passport Office in the Fifth District in order to acquire the actual passports. The lines here were also very long and it took Grete two days to get in the door and up to the issuing desk. She distinctly remembered the overpowering odors emanating from thousands of sweaty bodies packed together in the long narrow hallway. Upon showing the passport officer the many preliminary documents she had put together, she got the passports.

While these were not the only Reich documents (see below) necessary before taking the next step—applying to the representatives of the country the Jew wished to enter—it is important to note that each one of them was accompanied by an expiration date. Time was of the essence. If the emigrant was unable to complete the next steps of the process before these drop-dead (literally) dates, s/he had to start all over again.

Step Six: The Certificate of Moral Probity

Once visas were secured (see below), the Nazis' perverse process required Grete to go back to the Zentralstelle to secure five "Certificates of Moral Probity," a requirement that was just another invention designed to torment Jews and test their endurance. Two witnesses were necessary.

This was the first time Grete's instincts and ensuing good judgment proved wanting. She assumed erroneously that only two witnesses would suffice for all five certificates, so she brought two non-relatives who could vouch for all five family members. Upon arrival at Eichmann's office accompanied by her two witnesses, she was told that she could only receive one certificate for herself, but that she would need eight other witnesses to vouch for her parents and grandparents. The only thing she had correctly surmised was that they had to be unrelated to the applicant.

This setback was the first time during the ordeal that Grete panicked. Where was she going to find eight additional witnesses in a time when the Jews of Austria were afraid to go out of their residences and terrified of any contact with Nazi officialdom? Nevertheless, she went about finding people with determination and desperation.

Finding the first four witnesses was relatively easy. The remaining four proved to be more difficult. She reached out to the family's former chauffeur and maid, both of whom agreed to go with her. The last two were more of a problem. She finally managed to persuade her downstairs Gentile neighbors to accompany her in return for what amounted to a pay-off. In better times when they would interact with the Sobels, they had often remarked on the fine, large silver samovar in the kitchen in which Ernestine brewed tea for the ritual mid-afternoon *jause* (more than a snack; less than high tea) of which the Viennese were so fond. The samovar was the price of their cooperation. For Ernestine, this was like the final nail in the family coffin. Both Grete and her father feared the onset of another deep depression. Fortunately, they dodged that particular bullet.

Her second trip to the Zentralstelle was successful. Moral probity, as assessed by the most immoral regime in history, was achieved.

Step Seven: Proof of Residence

Two witnesses were also required to prove residence in order to obtain the most prized of all documents so far, the *Ausreisebewilligungen* (exit visa), the permission to leave Austria. This time, however, the Zentralstelle only required two witnesses for the whole family. Grete also had to supply a photograph of herself and each of her parents and grandparents in which their left ears were exposed (a bizarre, meaningless requirement designed solely as an eleventh-hour annoyance) and also register their fingerprints. She went home, had the necessary photos taken by a former patient who risked his livelihood by agreeing to come to the Sobel apartment, took her parents and grandparents with her to the Zentralstelle, and was issued five Ausreisebewilligungen. The *quid pro quo* was each family member's signature on a promissory document in which each had to pledge never to return to Austria again. Mother did not keep that promise, but no matter since by then the Nazis were history.

This was all that was required in order to get out of a country that rejected its Jewish population and was determined to beat them down with bureaucracy. However, having successfully negotiated this mind-boggling maze, Grete was not finished yet. The next steps she had to negotiate would prove as challenging.

Chapter 43
Getting In

> *"We can delay and effectively stop for a temporary period of indefinite length the number of immigrants into the United States. We could do this by simply advising our consuls to put every obstacle in the way and to require additional evidence and to resort to various administrative devices which would postpone and postpone and postpone the granting of the visas."*
>
> Assistant Secretary of State Breckinridge Long (advising U.S. consulates on how to stymie the visa granting process for European Jews)

Step One: The Affidavit of Support and Sponsorship

Successfully negotiating the Nazi emigration process was only half the battle. Two very daunting additional steps were required in order to emigrate to the United States. The first was an *Affidavit of Support and Sponsorship* that the American government demanded to be signed by a "responsible" (see below) U.S. citizen assuring that the immigrant would not become a burden on the government once in country. Six copies were required in addition to the original. This was the most important of the many documents required to get out of Austria and into the United States. It became the difference between life and death for innumerable European Jews.

For many Austrians, the Affidavit was an insurmountable hurdle because they did not know anyone in the U.S. For others, like Grete, there were already a handful of relatives who had made it into the U.S. years before, but none of them had yet been granted citizenship, so they could not issue Affidavits. The Affidavit of Support is still required to this day for entry into the United States.

To help with this requirement, the Quaker relief house in Vienna asked its home office in the U.S. for phone books so that Viennese Jews desperate to get out of Europe could scrutinize them for potential relatives in America who could provide the elusive Affidavit. When a handful of phone books arrived, they were quickly worn out and not replaced.

The list of documents Grete was required to submit in order to obtain the Affidavit was daunting; in addition to her birth certificate, and proof that her quota number had been reached on the waiting list, she had to provide the entire batch of documents obtained from the Austrian authorities that I described above. Plus another police certificate of good conduct was required that no one had mentioned to Grete until now. In addition, the Affidavit sponsor had to submit copies of his or her most recent federal tax return, affidavits from their banks regarding their accounts, and affidavits as to the sponsors' assets or commercial standing.

Grete, however, was fortunate that an uncle—Morris Brandwein—whom she had never met, had emigrated to the U.S. years before and married an Irish Catholic U.S. citizen in Boston. Grete wrote to him, introduced herself as his niece, and asked for Affidavits for herself and her parents and grandparents. Since Morris was not a citizen, it was his Irish-American wife—Aunt Margaret Brandwein—who immediately signed and mailed Grete five Affidavits and all of the supporting documents while simultaneously sending duplicate originals directly to the U.S. government.

> *"The Affidavits came from Aunt Margaret. She moved heaven and earth to get us out. She was a marvelous woman, a beautiful, blond, lovely*

Irish woman. I cannot forget her. She called the Nazis the 'nays-eyes.' The Brandweins were poor. They had a little restaurant and lived over it. She baked pies and they could hardly afford anything. But it worked. Through her efforts, we survived."

For the rest of her life, my otherwise stoic mother teared up whenever she talked about Aunt Margaret.

The Affidavit was the gold, platinum, and rare-earth element standard for any Jew seeking to escape from the Holocaust. People went to unusual, desperate and heroic lengths to obtain them. My father, Ernst Hermann, was one of them. The remarkable story of how he obtained one is related later in this book.

The Affidavit of Support and Sponsorship warrants additional comment because it became such an important immigration admissions test. The advent of the Great Depression prompted President Herbert Hoover in 1930 to direct the State Department to report to him about the impact of immigration on the Depression. The September 1930 report recommended that immigration visas be restricted even more severely than they had been in the 1920s under President Coolidge. The report recommended the following:

> *"Where there is not any reasonable prospect of prompt employment for an alien laborer or artisan who comes hoping to get a job or live by it, the particular consular officer in the field to whom application for a visa is made (upon whom the responsibility for examination of the applicant rests) will before issuing a visa have to pass judgment with particular care on whether the applicant may become a public charge."*

The report recommended that consular officers refuse to issue visas in such cases.

After receiving the report, Hoover issued an Executive Order to all consulates that

> *"if the consular officer [in any country] believes that an applicant [for a visa] may probably be[come] a public charge at any time, even . . . a considerable period [after] his arrival [in the United States] he must refuse the visa."*

The Executive Order made no distinction between applicants who wanted to come to America to work and those fleeing political or religious persecution.

The irony is that there is no evidence that a single recipient of an Affidavit of Support was ever investigated by U.S. authorities once they arrived on these shores to determine whether they would or had already become a public charge. The U.S. Holocaust Memorial Museum in Washington, DC was unable to identify even one refugee or sponsor with respect to whom an Affidavit was ever questioned or followed-up by the government. Thus, the Affidavit became a meaningless piece of paper. Its sole purpose in the late 1930s and 1940s was to prevent Jews from escaping to the United States.

The refugees were proud, hard-working people unaccustomed to living on handouts and indoctrinated by prior generations to help family and friends, relying on each other rather than the state. They had been through Hell more times than not and were good at survival and fending for themselves. Most of them had nothing when they stepped off the boat in New York harbor except a desire to work hard and invest whatever sweat equity was necessary to survive and succeed. And remarkably, almost all did.

Grete perhaps summed it up best, saying:

"The Affidavit for us was a door-opener and at the same time a huge obstacle for the people whose lives were at risk in Europe. But then, once we got here, the American government did not care, never contacted any of us to see what our condition was, never contacted any of the people who had provided the affidavits. I knew of no such case whatsoever. Once we got here, the incentive was to become a U.S. citizen as quickly as possible, so that we could feel protected and not fear being forced to leave."

Step Two: American Visas

Grete's next task was obtaining U.S. visas for the family. The Nazi authorities would not allow Jews to emigrate unless they were assured of some place to go, for fear that upon arrival they would be deported back to Austria.

An American visa was an incredibly hard-to-get document among the endless series of hoops a Jew had to jump through in order to leave the Old World for the New.

This was also a multi-step process and the biggest hurdle thus far she had to overcome. Once she obtained the critical Affidavits of Support, she went to the U.S. Embassy and another days-long wait in line.

Within months after Hoover's Executive Order, the number of U.S. visas issued for everyone worldwide plummeted by 75 percent. Immigration into the U.S. dropped from 241,700 in 1930 to 97,139 in 1931. President Roosevelt rescinded the Executive Order in 1936, but American consuls did not change their procedures and also began rejecting tens of thousands of visa applications because of technical flaws in the applications, procedural difficulties, or any number of other excuses. In fact, the number of permitted immigrants was miniscule from 1931 to 1945, coincident with the period that the desperate desire to come to the U.S. skyrocketed:

Year	Number of Immigrants
1931	97,139
1932	35,576
1933	23,068
1934	29,470
1935	34,956
1936	36,329
1937	50,244
1938	67,895
1939	82,998
1940	70,756
1941	51,776
1942	28,781
1943	23,725
1944	28,551
1945	38,119

The typical American consular officer shared the same background as the anti-Semites at State Department headquarters in Washington. Anti-Semitism almost certainly influenced their behavior when it came to decisions about granting visas.

Worse for the Jews of Austria and Europe, the entire visa process was overseen by Assistant Secretary of State Breckinridge Long, whose quotation introduces this chapter. Long was obsessed with the ridiculous notion that many Jewish immigrants were secretly German spies, as incredible as it sounds that a Jew would be spying for the government that was murdering his people.

Thus, for many European Jews, securing a U.S. visa was where the exhausting ordeal ended badly. Much depended on the individual U.S. consular officer before whom one appeared. The vast majority toed the State Department party line and treated Jewish applicants with skepticism and scorn, subjecting them to invasive interviews in order to find a reason—any reason, often flimsy—to reject their application.

U.S. immigration law at the time imposed a quota of only 27,000 Germans and Austrians (now that Austria was part of Greater Germany) a year to enter the country. Even in such desperate times, the annual quota limits were never reached because of the consular obstacles put in the way of these frantic people.

Once inside the U.S. Embassy, Grete faced a new, unanticipated barrier: the consular officer questioned the *validity* of her Affidavits of Support. The State Department had no uniform policy on validity, leaving the decision up to the judgment of each individual consular officer. Those serving in Austria were, with few exceptions, extremely strict about what they would deem a valid Affidavit of Support. In some instances, they would not permit a brother or sister to vouch for each other per the Affidavit because they did not consider siblings to be closely enough related!

Before getting to this validity check, Grete was first examined by an American doctor who gave her a clean bill of health. She fretted that Ernestine would flunk the physical examination, but remarkably, she did not. David, grandfather Liber and grandmother Julie also passed easily.

When Grete arrived back at the embassy for the validity check and visa, she was astonished to see that this time there was no line. The reason was because so few Austrians had been able to successfully make it through the ordeals described in this and the preceding chapter. She was given her visa without much hassle because the American consular officer took a liking to her, so she was smart enough to flirt with him.

While she could now leave for America, her parents and grandparents could not. Despite having lived in Vienna for close to a half-century and having become Austrian citizens before being stripped of citizenship after the Anschluss, David, Ernestine, Liber and Julie were not considered Austrian for U.S. immigration quota purposes. Under the *National Origins Act of 1924*, they were deemed Polish because all four had originally come to Austria from Poland. And since the annual quota for Polish immigrants into the U.S. was only 6,524 in 1939, they were denied visas. 1939 was the worst possible year to be considered Polish, especially after Germany invaded Poland on September 1. There were no spaces left and an impossibly long waiting list.

Step Three: The Shanghai Option

What should have been the moment of triumph for Grete was dashed by this new problem. Walking home from the U.S. embassy, she went over the options for them in her head.

Grete knew from her research that it was possible to obtain an entry visa from China for her parents and grandparents to go to Shanghai. Ho Fengshan, the new Chinese Consul-General in Vienna, was liberally doling out visas to Jews. Ho, a Christian who was very sympathetic to the plight of the Jews, helped over 4,000 reach Shanghai. Anyone who could show that s/he had a one-way steamship ticket automatically received a visa for Shanghai. The next day, Grete began putting together the means to buy four tickets. Once she had the money and purchased the tickets, she went to see Ho and obtained visas for her parents and grandparents. Despite my inquiries, she refused to tell me how she managed to come up with the funds to buy the tickets.

In the meantime, she did not want them to remain behind in Vienna, deeming it much too dangerous. The most viable alternative was to get them to Milan, where it was still relatively safe for Jews. There, they could stay with their Gottlieb relatives until they could board the ship from Genoa for China.

She next went to the Italian embassy, where she was easily able to obtain temporary visitors' (transit) visas to Italy. Additional black market jewelry sales bought them train tickets to Milan.

But then she ran into another problem.

Step Four: Baptism

Under pressure from Hitler, Mussolini suddenly tightened the screws on both his own Jewish population and would-be Jewish immigrants. He decreed that only *baptized* Jews would be permitted to enter Italy on any kind of visa.

For Grete, the solution to this oxymoronic mandate was obvious: She, David, Ernestine, Julie and Liber would have to be baptized. At first her parents and grandparents all objected. There was a great deal of weeping, shouting and hand-wringing in the apartment. Grete argued that her parents had never been very religious (although David usually fasted and occasionally attended services on Yom Kippur). Liber and Julie were another story. They had kept a kosher home until that became impossible post-Anschluss. Liber woke up every morning, donned *tefillin* and a *tallis*, and *davinned*, rocking back and forth in the Orthodox tradition while communing with his God.

One of Grete's former patients had been a priest in a nearby church, so Grete, undeterred by the family's objections, went to see him and found a sympathetic ear. She asked him if he would sign baptismal certificates for each parent and grandparent and also for her (the ship on which she had bought a ticket to America would also sail from Genoa), but he refused, saying that he feared the consequences if his complicity in the subterfuge was discovered. He suggested that, alternatively, the family undergo an actual baptism and convert to Catholicism.

However, money talks, so Grete asked the priest if it would be possible to make a substantial "donation to his church." His hesitation in responding was enough to encourage her to return home, unearth some more jewelry, sell it, and return to the church with the donation, which she handed to the priest. He left her sitting in a pew and returned several minutes later with five signed baptismal certificates.

When Liber saw the baptismal certificate with his name on it, he recoiled in horror and said: "I'm not going and that is that." Despite Grete's begging him to change his mind, her pleas were unpersuasive. He said that in any event he was too old to undertake such an arduous journey. He was adamant and could not be convinced to change his mind.

David and Ernestine accepted the baptismal certificates and left Vienna for Italy before Grete. However, their son, Otto, who was studying medicine in Switzerland, went to see his parents in Milan and refused to let them board the ship for China, fearing that such a cultural shock would have very negative consequences at best, and that at worst he and the rest of the family would never see them again. Consequently, Grete's parents stayed a year-and-a-half in Milan, surviving on what Grete was able to send them every week from her meager earnings in New York as well as loans from the family of their former landlord in Vienna who were now also Italian immigrants.

Grete did not know about these loans. She knew her father was unable to obtain an Italian work permit, but did not realize how destitute her parents were. She believed that the small amount of money she was able to send them every week once she obtained employment in New York City was sufficient.

> Author: "Did your father do anything while in Italy?"
> Grete: "No. There was no possibility of work. I made $25 a week, and I had to pay the employment agency a quarter of what I made. I kept $5 for myself and the rest I sent them. One day a young man appeared whom I had known, the grandson of our landlord in Vienna. Very rich people. They had emigrated to Italy and I found out that what I had sent to my parents was insufficient because of the inflation in Italy, which caused prices to rise. He said that his family had lent my parents money and he came to claim it, so I paid him what I could."

It took Grete several years to pay the rest of the money back to the landlord's grandson.

Step Five: Endgame

American visa in hand, Grete still had one more step to take. She was required to take her collection of documents to the Zentralstelle in the Palais Rothschild where she would be interrogated and have her entire portfolio of exit and entry documents reviewed by the Austrian authorities before they would issue the final piece of paper needed to leave the country: the Exit Permit.

When she got there at dusk (she had been advised that she would have to stand in line all night in order to have a hope of being seen the next day), there were two lines of would-be emigrants stretching back over a quarter mile. She got in the line labeled "Normal Jews" (the other—*Dachauer*—line was reserved for Jews who had been recently released from the Dachau concentration camp, distinguished by their shaved heads).

It took several days of sleeping in line for Grete to get into the building and up to the interrogation desk. Meanwhile, she was harassed daily by Nazi Blackshirts who walked up and down the line yelling insults, prodding emigrants with batons and rifles, and arbitrarily yanking some of them out of the line and taking them away.

Inside the Palais, she was interviewed by several officials. They were very rude. The issue of unpaid taxes was raised once again, causing Grete's heart to sink. Except this time, it was a different tax issue. Years before the Anschluss, David received a tax rebate from the Austrian government that amounted to quite a lot of money. Despite her explanations, the Nazis now reimposed the original tax. This time, there was no jewelry left under the floorboards of the apartment, so Grete went to her Uncle Shulman, who lent her the money to pay the bogus tax.

Money in hand, she went back to the Palais Rothschild and stood in line for days all over again.

The situation with the lines of frantic Jews had worsened. Wehrmacht troops and SS men began to chase people away and beat them up. When I asked if they beat her, her response was: "Not very much." She stood in line in her raincoat with deep pockets in which she stored some sandwiches and waited for many days.

Once inside the Palais for the second time, she was directed up and down a set of staircases and had to appear in different places in the building, ending up each time in front of a desk and an official wearing a swastika armband. Each desk officer asked her questions but did not wait for an answer. The culmination of this latest ordeal was that she handed over the tax money and her documents were finally stamped "approved."

It was time to leave her native land.

Chapter 44
War

Poland

Germany invaded Poland early on September 1, 1939. Its pretext was a fake attack on a German radio station at *Gleiwitz* in Silesia staged by Wehrmacht troops dressed in Polish army uniforms. Upon seizing the station, they broadcast a bogus incendiary challenge to Germany in Polish.

For the first time in his five aggressions—Rhineland occupation, Anschluss, Sudetenland, Czechoslovakia, Poland—Hitler met armed resistance. Nevertheless, the heavily outmanned and outgunned Poles were defeated in six weeks, their medieval horse cavalries overwhelmed by Germany's Panzers, and their hopes dashed by having to fight a two-front war against both the Germans and the Soviet Red Army, thanks to the late August Molotov-Ribbentrop Pact that created an alliance between the two totalitarian powers.

The invasion of Poland allowed the Nazis to take their war against the Jews to another level—the extermination of Poland's 3 million Jews. These murders were initially executed primarily by bullets. Tens of thousands of Polish Jews were immediate victims.

It is here that we see the first glimpse of the Nazi fantasy connection between Jews and Communism that was about to generate so much tragedy. To Hitler and the Nazis, the link was extensive, combining the two mortal enemies of Nazism into one stereotype. No matter that Stalin, too, was a virulent anti-Semite who had a long history of anti-Jewish activities, including state-sanctioned pogroms. By 1939, Stalin had purged almost all Jews from the Soviet leadership. Facts did not matter. In the Nazi worldview, it was Jews who pulled the strings throughout the Soviet empire.

Operation Barbarossa

The next major escalation of the Nazi war against the Jews had a defined starting date: June 22, 1941. At 3:15 AM that morning, three German Army Groups consisting of 3 million soldiers crossed into Soviet territory. Hitler's longed-for dream of carving out *lebensraum* (living space) for the expanding German nation into the emptiness of the East was launched. "Operation Barbarossa" represented the largest invading force in the history of warfare.

The spearhead of Army Group Centre and, for that matter, the entire German invasion, was General Heinz Guderian's Third Panzer Army. His troops jumped off from the Bug River near Kamianka-Strumilova (Liber and Ernestine's home town) on the Poland-Ukraine border.

Operation Barbarossa was launched 129 years to the day after Napoleon crossed the River Nieman and invaded Russia. Six hundred ten thousand French and allied soldiers crossed into Russia and advanced all the way to Moscow, where Napoleon watched helplessly as the city burned to the ground in the ultimate expression of a "scorched earth" policy. Napoleon's blunder was waiting until late June to launch an invasion of Russia, where winter often begins in September. Three years later, his surviving 9,000 troops limped back across the Nieman in one of history's most devastating military defeats.

Hitler's overweening delusion of his own military brilliance obviated any need in his mind to study the history of Napoleon's tragic mistake. Like his egomaniacal predecessor, he also underestimated how long it would take to conquer the largest country on earth (spanning 6,000 miles from East to West across 11 time zones), the traditional fierce resistance against foreign invaders of the Russian population, and the severity of the Russian winter. History, as it so often does, repeated itself: less than three years after invading the Soviet Union, the decimated German forces were in desperate retreat from Russia.

At the end of 1941, Hitler blundered once again, recklessly declaring war on the United States a few days after Pearl Harbor, when America's outrage and total focus was on Japan's surprise attack. By so doing, Hitler enlisted the overwhelming industrial capacity of the United States in the alliance against him and ensured his eventual defeat.

The War against the Jews

The three years that the Germans warred in Soviet territory were devastating for the Jewish residents of the U.S.S.R. Hitler felt that a special force was needed to eliminate Soviet Jewry. To deal with this non-threat, *Reichsführer* Himmler directed his deputy, the feared Reinhard Heydrich, to unleash the Einsatzgruppen. They followed behind the Wehrmacht as they made their way deeper into the Soviet Union in order to root out "enemies of the state." Einsatzgruppe A, attached to Army Group North, had around 1,000 men and was the largest of the four killing units. Einsatzgruppen B, C and D were attached to the other Army Groups and consisted of between 600 and 700 men each.

Three weeks before the invasion, Heydrich briefed the Einsatzgruppen leaders on their mission, charging them with killing Communist politicians, political commissars and Jews in the service of the party or state. On June 23rd, one day after the invasion, Einsatzgruppe A arrived in Kaunas, Lithuania, where they incited the local Lithuanian population to organize a pogrom against the city's Jews. Einstazgruppe A did not have to lift a finger. The enthusiastic locals clubbed Jews to death in the streets while crowds shouted "Beat the Jews!"

The pogrom lasted four days. Its work done, one of the killers climbed on top of a pile of Jewish corpses and played the Lithuanian national anthem on his accordion. By its end, 5,000 Jews lay dead. Many were tortured before they died. Another 30,000 were herded into a hastily contrived ghetto. In October 1941, Einsatzkommando 3, a subordinate unit of Einsatzgruppe A, murdered more than 9,000 Kaunas ghetto residents, including more than 4,200 children. According to eyewitnesses, they took special pleasure in killing babies by smashing them against trees, throwing them up in the air and impaling them on their bayonets, and then shooting them to make certain they were dead.

The local populations were eager to help. The Germans were treated like liberators and the enthusiasm of the indigenous population was easily manipulated against the Jews. It was an eye-opener for the Nazi leadership, confirming that their anti-Jewish prejudices were widely shared.

In mid-August, Himmler attended a mass shooting of Jews near Minsk in Byelorussia (today Belarus), newly fallen to the Germans and home to more than 50,000 Jews. In preparation for his visit, the local Einsatzkommando commander carefully selected 100 Jews, mostly men. After they finished digging a long ditch, ten Jews were ordered to jump down into it. They were shot and covered with dirt. Then another group of ten jumped down on top of the first group and were shot and covered. And so on until all one hundred were executed.

Himmler stood on the lip of the ditch and watched, fascinated. Later, he expressed concern that the shootings might traumatize the shooters and impair their psychological health. His concerns were possibly misplaced. Walter Mattner, a Vienna policeman, participated in the shooting of 2,273 Mogilev (Byelorussia) Jews, after which he sat down and wrote his wife:

"My hand was shaking a bit with the first cars. By the tenth car, I was aiming calmly and shooting dependably at the many women, children and babies. Bearing in mind that I have two babies at home, I knew that they would suffer exactly the same treatment, if not ten times as bad, at the hands of these hordes . . . The babies went flying through the air in a big arc and we shot them down as they flew, before they fell into the grave or into the water."

The "hordes" to which he referred were Jews. The babies were also Jews.

Several weeks later, Albert Widmann, a forensic chemist, and Arthur Nebe, an SS squad commander, traveled to an insane asylum in Mogilev and placed two pipes through a bricked-in window. Patients were herded into the room and the doors were closed and locked behind them. A car exhaust was connected to the pipes. When the car engine was turned on, its exhaust fumes were piped into the room. But the car was not powerful enough and, although the patients got sick, none died. It was a big disappointment to the Germans. But all was not lost. A nearby police transport van was commandeered. A hose was fitted onto the van's exhaust pipe and the experiment resumed. Within minutes, all of the patients fell unconscious. Ten minutes later, they were all dead. The Final Solution found its solution.

A month later, Rudolph Höss, the Auschwitz commandant, used Zyklon B (prussic acid) on humans—900 Soviet prisoners—for the first time. The gas crystals were flung into the room and the door closed. Someone yelled "gas" and a lot of shouting followed. The prisoners rushed the door in a vain attempt to break it down. There was no escape. Within minutes, they all died. Höss wrote that he was greatly relieved because, to that point, with the mass extermination of Jews about to begin, the murder bureaucracy had no idea how to carry out such an immense task. Now they had their answer.

Two weeks later, several hundred miles to the East, at a ravine outside of Kiev called *Babi Yar*, Einsatzgruppe C, along with Wehrmacht, SS and German police units plus local Ukrainians, carried out the largest single mass murder of the Holocaust. The following order was posted all over Kiev on September 26:

> *Kikes of the city of Kiev and vicinity! On Monday, September 29, you are to appear by 08:00 a.m. with your possessions, money, documents, valuables, and warm clothing at Dorogozhitskaya Street, next to the Jewish cemetery. Failure to appear is punishable by death.*

Over two days, 33,771 Kievan Jews were rounded up and trucked to Babi Yar, where they were ordered to undress and were then shot, their bodies dumped into the ravine.

The Einsatzgruppen eventually murdered more than 1.5 million Soviet Jews. Their usual *modus operandi* was to shoot all Jewish males when they arrived in a town. The directive to kill all Jews who were "enemies of the state" meant, in practice, all male Jews. The units did not bother with fine distinctions. It was easier to assume that every male Jew was an enemy of the German state. Following that, they concentrated on women and children. At least 20 of Grete's relatives were victims of the killing squads.

Chapter 45
The Final Solution Hits Home

Seventy-plus years after the end of World War II, when Americans say "the war," everyone still knows which war they mean. We have experienced many wars since then—Korea, Vietnam, Desert Storm, Iraq and Afghanistan—but none have embedded themselves into the national psyche to the extent of World War II. Perhaps that is due to the fact that (1) we won and (2) unlike succeeding wars, World War II required sacrifices from the majority of Americans.

Hitler, overconfident due to the success of his bloodless takeovers of Austria, the Sudetenland and Czechoslovakia, was convinced that Britain and France would also let him take Poland. When they did not, he was somewhat shaken, but the die had been cast. He understood that the equine-rich, but tank-poor, French army was a paper tiger incapable of defending *la patrie* and that woefully unprepared Britain, still haunted by the memory of a lost generation moldering in their graves in Flanders fields, was led by desperate appeasers—Prime Minister Neville Chamberlain who had already knuckled under to Hitler twice, and Foreign Secretary Lord Halifax (the "Holy Fox"), eager for accommodation with the Nazis.

In New York, Grete worried about what war would mean for the family, especially Liber and Julie, left behind in Vienna. She devoured newspapers. Every evening, she listened to Ed Murrow's CBS broadcasts from London that began with that stirring radio voice announcing: "This is London." The bombing of Britain worried her because her cousins, Lucy and Jules, were there thanks to the *Kindertransport*.

In fall 1939, Liber and Julie were forced to give up the Sobel's Vienna apartment. They went to live with elderly relatives in a cramped, two-room flat.

In October 1939, two thousand Viennese Jews were sent by train to the Majdanek concentration camp near Lublin, Poland, the first mass transport from Vienna to a death camp. A week later, another two thousand Viennese Jews were sent there. Eichmann stated that his goal was to create a "Judenfrei" (Jew-free) Vienna by March 1, 1940. It took longer.

Liber and my mother still corresponded. Grete begged Liber to try to find a way to escape. *"What,"* he wrote Grete, *"could the Nazis possibly do that could be any worse than what they have done already?"* He and Julie would find out.

In late 1941, the Reich's Jewish emigration policy was replaced by a new one: extermination.

On July 9, 1942, with the Final Solution in full swing, my great-grandparents' turn came. Liber and Julie were notified that evening that they would be leaving Vienna at dawn. They were allowed one suitcase each.

They reported to the *Westbahnhof* train station early on July 10, where they were herded at gunpoint onto Transport No. 30, a sealed train, by an Austrian SS unit. They were designated prisoners number 494 (Liber) and 495 (Julie). The train moved slowly through the Austrian countryside, paralleling the Danube on its way to Bohemia. The distance between Vienna and *Terezin* (the town next to the Theresienstadt concentration camp) is 466 kilometers (280 miles). The journey took 30 hours.

Late the next morning, after being crammed sardine-like into a stifling cattle car with no windows, no ventilation, no place to sit, barely room to breathe, and with only one bucket to serve as a toilet for over 500 people, the train arrived at Theresienstadt.

When the train doors slid open, people staggered out, blinded by sudden sunlight, gasping for fresh air, reeking with the stench of piss and shit, sweating bodies and death. Once the living were off the train, the guards removed those who had died during the journey.

Julie and Liber stood trackside for several hours while an official called roll. Then they were led at gunpoint into the camp.

Sixty thousand Jews, virtually all of Vienna's remaining Jewish population, were shipped to the camps in the summer of 1942. By fall, fewer than 7,000 Jews remained, down from 210,000 at the time of the Anschluss. The Germans forced the Jewish communities to pay for transporting their members to the camps. Add the massive amounts of money and treasure the Germans stole via confiscated bank accounts, stock portfolios, bonds, jewelry, works of art, and other property, and the Holocaust became a self-financing and very profitable enterprise. Most of these assets have never been returned.

Theresienstadt was unique among Nazi camps. It was considered the "model" camp, a "Potemkin" village smokescreen for what really went on behind the gates. Periodically, credulous International Red Cross representatives were allowed in to inspect conditions. A prison orchestra, staffed by prisoners who were internationally accomplished musicians, played in honor of their arrival. The naïve Red Cross representatives were shown art works produced by the prisoners, and visited clean and orderly barracks, mess halls and craft shops.

It was all a façade. The Red Cross inspectors actually reported that the Germans ran a "humane" camp system and commended them for its "cleanliness, orderliness, decent food and diverse cultural activities."

Julie and Liber endured 807 days in Theresienstadt. Grete received her last letter from Liber in summer 1943, after which even censored writing was prohibited.

My great-grandparents' final journey began on October 28, 1944. They were herded onto transport *Ev*, packed 700 people to a railroad car. The train carried them on a painfully slow journey to Auschwitz/Birkenau. They were designated prisoners 1022 (Julie) and 1023 (Liber).

When the train doors were slammed shut, the only light that came in was from narrow slits between the wooden slats on the walls. There was no room to sit or lie down.

The trip took four days. Sleep was impossible, jostling was constant, and relieving oneself depended on fighting to get to the corner and its single bucket. The stench and intense cold (the cars were unheated) overwhelmed the passengers. The air was virtually unbreathable. The only food was what the travelers had managed to bring along. Many people, especially the elderly and little children, died during the trip. Somehow, Liber and Julie survived.

When the train pulled up at the Auschwitz siding, soldiers with snarling German Shepherds and Dobermans opened the doors, screaming at the people who poured out: "Get out! Get out! Line up in groups of five! *Mach schnell!* Warm food waits!"

Those still alive staggered out, gasping. The old men almost all wore suits. Some even wore ties. Many of the women covered their heads with shawls. Children were still in school uniforms, tattered from their lengthy incarceration in Theresienstadt.

If this was a night arrival, blinding searchlights made it impossible for the prisoners to see much of anything.

Prisoners too weak to detrain were shot—a single bullet to the back of the head—a few minutes after the ambulatory ones left the siding. Then the dead were carried off the train. A cadre of prisoners in striped pajamas went into the train cars to clean up the urine, feces, brains and blood before the train returned to the west and south to pick up a new cargo of the damned.

There was much moaning, groaning, shouting and yelling during this process. In the minutes between exiting the train and being lined up by gun-toting SS men, prisoners fanned out and ran around looking for family members, friends and lovers from whom they had become separated during the voyage.

It was time-consuming to get people to line up properly. After being sealed in a stinking, confined compartment for so long, they were often too numb to follow instructions. Those who did not heed the line-up order quickly enough were truncheoned into compliance.

Young mothers with babies spread their shawls on the ground in order to change diapers. This was not permitted. Mothers were yanked to their feet and shoved into line, forced to abandon their babies. The mothers' cries and wails were heart-rending. It now suddenly dawned on many prisoners just what was in store for them, which did nothing to calm the tumult. Some babies cried, others just watched in silence as their mothers disappeared forever. The soldiers meanwhile repeated the lie that hot soup waited just down the line.

Once a semblance of order was achieved, the lines moved forward, prodded by guns and attack dogs. As the prisoners approached a man facing them, the more worldly ones could see that he was a physician by the *caduceus*—the coiled snake symbol derived from ancient Greece that designated a medical practitioner—on his lapel. A healer! A good sign.

The doctor pointed with his riding crop, directing some people to the right, others to the left. The young and fit, deemed suitable for slave labor, went to the left while the old and infirm went to the right, forming two columns as the line moved beyond him. SS Dr. Josef Mengele, whom history would label the "Angel of Death" for the grisly medical experiments he performed on Holocaust victims, was the physician present at the siding when Liber and Julie disembarked. My great-grandparents were ordered to the right.

The siding cleared, the soldiers and dogs not needed to move the selectees along stayed behind to deal with the babies lying on the ground. Disposal methods included shooting, stomping on their heads, or the most popular, swinging the child overhead like a hammer thrower, then letting it fly into the side of the train where its skull was crushed. This always produced wild cheers from the SS troops.

Meanwhile Liber, Julie and several thousand others were marched to nearby Birkenau and into a concrete block structure that the guards told them was a temporary stop for delousing and showering. The outside of the building displayed fresh flowers in window boxes. Inside, they were ordered to strip naked, remove any personal belongings, and remember where they placed their clothes so they could retrieve them after showering. Then they were steered into a cavernous room with a capacity of 3,000 people. Before the women entered, their heads were shaved. Unaccustomed to communal nudity, prisoners covered their private parts with their hands.

Once everyone was inside the chamber, the doors were sealed. Looking up, the captives saw multiple shower heads. What they could not see was that there were no pipes behind them connecting them to a water source.

Upon receiving the signal that the chamber was sealed, SS men on the roof removed hatches exposing wire columns that fed into the chamber. Zyklon B gas canisters were placed inside the columns and lowered into the room. Once the canisters reached the chamber floor, the roof hatches were sealed. Within minutes, toxic gas rose in a cloud and filled the chamber. Hysterical screams were quickly followed by the unimaginable agonies accompanying death by asphyxiation. Within minutes, Liber, Julie and the other victims were dead. With their dying breaths, the pious recited the "Shema," the ancient and most holy of Jewish prayers: "Hear Oh Israel, the Lord our God, the Lord is One." God, however, was not listening.

When the screams stopped, powerful fans embedded in the walls expelled the gas from the chamber. Following the murders, *Sonderkommando* work crews comprised of Jewish prisoners removed the bodies and placed them on a "corpse lift" for transport to the crematorium. Once the bodies were gone, the Sonderkommando re-entered the gas chamber and hosed away the blood, vomit, piss and shit that covered the floor, walls and even the ceiling.

The Nazis sold the best heads of hair they harvested for wigs, furniture and pillow stuffing. Socks went to U-boat submariners. Shoes, jewelry, clothing, gold fillings and other items were also taken.

The date was November 1, 1944. It was Liber's 79th birthday.

Regret turned into guilt. My mother never forgave herself for diagnosing Liber's 1935 colon cancer, which because it was caught early, was cured by successful surgery. She lamented that, if she hadn't caught the cancer and Liber had died in bed, he would have been spared the terrible ordeal he had to suffer nine years later. Grete's sorrow about Liber and Julie's fate was lifelong. She even spoke about it during her final days on Earth, quoting Heinrich Heine: *"Sleep is good, death is better; but of course, the best thing would be never to have been born at all."*

Liber and Julie were only two of Grete's relatives murdered by the Nazis. We never were able to piece together a precise tally. We were able to confirm 59 on both sides of the family, but that did not account for many who were never heard from again after the war. An educated estimate of murdered relatives is somewhere between 90-100 aunts, uncles and cousins.

Chapter 46
Mountbatten and Marriage

Although this book revolves around my mother, it is impossible to talk about her life without also providing a picture of my father, to whom she was married for 51 years.

A Case of Mistaken Identity

When I was born, my parents named me Richard after two people for whom my father had boundless admiration: his mother, Theresa, whose nickname was Rezl (pronounced *Ray*-zell); and Lord Louis Francis Albert Victor Nicholas George Mountbatten, First Sea Lord, First Earl Mountbatten of Burma, and the last Viceroy of Britain's Indian Raj. My father mistakenly assumed that Mountbatten's name was Richard because he was known as "Dickie" within the royal family after his uncle "Nicky," Russian Tsar Nicholas II. "Nicky" became "Dickie" because the royals felt one Nicky was enough. My parents did not realize their error until they read Mountbatten's obituary following his assassination by the Irish Republican Army in 1979.

Ernst's "Provenance"

Ernst was born in the Hollandstrasse building next to where Grete was born four months later. His father, Solomon Hermann, was a cobbler. His mother stayed home with Ernst and his younger sister, my Aunt Hedy (Hedwig).

Solomon was born in 1879 and grew up in Bratislava, Slovakia 35 miles down the Danube from Vienna. Like my maternal grandfather, David Sobel, Solomon was forced to leave home in his teens, in his case due to his strained relationship with his stepmother. He came to Vienna and was apprenticed to a shoemaker.

Ernst's mother, Theresa Jaul, was born in 1880 in *Wiener Neustadt*, about 40 miles south of Vienna. The Jauls were a large, clannish family that lived next to each other and the Blums, a large family of Jaul cousins. The two families were involved with each other in various businesses. They were very religious.

I don't know how Solomon and Theresa met, only that her family opposed their marriage, feeling that Theresa was "marrying down."

Solomon and Theresa never had much money and lived a modest existence. As I indicated above, Solomon was drafted into the Austro-Hungarian *Gemeinsame Armee* (Common Army) in July 1914. In August, Austria-Hungary, goaded by Germany, mobilized, and *Infanterist* (Private) Hermann went off in his field gray uniform, one of 3.35 million Austrian soldiers to serve in the First World War. As the trains pulled out of Vienna's *Sudbahnhof* station, thousands of Viennese cheered, certain their loved ones would be home by Christmas.

Solomon, age 35, was at the older end of draft eligibles. His draft status was established by a written questionnaire which, among more standard queries, wanted to know if a recruit could play a musical instrument and played any sport. No physical examination was necessary.

Theresa and her children could not survive in Vienna on the pittance paid to Austrian army privates (I earned only $102.30 per month as a buck private in the U.S. Army in 1969, so you can imagine what Solomon earned in 1914). She took nine-year old Ernst and five-year old Hedy and went back to Wiener Neustadt. There they ate reasonably well—the Jauls and Blums grew vegetables and fruit and kept some farm animals—and had a roof over their heads during the four long years of the war. When Solomon was discharged after four brutal years fighting in many bloody battles on the Isonzo Front, he came home and resumed his cobbling trade, and the family rejoined him in Vienna.

After grade school and gymnasium, Ernst entered Vienna Medical School a year ahead of Grete, in the same class as his friend, Viktor Frankl. Ernst graduated in 1930, but it was not a joyous occasion. Theresa, age 50, was dying of pancreatic cancer and passed away soon after graduation. The family was devastated. Even into very old age, Ernst could not speak of his mother without shedding tears.

Although Ernst romanticized Vienna, a love affair he maintained all his life, he was a realist when it counted. After watching Hitler march triumphantly into town in March 1938 to the cheers of hundreds of thousands of Viennese, he wasted little time planning his departure. He bought a ticket to Shanghai for himself and his father, the Chinese metropolis being the only place Jews could go in the world without a visa, but he had no real desire to go there. The Shanghai tickets were an insurance policy. Instead he looked toward Switzerland. (See Chapter 35 for Ernst's escape from Austria).

Zurich to Paris to London

When Ernst arrived in Zurich without a transit visa or any other sanctioned document, he sensed that the Swiss authorities would soon discover and deport him. He contacted a Gentile physician from Vienna, referred by a colleague. This doctor was a stranger, but my father persuaded him to loan him enough money to get to Paris. Sure enough, as the Swiss were closing in on him, he left the country for France, after securing a transit visa from the French consulate.

By 1938, France was once again awash in anti-Semitism. In April, Jewish Premier Leon Blum's Socialist government fell, brought down by anti-Semitism. Ernst arrived in France at the very moment when Jew-hatred became official government policy. His transit visa meant that he could not stay very long.

After only six weeks in Paris, with money left over from his Zurich loan, he secured a temporary British visa and bought a ticket to London. In Cherbourg, he boarded a cross-channel steamer to Dover. Upon arrival in England, this otherwise astute man did something incredibly stupid. Asked by the English immigration officer if he had any money, he said "no, I had to borrow money to get here." He was immediately escorted to an interrogation room, where he was grilled extensively about his intentions. He managed to talk his way into being allowed to remain in England for a maximum of six weeks, after which he would either have to leave the UK or risk deportation back to Austria.

Serendipity and Kismet

Ernst longed to get to America. However, he lacked the necessary funds as well as a visa and the all-important Affidavit of Support. This is where Ernst's story diverges dramatically from the typical tale of Holocaust escape into one for the ages.

One Sunday, he bought a copy of the *Times of London* and, for the first and likely only time in his life, read a frivolous article, a feature about the best-dressed women in the world. Number one on the list was Lady Edwina Mountbatten, wife of Lord Louis Mountbatten, the great-grandson of Queen Victoria and first cousin of King George VI. Ernst read that Edwina was raised by her beloved grandfather, Sir Ernest Cassel, a converted German Jew who rose to become the confidant of King Edward VII (he was the last person to see "Bertie" alive), friend of Prime Ministers, financier of the royal family, and one of the richest men in the world.

Ernst impulsively wrote a letter to Lady Mountbatten in his poor English, describing his dire situation and asking her for help. Remarkably, she responded and invited him to an interview with her later that week at Brook House, her 37-room London apartment.

Ernst took the elevator up to Edwina's penthouse, where a butler in resplendent livery received him. Ernst thought the butler must be Lord Louis and, bowing, addressed him as such, much to the butler's astonishment.

Ernst explained his plight to Edwina, who listened intently. After she asked him several questions about his background and aspirations, she lent him enough money to buy passage to America and told him she would help him get a U.S. visa (she gave him a letter of introduction to U.S. Ambassador Joseph P. Kennedy, which streamlined the visa application process) and an Affidavit of Support from her close friend, Frieda Schiff (Mrs. Felix) Warburg in New York. The Jewish Warburgs were one of the world's great banking families. Today, their house is New York City's Jewish Museum. Felix Warburg was the inspiration for Little Orphan Annie's "Daddy Warbucks."

Edwina warned Ernst that if he did not pay her back within six months, she would never help another Jew again. He did . . . and she did, in spades.

Ernst did not meet Joe Kennedy, but Edwina's letter allowed him to end-run all the usual bureaucratic obstacles. He obtained his U.S. visa the next morning. In December 1938, Ernst sailed for America on the *Empress of Britain* out of Southampton. A week later, he was in New York City.

Why Did Edwina Do It?

Why did Edwina help my father? He was a complete stranger to her, a nobody. If there was ever a poster girl for the idle rich (Edwina was the richest woman in England) leading an aimless existence, it was Edwina. Her life up to that time (age 37) was one of parties, frenetic travel, a succession of lovers, and shopping. She was one of the world's great materialists.

Everything changed for her right around the time she helped Ernst. She became deeply affected by what was going on in continental Europe. This *doyenne* of frivolity became a dynamo of caring and champion for ordinary people: bombing victims of the London blitz; soldiers, sailors and the heroic Royal Air Force flyers who saved England during the Battle of Britain; and others, including Jews. Left behind was her single-minded pursuit of pleasure.

Edwina threw herself into work with organizations like the German-Jewish Aid Committee and the Jewish Refugee Committee. She sent checks to refugees who had nowhere else to turn. She kept her good works to herself, never seeking recognition. Her transformation lasted the rest of her life and sealed her (and her husband's and the royal family's) place in the pantheon of my father's heroes.

I don't know what prompted Edwina to help Ernst, literally saving his life. My guess is that a combination of factors were involved in both her response to Ernst and her subsequent efforts to help other Jewish refugees:

1. She adored her Jewish grandfather.
2. Her awareness of her Jewish ancestry was awakened upon observing the persecutions visited on the Jews of Europe.
3. At about the same time, she began receiving letters from people she met on her travels asking for help for themselves or relatives: a dressmaker, Leopold Neumann from Vienna, who needed assistance escaping from Hitler; a "Dr." Tuttnauer, a facial masseur, who wanted to stay in Britain and needed a license to establish a practice in London; a professional dancer, Wilhelm Kassel, who, like my father, had to get out of Switzerland before being deported back to Germany.
4. Ernst Hermann was a very enterprising, charming and persuasive man.

Edwina after Ernst

Some of these people needed the intervention of Edwina's royal and tremendously well-connected husband, so she prevailed upon him to write dozens of letters to relevant British authorities. He always did so promptly, with energy and good humor.

After the war, Edwina became the last Vicereine of India, a country she grew to love more than her own. During her 15-months on the subcontinent, she and her husband undertook Herculean efforts to assure a peaceful transition for India to independence.

Unfortunately, they failed. Communal riots accompanied Britain's transfer of power at midnight on August 15, 1947. The wrenching division of the country into India and Pakistan drilled down into small villages as millions of Muslims, Hindus and Sikhs found themselves on the wrong side of the partition lines. For months after partition, Edwina marshaled her considerable persuasive and organizational assets and set about trying to feed, clothe, and shelter millions of its victims. She put her own life in danger moving about India and Pakistan while the three communities slaughtered each other, sometimes in her presence.

The two great leaders of India's independence movement—Mahatma Gandhi and Jawaharlal Nehru—became her friends and counselors and, in the case of Nehru, allegedly one of her lovers (although the evidence for this is thin). Nevertheless, for the rest of her life, Edwina and Indian Prime Minister Nehru exchanged hundreds of intimate letters, confiding in each other to an extent that they could not with anyone else. Whether their relationship ever resolved itself physically, it is not a stretch to say that Nehru was at least the intellectual love of her life. Lord Mountbatten respected his wife's complicated relationship with Nehru and did not object.

Edwina spent her last decade, the 1950s, traveling the world doing humanitarian work. In England, she used her prestige to influence politicians to change their policies toward the British colonies. She tirelessly raised funds for UNICEF, assisted thousands of Jewish orphans and other refugees, ran vaccination and nutrition programs, and established educational and medical services. She became one of the first citizens of the world.

Edwina wore herself out with her good works. She died in her sleep in 1960, age 58.

Her activities and outspokenness were often awkward for Lord Louis. He was occupied with two very important positions in the 1950s, first as Commander of Britain's Mediterranean Fleet, then as First Sea Lord, the uniformed chief of the British Navy, the position once held by his father and to which Louis aspired all his life. In both positions, he was a reformer. Despite his wife's often overt criticism of her own government and its allies (she was quoted in the newspapers as saying that NATO "had everything wrong with it" and that the UN was "a racket"), her husband never attempted to restrain or silence her.

Ernest (he "Americanized" his name upon arriving in the U.S.) shared a lot of this idealism. In addition to quietly helping many needy relatives, friends, and Jewish refugees who arrived in America after the war, he did volunteer work in a mental institution and served in a variety of volunteer capacities in his adopted home town.

Mountbatten's Assassination

In 1979, Lord Louis, age 79, was vacationing at *Classiebawn*, the Irish castle Edwina inherited from Sir Ernest, surrounded by his children and grandchildren. On the morning of August 27th, he took his 14-year old twin grandsons, his daughter Patricia and her husband, his son-in-law's mother, and a local Irish boy out in his boat, the *Shadow V*, to collect lobster pots.

As the boat pulled out of *Mullaghmore* Harbor, a 50-lb bomb hidden in the boat beneath Lord Louis' feet detonated, triggered either by remote control or a timing device. The boat disintegrated. Lord Louis was killed instantly, along with the local boy and Mountbatten's grandson Nicholas. His son-in-law's mother was fatally injured. The Irish Republican Army took credit for the murders in a press release. My father was devastated. Always an emotional man, his tears flowed freely.

In 1982, Ernest was energized by the Falklands War. His outspoken support for the British defense of these barren islands 8,000 miles from Great Britain, populated mainly by sheep, heavily influenced his 4-year old grandson, David, in the same Anglophilic direction. The two of them closely followed the war reports. The year before, my father set his alarm clock to wake him up at 2:30 AM on July 29th so he could watch the live broadcast of the wedding of Prince Charles and Diana Spencer. God forbid that I ever criticized the royal family in his presence.

Ernest paid Edwina back within three months of his arrival in America, borrowing the money from relatives.

Coming to America

Shortly after arriving in New York, Ernest passed the New York State medical examination and the mandatory English examination required of all émigré physicians. As a *quid pro quo* for the modest support he received upon arrival from the Jewish Agency ($50 in cash), he agreed to serve four years in a remote rural area of the state. The Jewish Agency sent him to Ellenburg, not far from the Quebec border.

His father, for whom he had managed to secure passage to America after he arrived in Ellenburg, joined him as chief cook and housekeeper. Ernest also acquired a significant other and her son, who moved in with him. His lady friend's son became quite famous in later life when he developed the first oral contraceptive.

In 1943, Ernest returned to New York City and began contemplating his future. He wanted to specialize in ophthalmology and applied for residencies in both San Francisco and Baltimore. While Johns Hopkins in Baltimore was the best eye residency program in the nation, Ernest was unimpressed by the shoddiness of 1940s Baltimore while, at the same time, dazzled by the natural beauty of San Francisco, despite the poor reputation of its residency program. In 1944, he left New York for the West Coast.

While in New York, he visited a friend in the hospital where Grete was working. He heard that this friend was sick from the anesthesia (to be expected) he received prior to his surgery. Ernest asked his friend: "Who gave you that bloody anesthesia?" His friend replied: "Dr. Margarete Sobel." My father said: "I met her once in Vienna and know her brother." He then asked his friend to help him contact her. Their first date was at the iconic Russian Tea Room on West 57th Street in Manhattan, adjacent to Carnegie Hall and just down the block from the legendary Carnegie Delicatessen. Grete arrived on time; Ernest was an hour-and-a-half late. As Grete was about to give up and leave, Ernest came walking down the street and the rest was, well, Kismet.

During his "second act" in New York City, Ernest rented an apartment in the Manhattan Beach section of Brooklyn. One of his upstairs neighbors was an aspiring prima ballerina named Margot Fonteyn. Another was the Hungarian composer, Bela Bartok. Ernest only had a nodding acquaintance with both.

Chapter 47
Endgame

The Reich Implodes

The fear that tethered Hitler's generals to him cost Germany several million unnecessary deaths as the war in Europe wound down. Completely unhinged by then, Hitler denied every single general's request to retreat. He would have none of it, and his followers were too fearful of his explosive wrath to push their positions.

The Americans and Brits in the West and the Red Army in the East gradually pincered Germany. For his last hurrah, Hitler adopted Richard Wagner's operatic *Götterdämmerung*—"twilight of the gods"—theme and applied it to his doomed Reich, his feeling being that if I have to go down, so do they all. His countrymen, he concluded, were not worthy of his genius. The Berlin Philharmonic presented its last concert, which included the *Götterdämmerung* finale, as the Red Army's artillery bombarded the city.

Hitler's edict that the Wehrmacht "fight to the last man and the last bullet" was, in reality, a relative concept. Instead, vital resources that could have been employed in Germany's defense were diverted to completing the job of killing Jews and other "undesirables." As the Allied armies approached, the horror of the entire 12 years of the Holocaust and war escalated to unimaginable levels of murder and degradation. The regime continued to systematically seek out and destroy the pariah populations to the last. Some of Grete's relatives who had miraculously survived until then died on forced death marches as the Red Army neared their concentration camps.

This diversion of men and materiel went on while the Wehrmacht was losing at least 350,000 men killed and wounded each month in 1944 and early 1945, the German civilian population was suffering the loss of 500,000 lives due to Allied bombing, and hundreds of thousands of German refugees lost their lives fleeing from the Soviet onslaught in the East. Nevertheless, the gruesome death marches from hastily abandoned death camps continued to the very end. The bureaucracy and machinery of death had become very finely honed by then, and it was important to the Nazi elite that the job be finished before Germany imploded. To their last days, the leadership held onto the delusion that the world would someday recognize that doing away with millions of *untermenschen* (sub-humans) was a heroic undertaking that history would applaud.

. . . To the Last Jew

The last major effort at mass Jewish annihilation took place in Hungary. Its victims included relatives of Ernst and also of Grete's sister, Rose, by marriage. Throughout the summer of 1944, as the Red Army advanced through Byelorussia, trainloads of Hungarian Jews, eventually numbering almost half-a-million, were transported to Auschwitz-Birkenau. The crematoria were under enormous strain, having to "process" 10,000 Jews a day for most of the summer. Smaller Jewish populations from the remaining Polish ghettos, Slovakia and Theresienstadt kept the gas flowing at Auschwitz-Birkenau throughout the fall of 1944.

In November, Reichsführer Heinrich Himmler, who bore overall responsibility for carrying out the Final Solution, announced that the "Jewish Problem" had largely been solved and ordered the closing and demolition of the camps. This was prompted by the imminent discovery of the camps by the advancing Red Army. The crime of the millennium had to be covered up as much as possible.

Meanwhile, propagandistic vitriol against Jews continued to spew forth from Josef Goebbels' media empire. Even while witnessing the tribulations of the Jews who were evacuated from the death camps and marched westward, the German population was, at best, indifferent to their horrific plight. The majority of Germans thought the Jews were receiving their just rewards for their supposed perfidy which had placed Germany in its current predicament.

For most Germans, the disappearance of the country's entire Jewish population was a footnote. Out of sight; out of mind. These emaciated skeletons suddenly parading before them on foot in their threadbare striped uniforms elicited no sympathy. Many Germans spat on them, beat them, and hurled invectives at them as they passed by to a fate obvious to all.

Not much positive has ever been associated with the February 1945 fire bombing of Dresden (ably documented in Kurt Vonnegut's novel, *Slaughterhouse Five*). Thousands of refugees and forced-march prisoners were crammed into this beautiful, classical city of 640,000. On the evening of February 13th, a British incendiary bomb attack, followed the next day by a lunchtime American air raid, created a firestorm that turned the city into a raging inferno.

However, something good actually did come of the Dresden bombing. The handful of Jews remaining in the city, having somehow survived 12 years of persecution, deportation, starvation, torture and death, had been scheduled for imminent transport to the death camps. The chaos following the firestorm enabled them to rip off the yellow stars they were forced to wear and blend in with the homeless Dresden masses, thus avoiding their fate. Consequently, a larger proportion of Dresden Jews survived the Holocaust than in any other German city.

As April turned to May and the war's end was imminent, Germans began "reinventing" themselves as anti-Nazis and resisters. The overwhelming majority got away with it, feigning horror at the atrocities. Swastikas suddenly disappeared and photographs of der Führer, which had adorned virtually every German household, were ripped from the walls and burned. Millions of pages of incriminating documents met a fiery fate.

The Greatest Mystery

The question that obsesses me more than any other about Germany's enthusiastic descent into the inferno is this: *Why were so many resources diverted to killing innocents when they were so critical to the nation's war effort and ultimately to Germany's very existence?* The answer is not easily forthcoming.

Here are the relevant facts:

- The United States Holocaust Memorial Museum calculates that there were around 20,000 death, concentration, slave labor, and satellite camps in German-occupied territory. Camps were established in Austria, Lithuania, Latvia, Estonia, Belgium, Bulgaria, the Channel Isles, Danzig, Denmark, France, Germany, Greece, Holland, Hungary, Italy, Norway, Poland, Czechoslovakia, and Yugoslavia. Approximately 600 were main camps; the rest specialized sub-camps devoted to specific forms of "medical" experiments, torture and death.
- We don't know exactly how many men and women were posted to these camps as administrators, prison guards, and support staff. Some estimates go as high as 2 million.
- Add into this latter figure the number of people who served the camp regimes as regional and central administrators, laborers, and transport officials and the number of people diverted from fighting the war rises even higher.

- Several thousand men were needed to staff the Einsatzgruppen killing units.
- Trains transporting victims to the camps had to be diverted from carrying troops and essential supplies to the Western, Southern, and Russian fronts. They numbered in the hundreds. Overall, approximately 5,000 railroad cars were in regular use for this purpose.
- Massive quantities of food, fuel, and other essentials were also diverted from the war effort to camp administration.

The striking thing about this mania for murder is that it did not abate even a little when the momentum of conquest ground to a halt in late 1942-early 1943 at El Alamein and Stalingrad, the two great inflection points that turned the tide against Germany. The war still had two-and-a-half years to run, but nothing was done to reduce the size of the camp administrations or to divert desperately needed resources to the beleaguered troops. The camps continued to be fully staffed and resourced despite desperate pleas to Berlin for fresh troops and supplies from front-line commanders.

None of this made sense given that Hitler's primary focus was on winning the war. He appears to have compartmentalized his obsessions to the point where he forgot about the vast human and other resources at his disposal that were used for a purely secondary purpose. Not even the existential threat of being crushed by both the advancing Red Army and the Western Allies could induce him to change his business model.

Chapter 48
Reckoning

As April turned into May 1945, the Allied armies cornered what remained of the Wehrmacht, Waffen SS, and hastily cobbled together *Volkssturm* (Home Guard) (comprised of teenagers and the elderly) into a narrow sliver of Germany. Both the Red Army and the Western allies encountered the death camps, horrified by what they saw. After liberating them, they routinely moved the inmates to the nearest town to be fed, clothed, and housed. Tens of thousands of them died from eating food too rich for systems accustomed to years of starvation diets. Many others perished from either the shock of liberation or the vulnerability of their weakened bodies to disease. They often expired with a smile on their faces, knowing they were dying in freedom.

With few exceptions, Jews transported to adjacent towns were spat upon by the locals and subjected to verbal abuse. Germans did not suddenly become philo-Semites. "Death to the stinking Jews" rang out all over the country. It appeared that the World War I "stab-in-the-back" libel so effectively promoted by Hitler was poised for a return engagement.

Wisely, the Western allies' magnanimous treatment of the defeated Axis nations contrasted sharply with the way the victors treated Germany and Austria after World War I. Taking a lesson from President Lincoln's plans for the South following the Civil War, plans never executed due to his assassination, America and to a lesser extent Britain overwhelmed Germany, Austria and Japan with kindness.

Only around 1,000 Jews were still alive in Vienna at the end of the war. This amounted to fewer than ½ of 1 percent of the pre-Anschluss Jewish population. Most of the survivors were partners in mixed marriages. A handful survived in hiding, sheltered and fed by sympathetic Christians.

Estimates of the number of Viennese Jews who died in the camps range from 65,000 to over 100,000. Fewer than 2,000 camp inmates survived, a handful of whom returned to Vienna. One of them was Ernst's lifelong friend, Viktor Frankl, who lost his entire first family in the camps. He remarried and spent the rest of his life in Vienna, practicing psychoanalysis and writing and lecturing about his Logotherapy construct that garnered him world-wide fame.

Ernst's intellectually disabled Aunt Hilda returned to Vienna from England and lived out the rest of her life on a small pension. Her sister, Aunt Rosl, a flamboyant woman who married often and well (twice to Vienna's leading newspaper publishers), also came back. Before escaping to England, Rosl moved in Vienna's rarified circles and was friends with both the leading Jewish and Gentile families. Among them were the Bloch-Bauers and Altmanns of *Woman in Gold* fame. Rosl was present at the wedding depicted in the *Lady in Gold* movie about the famous Gustav Klimt masterpiece starring Helen Mirren and Ryan Reynolds.

Grete's first cousin, Rudi Shulman, who also had an intellectual disability, never left Vienna, having been abandoned by his parents when they left for Shanghai in 1938. He miraculously survived and continued to live there afterwards. We never found out how he managed it.

Vienna did not shed its deeply ingrained anti-Semitism after the war. The University of Vienna was almost as hostile to Jews after the war as before. The head of the Christian People's Party campaigned for office, proudly declaring that he had "always been an anti-Semite." He was easily elected the first president of the post-war Austrian parliament.

Despite its continuing anti-Semitism and drumbeat of lies about its phantom victimhood, Austria was the greatest beneficiary of U.S. largesse after the war, receiving more

Marshall Plan money, *per capita*, than any other European country. Some U.S. taxpayer money provided pensions to Austrian Wehrmacht and SS veterans; none went to its Holocaust victims.

Everybody in Germany and Austria, certainly, as well as in the conquered territories, knew about the Holocaust while it was ongoing. A large number of captive nation residents enthusiastically assisted the Germans in terrorizing and exterminating their Jewish neighbors.

Millions of Wehrmacht soldiers, Waffen SS, Einsatzgruppen units, and bureaucrats involved in identifying, classifying, transporting, guarding, administering camps, and executing Jews, gypsies, disabled persons, homosexuals and others knew exactly what was going on.

Most camps were near populated areas. The stenches fanning out from them were intense and noxious. People knew what death smelled like.

Chapter 49
Selective Punishment

Few of the Germans, Austrians and many others who participated in the Holocaust were punished after the war ended. Of more than 6,500 camp guards and administrators at Auschwitz-Birkenau alone, only 750 received any punishment. Punishments generally amounted to little more than slaps on the wrist, after which the perpetrators were able to live quiet and often prosperous lives.

Thousands of Nazi butchers evaded or successfully survived the Allies' halfhearted "denazification" program. Many were even rewarded despite their misdeeds. Kurt Waldheim, the United Nations Secretary General and later Austrian President, is one of the more notorious exemplars of this craven crowd. During the war, he served in Yugoslavia and likely participated in some of the many daily atrocities that took place there.

One of the most blatant miscarriages of justice was the non-punishment of Hans Globke, post-war German Chancellor Konrad Adenauer's State Secretary, one of the most powerful positions in the Federal Republic. From 1933 on he developed the "legal" basis of anti-Semitism, including the official commentaries accompanying the Nuremberg Laws. His participation in the persecution of the Jews was conveniently overlooked by the Allies.

The Nuremberg trials were the showpiece of the punishment phase of the "closure" following the war. Only a handful of high-ranking Nazis were tried, convicted, and hung.

In my first job out of law school at the Pentagon, I got to know a retired Army sergeant who served as one of the Nuremberg hangmen. He showed me photos he had taken of Nazis dangling from their nooses. He also shared with me an original letter Joachim von Ribbentrop, Hitler's foreign minister, wrote to his daughter the night before his execution. It was touchingly written, but I was anything but touched. Although he promised Ribbentrop he would send it, he never did.

Worse, the United States made what can only be labeled a deal with the devil. The U.S. Army, the Office of Strategic Services and its successor, the CIA, spirited hundreds of Nazi scientists out of defeated Germany and spent the post-war years protecting them and "sanitizing" their war records, which included crimes against humanity.

The U.S. government's rationale was that their scientific expertise was needed to win the Cold War against the Soviet Union. To this day, tens of millions of pages of documents detailing this country's employment of pampered Nazis who escaped justice remain classified. My *Freedom of Information Act* requests for some of these documents were uniformly denied.

In addition, thousands of former SS officers and Gestapo functionaries were recruited by the U.S. to be advisors and foot soldiers in the Cold War. Many were murderers whose crimes were well-known and well-documented. No matter: "national security" justified anything.

The Army, State Department and CIA each had a special program that brought Nazis and their Eastern European collaborators to the U.S. or placed them on the U.S. payroll abroad. Presumed knowledge of the Soviet Union excused everything. The CIA's efforts at covering up its use of Nazi murderers went so far as to reinvent their histories as "freedom fighters" against the Nazis and heroes of the Cold War. Many such recruits came from the Einsatzgruppen.

The U.S. government even conferred citizenship on thousands of recruited Nazis ahead of Holocaust refugees. President Truman authorized this program.

Disgraced Senator Joseph McCarthy (R-WI) employed a secret espionage unit, some members of which were ex-Nazis, to ferret out alleged Communists in the U.S. government.

The CIA used funds it confiscated from Nazis to fund its Nazi recruiting efforts. A large portion of those funds was money confiscated from murdered Jews. Their families were never compensated.

The CIA did not stop there. As the Italian elections of 1948 approached, it appeared that the Communists might win. To counter that potentially disastrous outcome, the CIA diverted several hundred million dollars of confiscated Jewish assets to barrage Italian voters with pro-American, anti-Communist propaganda. The CIA also turned over tens of millions of its "black budget" of looted Jewish funds to the Vatican for use in the 1948 elections.

Those same elections prompted the CIA to develop intimate ties with the Vatican, which was panicked at the prospect of a Communist takeover of Italy. The Church established a Catholic lay organization—Intermarium—comprised primarily of East European exiles, many of them Nazi collaborators, to influence the elections, after which some of them moved on to become prominent in the CIA-sponsored Radio Free Europe and Radio Liberty.

The oft-feted rocket scientist, Wernher Magnus Maximilian Freiherr von Braun, was the case in point. Von Braun headed Germany's V-2 (the "V" stood for "Vengeance Weapon") rocket program that killed hundreds of British civilians. His V-2 plant in *Peenemunde* employed thousands of slave laborers, many of whom died under brutal conditions that von Braun sanctioned as the price of success.

Despite his war crimes, von Braun and his entire rocket team were spirited to the U.S. at the end of war and set up in plush working and living conditions in Huntsville, Alabama, where they became the centerpiece and prime movers of America's ballistic missile development program and, later, NASA's space program. Von Braun became an American icon and hero despite his despicable criminal past, a past his American enablers conveniently sanitized. Von Braun's transformation from Nazi murderer to all-American hero is a permanent blot on this country.

Part Three
Bi-Coastal, 1939-1948

The first two-thirds of this book focus on the first trimester of my mother's life, her European phase. The remaining third is about the last two-thirds of her life—her American era—that happily lacked the intense drama of that first trimester. Economic devastation, starvation, and death as daily possibilities went away. Overt anti-Semitism faded. Her American life was always interesting and sometimes frustrating, but largely secure and mercifully not as eventful.

I have divided Grete's American tenure somewhat by geography. Her last 68 years were spent in New York, San Francisco, New York again, Canandaigua (NY), Miami Beach and Arlington, Virginia. The rest of this book follows that geographic script.

Chapter 50
In Transit

My mother's European life was at an end. Her new life in the New World was about to begin.

Saying goodbye to Liber and Julie was, Grete said, the worst moment of her life. When she walked out of the apartment and down the stairs to Hollandstrasse, she was inconsolable. The intense pain she felt was still with her until the day she died 68 years later.

Milan was a principal way station for Austrian Jews escaping from Europe. It was relatively easy to obtain a transit visa at the Italian embassy in Vienna. It took Grete only one visit lasting only a few minutes to secure transit visas for herself and her parents.

Max and Bertha Gottlieb, Grete's aunt and uncle, opened their Milan apartment to their fleeing kin. Grete's sister, Rose, had briefly stopped there on her way from Vienna to Buenos Aires to join her new husband in 1938. After a week, she boarded the *Conta Grande* out of Genoa for Argentina.

Grete stayed with Max and Bertha for several weeks awaiting the departure of the *Rex*, also from Genoa, in late February 1939. Otto, Grete's youngest brother, was an intermittent visitor to Milan in 1939 and 1940, coming from Switzerland to see his parents, who lived with their cousins from early 1939 until May, 1940, greatly exceeding the time limits of their transit visas. The Italian authorities never checked on them.

David and Ernestine left Milan just days before the "phony war" in the West turned into the real thing, making travel across the Atlantic a much riskier proposition. In Genoa, they boarded the *Conte di Savoia*, the class of the Italian Line. It was the last ship permitted to leave Italy for America (immediately following this voyage, the ship was commandeered by the Italian Navy).

They escaped from Europe a few days before Mussolini entered the war and began rounding up and incarcerating Jewish refugees in Italy. Few survived. Max and Bertha were among the lucky ones who did.

A month later, the British Royal Air Force bombed Milan, destroying many buildings in the district where Max and Bertha lived. They survived the bombing and eventually made it to the United States via forged papers that got them through France and Spain to Lisbon. Once in America, they were interned in a refugee camp in Oswego, New York on Lake Ontario with more than 1,000 other Jewish arrivals. Bertha died there in 1945.

The *Conte di Savoia* and the *Rex* (see below) were sister ships considered the epitome of ocean liner luxury during their sailing salad days in the 1930s. Grete and her parents, however, sailed third-class (what used to be called steerage), the lowest rung on the ships' ticket hierarchy and, for them, the only affordable one.

Grete traveled to Genoa by train from Milan with mixed feelings and considerable trepidation about America. She could not stop thinking about Liber and Julie in Vienna. She said her tearful goodbyes to her parents in Milan, boarded the train, and headed for Italy's great seaport.

She arrived in Genoa in mid-afternoon and spent the hours before boarding the *Rex* wandering around the harbor from which the young Christopher Columbus had first ventured out to sea almost 450 years before. She found Genoa quite beautiful (locals call their city *Genoa La Superba*) and remarkably calm. Mussolini's Black Shirts and squads of armed *Carabinieri* were everywhere, but they seemed very laid back. Many tipped their hats to the pretty *signorina* as she passed. She went to the city's magnificent cathedral and walked from there to the *La Scala* opera house and then to the convent of *Santa Maria della Grazie* to gaze in awe upon Leonardo da Vinci's *Last Supper*.

At 7:00 PM, Grete went on board the *Rex*. Two hours later, it sailed out of Genoa's great natural harbor into the Tyrrhenian Sea and made for the Mediterranean. Grete shared a cabin with two other young women, one English, the other American. They paid no attention to her, preferring to speak with each other in their common language. The seas were calm and the ship made good time to Gibraltar. Grete wandered the decks, luxuriating in the salt sea air. She felt relaxed and alive for the first time since the Anschluss. She looked forward to the remainder of the voyage.

Then everything changed. As soon as the *Rex* cleared Gibraltar and Portugal's Cape St. Vincent, the southwesternmost point of continental Europe, the calm waters of the Mediterranean gave way to the rough churn of the Atlantic. The next five days were a living Hell. Grete became ill as soon as Europe disappeared aft and spent the rest of the crossing in bed, eating nothing and intermittently vomiting bile. By the third day out from Europe, she felt so miserable that she wanted to die.

Grete's roommates ignored her distress. They did not even offer to bring her water and disregarded her plea to request a house call from the ship's doctor. Stoic as always, Grete kept her mouth shut for the rest of the trip, opening it only to throw up.

She survived the voyage and lived in America for another 68 years. The *Rex* was not as fortunate. On September 12, 1944, this ship that held the *Blue Riband* (awarded to the fastest trans-Atlantic liner) from 1935 to 1938 was hit by 123 rockets launched by the Royal Air Force just off of Slovenia's cramped Adriatic coast. She caught fire along her whole length and, after burning for four days, rolled onto her port side and sank.

Chapter 51
The New World

Grete was still in bed when the *Rex* entered New York harbor. Unlike millions of immigrants, she did not get to see the Statue of Liberty. When I asked her about what the experience of arriving in the United States was like, she said she was so sick she could hardly remember having gone through it. Until the ship docked, she stayed in her cramped berth. When she wobbled down the gangway, she had not eaten for more than a week.

My mother staggered through customs and immigration without incident. Her cousins were waiting for her at Manhattan's West Side pier. When they saw what she looked like, the first thing they did was take her to one of the Horn & Hardart automats that peppered Manhattan until the late 1950s and forced her to down some food and drink. Horn & Hardart was her first memory of New York, one she treasured until her dying day. When we would visit New York City in the 1950s, we always made at least one "pilgrimage" to the automat to eat what amounted to a ritual meal of remembrance.

The cousins quickly embraced her into their family fold. America, in contrast, did nothing to help her. There were no government-sponsored programs for Jewish refugees escaping certain death in Europe. No language classes; no welfare payments; no job assistance. America made it difficult for these refugees to assimilate, much less survive economically. If the Jewish refugees from Hitler were going to make it in America, they would have to do so on their own.

It was not easy. Grete was 33 years old, suddenly stateless, having lost her occupation, her language, her connection to anything familiar, and her self-confidence.

Her first two weeks in America, she shared a small bed in her cousin Hilda's apartment with Hilda's young daughter, Edie. The sleeping arrangement was less than ideal because, according to mother, "Edie kicked out in her sleep and had gas."

Grete was unable to resume practicing medicine until she could get over two hurdles: the New York State Medical Board examination and the required English exam. It would take her a very long time to get through these obstacles.

> *"One day at the U.S. Embassy in Vienna, while I was waiting to be interviewed, I heard a girl tell another girl that, in America as a doctor from Europe, although you could not practice medicine, you could get a position quickly as a practical nurse, and that gave me my idea."*

Her "idea" was to visit employment agencies and apply for private nursing jobs. Within two weeks, she secured one. She was able to move out of Hilda's apartment and live in the homes where she worked. The standard duty day was 20 hours, with four hours off. Early on, she often left during her off time to visit her relatives. Sleep was of secondary importance.

Grete's first job was in the Bronx, caring for a girl who had recently had a mastoidectomy, a surgical procedure wherein cells in the hollow spaces behind the ear that have become infected and spread into the skull are removed. Next, she was assigned to care for an elderly man with tertiary syphilis who lived on posh Central Park West. He was a mess, the syphilis manifesting itself through open skull sores. His bones were severely affected and had formed craters. He was far gone mentally and did not talk. Although his embarrassed family did not reveal what was wrong with him, Grete was able to diagnose his condition right away. She frequently took him to

Mt. Sinai Hospital in his chauffeured car for check-ups and when she mentioned her diagnosis, the doctors were impressed.

During her down time, she devoured three newspapers a day—the *New York Times*, *Herald Tribune*, and *New York Post*—which helped her with her English. This job lasted for several months, until her charge died. From then on, she was assigned a series of jobs, each one lasting only a short time.

She continued working as a practical nurse until 1943. Although she easily passed the state medical board exam (in English) in late 1939, she was unable to get through the English exam for four more years, flunking it four times.

Sunday, December 7, 1941 was a rare day of rest for Grete. Her parents had now been safely in the United States since June 1940, and David had found work in a men's clothing store on the lower East Side of Manhattan. His only complaint was about his 90-minute subway commute to work, traumatic for someone whose working life back in Vienna meant walking downstairs from his apartment to his store.

Grete had only recently been able to cut back on her 20-hour-a-day, 7-days-a-week work schedule and could now spend Sundays at home with David and Ernestine in their tiny basement apartment at 104 Elliott Place in the Bronx, nine short blocks north of Yankee Stadium.

It was a beautiful day, sunny but cold. Grete and her parents were hosting a neighbor, Frau Glazer, for tea in mid-afternoon when they noticed people running down the street toward the Grand Concourse, the Bronx's main thoroughfare just two blocks away. David went outside to find out what was going on and came back in, ashen-faced, saying, "The Japanese have bombed Hawaii." The family spent the rest of the day huddled around their RCA radio, listening for updates about Pearl Harbor.

Three days later, Adolf Hitler made his second worst mistake as Germany's Führer (invading the Soviet Union six months earlier topped all the others), recklessly declaring war on the

United States. Germany and Japan had only orally agreed to support each other's war efforts *if either country were attacked*. Germany now provoked the United States to join the European conflict.

Knowing what the Nazis were doing to the Jews of Europe, the Sobels worried that the fate they thought they escaped when they fled Austria might befall them anyway.

Chapter 52
Following Her Heart

"One day if I go to heaven . . . I'll look around and say 'It ain't bad, but it ain't San Francisco'."
Herb Caen (legendary columnist for the *San Francisco Chronicle*)

Following their near-miss of a first date, Grete and Ernest quickly fell in love and, after only a few months, decided to marry. There were delays, however. Ernest left for his ophthalmology residency in San Francisco in August 1944. His decision to opt for San Francisco over Baltimore haunted him for the rest of his professional career. He felt his training was inadequate, inferior to what he would have received at Johns Hopkins. He agonized before every eye surgery to the point where he became a frequent taker of strong sleep medications that knocked him out the night before a morning operation. Probably a good thing that his surgical patients knew nothing of this.

Grete stayed behind in New York. She had finally become licensed to practice medicine in New York State in late 1943 and stayed when Ernest left in order to continue to gain experience administering anesthesias. She did not join Ernest in San Francisco until February 1945.

My parents were married by the San Francisco County Clerk a month later. Their witnesses were the two Professors Kraus, their respective former gymnasium teachers. Both Grete and Ernest wore gray suits. Their wedding photo conveys serene joyfulness and hope for the future.

There was no time for a honeymoon. Ernest had to go right back to his residency and Grete, who got a job in a local hospital, also had no time off.

Seven weeks after the wedding, VE Day marked the Nazi defeat. Grete and Ernest did not get caught up in the wild celebrations that erupted in downtown San Francisco. Instead, they stayed home, quietly remembering the relatives they lost in Europe.

Three months later, Japan surrendered. This time, with no "skin" in the Pacific war, the newlyweds joined in the street celebrations.

Ernest fell in love with San Francisco, its unique topography, and primarily its spectacular vistas. He would have happily settled there for the rest of his life. Grete, in contrast, was less impressed. She missed her parents and siblings in New York (by this time all three—Ben, Otto and Rose—had made it to the U.S.). Moreover, despite her difficult life in New York, she had grown to love the city that offered her life and hope after Vienna.

Chapter 53
It Was San Andreas' Fault

Grete gave no thought to the instability of California's geology when she moved to San Francisco. She was in love, living in one of the most romantic settings on the planet, and starting a new, very happy life. Geology was not on her radar screen.

Ernest, eternally curious, was always eager to go somewhere to see something new. A week did not go by that Ernest and Grete did not hop in their used, dark-blue Chrysler New Yorker and travel somewhere—Sausalito, Berkeley, the Muir Woods, Napa, Sonoma, Sequoia National Park, Yosemite (I found out years later that I was conceived there). It was only a matter of time before Ernest would get curious about the San Andreas Fault and drag Grete to see it one weekend in January 1946.

Big mistake. Grete was pregnant, almost 41 years old, during an era when middle-age first pregnancies were uncommon and were believed (with good reason) to be quite risky. She told me years later that, although she very much wanted at least one more child, I never had a sibling because she feared she was too old and felt she had dodged a bullet with me.

She had great trepidation about getting pregnant at all. Her obstetrical training in medical school made her well aware of the risks. Ernest, however, was a very persuasive husband. He was able to wear Grete down and they decided to try to have a child.

She had never heard of the San Andreas Fault, the 810-mile ditch that extends the length of California and marks the spot where the Pacific and North American tectonic plates meet and occasionally cause the Earth to shudder. Grete still suffered from morning sickness deep into her second trimester. She was grumpy and tired, but in traditional European wifely mode did not want to rein in her husband's enthusiasm or bother him with her female troubles. So when Ernest said they needed to visit the famous ditch, she did not protest.

When they arrived at a good viewing site just west of Palo Alto, Grete was shocked. The fault was not only visible; it was an actual fissure in the earth, and it scared her. She promptly announced that they had to move back to New York as soon as Ernest's residency ended in May. There was no way, she proclaimed, that she would bring a new life into the world on top of an instability that might crack any day and consume the entire West Coast.

When they got home, she went to the San Francisco Public Library and took out books about the fault and about the 1906 San Francisco earthquake that destroyed 80 percent of the city and killed 3,000 people. She insisted on reading the relevant disaster passages aloud to Ernest while he ate dinner.

Ernest was accustomed to the male European notion that his dutiful wife would always accede to her husband's wishes. However, for one of the few times in her life, Grete defied her husband. She was adamant about leaving. She presented him with an ultimatum. Either her and the baby or San Francisco. Take your pick. It was no choice. They newlyweds prepared to move.

Ernest, however, insisted on one last hurrah before leaving California behind. He had to see Death Valley. They left San Francisco for New York in late May, 1946 in their aptly named Chrysler New Yorker. The car had no air conditioning and its shotgun passenger was 8-months pregnant and very uncomfortable. Death Valley was probably not the wisest route under the circumstances. Nevertheless, Ernest was undeterred in his determination to experience it.

They left very early in the morning and drove southeast, stopping for lunch in Fresno. By mid-afternoon, at the height of the day's heat, they entered Death Valley. It was 120 degrees F. Grete became quite ill. Meanwhile, Ernest, always excited by nature's marvels, kept stopping to take pictures. My mother kept quiet despite her suffering, deeming it the price she paid for her husband agreeing to return to the East Coast.

Once through Death Valley, the trip became more tolerable despite their taking a Southern route across the U.S. However, when they crossed the Mississippi River and stopped for the night in Memphis, Grete began to experience what turned out to be false labor. Ernest drove her to a local hospital where Grete was convinced she would give birth. She did not. Sam Phillips' loss (me) proved New York's gain.

My parents arrived in New York City On May 31st. Nine days later, Grete's real labor pains began. I entered the world the next morning in the maternity ward of Manhattan's Gotham Hospital. The hospital no longer exists. June 10 was grandmother Ernestine's birthday. My mother said that my grandmother came out of her latest (and last) clinical depression as a result of my arrival on her birthday.

We lived with my grandparents in their cramped, one-bedroom Bronx apartment for several months. In early August, Ernest and Grete bought half of a duplex in Flushing, Queens for $4,000. It was a house that they both loved, but they were not destined to stay there long.

Grete arrives in New York aboard the Italian liner, *S.S. Rex*, February 1939.

Horn & Hardart automat, where Grete ate many inexpensive meals during her early years in New York. (*Source: New York Public Library*)

Edward R. Murrow, one of Grete's heroes, broadcasting from London during the Blitz. [The author was a college classmate of Murrow's son, Casey.] (*Source: PBS*)

Lady Edwina and Lord Louis Mountbatten. Edwina made it possible for Ernest to emigrate to the United States. (*Source: wn.com*)

Grete's sister Rose and her husband Ted Williams, circa 1945 upon arrival in the U.S. from Argentina [Note: these photos were charred in the apartment fire that killed Rose in 2011]
Author's collection

Grete's brother Otto Sobel
Fort Smith, Arkansas, 1944
Author's collection

Grete's brother Ben
and his wife, Mildred
Author's collection

Grete and Ernest's best friends,
the Buxbaums (L to R: Henry,
Mimi and son Richard)
Author's collection

Chapter 54
Choosing Poorly

"You always pass failure on your way to success."
                                        Mickey Rooney

"You can spend minutes, hours, days, weeks, or even months over-analyzing a situation; trying to put the pieces together, justifying what could've, would've happened . . . or you can just leave the pieces on the floor and move the fuck on."
                                        Tupac Shakur

My parents began their new life with little money, a baby, and the need to build a medical practice at a time when this was a much iffier proposition than it is today. Ernest had spent the months at his in-laws' apartment studying for the ophthalmology board examination, which he took and passed just before moving to our Flushing house. Now it was time for him to earn a living.

Ernest foolishly rented office space on Manhattan's Park Avenue, the priciest address in New York. His choice of office location was heavily influenced by a colleague, a Viennese refugee psychiatrist whose successful practice was the result of (1) promoting that he had studied under Sigmund Freud, and (2) being from Vienna, the shrink Mecca, both cachets guaranteeing a good practice. Dr. Reininger told Ernest that Park Avenue was the only reasonable place in which to establish a successful medical practice in the city. Reininger may well have been correct had Ernest been a psychiatrist. Ophthalmology was a different breed of cat.

Ten years later, Grete, believing me to be mentally challenged, drove 350 miles so that I could be examined by Reininger. Her concern was prompted by my lack of interest in the high culture she and Ernest had grown up with in Vienna, along with my reading habits. At age ten, I had not yet developed an interest in the great literature—Dostoyevsky, Thomas Mann, Goethe, Schiller, Proust, etc.—that had meant so much to Grete. Instead, I was into The Hardy Boys, Tom Corbett Space Cadet, Sport Magazine, Sports Illustrated and Mad Magazines, and each year's new edition of the Information Please Almanac, which I devoured and virtually memorized. For Grete, this was not normal. She discounted my good grades in school because she believed American education was seriously deficient. Reininger told her I was a perfectly normal American boy. She was relieved but not convinced.

While a German accent was a powerful come-on for psychiatric patients, it was a significant deterrent to the acquisition of a patient base following a world war against Germany. Ernest spent many days and hours idling his time in his expensive office. He received a few patients as a result of referrals from Reininger, but that was it.

Chapter 55
Searching for Shangri-La

Ernest could not make a go of his Park Avenue practice. Physicians in the early post-war years did not make remotely close to the huge incomes they enjoyed from the mid-1960s on. Third-party payers—health insurance companies and the federal government—had not yet arrived on the payment scene to any significant extent. Most patients paid doctors out of their own pockets.

In Ellenburg, Ernest was often paid in kind—chickens, a side of beef, eggs, pork (his formerly Orthodox Jewish father/cook/housekeeper was horrified), lamb chops, etc. His patients were dirt poor and cash was a pipedream. In New York City in contrast, his few patients paid in cash. However, there were never enough of them. Meanwhile, money was hemorrhaging via mortgage payments, Park Avenue rent, food and baby expenses. Savings were fast being depleted. Something had to be done.

My parents believed they needed to relocate. So we began to spend weekends searching for a new location. We piled into the car early on Saturday mornings and drove around, looking for a place where ophthalmologists were in short supply. We returned home every evening in order to save money, then began the search again early on Sunday.

At first, Ernest focused on places close to New York City, beginning with Staten Island and Long Island. Grete fell in love with Staten Island and its bucolic environment. Ernest not so much. They argued about settling there, but Grete gave in quickly, a combination of guilt about forcing Ernest to leave his beloved San Francisco and concerns about having to take a ferry boat every time they wanted or needed to go to see family in the Bronx, Brooklyn (Ernest's father and sister were now living there) or Manhattan.

When we exhausted close-in locations (Nassau County on Long Island was quickly rejected), we expanded out in concentric circles; first Westchester, then Suffolk, Dutchess, and Putnam Counties. All were overflowing with ophthalmologists.

The roads were not great in the late 1940s and a trip to the suburbs and exurbs took much longer than it does today. It became increasingly difficult to make it back to Flushing by nightfall. It was time for a wider search strategy.

So, Ernest then went off by himself every weekend, ranging farther and farther out from the city. He stayed overnight Saturday on the road, usually in a boarding house, and returned late Sunday. Grete and I stayed home.

Ernest traveled as far as Oneonta, Oneida Lake, the lower Adirondacks, the Capital District around Albany, Lake George, etc. Nothing. Ophthalmologists were everywhere. Always subject to fleeting fits of depression, he began to despair.

And then, suddenly, a glimmer of hope.

Sometimes it takes years to recognize when opportunity knocks. Just weeks after Ernest arrived in Ellenburg in 1939, there was a vigorous knock on his door. He opened it and was confronted by a man about his own age with wild dark hair, pant cuffs tucked into high socks, and an intense German accent. Dr. Henry Buxbaum, himself a Jewish refugee physician posted by the Jewish Agency to Northern New York, came from Malone, about 35 miles west of Ellenburg. It was the beginning of a beautiful, and often tumultuous, 40-year friendship—one that would have a major influence on my own life as well as on my dad's.

Dr. Buxbaum heard that a Jewish refugee physician had been sent to Ellenburg and wasted no time getting there. Ernest was delighted to find a *landsman* nearby. Solomon put out a plate of cold cuts, cheese and bread, and Henry and Ernest were soon talking as if they had been friends since childhood.

Several hours later, there was another knock on the door. It was two FBI agents. Buxbaum had asked a local resident for Ernest's address and his heavy German accent aroused suspicions. After pointing Buxbaum in the right direction, the gentleman phoned the FBI office in nearby Plattsburgh and told them he had just encountered a German spy.

The FBI politely questioned both Buxbaum and Ernest, concluded they were not Nazi operatives, and apologized for the intrusion.

Segue to nine years later: Ernest was desperate. His quest for a place to relocate had reached a dead end. He thought his only alternative was to move to another state, take that state's medical board exam, and hope for a better outcome.

The future appeared bleak when Henry Buxbaum called Ernest from Canandaigua, a small city in Western New York's Finger Lakes region, where he had settled following his Jewish Agency tour of duty in Malone. Henry was making a go of a general medical practice, and discovered that Canandaigua and some of the neighboring counties lacked a board-certified ophthalmologist.

Buxbaum urged Ernest to drive the 350 miles from New York City to Canandaigua to scope out the opportunity. Ernest by now was eager to grasp at any straw, Grete less so. The distance from family seemed to her enormous and Canandaigua appeared as remote as the Arctic Circle. At least the towns they had looked at were all within a few hours of the city at the most. Canandaigua was another world altogether.

Nevertheless, she deferred to Ernest and sent him off to Western New York. He came back enthusiastic. While in Canandaigua, Buxbaum introduced him to a longtime local physician—Harvey Jewett—with impeccable "American WASP" credentials, who had helped Buxbaum when he first arrived and who pledged to refer patients to Ernest.

Ernest left for Canandaigua soon after, leaving Grete to sell the Flushing home. It took her several months to complete the sale (at a loss), whereupon Ernest returned to collect us and begin a new life.

Part Four
Small-Town America, 1948-1978

"The window, in the provinces, replaces theaters and promenading."

Gustave Flaubert, *Madame Bovary*

Chapter 56
Into the Provinces

Culture shock understates Grete's reaction to Canandaigua. Having only lived in three of the great, cosmopolitan cities of the world—Vienna, New York and San Francisco—she suddenly found herself in a tiny, provincial town at what seemed to her to be the outer edge of civilization. Moreover, she went from a house—albeit a modest one—to two rooms on the upper floor of a boarding house.

The rush-rush dynamism of New York City was replaced by the placid quietude of Canandaigua. In 30 years there, Grete never really became comfortable with her new surroundings. Ernest, who had experienced small-town life in both Wiener Neustadt and Ellenburg, took to his new surroundings like a bee to honey.

A Little History

Canandaigua was not always a backwater. The town dates to the fifteenth century when Native Americans settled there at about the time the real Hiawatha (not the fictional Longfellow creation) united the five Iroquois tribes. It became the Seneca capital, the "Western Door" of the Iroquois Confederacy.

The Senecas sided with England during the Revolutionary War. They were enough of an irritant that George Washington sent Major General John Sullivan on a punitive raid into the Finger Lakes in 1779, during which he burned Kanandarque (the original Seneca name), killed most of the braves and burned their crops. Many women and children died of starvation over the ensuing winter.

The "Finger Lakes" consist of 11 north-south lakes that splay out south of Lake Ontario between Rochester and Syracuse. Their digital shapes were carved out by retreating Ice Age glaciers that left behind very deep lakes (Canandaigua Lake is deeper than Lake Erie).

Canandaigua became the major settlement and county seat of all of Western New York following the Revolution and the site of the land office for the sale of formerly Seneca lands. Robert Morris, the Jewish financier of the continental army and close friend of George Washington, sent his son Thomas to Canandaigua to administer the illegal land sales. In 1794, the U.S. signed the Treaty of Canandaigua with the Iroquois that affirmed Indian land rights in New York. To this day, the U.S. government makes an annual payment to the Indians of a few bolts of calico cloth.

Canandaigua's most prominent citizen, Gideon Granger, arrived in 1814 after serving as U.S. Postmaster General under Presidents Jefferson and Madison. His portfolio included keeping tabs on Vice President Aaron Burr as he traveled the continent scheming to establish his own empire. In facilitating his mission, Granger built the post roads, the nation's first interstate highway system, and managed to make the postal service profitable.

Canandaigua reached its apogee in the first three decades of the nineteenth century. Then along came the Erie Canal, which ran 15 miles north of town and leapfrogged Rochester ahead of Canandaigua. The idea for the canal came from the pen of Jesse Hawley, a local grain merchant, while he was in debtor's prison in Canandaigua. His essays spurred New York governor DeWitt Clinton to build the canal.

Canandaigua gained additional notoriety in 1826 when one William Morgan was expelled from the Masonic Order. Vengeful, he wrote a book revealing the Masons' secrets. This did not sit well with the Order. They had him arrested and jailed in Canandaigua on a bogus bad debt charge. The next night, four vigilantes took Morgan to Fort Niagara. He was never seen nor heard from again. Weeks later, a badly decomposed body washed up on the Lake Ontario shore. The body was identified by a Canadian woman as her husband, but that did not stop talk that it was really William Morgan.

Morgan's disappearance prompted publication of his book, which became an overnight best seller. It also launched a new political movement, the Anti-Masonic Party. The party ran candidates for president in 1828 and 1832 before disappearing from history, but not before it had gained the support of luminaries like John Quincy Adams and William H. Seward, who lived just down the road in Auburn, New York.

Canandaigua's involvement in the story was not over. A leader of the anti-Masons was Gideon Granger's son, Francis. In 1830, he unsuccessfully courted Morgan's widow. The comely Lucinda instead chose to become one of the multiple wives of another area resident, Joseph Smith, founder of the Church of Jesus Christ of Latter Day Saints (a.k.a., the Mormons).

When the Anti-Masons were absorbed into the Whigs, Francis became a Whig and rose to national prominence. In 1836, he was the Whig candidate for Vice President, running with General William Henry Harrison. This was the only time the election of the Vice President was thrown into the U.S. Senate for resolution, as no candidate won a majority of Electoral College votes. The Senate chose Richard Johnson over Granger to serve as President Martin Van Buren's Vice President.

Four years later, Harrison again was the Whig standard bearer. He wanted Granger to run with him again, but Francis declined. This proved a monumental mistake. Harrison's second choice, John Tyler, succeeded him as president 32 days after the inauguration (conducted in a driving snowstorm and lasting more than three hours) when Harrison became the first president to die in office. Tyler appointed Granger to his father's old post, a job he abandoned after only six months.

Non-religious Grete now found herself in a region where religion was a central preoccupation as well. The number of churchgoers in Canandaigua was something she had never encountered, not even in fervently Catholic Vienna, where secular sophistication tempered Sunday church attendance. In Canandaigua, it seemed as if every resident spent Sunday morning communing with his or her maker.

This was nothing new to the region. The Finger Lakes earned its nineteenth century appellation—the "Burnt-Over District"—as a result of the white-hot religious intensity that consumed Western New York. The area's religious zeal took root very early. Several movements that originated here deserve mention.

The Publick Universal Friend

Jemima Wilkinson styled herself the "Publick Universal Friend." She was one of the first to realize that one could make a lucrative career out of prophesying.

In 1774, age 16, she became so ill that she was laid out in her parents' parlor, surrounded by grieving relatives in anticipation of her imminent death. At the stroke of midnight, she opened her eyes, leaped out of bed, knelt in prayer and proclaimed in a different voice from before that she had been raised from the dead and was now infused with the divine spirit. She said she had a calling to preach God's word. For the next 13 years, she traveled all over Connecticut, Pennsylvania and New York accumulating followers, riding in a horse cart with "P.U.F." engraved on its side.

In 1789-90, she sent scouts to look for land upon which to build the "New Jerusalem." They reported that the Finger Lakes were ideal. The "Friend" and her followers relocated to the shores of Keuka Lake, a few miles from Canandaigua. Jemima now turned to converting the Iroquois. She was unsuccessful, having built "Jerusalem" on land purchased from speculators without bothering to settle Seneca claims.

She published a book, *Friend's Advice*, full of empty aphorisms that make Mao Tse-tung's *Little Red Book* seem like a wellspring of deep thoughts.

Jemima shunned hard work. Like Tom Sawyer, she was skilled at getting others to toil for her. Nevertheless, she proclaimed that Jerusalem was open to all who were willing to work hard. Meanwhile, she lived sumptuously.

She ruled with a firm fist. Her followers were prohibited from marrying; those already married had to live apart. Her purpose was to become her followers' sole heir; many left her all of their property. Unfortunately for her, the frontier was rapidly becoming one where the rule of law prevailed. A Canandaigua court invalidated many of these dubious bequests.

Jemima's courtroom experiences did not end there. An acolyte she labeled the "Prophet Elijah" put on a tight girdle before publicly preaching. During his presentations, his stomach swelled from the constricting girdle, a "miracle" he attributed to being "filled with prophetic visions." This was too much for the authorities. Jemima was tried for blasphemy in Canandaigua. She was acquitted on a technicality.

She was the "Publick Universal Friend" in one sense. Despite publicly renouncing sex, she was insatiable, frequently caught *in flagrante* with both sect members and outsiders.

Jemima died for real in 1819 and her Friends' movement (not to be confused with the Quakers) soon disappeared.

The Mormons

In 1827, young Joseph Smith announced to the world that he was the prophet of a new religion. In September 1823, Smith, who lived just north of Canandaigua, was hiking on Hill Cumorah, a low-rising glacial drumlin adjacent to the Canandaigua Road. Reaching the summit, he fell asleep and received a vision in which the Angel Moroni appeared and told him where to find a buried set of golden plates containing the Book of Mormon.

This did not create quite the stir that Smith anticipated. The Finger Lakes had a long history by then of being a hotbed of new religions and the occult. Crying Madonnas, channelers, oil stains on the roads resembling Jesus, rapping interpreters and assorted others were abundant.

Smith had tried his hand at a number of entrepreneurial ventures: alchemy, divining rods, and so forth. They were non-starters. This time he felt he had been guided by a divine hand.

Western New York's disinterest was ultimately Utah's gain. Smith left the area and set up shop first in Ohio, then Missouri, and finally in Nauvoo, Illinois where he and his brother were killed by a mob. He was mourned by his 44 wives and indeterminate number of children. Following his death, Brigham Young took over leadership of the movement as well as many of Smith's wives and children and led them into the Utah desert.

The Mormons come back to the Canandaigua area every summer where they stage an impressive, 800-actor sound-and-light show on Hill Cumorah.

Who's That Rapping?

Spiritualism garnered two million followers worldwide before fading into obscurity. The movement derived from rappings heard by the two Fox sisters of Newark, a few miles from Canandaigua, and the foresight of a third sister who took the rapping show on the road and charged admission. The sisters claimed the rappings were made by one John Bell, who told them he had been murdered in their home years before. When the house was eventually torn down, a skeleton was unearthed beneath its foundation.

Millenarianism

The Burnt-Over District was not done. Another global religious excitement, still thriving today, also originated there. In 1818, William Miller announced that the Second Coming was just down the temporal road. His Old Testament studies revealed that the end of the world would occur in 1843. His prediction led to a paid national lecture tour.

As the End Time neared, Miller's predictions became more precise. The last day was going to be April 21, 1843. As the date approached, his followers gave up all of their worldly possessions, ignored their children, neglected their farms and abandoned their businesses. That evening, they went to bed convinced they would wake up in heaven.

When they woke up in their own beds the next morning, they were understandably disappointed. Miller, however, was ready with an answer. He said he had erred in his calculations because he had mistakenly used the Hebrew rather than the Roman calendar. The new Advent would take place on October 22, 1844.

Possessions were divested in anticipation of The Rapture. On October 23, deep disappointment set in once again.

Miller apologized, blamed another calculation error, and threw himself on the now less-than-tender mercies of public opinion. Amazingly, the doubling down that should have aroused skepticism did not. The next year, Miller's remaining followers held a convention and broke up into several groups distinguished by subtle doctrinal disputes. The most successful became the Seventh-Day Adventists.

The religious fever that consumed the Finger Lakes subsided, but not totally. The locals not only took their religion very seriously; they also tried to impose their theological preferences on others, including the handful of Jews living among them. Grete, Ernest and I experienced this occasionally. It made for some discomfort and isolation, although my father dealt with it very well, essentially by ignoring it. Grete not so well.

Grete and God

Grete's religious indifference began early. She and her siblings never went to synagogue, although her father did on occasion. Home life did not include candle lighting on Friday nights or even during Hanukah. Passover seder rituals were cut short by tempting kitchen smells.

Well into her nineties, Grete fasted on *Yom Kippur*, the Jewish Day of Atonement. Her atoning had little to do with religion, however, but rather with survivor guilt.

The Holocaust squeezed whatever remnant of religious belief she might have retained out of her forever. Because I was around, Ernest paid lip service to Jewish ritual, which largely amounted to lighting Hanukah candles and singing "Rock of Ages" in Hebrew. My parents sent me to Sunday school at the makeshift temple (a former Hobart College fraternity house) in nearby Geneva that served the sparse Jewish population of five counties. I stayed with it until my Bar Mitzvah. Grete, not very up on Jewish dietary taboos, served German potato salad spiced with bacon bits at my post-Bar Mitzvah temple reception. The rabbi told her it was the best potato salad he ever tasted.

An incident in the mid-1950s confirmed Grete's contempt for what she considered irrational Jewish religious practices. Ernest's maternal Uncle Shani and Aunt Therese ("Rezi") had escaped from Wiener Neustadt and ended up in Washington Heights in upper Manhattan, at the time heavily populated by Jewish refugees. They looked like caricatures of Eastern European *shtetl* Jews, dressed from head to toe in black with all of the Orthodox trappings.

On a trip to New York City, we visited them and, at Uncle Shani's urging, took Aunt Rezi back with us to Canandaigua for several weeks. The next Saturday morning, Grete and I went out in our backyard to do yard work. Sweaty and filthy, we went back to the house at noon for a lunch break. However, the kitchen door automatically locked when closed and Grete had forgotten her keys. We saw Aunt Rezi through the window sitting on a chair facing us. We banged on the door and shouted that she should unlock it and let us in. "I cannot until sundown," she said. "It's *Shabbat* (Sabbath)."

Aunt Rezi interpreted the prohibition on working during Shabbat to mean that she could not even open a door. Despite our entreaties, she would not budge. We did not get back inside until Ernest came home at 7 PM and had to restrain my mother from throwing Aunt Rezi out on the spot. Grete invoked that incident for years whenever she felt the urge to inveigh against Orthodox Judaism and its lack of relevance to the real world.

Despite her antipathy to organized religion, Grete had some spiritual inklings. She occasionally read a book about a particular religion and expressed admiration for its inherent logic, always adding that it was a stark contrast to the world's major organized faiths. Buddhism and Bahai'ism intrigued her. She even had a brief flirtation with Unitarianism. Despite these occasional temptations, she never took an affirmative step toward any of them. Strangely, she and Ernest visited Catholic shrines—Lourdes, Fatima, Sainte-Anne-de-Beaupré—more out of curiosity than otherwise.

Canandaigua Post-Burning

Life in Canandaigua calmed down a bit after the Burnt-Over District largely burned itself out. Alexis de Tocqueville visited in 1831 during his tour of American prisons. He was hosted by John Canfield Spencer, a local lawyer with two daughters so alluring that de Tocqueville cut short his visit and left town abruptly, unable to concentrate on his work in the face of such beauty. Back in Paris, he wrote the classic, *Democracy in America*. Spencer became his American publisher.

Stephen A. Douglas graduated from Canandaigua Academy in 1831, studied law under a local attorney, and spent several years practicing in town before moving to Illinois.

Eleven years later, Spencer's son Philip, also a Canandaigua Academy graduate, was a 19-year old ensign serving on the *U.S.S. Somers*, a Navy ship returning home from Africa when he was accused of mutiny and hung from the yardarm without a formal court-martial. This was and still is the only mutiny in U.S. Navy history. At the time, his father was U.S. Secretary of War. Young Spencer's hanging had two major impacts: Herman Melville took the story—heard from a cousin aboard the Somers—and based his novel *Billy Budd* on it; and the U.S. Naval Academy at Annapolis, Maryland was established to train young naval ensigns so that they might avoid Philip's fate.

Nothing much of interest happened again in Canandaigua until 1873, when Susan B. Anthony was tried and convicted in Canandaigua's county courthouse for voting in the 1872 presidential election, an illegal act at the time. The Women's Movement began in nearby Seneca Falls in the 1840s under the joint leadership of Elizabeth Cady Stanton and Ms. Anthony. Today, the Women's National Historical Park in Seneca Falls is run by the National Park Service as a shrine to the movement.

Canandaigua in the twentieth century receded into backwater status. Humphrey Bogart spent his childhood and adolescent summers on the lake. His parents owned a mansion there and his grandparents ran the Canandaigua Hotel. Howard Samuels, a local friend of both Ernest and my father-in-law, Jim Canali, ran for Governor of New York after he and his brother made millions inventing the plastic clothes line when they returned from the Second World War. That was about it.

Chapter 57
The Chosen People in the Chosen Place

In the Seneca language, "Kanandarque"—Canandaigua—means "the chosen place." Grete could not imagine what the town could possibly have been chosen for other than incessant gossip. For Grete, life in a little American town was like living in another universe. She never got over that feeling. She was always a big city girl through and through.

Canandaigua had one big advantage: natural beauty. Its location on the north shore of its namesake lake is gorgeous. From its stately Main Street leading down a gently sloping hill to the lake, to its Sonnenberg estate built by Frederick Ferris Thompson (one of the founders of both J.P. Morgan and what is now Citigroup), to its campus-like Veterans Administration Hospital that has been home to thousands of veterans with mental problems, Canandaigua was and is a very pretty little town.

Driving south along the lake, the scenery is spectacular. The Helderberg Escarpment rises 2,000 feet above the waters. Europeans who visit call the lake the "Rhine of America."

The area's natural beauty, however, was not enough for Grete. She arrived in town with all the preconceived notions about the provinces and never really gave the locals a chance. It was not easy in 1948 being a newly-arrived refugee with a heavy German accent, Jewish to boot, and without a driver's license, toting around a baby, living in two small rooms, and trying to lend support to a husband struggling to earn a living.

Being Jewish in a community that had little knowledge of or interaction with Jews was discomfiting. We viewed ourselves as separate from the majority, Grete and I more so than my father. She believed she lived among strangers who would never understand her.

Despite being a physician and specialist, she was never able to achieve co-equal status with her husband. Instead, her husband's health, well-being and comfort became her priorities.

Professionally, she was frustrated. Although she was the only trained anesthesiologist in the area, she was rarely asked to assist in surgeries. Gender discrimination was rampant among the local physicians. Instead, outside of Ernest and one or two others, the local surgeons used their untrained male pals who messed up many an anesthesia. Grete never lost or disabled a surgical patient.

Her light surgical load prompted her to look for other ways to supplement her limited hours. One was to work in Ernest's office in an administrative and nursing capacity, which she did for approximately ten years. Until I became old enough to take over, she also was the office janitor, going in on Sundays to sweep, dust, and mop.

She took a part-time job as the Canandaigua Academy (my alma mater) school physician. I pumped her for information about what certain girls looked like *déshabillée*, for which I invariably received a dope slap on the head. She kept that job until Ernest retired.

Chapter 58
Friends

Grete did not make friends easily and never had very many in Canandaigua. However, she was very close to the friends she did make. Her best friend was Mimi Buxbaum, Henry's wife. Mimi was a martyr, putting up with Henry being a test of character . . . or something. He was the most impulsive human being I have ever met while also being one of the best and most fascinating. He treated me like a son and was always there for me, especially when my parents were away. When my back went out one summer, Henry appeared several times a day with medications and food. One day he came in with a basketful of grapes he had helped himself to from a fruit farm, dodging grapeshot from the farmer's shotgun.

Late in life, Henry became obsessed with art and began collecting, overwhelming his house with paintings, sculpture and artifacts. His tastes were eclectic because he was literally interested in everything. He haunted Madison Avenue galleries in New York, as well as Sotheby's and Christie's art auctions, and amassed a collection that became very valuable. On one of his trips to New York, he encountered an impoverished German expatriate artist, Carl Heidenreich, a talented modernist whom he brought home with him. Mimi had no say in the matter. Heidenreich lived with the Buxbaums for several years and left Henry several hundred of his works.

Henry was not only my father's best friend, but one of mine, too. He was acquainted with a fascinating cast of characters, including Vladimir Nabokov (the author of *Lolita*) and

Professor Hannah Arendt (author of *Eichmann in Jerusalem: The Banality of Evil*). I got to meet and talk with both of them through Henry.

He had enormous respect for my mother and demonstrated that in many ways, asking her advice on a range of topics, both personal and professional. While my mother and Henry were great friends, Grete sympathized with Mimi's plight and became her go-to person whenever the pressure of living with Henry became too much.

Marie Graham was the first Canandaiguan who befriended Grete and became Ernest and Grete's first landlord. She was a Christian Science elder. Years later, when we lived across the street from the Church of Christ Scientist, Grete volunteered me to shovel its walkway and steps early every Sunday morning in winter. I was not paid and fantasized about spreading aspirin in front of the steps so that the worshippers would not be able to cross the threshold.

Marie was a very aristocratic lady. The fact that Grete and Ernst were both Jewish refugees from Europe who spoke English with heavy accents was immaterial to her.

Blatant prejudice was not very common in Canandaigua, principally because there were few objects against which it could be directed: organizations that were closed to Italians, Jews, and Blacks; a handful of Jews; and only one, very poor African-American family. Grete would from time-to-time put together a bag of clothing or groceries to give to the mom. Grete never thought in terms of someone's pride being an inhibitor to good works. If she saw that someone needed something, she did whatever was necessary to see that they had it. She performed her charitable work privately and unobtrusively, never seeking recognition or praise for it.

Another friend was a seemingly jovial woman who often brought produce from her garden to Grete. Their friendship blossomed over the years into a mutual admiration society. In the late 1970s, prompted by a severely strained marriage, the woman poured gasoline over herself in her yard and lit a match. Grete was devastated. Despite having endured so much death and destruction in her life, her friend's suicide shook her to her core.

This friend was one of several who took their own lives. Lola, a Holocaust refugee, was the wife of a physician 30 miles north of Canandaigua on the shores of Lake Ontario. This good-looking, boisterous, heavy-set woman shocked Grete when she saw that Lola had become a shadow of herself, thin to the point of anorexia, her *zaftig* figure a distant memory. Grete worried a great deal about her and was not all that surprised when she took her own life.

One of Grete and Ernest's friends who visited us several times in the early 1950s was a very handsome Viennese man named Max. He had gone through school with Ernest. He failed to revive his acting career after escaping from Europe. In 1955, he sat in a bathtub, put a plastic bag over his head, and suffocated himself. His suicide note said he had nothing to live for anymore.

Chapter 59
Refugee Quest

Standard Refugee Operating Procedure

Ernest and Grete made it a point to seek out the broader European refugee community scattered around Western New York. Their procedure when they heard of a new refugee family in the area was to pick up several bags of groceries and sweets and head out on Sunday afternoon to track down the newcomers. Grete believed heaps of food were the most effective icebreaker when meeting new immigrants whom she was certain had experienced hunger and even starvation in the years prior to their arrival on these shores.

This way my parents accumulated a large and diverse circle of friends, many of whom had survived the Holocaust. They numbered Jews and non-Jews from all over Europe—Germany, Austria, Scandinavia, Britain, the Low Countries, France, Italy, Spain, Russia, Ukraine, Poland, Czechoslovakia, Yugoslavia, Bulgaria, Romania, the Baltic States, even Turkey. Most were either highly educated or had seen their education frustrated when the Nazis marched into their countries. They included physicians, lawyers, scientists, typesetters, piano tuners, journalists, musicians, dancers, and many others.

The discussions that dominated these get-togethers ranged all over in terms of geopolitics and touched on science, mathematics, politics, and even sex. I would sneak around our house listening in, fascinated by their stories.

Back in the DDR

One family, the Ks, materialized in Canandaigua around 1950. They left Germany in the late 1930s and wandered all over Europe with their two very young children, hiding out for years while the Nazi killing machine tried to track them down. For a time after the war, they were in a displaced persons camp in Europe.

Dr. K was a psychologist at Canandaigua's Veterans Administration psychiatric hospital. The job paid a respectable wage and came with subsidized housing on the VA grounds.

The parents were a dour, embittered couple, angry and dissatisfied with everything—American society, their occupations (I don't remember what Frau K did), the schools, the lack of culture, etc. They were outspoken defenders of Communism, which begged the question why they had not headed East. They pronounced every aspect of American life decadent and deemed American society rotten to the core. Their criticisms reached a crescendo one Sunday afternoon at our house, both of them literally shouting their condemnations of America, which elicited considerable push-back from the other guests.

Two weeks later, they were expected at another gathering of the regional refugee group, but did not show up. The next morning, Dr. K did not show up for work. No one knew what had happened to them until, several weeks later, they and their children appeared on the nightly television news, paraded in front of the cameras by Walter Ulbricht, the premier of the Soviet East German puppet state! The Ks had defected to East Germany. This was the 1950s, when thousands of East Germans were escaping to the West every week, risking their lives to get to freedom. Very few people traveled in the other direction.

Newark State School

Ernest was the visiting (volunteer) ophthalmologist at Newark State School, a mental institution in neighboring Wayne County. The institution's original name was "Newark State School for Mental Defectives." The "school" was actually a campus with four large main buildings and a number of Quonset huts that provided temporary housing for staff.

I often accompanied my father to Newark when my mother was working. By the 1950s, the place had been "humanized" to some extent, but straitjacketed patients and residents who roamed the halls aimlessly or crouched against the corridor walls staring vacantly and babbling incoherently or screaming were routine sights.

For its time, Newark State School was considered a progressive institution. Many residents were trained in basic occupational skills and were able to move into group homes and work at low-skills jobs such as cleaning houses and in hospital housekeeping departments.

Sidebar: Ernest harbored a certain morbid fascination for mental institutions. Once, while visiting a refugee physician in Beacon, New York, a small city on the east bank of the Hudson River, our host took my father and me on a tour of Mattewan State Hospital for the Criminally Insane. This Dickensian institution made Newark look like a luxury spa.

The Grandparents and the Vampire

Through his work at Newark, Ernest met two other Holocaust refugee doctors, Dr. J from Ukraine and Dr. S from Transylvania, that land of darkness and castles perched precariously on Carpathian crags. Grete and Ernst welcomed both families into the refugee circle.

We spent many a pleasant Sunday afternoon and evening at the Js' Quonset hut home on the Newark grounds. Unlike many treks around the region to commune with refugees, I always looked forward to these visits because Dr. and Mrs. J. were like grandparents to me, taking an interest in my activities and saving postage stamps from their world-wide correspondence for my collection.

Despite suffering under the Soviet regime, followed by the Nazis and their brutal Ukrainian allies, and then once again under Stalin, the Js were "glass-half-full" people. They were eternal optimists, convinced that a better world awaited them and their three-generation family in the United States. They were grateful to have survived and made it to the Land of the Free.

Dr. S was their polar opposite. He was a miserable character who took every opportunity to bad-mouth his adopted country and its "shallow, superficial, ignorant, uncultured" people. Nothing was as good as it had been in Romania.

This was pretty astounding given that he, his pretty little wife and daughter had survived the war because of the remoteness of their mountain village with only one road in and out. Even at a young age, I could tell that something was not right between him and his wife. At social gatherings, he spoke in a deep bass reminiscent of every Dracula B-movie ever made, while she kept quiet, a meek little background figure, a nodding prop to his ravings.

The very first time we encountered him, we arrived in front of his Quonset hut with a load of groceries. It was just after sunset on a moonless night. As we pulled up in front of the hut, a tall, angular figure burst out of the front door and approached the car. To my fertile imagination, it appeared that he was floating just off the ground because I could not see his feet over the car window sill. He was uncommonly pale, his face a stark contrast to his black garb and the blacker night. He wore a billowing black cape with a high collar. He opened the passenger side door and put out a bony white hand with long fingers for Grete to take. Baring his sparkling large white teeth, he said "Good evening" in a heavy East European accent. Straight out of central casting.

While Dr. S and his family attended events hosted by their neighbors, the Js, they never made the short drive to Canandaigua to attend the refugee gatherings at our house.

Several years later, Dr. S's wife filed for divorce. She alleged that he beat her and their daughter and was a merciless domestic dictator. They moved away and that was the last we heard of them. I don't recall ever seeing teeth marks on her neck.

Savona Roland

One of our Sunday excursions into the hinterlands in search of newly-arrived refugees was to Savona, a small village about 90 minutes from Canandaigua isolated deep in New York's Southern Tier. How a Holocaust refugee doctor wound up in such an out-of-the-way place remains a mystery.

The trip turned out to be the second and last failure in Grete and Ernest's quest for new members of the refugee circle (Dr. S being the first). Savona and this physician and his family were not exactly a match made in heaven.

The family surname was "Benedict," not the best name to bring to the American provinces. The only Benedict known to the locals was Benedict Arnold, the Revolutionary War traitor. But that was only the tip of the really bad karma iceberg. Dr. B's first name was "Adolf," the most despised first name on the post-war planet.

Could it get worse? Absolutely! Not only did Dr. B share Hitler's first name; he could have been his twin. The unruly shock of black hair falling over one eye. The funny little square, black mustache. The abrupt arm gestures. All that were missing were a swastika armband, jodhpurs and jackboots.

Dr. Benedict was also Jewish. (You see, Einstein, God does play dice with the universe).

When we arrived at the B's home, I was sent outside to play with their son, who was burdened with the singularly un-American name of "Roland." When it was time for dinner, his mother stood on her front stoop and shrieked at the top of her ample lungs: "ROWWW-LANT! MALZEIT!" (supper time). Yet another way not to endear oneself to suspicious provincials.

The dinner was awkward and came to an abrupt end when Ernest, who often lacked a filter, suggested to Dr. B that he consider changing his hairstyle, shaving off his mustache, and toning down the mannerisms. We were quickly ushered out and never saw the Bs again. A few months later, we heard that they had left Savona for parts unknown.

Stern, Stürm und Drang

Most of the refugee circle, in contrast, consisted of people who got on quite well with Grete and Ernest and one another. There were the Korpells, who lived in a Rochester suburb an hour away. Grete Korpell had been one of Ernest's girlfriends in Vienna. She was a talented potter. Her husband, Fred, had been in the middle of his medical school education when the Nazis marched in and dismissed all Jewish students from the University. Once in the United States, he was too poor to resume his studies, so he became a printer and tuned pianos on the side. His incomplete education vexed him, but he was too proud to show it. He was largely self-educated and knew a prodigious amount about a great many subjects.

Like so many parents, he and his wife lived vicariously through their children's accomplishments. Both kids, an older boy and younger girl, were gifted musically and were also excellent students. The boy became a psychiatrist. The girl became a professor at a Midwest college and married another academic.

Franz and Doret S and their son, Danny, were also unusual, not at all fitting in with the expectations of rural America. Franz was German-Jewish, carried himself like a caricature of a

Prussian Junker replete with head thrown back to support a monocle, and strutted around with a pocket watch and chain hanging from his vest.

Doret was fascinating. She was part Jewish, part Turkish, and looked like a hot (very hot) Circassian or Gypsy beauty, with smoldering black eyes, a fabulous complexion and reddish-blond hair atop a terrific body. Her volatility added to her allure. I witnessed many arguments over nothing between Franz and Doret, all of which ended with her storming out of the room, sashaying her hips in a way that halted all conversation among the men present.

The S's also came burdened with financial problems, unable to rise to the same economic level they had enjoyed in Europe. I suspect that their many clashes had a lot to do with their financial circumstances.

Danny was the apple of their eyes, just like the Korpell progeny. He was a musical prodigy and enjoyed a career as the conductor of a symphony orchestra. His daughter is today a virtuoso violinist.

The Einstein of Granger Street

Max and Juliana Bruck became very close friends of Grete and Ernest. They started their American saga in tiny Naples, New York, the town at the southern tip of Canandaigua Lake (I was going to say the "foot" of the lake, but the southern ends of the Finger Lakes are actually the heads—water flows into the lakes from streams to their south and flows out into streams at their north ends). After a number of years, they moved to Canandaigua and lived around the corner from us. Max was a psychiatrist at the VA Hospital and Juliana was a nurse at our local hospital. This was a second marriage for her, her first husband having perished in the Holocaust. She had one son, Leo, who, following a succession of boarding schools, including military academies, moved to Switzerland and became a hugely successful international oil trader.

Juliana was a wonderful woman who became my *de facto* aunt. She was selfless, always upbeat despite the tribulations she had endured, and was a warm-hearted, non-judgmental human being of the finest character. Grete liked her very much.

Max was, well, a character. Psychoanalysis was his vocation, but mathematics, puzzles and daydreaming "Big Thoughts" were his much more interesting avocations. Whenever I was at his house, he challenged me with puzzles and math problems. He also had a lively correspondence with Thomas Szasz, a world-renowned psychiatrist, and also with Albert Einstein. In later life, Max claimed credit for having given Einstein the idea that led to the General Theory of Relativity.

My mother labeled Max "a typical German oddity." My grandfather, David, offered a livelier description that requires some knowledge of both Yiddish and German idiom: "*Nicht ein großer Chochem und nicht ein kleiner Narr.*" Translated: "Not a great wise man and not a little fool."

Mensa and Nonsense

Some refugee acquaintances stayed just that—acquaintances—never really becoming friends. One such family lived in Ithaca, 75 minutes from Canandaigua. I don't remember their names, only their pretensions. The father was a Cornell professor; the mother worked in the university's administrative office. Their only child, a son, was yet another musical prodigy. Both parents were members of Mensa, the society of egotists whose membership qualification is a high IQ. Forget for the moment that IQ tests have been largely debunked. Just like the Scholastic Aptitude Test, it has been shown time and time again that you can study for an IQ test and improve your score which, of course, undercuts the whole notion of a measurable IQ that means much.

The Ithaca Mensa-ites were insufferable. They literally had Mensa'd their house to a fault, decorating it with all sorts of silly-looking plaques and mementos announcing their superior intellects to their guests. When we left and drove home, Grete said: "I hope we never have to see those obnoxious people again." For her, that was a resounding condemnation completely out of character. Our first visit to their house was also our last.

The Jewish Anti-Mother

At this time in my young life, my mother was convinced that, with good fortune, my intellectual and cultural mediocrity would not hold me back so far that I would have to be institutionalized. Grete and Ernest were old first-time parents and their attitudes toward children were formed by their own experiences growing up in a sophisticated city awash in high culture. In their eyes, they had tried and failed to mold me into an intellectual. This was despite dragging me to operas, symphonic concerts and art museums. Nothing stuck. Mickey Mantle's 1956 triple crown meant much more to me than an evening with Pierre Monteux or Rembrandt van Rijn. The sports section of the *New York Times* was my principal reading material in those years, not the great literature, art and music compendia that dominated our bookshelves.

They thought I was a hopeless case. Whenever this was underscored by a visit to the home of a prodigy whose parents bragged incessantly in front of us about junior's epic achievements, Grete cringed and looked at me with what I can only term pity, whether for her or me I don't know. When I first saw *I, Claudius*, the wonderful public television series about ancient Rome, I was probably one of only a handful of viewers who identified closely with the bumbling, stumbling Claudius (played so brilliantly by Derek Jacoby).

I have only touched upon a handful of the refugee circle personalities my parents cultivated. There was a Greek accountant and his very alluring physician wife who obviously disliked her husband and flirted with everybody, including me when I became old enough to be interesting. Another member,

Karl Drechsler, was a lifelong friend of Ernest's dating back to his kindergarten days. Karl was an attorney who wrote labor law summaries for Lawyers Cooperative Publishing Company in Rochester (now a subsidiary of Thomson Reuters, the same company that bought my business). His much younger, stunning wife Irene was a delightful woman and the perfect mate for Karl.

Having lived in the Washington, DC area for most of my adult life, I have to marvel at the stimulating, vibrant circle that Grete and Ernest brought together in the American hinterlands. While I have an interesting and terrific group of friends, neither their diversity nor their histories can match my parents' refugee circle.

Chapter 60
American Provincial

For many years, we were the only 100 percent Jewish refugee family in Canandaigua. Both Grete and I felt out of place (Ernest not so much), a feeling reinforced on occasion by contact with other townsfolk. I was ashamed of (1) being Jewish, (2) having foreigners for parents, (3) that my parents were so much older than those of my contemporaries, and (4) that kids asked me why my parents "talked funny." I ached to be a 100 percent American boy. It took leaving town for college to open my eyes and allow my pride in my Jewish and foreign heritages to blossom.

The local school system did little to acknowledge that there might be students who were not practicing Christians. Christmas trees were ubiquitous in every classroom and carol singing at holiday time was mandatory. Oddly, my mother enjoyed being serenaded by the groups that came around at Christmas singing carols. It seems she and her sister Rose spent their youths going to Vienna's *Stephansdom* at holiday time for the singing.

The older I got, the less I participated in these public celebrations. My strategy was, first to mouth the words to the Christmas carols, then later to keep my mouth shut.

Mothering

Grete was both an older wife and mother and a *European* one, a decidedly different species from her American counterparts. Her notions of spousal responsibilities were those she brought with her from Europe: subservience to her husband; total responsibility for the home, including cooking and cleaning; and only rarely debating her spouse or challenging and countering his opinions with her own.

This led to some extreme behaviors, many of which were out of character for someone who had demonstrated her mettle first in a male-dominated medical school and later in getting her parents and herself out of Vienna.

For example, she did not learn to drive or obtain a driver's license until she was in her early 50s. Until then, she was wholly dependent on Ernest for transportation. However, she did not dare ask him to drive her anywhere. In her early years in Canandaigua, she walked two miles down a hill to the A&P supermarket once each week for groceries, with her little boy in tow, and then carried heavy grocery bags back up the hill with a whiny child clutching her skirts, demanding to be carried. It would have been a simple matter to ask Ernest to drive her when he came home from his office or on a Saturday afternoon after his work week was over. It never occurred to her to make the request.

Her mothering philosophy was also European, Viennese to be more precise. She grew up in a music-saturated environment in which opera was as central as Major League Baseball is to us, concert-going as obsessive as Sunday football on TV, and the great Viennese composers—Mozart, Beethoven, Shubert, Brahms, the Strausses, Mahler et al.—were the iconic equivalents of Joe DiMaggio, Jim Brown and Bill Russell. She failed to understand that my interests gravitated toward Yankee Stadium rather than Carnegie Hall and threw up her hands in despair when she saw me reach for the sports section when Ernest came home with the *New York Times* in tow.

Most European parents paid little attention to their children until they became sufficiently interesting as late teenagers and young adults able to discourse intelligently. Grete, however, did the opposite because she perceived me to be on a path to perdition. She became very "hands-on," in modern parlance a "helicopter" parent when it came to academics and culture. She read to me and forced me to read "serious" literature on my own (along with my "low-brow" material). She encouraged me to collect stamps and wrote to her friends and relatives around the world to save their country's stamps for me. I did not need much encouragement, being avidly interested in the stories stamps could tell. I learned more about history, geography and current events from stamps than I ever learned in 20 years of formal education.

My mother never attended a PTA meeting, did not involve herself in any school activities, and only came to one of my school athletic events (and embarrassed me when she ran out of the bleachers to take my pulse after I won a 440-yard race and broke the school record). She fretted that my education was not up to the European standard. She was absolutely correct about that—in my last semester of high school, I had two classes and six study halls. Her stop-gap solution was to assign me readings at home—*Crime and Punishment*, a heavy dose of Kafka, *The Rise and Fall of the Third Reich*, Proust's *Remembrance of Things Past* (I never got beyond page 8)—and forced two years of Latin on me, for which she borrowed books from my school and taught me herself.

Gregarious Ernest, in contrast, became quite the community leader. He served several terms as president of the American Field Service, a high school exchange program, taught a volunteer Physiology course at the high school in summer, and was an active Rotarian. His social skills were in marked contrast to Grete, who was very much a loner, was uncomfortable in public, and consistently fretted about social *faux pas*.

My parents' indifference when it came to my outside activities extended to the college application process, in which they played no role whatsoever. It was completely up to me where I applied. I visited a number of colleges by myself, and it never occurred to me to run my applications and essays by my parents. When I was accepted at Yale, Ernest's only comment was: "Too bad, I was hoping you would choose Cornell and its beautiful campus." Grete had no comment at all.

I did not discover how different my upbringing was, by American standards, until I was able to compare it with my college friends and Army buddies. As a child and adolescent, I was mortified by being different. It took maturity and exposure to the world outside Canandaigua to make me appreciate my parents and how they raised me.

Chapter 61
Making It in America

The Early Years

Our image of physicians today is of Mercedes, Porsches and Jaguars populating hospital parking lots. Despite their gripes about school loans et al., it is a fact that doctors today earn very good incomes. The average salary of anesthesiologists in 2017 was $370,000; ophthalmologists - $350,000. Not bad.

That was not always the case. When Ernest arrived in Canandaigua as the only board-certified ophthalmologist in a multi-county region, patients did not line up at his office door. He had to rent office space (for $80/month) in a run-down, dark, decrepit building. His patients had to negotiate 30 steep stairs, largely in the dark, to get to his floor, where they sat in a waiting room that looked more like the ante-room to a prison death chamber than a doctor's office. The furniture was second-hand and, in order to pay for equipment and instruments, Ernest had to beg, borrow and rely on the good offices of Henry Buxbaum and Harvey Jewett. Dr. Jewett took Ernest under his wing. He introduced him to local doctors as well as the staff at Canandaigua's Thompson Hospital and Rochester General Hospital.

For the first year of Ernest's practice, the only referrals he received were from Jewett and Buxbaum. There was suspicion among the locals about a Jewish refugee physician with a German name and heavy German accent suddenly appearing in a community dominated by White Anglo-Saxon Protestants and Irish and Italian Catholics, many of whom had never had any contact with Jews, much less German speakers, other than those who shot at them during the war. Religious discrimination was rarely overt, but the undertone was there. The irony, of course, was that Ernest and Grete were from Austria, not Germany, and barely escaped the Germans with their lives.

Nevertheless, as Ernest's capabilities came to be appreciated by his colleagues and the community, and as the temporal distance from World War II increased, his economic prospects improved. His engaging personality and avid curiosity about other people helped immensely.

The same kind of acceptance was never granted to Grete. In her case, the discrimination was primarily gender-based. She was rarely asked to assist with surgeries other than Ernest's and never came close to earning more than a pittance.

Despite straightened circumstances, Ernest impulsively bought a house in late 1948, exhausting his meager savings and borrowing the rest of the down payment of $3,200 from Grete's brothers. The house cost $14,000 and was located in one of the nicer parts of town, its expansive back yard bordered Canandaigua Academy, the local public high school.

The sellers were a family who had recently suffered a devastating loss: the death of their 16-year old daughter in an automobile accident just before dawn on Easter Sunday. Her father was president of a local bank. Neither he nor his wife could abide continuing to reside in Canandaigua. They had to get out and sold for a price significantly below market value.

The house was a large home with an interesting history. It was built in 1910 by John North Willys, a Canandaigua native who founded the Willys-Overland Automobile Company, for his mother. Willys later invented the Jeep, one of which I drove and loved during my Army service.

The house itself was originally constructed with moneyed people in mind. A huge basement contained a cast-iron boiler that would not have been out of place in Dr. Victor Frankenstein's basement laboratory. Ernest and I played table tennis next to the boiler, a before-dinner ritual I savored because it was the only sport my dad and I ever did together.

The most interesting feature of the basement was a 13-foot long Swiss *Alpenhorn* that was singularly out of place in Canandaigua. I never could get a sound out of it. The only time it got played was when we hosted 17-year old Felix Kraus, the son of Herr and Frau Professors Kraus, Ernest and Grete's gymnasium teachers from Vienna. Felix was yet another musical prodigy and spent his career playing the oboe and English horn for the world-renowned Cleveland Orchestra.

The house had 10-foot ceilings, a large kitchen with a breakfast nook, a big walk-in pantry, large dining room, living room, music room, bathroom and three sizable porches on the first floor. The second floor had five spacious bedrooms and a sleeping porch, as well as two full bathrooms. The attic, which had been servants' quarters when Mrs. Willys lived there, had four additional bedrooms and a bathroom. It was much too big for a small family.

The former presence of servants was evident in several house features: a dumbwaiter, an intercom system that didn't work, a bell rung by a long rope chain used to summon the servants to the kitchen and best of all, a hidden stairwell that went from the kitchen all the way up to the attic, skirting the second floor so that the servants could go between the two without intruding on the family's private quarters. A terrific place to play for a kid.

While the house had more than its share of unique features designed for an era long-gone, it was run down, which contributed to its low price. It needed a great deal of work, most of which never got done in the 15 years we lived there. Nevertheless, it was a wonderful house in which to grow up and its many oddities and mysteries contributed a great deal to the development of a child's fevered imagination.

"Socialized" Medicine

My dad's avid interest in other people had two consequences: first, we never ran out of table topics (I don't remember a single instance of an awkward pause in any dinner conversation); and second, Ernest's medical practice never reached the financial heights that post-war doctors, eventually fueled by Medicare, took for granted as their birthright. He spent so much time "schmoozing" with patients that he never was able to see very many in a day. By the time a patient left his office, Ernest had thoroughly imprinted his or her life story in his mind. When he came home after work, he regaled Grete and me with what he had learned. This added greatly to the rich tapestry of our lives.

Money was important, but only to the extent it was needed to provide the basics of existence plus a little extra. I discovered many years later that Ernest and Grete's highest combined annual income was $60,000 in his last year in practice (1973), much more than enough for a very comfortable life. He achieved that thanks largely to Medicare, which was launched in 1965.

One of the means that the U.S. Department of Health, Education and Welfare (HEW) employed to determine how much to pay healthcare providers for specific Medicare services was a questionnaire. One question asked how much Ernest charged for cataract surgery: $200. Several months later, a form letter from HEW Secretary Joseph Califano arrived, informing physicians what they would receive for their services from Medicare. For cataracts, the government would pay $600 in Western New York. Ernest was stunned and wrote Califano, stating that Medicare would be grossly overpaying providers. He got no response. The American Medical Association, which had fought Medicare tooth-and-nail ever since 1948, arguing that it was "socialized medicine," kept mum.

Medicare cost taxpayers $3 billion in 1966. The government estimated that, allowing for inflation, it would cost $12 billion by 1990. In 1990 Medicare actually cost $107 billion. Today: $579 billion.

Impulse Buy

In 1955, a new patient, Tom Roberts, came to Ernest's office to have a foreign body in his eye removed. Extracting the offending item took only a few minutes, but Mr. Roberts was in the office for over an hour while Ernest cross-examined him on his history. Roberts had been New York Governor Thomas E. Dewey's Secretary of Labor and now owned a summer home on Canandaigua Lake.

Much more interesting to my dad was the fact that Roberts was desperate to sell his lake property and move to San Diego where he and his wife (novelist Rae Potter Roberts) had a daughter and grandchildren. The house was not yet on the market, but Roberts was under great pressure from his wife to find a buyer.

Ernest was not usually impulsive. Before making a big decision, he would sit by himself in a quiet room and weigh the pluses and minuses, often toting the pros and cons in writing. Nevertheless, for possibly only the second time in his life (the first being reading the London *Times* article about Lady Mountbatten), he acted impulsively, telling Roberts he might be interested in buying his cottage. They met there as soon as Ernest cleared his waiting room.

Ernest bought "Idlewood" (Canandaigua Lake cottages often had names . . . my wife spent her summers at her extended family's "Maintop") on the spot for $11,000, a bargain. This time he did not need to borrow money. He had paid Ben and Otto back for their 1948 home loans years before. In the interim, he had saved and invested well and had enough cash on hand to write a check to Roberts. Only years later did Grete discover that, in so doing, Ernest had depleted their savings.

He came home that evening and announced that we now owned a lake house. Grete was shocked, angry that Ernest would do such a rash thing without consulting her first, a resentment that transferred to her never really liking the place.

As if one unusual house was not enough, now my parents had added another. Idlewood was the oldest farm house on Canandaigua Lake, dating from the mid-nineteenth century. And it looked it. If the Main Street house was run down and needed an upgrade, Idlewood was a dump. It had no central heating. Water for bathing and flushing came directly out of the lake via a pump. The house did not need central air conditioning (unusual at that time anyway) because it was shaded by tall oaks, elms, maples and pines. It sat on a bluff overlooking the east side of the lake. Its 140 feet of lake frontage was accessible by a flight of stone steps leading down to a shale beach. One of its best features was a hard-packed, sandy lake bottom.

The lake back then was very clean. When swimming on a calm day, you could clearly see the bottom even in 20-30 feet of water. The lake is nowhere near as clean today, due to massive private development and escalating agricultural runoff.

The house came with all of its furniture and kitchen items, and included an extensive library that provided me with hours of reading pleasure. The layout was "farm-oriented," with a huge country kitchen, a large dining room with a heavy oak table that seated 16 people, and a big living room that ran the entire width of the house and led to an expansive porch overlooking the lake. The second floor, warped floors and all, contained seven bedrooms, three good size and four quite small. Those four did not have walls that went completely up to the ceiling, which meant that privacy was an issue. Female visitors dressed and undressed in them at their peril, given that there were often adolescent boys around adept at peeking over walls.

A chest at the foot of my bed contained memorabilia documenting Secretary Roberts' political career, including personal letters from Governor Dewey, Presidents Truman and Eisenhower, FDR's Labor Secretary Frances Perkins, Wendell Willkie and many other prominent people. Unfortunately, Grete, who abhorred clutter to the point where she spent much of her American life divesting herself of it, threw all of these collectables away.

When I came home from the Army, I found virtually all of my collections gone. My mother donated my library to the local community college. My baseball cards, shells, minerals, butterflies, sports trophies and other collections were gone, even my roll-top desk. Her justification: "I thought that if you got killed in Vietnam [my 'Nam orders were rescinded at the last minute], you would not need all this stuff." Strangely, the only trophy she kept was the "Proud Rifle" statue I received for being the top boot camp soldier at Fort Dix. She said that, if it had not been for mothers like her who had also discarded their sons' baseball cards, my collection—which included a 1951 Mickey Mantle Bowman rookie card and three 1952 Mantle Topps cards (today worth big money)—would be worthless!

Idlewood had an in-law "suite" off the kitchen, a long and large "ell" with a sunny bedroom/sitting room, its own bathroom, kitchen and dining area. It was a great place to hide out when I needed some privacy.

Idlewood's south side was a rat's maze of patios and grilling areas with a giant, built-in grill, worthy of the legendary Frank Pepe's New Haven pizza restaurant's monster oven. My parents never once fired it up, barbecuing not exactly being a Viennese Jewish pastime.

Ernest insisted on staying out at the lake even as the seasons changed, the weather turned inclement, and the house became colder. By the time we returned to our town home, it was often early November which, in those pre-global warming days, was frequently well into snow season. We ate some Idlewood meals wrapped in blankets.

By the time she approached her 60th birthday, Grete had become tired of carrying household items back and forth between the two houses. I kept asking Grete why she resisted having two sets of household items, one at each house? Her answer was illogical, but obviously deeply seated in the privations she and her family had suffered. There was no convincing her that a modest investment that would enable her to move seamlessly back and forth between houses without countless trips to town and back twice a year, hauling plates, cutlery, pots, pans, clothing, etc., was worth pursuing. She also was tired of traveling back and forth frequently for drinking water. She could not be convinced that a business-size water cooler could save her numerous trips.

One other problem Idlewood caused in Grete's mind was its attractiveness to visitors, principally family guests, some of whom—unlike Uncle Julius and Aunt Hedy and the Hirsely cousins from Chicago, all of whom we were always eager to see—arrived uninvited and stayed long. These visits generated a great deal of work for Grete, especially when guests would stream into the kitchen at all hours of the morning and want breakfast.

Consolidation

Ernest eventually succumbed to Grete's complaints and agreed to put both houses on the market and try to find a year-round home on the lake. I opposed my parents' intention to sell because I loved both houses and wanted to keep them in our family. They bought a relatively new house close to the north shore of the lake and moved in on the weekend immediately following the assassination of President Kennedy.

I don't know what the Main Street house is worth today, but the last time Idlewood changed hands, it was for $1.8 million. Whenever I pass by either house, I feel a sense of loss.

Grete and Ernest on their wedding day,
March 17, 1945, San Francisco
Author's collection

The San Andreas Fault,
the impetus for Grete insisting
that she and Ernest move
back to New York.
(*Source: maravilhas-
naturais.webnode.pt*)

South Main Street, Canandaigua, New York in the 1950s, where Grete and Ernest
lived for 30 years from 1948 to 1978.
(*Source: playle.com*)

Winter, 1947-48   Grete the "mom"   Summer, 1947

Ernest's father, Solomon Hermann, with (L to R) the author and Ernest's nephew, James Friend

Grete's father David with the author

Grete's mother Ernestine (a.k.a. Esther, a.k.a. "Grandma Tinnie") with the author

photos from author's collection

Chapter 62
Going Back

I never understood how Vienna's Jewish refugees could wax nostalgic about the city that, first, never fully welcomed them, abused them while they lived there, and then tried to kill them. Yet many ached for Vienna. Ernest certainly did. He was misty-eyed about its glories and did not want to think about its dark side.

Grete and Ernest first went back to Vienna in 1954. Like Germany and Berlin, Austria and Vienna had been partitioned among the victors of World War Two. The surprising difference was that the Soviets actually left Vienna and Austria voluntarily in 1955.

The Red Army captured Vienna on April 13, 1945 and established a Communist puppet government. The Allies objected, but the Soviets refused to allow Western power representatives to enter Vienna unless both the country and city were partitioned into four occupation zones. A partition agreement was reached on July 4. It differed in one respect from the parallel Berlin agreement, dividing Vienna into *five* zones, one each for the U.S.S.R., the U.S., Britain and France, and an International Zone that alternated among the four powers.

Austria was too small and insignificant to obsess even paranoid Joseph Stalin. It did not share a common border with the Soviet Union. It was not important enough for the Soviets to go to the trouble of subverting the government. Moreover, Stalin was persuaded by the KGB and GRU (Soviet Military Intelligence) that Austria's geographic position made Vienna an ideal place for "spy vs. spy" activities (they could not have been more correct). Consequently, the Soviets agreed to leave ten years after the occupation began.

Austria tried to pass itself off as Nazi Germany's first victim, a false proposition that the Austrians milked for all it was worth. They conveniently "forgot" that they welcomed the Nazis with wild enthusiasm unmatched anywhere else, Germany included. Moreover, after the war, more than 500,000 Austrians were subject to "denazification," a huge percentage of Austria's tiny population and, proportionately, far exceeding every other European country subject to Nazism, including Germany. Denazificiation, such as it was, had exhausted itself by the end of the four-power occupation in 1955.

This worked to Austria's advantage. Its denial of any guilt for what it had done to its Jews and other victims made it resist paying any reparations to them. It took more than 50 years and Herculean efforts by Stuart Eizenstat, President Jimmy Carter's chief domestic policy advisor, to persuade Austria to pay even nominal sums to only a handful of the people it persecuted, expelled or murdered beginning more than 60 years after the end of the war. By then, many of its victims were dead. The reparations were miniscule compared to what Germany, in contrast, felt was its moral obligation. Grete received $7,000 to compensate for the loss of her home, medical practice, her father's business, etc.

By the time Grete and Ernest returned to Vienna, Austria was doing quite well relative to the rest of Europe. Thanks to the Marshall Plan kick-starting the Austrian economy, its Gross Domestic Product increased 400 percent in just six years, and its location at the crossroads of Europe conferred numerous advantages. Western companies eager to do business with the Eastern Bloc congregated in Vienna, adding to the local economy and general prosperity.

Seeking the Vaunted Days of Yore

My parents stayed in Vienna for three weeks, walking through the rubble that still marked sections of the city, checking out old haunts, for which they had to show their passports and identity cards since Leopoldstadt was in the Soviet Zone. Their return was traumatic for both of them, but much more so for Grete.

In addition to spending time with Ernest's Aunts Rosl and Hilda, they were entertained by Viktor Frankl and his new wife. Ernest and Viktor reminisced about "old Vienna" while Grete watched, incredulous, at their *"herz-schmerz"* (literally "heart pain," but the broader meaning is the heartache accompanying Viennese sentimentality) tango. She could not understand how they could have any positive feelings for this town without pity that had done them so wrong.

Ernest came back to America pining for Vienna. He wallowed in the Viennese penchant for over-sentimentality. It did not take much for his eyes to well up over things most people would deem superficial. He even began making noises about returning to Vienna to live. Grete told him if he did, he would go alone.

Grete had no interest in ever going back again. Although she rarely stood up to Ernest (the San Andreas Fault aside), this was one issue where she took a stand. Every time my dad became wistful about Vienna, she reminded him in excruciating detail why they left. She was a cold-blooded realist about Vienna and every other aspect of life. She had no illusions about the state of the world, humanity, and the so-called advance of civilization, all of which she viewed with considerable skepticism. Give her Kafka over Schnitzler, Josef Roth over the over-emotional literary luminaries of the era.

Viktor Frankl

When I got to Vienna 12 years later, my main purpose was to find an answer to the perplexing question of Vienna's attraction for my father and his friend Viktor Frankl, the most eminent personage from his circle, who returned there after years in Auschwitz and other death camps. Viktor told me then that Vienna is the only "livable place conducive to my personality and work."

Viktor and Ernest continued to see each other whenever Ernest went back to Vienna, which he did frequently from 1954 on. Grete refused to go back again until 1966, when she did so only in deference to my desire to see her home town.

Viktor survived Auschwitz, attributing his defying death to the "self-therapy" he devised while incarcerated, from which he derived his best-selling work, *Man's Search for Meaning*, the "bible" of Logotherapy. I made sure to read the short book before meeting him and, frankly, got little out of it; upon rereading it much later in life I came to appreciate it more.

Rosl, Romy and Karli

Aunt Rosl—the youngest child of my dad's grandfather Edward Hermann's second marriage—moved back to Vienna from England after the war. Ernest and Aunt Rosl were very close, being only 10 years apart in age.

Rosl was still a beautiful woman in her early 70s and was on her fourth husband, a prominent Viennese newspaper publisher. The family scuttlebutt, true or not, was that Rosl had either been married to, or been the mistress of, all of the major Viennese newspaper publishers, a status that got her and her sister, Aunt Hilda, a pass to remain in England during the war.

After dinner at her lovely apartment, she treated us to tickets to the *Burgtheater*, where we saw Shakespeare's *Twelfth Night* performed in German. Seated directly in front of us was the international movie star, Romy Schneider, to whom we were introduced by Rosl during intermission. Romy was drop dead gorgeous, notwithstanding being seven months pregnant. Although she spoke English very well, I was speechless in her presence. I have absolutely no recollection what we talked about at intermission, only that she declined Ernest's offer to get her a glass of wine. Sadly, both Romy and the son she was carrying when we met her both came to a bad end, dying much too young.

The other Viennese whom we met and spent time with was a former neighbor of Grete and Rose growing up. Karl "Karli" Bauer was a Gentile *bon vivant*. We met him at the Hotel *Sacher* for tea and a slice of *Sachertorte*. I had never met anyone like him. He was dressed in a silk shirt with cufflinks that appeared to be pure gold, a blue polka-dot tie that would be the envy of Giorgio Armani, and a perfectly tailored blue blazer. He was a handsome 50-something, a rogue with wavy blond hair and a year-round tan. He was being "kept" by a Hungarian countess in a palace just outside Vienna and did not seem to have any gainful employment. The best we could get out of him was that he brokered "deals." When we parted, both Grete and Rose speculated that he had something slightly underhanded going on that had to do with espionage, not unusual in 1960s Vienna.

Impressions

By the time I left Vienna, I hated it and despised the Viennese even more than before. I found them fake and oily, oozing false empathy as easily as if it were sweat. It disgusted me that they greeted each other with "*Servus*," which translated means "your slave." Diminutives were rampant, too. Everyone seemed to have a "cutesy" nickname.

Grete took one book with her on our trip to Vienna: Joseph Roth's *The Radetzky March*, a poignant picture of the bygone world of Habsburg rule, a world that in some respects never existed and certainly did not exist for most Viennese Jews. Roth was so anguished by this "loss" and his inability to traverse the cultural abyss that foreclosed full Jewish participation in Austrian life that he drank himself to death in Paris in 1939 when he was only 45 years old.

The book takes its title from Johann Strauss the Elder's 1835 composition dedicated to Field Marshal Josef Radetzky, the most famous Austrian military leader of the nineteenth century. It is a stirring piece of martial music that still moves the easily moved Austrians to this day and is by tradition the last encore of the annual Vienna New Year's Concert performed by the Vienna Philharmonic, during which the conductor faces the audience and leads the enthusiastic Viennese in loud clapping to accompany the performance.

Clueless About the Nazi Hunter

Grete and I came away from our Vienna visit with one regret, although we did not come to regret it until years later. Our second evening at Viktor's apartment, we met a taciturn, rather grouchy man who did not say much and seemed consumed with a rage so deep that it colored everything about him. He was totally standoffish. We did not pay him much attention, and that proved to be one of the biggest mistakes of my life. His name meant nothing to me in 1966. He was Simon Wiesenthal, the great Nazi-hunter who devoted his post-war life to bringing Nazis to justice. It took my mother to remind me much later that we had actually encountered the great Wiesenthal that evening at the Frankls. It took the 1976 Ira Levin novel and the 1978 movie based on it—*The Boys from Brazil*, starring Gregory Peck as Dr. Josef Mengele and Laurence Olivier as the Wiesenthal character—for me to comprehend what we had missed. I have regretted my lack of curiosity to this day.

Chapter 63
Politics: Madly for Adlai

Politics, public affairs and international doings were very important to Ernest, less so to Grete. She bristled every evening when Ernest came home and we ate dinner while watching the evening news. Dad swiveled the television around from the living room into the dining room and forbade us from talking while we watched NBC's John Cameron Swayze, then Chet Huntley and David Brinkley, and/or CBS's Douglas Edwards, then Walter Cronkite (Dad disdained ABC News for reasons unknown).

Grete viewed TV's intrusion into family time as an affront. She would gobble down her meal and head directly for the kitchen. Ernest barely noticed.

When the news was over, Ernest "discussed" with me the stories we had just heard. Before I hit double digits (age 10), I found these monologues boring and largely irrelevant to the central concerns of my life: sports and fitting in with Americans. As I grew older, however, I began to value them. My dad and I had little in common until I became old enough to participate in post-news debates and became interesting to him. Grete never had much to say, but when she did, her observations were very much her own.

It was a shock to learn much later that Grete had once registered Republican. Also that she considered voting for Dwight Eisenhower in 1952.

My earliest memory of public affairs was the Korean War. Grete and Ernest were very upset that the United States was once again fighting a war just five years after the most horrible conflict in history had ended. Nevertheless, they cut President

Truman considerable slack. It was still an era when people deferred to the supposed greater knowledge of those in power.

In the 1952 presidential election, Ernest was "all in" for the "intellectual" governor of Illinois, Adlai E. Stevenson. It also appealed to him that, like Ernest, Stevenson was bald and wore shoes with holes in the soles. During the campaign, Grete gradually warmed to Stevenson, sensing that Eisenhower's ideas of governance were unformed. Ernest said: "All that man has is a smile."

The other reason Stevenson was elevated to iconic status in our household was because he was enthusiastically endorsed by Eleanor Roosevelt, to Grete and Ernest the most revered woman in the country. For a time, a framed photograph of Stevenson hung on our wall between portraits of Johannes Brahms and Gustav Mahler.

In 1956, both Grete and Ernest supported Stevenson again. Eisenhower won by a landslide. Both in 1952 and 1956, his victories shocked my dad. He was certain that the American public could not possibly favor Ike over his intellectual hero.

There was another reason why Grete and Ernest were disinclined to support Eisenhower: his running mate, Richard M. Nixon. My parents loathed Nixon. That did not change throughout his political career. To them, he was evil incarnate. His crimes—in their eyes—included: (1) his conjuring of Red scares in his 1946 House race against Jerry Voorhis and senatorial contest versus Helen Gahagan Douglas in 1950; (2) his service on the despised House Un-American Activities Committee; and (3) his general demeanor and affect. They thought he was a manipulative weasel. They were appalled that Eisenhower would select such a man as his running mate. In their view, Nixon was reason enough to vote against Eisenhower. For more than two decades, my father kept saying: "Someday that man will get his comeuppance."

Looking back, what amazes me about that 1952 election was that here were two recent immigrants who had by then been completely "Americanized" politically, to the point where they felt no qualms about expressing their opinions. Only a few years before in Austria, going public with political opinions would have meant a death sentence.

Nixon hatred became embedded in Grete's and Ernest's DNA. It carried over to his 1960 run against John F. Kennedy, despite their viewing JFK as a usurper of what should, in their eyes, rightfully have been a third presidential nomination for Stevenson. Nevertheless, they grudgingly voted for him in large part because he was not Nixon. My father was probably more favorably disposed than Grete toward Kennedy because obtaining his U.S. visa was greased by JFK's father, Joe Kennedy, at the behest of Lady Mountbatten.

When I asked Grete years later if she had ever actually voted for a Republican, she invoked the sanctity of the secret ballot and refused to answer. I found out later that she had told my wife that, although she always voted for the person, not the party, she had never found a Republican who was the better person.

Chapter 64
Books

Books were central to my mother's life. She was a voracious reader, always with her nose in a book. Her reading interests were wide-ranging and eclectic. From when she was first able to read a complete sentence until almost her 101st birthday, she never stopped reading. When her macular degeneration advanced to where she was no longer able to read, my wife and I read to her.

Grete not only read; she processed what she read, dissected it and discussed it, testing the authors' assertions. Over the years, she and I had countless exchanges and debates about a diverse range of topics and issues from her readings.

In trying to understand my mother better and "get into her head" for the purposes of this book, I embarked on a "Grete-reading program," incorporating the books that she consumed as she was growing up and as an emerging adult.

Goethe and Schiller were the platform from which her reading list took off. I struggled to read Goethe, enduring *The Sufferings of Young Werther* and *Faust*, but could not slog through *Götz von Berlichingen* or *Italienische Reise* (which I attempted to read in German). Schiller was easier on both my mental state and interest level, and I came away from *Maria Stuart*, *Wilhelm Tell*, and especially *Wallenstein* greatly impressed and appreciative of Grete's excitement about these seminal works.

Most of Grete's early literary exertions were restricted to the great—and some not so great—German-language writers of the nineteenth and early twentieth centuries: the "Biedermeier" School of frivolous writers, especially Franz Grillparzer; the Brothers Grimm, whose fairy tales plunge into the darkest side of the German soul; Arthur Schnitzler, whose dreamlike stories capture the late nineteenth century and *fin-de-siècle* Austrian obsession with sex, love, aimlessness, despair and death; the biting satirist Karl Kraus, whose *die Fackl* periodical stripped naked the illusory façade that Vienna held on to in its declining Habsburg years; Johann Nestroy; Robert Musil, obsessed with the uniquely Viennese obsession with . . . obsession; Elias Canetti; Hugo von Hoffmansthal; Thomas Mann; Stefan Zweig; Franz Kafka; Karl May, whose formulaic "Westerns" bedazzled Austrians with tales of an American Wild West that May himself never visited; Lion Feuchtwanger, whose *Jud Süss*, which portrayed the ambivalent position of Jews in German society and served as the model for Joseph Goebbels propaganda film of the same name (see above); Franz Werfel; and the supremely tragic Joseph Roth.

She also read widely among the great Russian authors—Pushkin, Tolstoy, Dostoyevsky, Gogol, Turgenev, Goncharev, Solzhenitsyn, Pasternak—and the French—Balzac, Hugo, George Sand, Proust—and other European authors of note, such as the Brontë sisters, Thackeray and Thomas Hardy, whom she especially revered. American authors were for the most part missing from her march through the Western canon. The only exception was plays. She read American drama extensively.

As Grete aged, her reading became all-consuming. Nighttime sleep became increasingly problematic, so she spent large chunks of each night reading. In her 90s, she began taking afternoon naps for the first time, compensating for her inability to sleep at night.

Grete's love of reading contrasted with Ernest. He scanned the daily newspapers but rarely read articles in depth, quickly losing interest. I only occasionally saw him with a book. Ernest had a compulsive need for company. For him, talking—schmoozing really—was more essential than the written word. Grete, in contrast, was content to be by herself buried in a book.

Chapter 65
Caring

Post-War Rudi

Helping others was paramount for Grete. She prepared "care packages" for two of the only three relatives who still resided in Vienna after the war—cousin Rudi and Aunt Hilda, both intellectually challenged and living on very little.

Rudi, as I indicated earlier, somehow survived the Holocaust and war in Vienna after being abandoned by his family. He was one of the few disabled individuals who did not perish in the Nazi's program to rid Europe of what they labeled "mental defectives" and "useless eaters." Disabled persons were both the first target of Nazi extermination policies and the pilot program for the subsequent mass murder of Jews. How a disabled Jew avoided detection by the Nazis' extermination bureaucracy is unfathomable.

His situation became even more dire as the war wound down in 1945. The end in sight, the Gestapo employed thousands of *Juden Greifer*—Jew "catchers"—Viennese civilians whose mission was to snare Jews who had somehow survived. They never found Rudi.

Grete lost contact with Rudi in the early 1970s when her care packages began being returned stamped "undeliverable." Neither the Austrian government nor the Viennese authorities could provide any information about Rudi's fate.

Hilda and the Harrimans

Aunt Hilda was also mentally challenged. She was Ernest's aunt, a daughter of his Bratislava grandfather Edward Hermann's second family. She was a sister of Aunt Rosl, whom we met earlier in this book. At the beginning of the war, Hilda was able to go to England, thanks to Rosl. She worked as a downstairs scullery maid in an aristocratic household. At the end of the war, Rosl took her back to Vienna and found her an apartment. She lived on help from Rosl and my parents. In the early 1960s, she was institutionalized. She died several years later.

The other family members whom Grete supported with packages and regular checks were the Harrimans of Worthing, Sussex on England's south coast. Kurt Harriman and his brother, Ernest's first cousins, came to England in 1938 as teenage refugees from Vienna. After six months in an internment camp, Kurt's brother joined the British Army. After that, I do not know what happened to him, except that he died young.

Kurt was too young for military service. He was advised to "Anglicize" his name from Hermann to Harriman, went to work for the British Defence Ministry, and married Shirley, the daughter of a Welsh minister and a true, selfless saint. They adopted a baby girl, Johanna, who suffered from what today would probably be diagnosed as Attention Deficit Hyperactivity Disorder. Her hysterical outbursts drove her father into seclusion in his upstairs bedroom.

Although Shirley was anguished about Johanna's condition, she was an attentive mother, but she suffered greatly from Kurt's European perception of wifely subservience. Shirley was at his constant beck and call, despite a permanently collapsed lung that made climbing the steep stairs to wait on him difficult. The two times I visited them, Shirley climbed up and down those stairs at least 20 times a day, responding to Kurt's demands.

Kurt suffered from angina and also was a hypochondriac. He often took to his bed after coming home from work. He retired early on disability and the family moved from the London suburbs to Worthing, where they purchased a small, attached house.

In 1960, the Harrimans "enjoyed" their 15 minutes of fame when they received a visit from the Hungarian Prime Minister, Ferenc Munnich, who was married to their (and our) cousin. Munnich was very briefly (four days) a member of the Imre Nagy government that defied Soviet rule and launched the 1956 Hungarian revolution. When he saw which way the wind was blowing (toward Russia), he fled Budapest for Moscow. Nagy and many of the senior members of his short-lived government were executed when the Soviets crushed the uprising. Munnich was then brought into the Hungarian government serving as both Interior and then Defense Minister. In 1958, he was elevated to the top post.

In 1960, the Munnichs made a state visit to England. After Munnich's London meetings with senior British officials, he and his wife detoured to Worthing to visit Kurt and Shirley. When his limousine pulled up in front of their house and armed security guards spread out up and down the street, the Harrimans became the talk of the town.

The visit was awkward. Kurt, after greeting his cousin and her husband, retired upstairs to his bedroom, leaving Shirley to entertain the Hungarian luminaries. Mercifully, the Munnichs did not stay long. They left and were never seen again by any Western family members. By 1961, Munnich was out of office and disappeared into the maw of history.

The Harriman's great tragedy occurred just before Christmas, 1979. Now grown-up Johanna went missing. She was last seen leaving a Worthing pub with a young man at 11:20 PM. At midnight, screams were heard coming from a cemetery. Five days later, her body was found under a leaf pile, wedged between a crucifix headstone and a wall in St. Andrews churchyard cemetery in nearby West Tarring. She had been raped, then strangled. Johanna, who had grown from gawky teenager into a very good-looking young woman, was only 22.

Several days later, the police arrested Edward Albert Stanley, 28, with whom Johanna had been talking at the pub. He was sentenced to 25 years in prison for my cousin's murder.

A life marked by constant struggle and tragedy became more than Shirley could bear. She died in the late 1980s and Kurt moved to Manchester to a retirement home, where he died seven years later.

The Polish Phantom

Grete quietly undertook many other charitable works. She and Ernest were generous to one and all. They took in all comers, relatives, friends and even strangers.

One of Canandaigua's only industries was a winery. Marvin Sands, the owner and CEO, was one of the few other Jews in town. Sands launched his company as a 21-year old just back from the war in 1945. By the mid-1950s, the company had added kosher wine to its product line (in 1987 it acquired Manischewitz). That meant that it required a *Mashgiach*, an Orthodox Jewish certified expert to supervise the rule-driven, tedious and difficult kosher wine-making process.

Mashgiachim were not exactly abundant in Canandaigua or Western New York. Sands looked far and wide and eventually was able to coax a Mashgiach who was a recent Polish Jewish refugee who had survived the war and Holocaust to relocate from New York City to Canandaigua and take the job.

Zygmunt Hess needed a temporary place to stay while he adjusted to the alien world of rural, small-town America and his new job. Sands asked Grete and Ernest to put him up for a few months until he got his feet on the ground and could bring his wife and young daughter to join him. My father agreed to help his friend.

My mother and I waited at the bus stop on South Main Street. When Mr. Hess stepped off the bus, he looked like the caricatures I had seen in books about the Holocaust that derived from Nazi rags like the *Völkischer Beobachter* and *Der Stürmer*. These "newspapers" depicted Jewish men dressed all in black with wide-brimmed hats, white short-sleeve shirts, caftans, and with sidelocks (*pi-kes*) and other religious accoutrements. These cartoon Jews all had exaggerated hooked noses and beetle brows. Mr. Hess looked like a Josef Goebbels fantasy. Coming from *shtetl* Poland to the bosom of the Polish Jewish community in New York City must have been a shock. Coming from there to Canandaigua was shell-shock. In all the time he was with us, he never lost his deer-in-the-headlights expression.

Hess's English was non-existent. Having grown up in a household of two Polish Jewish parents, my mother could haltingly communicate with Mr. Hess using an ersatz combination of the smattering of Polish and Yiddish that she had picked up as a child and young adult. Ernest tried to engage him in conversation using a combination of English, German, sign language and shouting. Nothing worked, so he gave up and grumbled that we were harboring a Sphinx.

We lodged him in a guest room across the hall from my bedroom. His loud and fervent evening prayers could be heard all over the house.

Every day, Mr. Hess walked the mile to and from work. He never deviated from his costume and caused quite a stir among the locals. He ate his meals alone in his room, and had his own cooking utensils, plates and cutlery, as well as a ceramic plate-like thing that he placed on top of our gas burners as a buffer against non-kosher "pollution" when he cooked. He washed his culinary items only after my mother cleaned up and left the kitchen.

Six weeks after his arrival, Hess's wife and little daughter suddenly appeared with no notice. We had no choice but to take them in as well. They were even more overtly intimidated and terrified by their abrupt relocation to American country life than their *pater familias*. They also dressed entirely in black and quavered around the house as if they were walking on eggshells. Whenever I looked at them, they trembled. The little girl, who was probably about seven, viewed me like Beowulf probably first viewed Grendel. Every time I was anywhere near her, she ran and hid. They all slept in the guest bedroom in the same large bed, even though that would not have been necessary. We had a second guest room next to Hess's bedroom where the girl could have slept.

We began to feel that we were living in a fish bowl, every move scrutinized by alien life forms.

A month after his family arrived, the day came when Mr. Hess did not come home after work. Suppertime came and went and none of the three transplants showed up in the kitchen. Grete went upstairs, knocked on their bedroom door, got no response, and opened the door to see what was going on. No one was there and all of their possessions were gone.

Ernest called Marvin Sands that evening, only to discover that Hess had not shown up for work that morning. A week later, Marvin told Ernest that the dispatcher at the bus station had sold three tickets to the Hesses (they were, after all, the most easily identifiable and memorable people in town) on the New York bus that left Canandaigua the morning of their disappearance.

Marvin, I found out years later, had offered to pay Ernest and Grete for hosting Hess and his family, but they refused. Instead, Marvin sent over multiple cases of wine that my teetotaling parents let sit unopened in our basement.

With or without a Mashgiach, the winery continued to thrive. Today, under the leadership of Marvin's sons, Constellation Brands is the largest wine company in the world.

Chapter 66
Suddenly It's 1960!

Sputnik and Scholarship

"Suddenly it's 1960" was the theme song of a successful 1957 Plymouth TV commercial. Apparently, Chrysler Motors could not wait for the real change of the decade to kick in. Neither could the rest of America.

On October 4, 1957, the Soviet Union launched a 28 lb. beeping metal ball into orbit. The U.S. reaction was utter panic. We were losing the space race! American education was found wanting. We were not churning out enough scientists, engineers and mathematicians. The feeling was that the American Century had come to a screeching halt.

The press and even Congress began to identify the weaknesses that contributed to our failure to match the Soviets. Science and math education was the culprit. Articles extolling the quality of Soviet STEM education proliferated.

A plan was rapidly cobbled together to kick-start American education and play catch-up. It was poorly crafted and did not roll out very well in Canandaigua. Around thirty sixth graders were selected to attend extra science classes before the official school day. I was one of them.

Grete was delighted, believing that the much maligned (by her) U.S. education system was finally doing something right by me, although she found it hard to understand why I was selected.

The acceleration of science—eventually math and language education were added to the mix—was intended to go through 12th grade. Maybe it did in much of the country. But in

Canandaigua, it fizzled by the time I was a high school senior. After just one day of class, the school board cancelled my Organic Chemistry class because there were only three of us left in the program. My full-year calculus class ended after only one semester because the few students remaining were not deemed worth the expense. The Soviets breathed a sigh of relief. Their STEM dominance was not going to be threatened by any Canandaiguans.

Grete was particularly annoyed by the abandonment of accelerated classes. When she discovered that in my last high school semester I only had two classes and six study halls, her contempt for American public education was set in stone. She rued the day she did not send me to a private high school.

My parents were completely detached from anything I was up to in school. They never joined the PTA and did not attend school functions. That was how it was done in Europe.

Despite competing on the high school track team for four years, my parents never came to see me run or jump until Grete showed up for my last home meet of my senior year. I was sufficiently excited that I broke two school records, running the 440 in 52 seconds-and-change and long-jumping just over 21 feet. That excitement quickly dissipated when, as I have mentioned, after breaking the tape in the 440, my mother came running out onto the track, took my pulse, and very vocally expressed her concern that I was out of breath. I quickly forgave my parents' lack of interest in my athletic career.

Grete's First Health Scare

Grete had always been inordinately healthy. She rarely had even a mild cold. Then, in the late 1950s, she began to experience vision problems. Ernest diagnosed a rapidly expanding cataract in her left eye, but did not want to operate on his wife. Instead, he sent her to a highly respected ophthalmic surgeon in Rochester who was also on the teaching faculty at the University of Rochester Medical School.

The surgery was a disaster. Shortly after her eye was stitched up, it began to hemorrhage. From then on to the end of her life, she had only limited vision in that eye.

She was a very young candidate (early 50s) for cataract surgery. So too for her other eye. She had successful surgery on that eye (performed by another doctor) just a few years later. Going into the operation, we were terrified that if the second surgery also failed, she would be virtually blind.

Passing the Torch

As the 1960 presidential election approached, politics became our obsessive dinner table topic. Ernest's second choice for the Democratic nomination, should it be denied to Stevenson, was Missouri Senator Stuart Symington, who probably looked more like a president than any American politician since Warren G. Harding. Grete was smitten with Minnesota Senator Hubert Humphrey, whose civil rights speech to the 1948 Democratic convention impressed her. None of these wannabes, however, could survive the Kennedy juggernaut.

On September 26, 1960, I watched the first-ever televised presidential debate with my father. We were both impressed with Kennedy's performance, pronouncing him the clear winner over the reviled, shifty-eyed, heavily perspiring Richard M. Nixon. Grete listened to the debate on the radio in the kitchen while she tidied up after dinner. When it ended, she came in and said it was a shame Nixon had won. Ernest and I were shocked, which goes to demonstrate the enormous power of visual imagery. Kennedy's looks and demeanor were made for TV, while Nixon had a face for radio. Don Hewitt, who directed the debate for CBS, said Nixon looked like "death warmed over." The fact that more Americans watched the debate on TV than listened to it on radio was probably determinative of one of the closest elections in American history.

We watched JFK's inauguration on January 20, 1961 in fascination. His eloquence got our pulses racing. Both Grete and Ernest were impressed by the theme of the advent of a new generation and new leadership. Ernest was especially hooked. He sensed that Kennedy had expressed precisely what he himself felt about being an American, something that imprints in the immigrant DNA and makes them and their children believe that the founding fathers are, in fact, *our* founding fathers too, and that their travails and history are shared with us.

But not Grete. JFK almost won her over, until he expressed the prophetic words that gave her pause and would cause this country so much anguish in the years to come:

> *"Let every nation know, whether it wishes us well or ill, that we shall pay any price, bear any burden, meet any hardship, support any friend, oppose any foe, in order to assure the survival and the success of liberty."*

Despite constantly underplaying her knowledge of politics and world affairs, Grete's instincts were astute. She turned to Ernest and said: "What do you think he means by that? I don't like it." She figured out right away just exactly who would bear that burden.

Her concern was, of course, soon justified by America's Vietnam misadventure, followed years later by the folly of the Iraq War. My admiration for her political sagacity skyrocketed with every new American blunder.

With Kennedy safely in Camelot, Grete and Ernest settled down to what was to be the last three years of the American post-war idyll. The bubble delusion of permanent peace and prosperity was about to burst.

Chapter 67
November 21, 1963

The post-war world Americans had come to take for granted reached its zenith on November 21, 1963. The United States was the dominant world power, both militarily and economically. Americans went to bed that night a supremely confident people who envisioned a future even more promising than its glorious recent past.

The Hermann family went to bed that night on the cusp of a major life change. In three days we would move from our North Main Street and lake houses to a year-round home on the lake. Grete was excited because it meant one less house to worry about and liberation from *schlepping* stuff back and forth twice a year.

The next day at 12:00 Noon Central Time, everything changed.

Few events of global significance in a person's life imprint themselves so deeply on the psyche that you remember in detail where you were and what you were doing when the news broke. The assassination of John Fitzgerald Kennedy was such an event. For my parents, this was the third event of that magnitude, the others being the Anschluss and Pearl Harbor.

Ernest was in his office when Jean, his assistant, burst in and told him about the shooting in Dallas. He continued to work through the afternoon and even treated my future wife, Anne.

Grete was just getting home from her school physician job. She turned on the radio while packing in preparation for the move and heard the news. She turned on the TV just in time to see Walter Cronkite report that President Kennedy had died at Parkland Memorial Hospital.

Americans sat riveted to their TVs, for the first time in history sharing a national trauma unfolding in real time. My family's immediate reaction was that something fundamental had changed. It was the end of an era and the beginning of a scarier, more unpredictable world.

Chapter 68
College Unbound

The new house came saddled with unanticipated baggage. Its hidden structural problems became apparent very quickly when (1) the entire basement flooded after a rainstorm, and (2) cracks appeared in the basement ceiling and house support joists, all of which the home inspector had failed to notice. The repair work included an elaborate re-digging and retrofitting around the entire foundation in order to alleviate the basement water problem, which nevertheless continued to vex the property for years. Following that project, the entire upper floor support system had to be reinforced. Ernest was not happy.

Despite these serious issues, Grete loved the house. It had a modern kitchen—a first for her—and required little routine maintenance. About the only thing that irritated her following the move was that Ernest began bringing enucleated eyes home from the hospital where he had extracted them from the corpses of people who had made organ donations. He stored them in a glass jar in our refrigerator, which made opening it quite the adventure.

I went through the college application process that fall on my own. Grete and Ernest knew nothing about the American college system and what was involved in the admissions game. I did it on my own and thought there was nothing unusual about that. I opted for Yale (my first choice), a great disappointment to my dad, as I have mentioned. Grete drove me to school after Labor Day, a trip that took inordinately long because she was both a careful and slow driver, hampered by her vision problems while also being directionally challenged.

For whatever reason, she refused to let me drive. We got lost several times along the way.

When we finally arrived in New Haven, she was appalled by the drafty old buildings on the Old Campus where the freshmen reside. When she saw the threadbare furnishings my new roommates and I had purchased from the prior residents, she was even more aghast. What really set her off was the phalanx of cockroaches that inhabited the sofa. They scattered whenever anyone sat down. My mother engaged in a lifelong jihad with roaches and spent many quality hours researching anti-roach treatments everywhere she lived. For the next four years, she sent me the information she had discovered about anti-roach strategies and ads for roach control products.

Consequently, her first experience with an American college was not a positive one. Having lived at home while she attended medical school, it was difficult for her to understand the American campus scene. When she got in her car for the drive home, her last words to me were: "I wonder if Cornell has a roach problem."

Over my four years in New Haven, Grete came to appreciate that I was receiving a top-notch education. She and Ernest only visited me once, on Parents' Weekend my senior year, when they attended their first and last football game, Yale vs. Cornell or, as we labeled it, The "Battle of Culture vs. Agriculture." Yale stomped Cornell 41-7 and my mother actually enjoyed herself. Dad not so much.

My father finally did come to watch me compete at my last Heptagonal Games (mislabeled as the competing schools include the eight Ivy League schools plus Army and Navy) at Cornell's Barton Hall. I ran the 220 as a sacrificial lamb (Cornell had a world-class sprinter who destroyed the field and whom my father cheered on to victory) and long-jumped a rather pedestrian 22 feet and something and finished off the podium. My teammate Calvin Hill easily won the event, after which my dad came up to him and warned him that if he jumped that far, he risked breaking his ankles. Hill went on to become the NFL rookie-of-the-year, beating out O.J. Simpson.

Chapter 69
The Sixties

The remaining years of the 1960s were more disruptive than anything that had affected America since the war. For our family, three issues stood out.

Civil Rights

When I was six years old, we drove to Florida over spring break. Dad tired of the drive as we approached Richmond, Virginia, so we parked the car at Union Station (known locally as Broad Street Station) and bought train tickets to Miami.

Awaiting the train, I went to the nearest water fountain and took a drink. The basin was filthy and the spigot was rust-covered. Suddenly, in mid-sip, I was dragged away by a man in a uniform who told me I shouldn't drink out of this particular fountain. Instead, he dragged me by the arm over to the other side of the waiting room to a much cleaner water fountain with gleaming silver-colored fixtures. I had no idea what was going on.

My mother appeared and got into some kind of argument with the man, who turned out to be the station master. I did not completely understand what they were shouting at each other about. I never heard her tell anyone else to "go to Hell." It was only when we boarded the train that my mother explained to me that, in the south, white and colored people were not allowed to drink from the same fountain. It was my first encounter with segregation. I was shocked.

Despite her difficulty adapting to the political correctness movement and learning to call African-Americans that appellation or, alternatively, "Black" (she could not train herself to refer to them as anything other than "colored people"), Grete was an avid supporter of the civil rights movement. The Supreme Court's *Brown v. Board of Education* decision impressed her, although she could not understand what had taken America so long to recognize "the obvious." Emmet Till's lynching pushed her completely over into the civil rights camp.

She often expressed her irritation at the snail's pace at which integration was bumbling along and at the stupidity and waste of time and energy displayed by people on the wrong side of history—the Ku Klux Klan, southern white politicians, and what she called "ignorant people." Ernest held similar sympathies, but rarely expressed them.

Grete encouraged my interest in civil rights, both because I endorsed her views and was "finally reading serious stuff" like Ralph Ellison's *The Invisible Man* and Harper Lee's *To Kill a Mockingbird*. As my high school graduation approached, I announced to my parents that I intended to go to Mississippi to register Black voters during the "Mississippi Freedom Summer." Grete was not opposed to the idea, but Ernest was adamantly against it. My arguments got me nowhere. His threats escalated, the clincher being that he would disown me and not pay for college. I relented, but my dad and I did not speak for several weeks.

Soon thereafter, three young civil rights workers—James Chaney, 21, a Black Mississippi native, and two New York Jews, Andrew Goodman, 20, and Michael Schwerner, 24, were murdered and buried under a dam near Philadelphia, Mississippi. They were there registering black voters. Arrested on bogus charges, they were released to the tender mercies of the Ku Klux Klan, who tortured and killed them. I endured a summer's worth of "I told you so's" from my dad. My mom was upset that she had not objected to my desire to head south.

Although I fantasized about rebelling, I was a conventional adolescent. I stayed home and took a summer job working at the local amusement park. While other people my age were risking their lives, I was flipping burgers, running bumper cars and handing out skee-roll tickets.

Vietnam

The issue that dominated our dinner table discussions for the next four years when I was home from college was Vietnam. In early August 1964, President Lyndon Johnson announced that two U.S. Navy destroyers had been attacked twice by North Vietnamese torpedo boats in open waters in a place called the Tonkin Gulf. Johnson ordered air strikes on the torpedo boats' home port. He also asked Congress to approve a resolution that would express support "for all necessary action to protect our Armed Forces." After only a few hours of committee consideration and floor debate, Congress approved the Gulf of Tonkin Resolution. The vote in the House of Representatives was 416-0. The Senate approved the resolution by a vote of 88-2, with only Democrats Ernest Greuning of Alaska and Wayne Morse of Oregon objecting. They immediately became two of my three political heroes (Eugene McCarthy joined the pantheon three years later). A 2005 National Security Agency report stated that the second attack was a fiction.

The Resolution triggered our first of many heated family debates about Vietnam. Grete at first hesitated to voice her opinions. Years later, she said that although she had doubts, she had deferred to the greater knowledge and access to information that she assumed our leaders possessed.

Ernest was 100 percent behind the President, a position he held firmly to for the next three years. He and I had shouting matches about that.

Our friend, Henry Buxbaum, came over frequently and, every time I was home for one of his visits, he and Ernest went at each other over Vietnam with so much passion and occasional rancor that I feared for their friendship. Looking back, I think it did have a negative impact, and I may have been at least partially to blame for that. I invariably sided with Henry, with whom I had become increasingly close. Now we were two peas in the same political and ideological pod.

The years of Vietnam escalation saw Grete's opinions evolve along with her willingness to assert herself about them. As America sank deeper into the Southeast Asian quagmire, Grete became more outspoken in her opposition to the war and less inclined to defer to her husband. By 1967, Ernest felt beleaguered and much put upon by his wife, his son and his best friend.

Then abruptly, in mid-1967, Ernest changed his views. He realized with a sudden start that I was very likely going to be at some risk after graduation.

What altered Ernest's views, in addition to his sudden realization that I might have to go to war, was Senator J. William Fulbright of Arkansas, a man Ernest greatly admired. Fulbright was Chairman of the Senate Foreign Relations Committee, with the power to hold hearings and grill administration and military officials about the war. His hearings painted an increasingly ugly picture of American involvement and received wide play in the news, often accompanied by graphic television images of death and destruction.

Ernest suddenly became a vigorous opponent of the war and even apologized to me for his earlier views. I told him it was OK. Grete, however, came down rather hard on him and, for years, kept raising his prior pro-war advocacy whenever it suited her purposes.

As my senior year in college proceeded, my parents both became, for the first time, engaged with me about what I was doing, specifically how I was going to avoid the military draft. Grete urged me to declare myself a conscientious objector, but that required my rejecting *all* wars. I told her I could not do that because I felt that there might be just wars in which I would participate. She argued that with my life on the line, that attitude was stupid.

Her next stratagem was to urge me to go to Canada. I never considered that an option, fearing I might not be able to return and that it would be a black mark on my career aspirations.

By this time, Grete thought I was a naïve romantic with a death wish. She could not understand why her arguments made no headway with me. So she invoked her last resort: I should defy the draft and go to jail. I said no, not being keen on becoming some lifer's bitch.

I countered by looking into several less risky alternatives like the U.S Coast Guard and VISTA (Volunteers in Service to America). For one reason or another, neither worked out for me. I graduated on my birthday. That morning, I and most of my classmates received notice that our draft deferments had ended. We were now "1-A," draft eligible. By mid-December 1968, I was in the U.S. Army.

Assuming I would go to Vietnam, I took boot camp at Fort Dix, New Jersey seriously, so much so that I wound up becoming the "Trainee of the Cycle." This won me an afternoon tea with the base commanding general, who said the Army would fly my parents down for the graduation ceremony and put them up in his house. Ernest was eager, but Grete nixed the offer, saying "I am not about to support a war machine." I was relieved they were absent.

When I received orders for Vietnam several months later, I did not tell my parents. I only revealed that to them when those orders were abruptly rescinded in favor of nuclear weapons school.

Israel

Neither Ernest nor Grete were Zionists. Neither thought seriously of escaping from Holocaust Europe to Israel. Their attitude was significantly different from many members of their Leopoldstadt generation. Both had many friends who were fervent Zionists who dreamed of life on a *Kibbutz*.

Ernest enjoyed his creature comforts and Israel came packaged with a hard-scrabble, low-paying existence, even for professionals. Moreover, he was determined to get his father out of Europe and feared that, at his age, he would have a difficult time transitioning to Israel. While his sister, Hedy, went to Israel, that was a practical decision prompted by the job that awaited her husband, Julius. I never heard Aunt Hedy or Uncle Julius express any Zionist tendencies, either. They were realists, not dreamers.

During the hours Grete spent researching locations at the main Vienna library, she never looked into an Israeli solution.

Growing up, I had been exposed to the heroic image of Israel through books and movies like Leon Uris' Exodus, and had read much about the dogged, idealistic people who made the desert bloom and twice (1948 and 1956) fought successfully for survival against impossible odds.

By May 1967, there arose yet another existential threat to the fledgling nation. The surrounding Arab nations—80 million strong—once again geared up to throw Israel's two million Jews into the sea. The impetus was Egypt's reckless leader, Gamal Abdel Nasser, a man desperate for a victory (Egypt's economy was in shambles and it had just been burned in a no-win, quagmire war in Yemen). Nasser was also being goaded by the Soviet Union that now was the most propitious time to strike at Israel and make his case for pan-Arabism under his leadership. Nasser moved his troops across the Suez Canal and ordered UN peacekeepers out of the Sinai Peninsula. He then persuaded Syria and Jordan to join him in his mission to annihilate Israel. Israel's Foreign Minister hopped from one Western capital to another seeking help. None was forthcoming.

As the crisis reached a boiling point, I had been having discussions with Jewish friends at college about what we could do to help Israel. We decided we needed to go there.

When I told my parents my intent, their reaction, to say the least, was not supportive. Grete's comment was: "Mississippi all over again!" Ernest, being less constrained, said: "You're crazy. You could get killed. I forbid you to go. I'll disown you. And that's that."

I decided to negotiate. "What would you say," I proposed, "if I went to work on a Kibbutz so an Israeli could leave and go fight?" For Grete and Ernest, that too was not an option. They pointed out that no place in Israel was safe from bombs and rockets.

Again, I was too much a member of a respectful generation. Defiance was not an option. I groused a lot, but stayed put. A week later, the Six-Day War came and quickly went. By June 10, my birthday, Israel had routed the Arab armies once again. While Israelis my age were fighting for their lives and dying for their country, I went home to an internship with the Rochester City Manager. Instead of rolled-up sleeves, a spade, or an Uzi, I sported a coat and tie and wielded a pen and paper.

Israel's stunning victory was incredibly inspiring. For the first time in my life, I was bursting with pride at being Jewish, even at home in Christian Canandaigua. My dad was equally excited, but my mom never commented on the triumph. She always worried that if Jews became too "loud" or boastful, we were opening ourselves up to a repeat of the Holocaust. She was always worried about things like that. For example, when Henry Kissinger became such an influential force in the Nixon administration, she became concerned that he might attract too much attention to Jews in power, which would redound to the discredit of the rest of us.

Chapter 70
Animal Magnetism

Grete had a passion for cats and birds. We always had one or more pets of either species, sometimes both simultaneously. The first was Rusty, a big, slow-moving tiger cat who was with us for five or six years, then ran away, only to be discovered by accident five years later on a hilltop a few miles from our home. Rusty's distinctive oil-slick pattern down the middle of his back identified him. He was bedraggled, but Grete nursed him back to good health, the first of many such amateur veterinary medical triumphs.

By then, we also had Goober, a feisty little cat who was Rusty's opposite. Goober was a manipulator, able to get his own way by alternating moods of extreme expressions of feline love with fits of intense pique when he would ignore Grete and go off in a corner to pout. Like all our cats, he favored Grete. He knew who truly loved him the most.

Goober and Rusty worked out a *modus vivendi* upon Rusty's return, establishing a demilitarized zone in the hallway between the kitchen and living room. Goober claimed the kitchen, pantry and dining room, while Rusty idled his days away in the living room, music room and front porch. While Goober invaded Rusty's space with impunity, Rusty never crossed the DMZ.

Sometime during the Rusty-Goober era, our cleaning lady, who raised parakeets, gave one to my mother. This was Plato, named by Grete after the Athenian philosopher, the disciple of Socrates and mentor of Aristotle. Why Plato? Because *Platys* in Greek means "broad-shouldered," which described this deformed bird perfectly. In the evenings when she could sit down and relax, she let him out of his cage and he flew around the living room, eventually perching on her head. The cats were intensely interested in Plato, but never managed to nab him. Plato ignored them and went about his avian business unintimidated. This was either a sign of incredible bravery or appalling stupidity.

Rusty eventually expired and Goober one evening did not come home. Plato died after a few years and was immediately replaced with Plato II, who was neither broad of shoulder nor particularly self-confident. But Grete loved him nonetheless.

Grete quickly replaced Goober with Goober II (it took her years to become more creative in naming her pets), and the circadian rhythms of our household proceeded as if nothing had changed. Goober II's crowning moment came when he followed me to a high school football game and ran out on the field at a most inopportune moment, tripping a Canandaigua Academy running back on his way down the field to a certain touchdown. Canandaigua lost the game by a few points.

Goober II disappeared one weekend just before our 1963 move. Plato II died earlier, but he was so unassuming that we hardly noticed his demise. Grete attributed his death to a heart attack brought on by Goober II's unwanted attentions. Grete by then had had enough of birds.

Soon after our move, a much-abused adult cat appeared on our doorstep, and for both Grete and the cat it was Kismet. She adopted Katrina, but kept her outside, having finally acknowledged that both Ernest and I were highly allergic to cat dander and had suffered miserably for years on account of Rusty and the Goobers. On particularly inclement days, however, Katrina and her numerous progeny hunkered down in the laundry room, closed off from the rest of the house.

Katrina was with Grete for many years, and you could see how much the cat worshipped her by her behavior. She had eyes for no one else. It was a mutual admiration society. Katrina slept around and year-after-year presented Grete with a new litter. At several times, Grete was happily nurturing six or seven cats and kittens at once.

Five of Katrina's progeny stood out. Napoleon, the runt of one of Katrina's litters, was at first unable to nurse because he could not climb the front steps to the cats' bed on the porch. Grete's solution was to patiently exercise him to the point where he was able to compete for his mother's milk. He became so robust that, as an adult cat, he was able to leap to prodigious heights, including finding his way to the garage roof.

Molière, another of Katrina's brood, broke his leg. Refusing to put him down, Grete devised a splint and limited his movement by putting him in a deep box. She checked on him many times a day, fed him, adjusted his splint, entertained him and, miraculously, nursed him back to health.

Another of Grete's feline triumphs occurred when a friend wanted to find a home for a beautiful gray kitten. Grete agreed to take it in, but was concerned that Katrina, who had also just given birth, would reject and perhaps even harm the new kitten. When the kitten arrived, Grete poured milk on its back and presented it to Katrina, who immediately began licking the milk. An intense bond was instantly formed. Thereafter, Katrina showered more love and attention on the adoptee than on her own flesh and blood.

The final episode in Grete's cat saga concerns the last two kittens to result from Katrina's nightly couplings (Katrina died shortly after giving birth). Discerning the sex of a kitten is not easy. Grete made two mistakes. She named the male Griselda (Grizzy) and the female Itchy Brother (Itchy).

Psychologists ponder the influence of names on personality. Grizzy's and Itchy's misnaming may be the best evidentiary argument. Grizzy was effeminate, fearful of everything and utterly dependent on his sister for protection. Itchy, in contrast, was brave, bold and decisive, all male characteristics if you buy into the stereotype. She was overprotective of her brother and maintained a constant, but not always successful, vigil designed to keep him out of trouble.

Like all of the other cats, Grizzy and Itchy adored Grete. They once expressed their adulation by cooperating in dragging a large, dead fish from the lake to her doorstep and then meowing incessantly until she came out to thank them for the great gift.

Grete had no experience with dogs until she and Ernest moved in with us in old age. By that time, our West Highland White Terrier, Baskerville (Baskie), reigned supreme in our household. We admonished Baskie to refrain from jumping up on my then almost 90-year old parents, which Baskie interpreted to mean avoiding contact altogether, a demeanor that frustrated Grete. While Ernest was still alive, but suffering from increasing dementia, he would furtively throw food down from his plate to a waiting Baskie, who learned very quickly to park herself under his chair.

Grete liked to sit in our living room and read. While she sat in one rocking chair, Baskie napped in the other. When the sun moved from one chair to the other, Baskie would jump down and stand directly in front of Grete, staring at her until she relinquished her chair to her canine tormentor.

Shortly after Baskie died, our daughter Elizabeth rescued a pit bull in Brooklyn, whom she named after the borough. Grete was appalled that a pit bull had been brought into the family fold, but soon discovered that Brooklyn was a pit in name only. This gentle, loving creature's mournful affect melted her heart. When Grete sat on the sofa, Brooklyn would jump up and lie down with her head in Grete's lap. Once again, late in life, Grete entered into a loving relationship with a pet.

Growing up, Grete and her siblings never had any pets. The closest they came was the large carp their mother bought and kept in the bathtub prior to killing and cooking it.

Chapter 71
Enemy Territory

Beer and Brats

I pondered how to tell my parents that I had received an Army assignment to Germany, the land of our enemies. I was astonished when they did not bat an eye when I told them. Grete had visited Bavaria upon graduation from high school (see above). Ernest had never been to Germany. I suspect they were relieved I was not going to Vietnam.

Reunion

Grete and Ernest visited me during my last year in Germany. I met them in *Grindelwald* in the Swiss *Berner Oberland*, which has some of the most spectacular Alpine scenery in the world.

Seeing my parents after such a long separation was marred by two pieces of news they brought with them. Two friends of mine had died suddenly in accidents. One, Tom, died in a naval aviation training accident in Pensacola, Florida. He was flying his aircraft and lost his bearings, unable to determine his position relative to the sky and the sea. He panicked and ejected, unaware that his plane was upside down. He slammed into the ground, leaving a young wife and newborn son. The other, Diane, died due to a car accident.

I was overcome by the news and left our dinner table to wander by myself for the rest of the evening. Grete and Ernest did not try to restrain me.

After Grindelwald, we drove to Germany and first traveled down the *Romantische Strasse*, the medieval Romantic Road. In *Dinkelsbuhl*, we went to a Christian Socialist Party campaign rally at which party chief and candidate for German chancellor Franz-Josef Strauss, a.k.a. *Der Dicke* (the fat man), demagogued his fervent followers with a diatribe worthy of a certain World War II German chancellor. Ernest's wallet was stolen during the speech, and he and I spent the night in the local police station while a cop typed out a report using only two fingers.

After the Romantische Strasse, we traveled to Nuremberg, just 35 miles south of my base at Bamberg. Grete did not want to go to the Nazis' holy city, but Ernest insisted. Grete became ill and stayed in our hotel room the entire time we were in Nuremberg. I am sure the illness was psychosomatic.

From Nuremberg, I put my parents on a train to Munich, from where they went on to Salzburg, Vienna and then home. As I waved goodbye, it hit me that Ernest had actually enjoyed Germany. Grete hated it. As for her return to Munich, I am certain she would have agreed with German Chancellor Otto von Bismarck's take: "*A Bavarian is a cross between an Austrian and a human being.*"

Part Five
Miami Beach, 1978-1994

"Miami Beach is where neon goes to die."
Lenny Bruce

"Old age is no place for sissies."
Bette Davis

Chapter 72
Following the Sun

In 1972, Ernest, age 67, suffered a major heart attack on the Byron Hotel balcony in Miami Beach where he and Grete had begun spending several months every winter. Had Grete's brother, my Uncle Ben, a general practice physician, not been just down the corridor, Ernest probably would have died.

The next winter, Ernest was diagnosed with a malignant, life-threatening brain tumor. He went to Los Angeles for a radical new surgical technique during which 50 percent of patients died on the operating table. He had no choice. Without the surgery, the rapidly growing tumor would have killed him. Many years later, I discovered that a professional colleague of mine underwent the same surgery in Los Angeles, performed by the son of my dad's surgeon, the physician who had invented the procedure.

The surgery was a success, but took so much out of my father that he decided to retire. He and Grete began spending entire winters in Miami Beach, renting a small housekeeping apartment a few blocks from the beach. They enjoyed spending time with relatives: Grete's sister and brother-in-law, Rose and Ted; Ernest's cousin Fred Hirschl, a tailor originally from Wiener Neustadt and his Viennese wife, Hilda; Grete's brother Ben and his wife Mildred. Uncle Julius and Aunt Hedy (Ernest's sister) visited on the few occasions they were able to come to Florida.

Grete and Ernest relocated permanently to Miami Beach in 1978. Ernest was after warm weather and the Florida "lifestyle," which in his version meant taking long walks and sitting around a pool deck conversing with interesting and not-so-interesting people. His deep interest in other peoples' lives and histories kept him marginally content despite increasing hearing loss in his remaining good ear.

Rose and Ted

For Grete, the Florida attractions were different. She was never much affected by climate concerns. Instead, the draw was her sister Rose and Rose's husband, "the other" Ted Williams (nee "Wilhelm" from Budapest), long-time Florida residents.

The Williams wound up permanently in Florida in 1950 after a 12-year journey from Vienna that took them first to Buenos Aires, where Rose quickly achieved Spanish fluency, then to Havana and, following the war, to New York City. Both had little education, but Rose was very bright and a lightning quick learner, and never had a problem finding and holding jobs as an executive secretary. Ted, on the other hand, bounced around in sales jobs, mainly in the textile, notions and apparel industries, where he earned very little.

Grete's cousin Fred Holman, a podiatrist, was already there and was a recreational tennis partner of the great Pancho Gonzales. Florida in 1950 was one of America's great lands of opportunity in that optimistic era. For the Williams, however, that was not to be until many years later.

They were frustrated visionaries slightly before their time. On arriving in Miami, they threw all of their meager savings into the purchase of a South Beach Hotel, one of those art deco buildings that now command tens of millions of dollars, an upscale clientele, and a hammerlock on hipness and cool.

In the 1950s, South Beach was a repository for elderly Jews from Eastern Europe via New York, primarily from the lower middle classes, seeking cheap accommodations in seedy apartment hotels. Grete's and Rose's father, David , spent a number of his later years in these run-down establishments, his days filled with low-wagering card games on hotel verandas with other *alter Kockers*, interwoven with alcohol and knocking around the beach with biddies seeking a last fling.

The Williams' 40-room Parkside Hotel was never home to more than a handful of guests. In those days, tourists preferred one of the new hotels farther north along Collins Avenue like the Casablanca, McFadden-Deauville, or the dazzling new Fountainbleau and Eden Roc.

My parents and I visited the Williams over the Christmas-New Year holiday in 1950-51 and were the only human guests at the Parkside. A gentle mama cat, Mitzi, and her litter of six kittens, all of whom nestled together in a drawer filled with soft blankets, were the only other patrons.

After four years of losing their collective shirts, the Williams exited the hotel business selling out for a song. Today, the former Parkside, just off Ocean Drive in the center of the South Beach action, is a very hot property. The last time it changed hands, the purchase price was $38 million.

Rose and Ted spent the next 12 years barely keeping their heads above water, relying primarily on Rose's organizational and language talents. She became the indispensable executive secretary to a company that did business throughout Latin America, while Ted bounced around selling this and that without much success. They saved enough to buy a small house in Northeast Miami just off Biscayne Boulevard, a pleasant, quiet neighborhood that went south quickly in the late 1970s and early 1980s when Miami became the nation's drug, murder and prostitution capital. A safe walk up the boulevard to 79th street for a delicious dessert at Junior's abruptly became a dim memory as prostitutes, pimps and drug dealers took over the thoroughfare.

In 1966, a combination of luck and recognition of competence finally brought the Williams the success they deserved. A North Carolina textile mill made them its South Florida representatives. Rose's management skills plus Ted's engaging personality and high-level interpersonal skills were the perfect combination, and they were able to earn multiples of what they had eked out up to then. They were so successful that, in seven years' time they put together enough to retire comfortably. They began taking long trips to Switzerland, Italy and the Austrian Alps.

Sadly, Ted did not get to savor retirement for very long. In 1977, he required emergency intestinal surgery in Innsbruck and, two-and-a-half years later, succumbed to a botched quadruple heart bypass operation. From Thanksgiving 1979 to just after New Year's 1980, he lingered in a coma, eyes half open and unresponsive. Grete and Ernest stayed with Rose every day of the vigil, and Grete stayed with her overnight.

In 1980, Rose, recently widowed, sold her house for substantially less than its value only a few years before. She moved into a rental condo on the ocean in Miami Beach that Ernest found for her. Rose lived in her beach condo for the next 30 years before burning herself to death in a cigarette-induced fire that took her life just five months before her 100th birthday.

The Languid Life

Grete and Ernest lived in Florida for 16 years. When their building converted to condos, they moved across the street to another apartment, which they purchased a year later for $40,000.

Ernest made friends easily, his openness, friendliness and consuming interest in other people's family histories constantly on display. They accumulated a large circle of acquaintances that, while never quite up to the caliber of their hugely interesting Western New York refugee crowd, had its share of compelling characters. Several stood out:

- Nobel laureate Isaac Bashevis Singer became an occasional visitor to Grete's and Ernest's apartment, and vice versa. Grete and Singer's wife found a mutual attraction. Grete felt a European wifely kinship with the much-put-upon Mrs. Singer, who had to endure life with a world-famous literary giant and demanding egomaniac. While Ernest was hardly in Singer's category, he was a traditional European husband who expected wifely submissiveness and rarely lifted a finger to help around the house. It always galled me that my father, such a gentleman and decent human being in every other way, treated his intelligent professional spouse as if she were put on this Earth to serve him and keep him comfortable.

Singer often sought Ernest's medical advice—he was a classic hypochondriac—which my father was eager to provide, much to Grete's annoyance. Her objections were that Ernest was (1) not admitted to practice medicine in Florida, (2) out of touch with medical advances since his retirement, and (3) exposing himself to possible liability. Although she was very vocal about it, Ernest could never bring himself to stop playing the Herr Doktor role. He spent his life being admired by the extended family for his achievement and he exulted in it. He loved being called "doctor" and he loved the "MD" on his license plate. Just ask any cop or trooper in Canandaigua who stopped him when his heavy foot far exceeded the speed limit . . . the MD always got him off.

- Henry Zeizel was a friend dating back to Ernest's kindergarten days in Vienna. A promising architect, he escaped from Austria at the end of the 1930s, settling in Baranquilla, Columbia. His career thrived until the late 1970s, when he was blamed for the collapse of a major apartment building that resulted in a number of deaths. Henry and his wife fled from Colombia to avoid

potential prosecution and settled in Miami. Grete and Mrs. Zeizel hit it off immediately and became fast friends.
- Another friend, whose name I have forgotten, was an international trader with a less than totally above-board business past who was of Czech origin with a very retiring Peruvian Mestizo wife. He was outspoken and had an opinion—usually an extreme one—about everything. He became Ernest's debating substitute for Henry Buxbaum.
- Grete was friends with a neighbor who was a first cousin of Barbara Walters, an occasional visitor. She also made friends with a Mrs. Levy, whose son served as New York City's Schools Chancellor until Mayor Rudy Giuliani fired him.
- Another neighbor had a son who owned a motorcycle shop in Canandaigua.

Days in Florida passed unhurriedly with little to do and filled with back-and-forth among friends and relatives. Ernest became increasingly glum. His hearing had deteriorated and social interaction became difficult. He felt diminished, pining for his glory days practicing medicine and being widely known as a physician. He could no longer really enjoy television, theater, or music. He became depressed.

Grete, in contrast, thrived in Miami. She loved getting to see her sister almost daily and enjoyed Hilda's company at least once a week.

Ernest's sister, Hedy and her husband, Julius Friend at their 50th wedding anniversary celebration
Courtesy of James Friend

Grete and Ernest's friend, Nobel Laureate Isaac Bashevis Singer
(Source: britannica.com)

Ernest's friend, Viktor Frankl, renowned philosopher and psychotherapy pathfinder.
(Source: pbs.org)

Arlington, Virginia Public Library, where Grete went almost every Saturday morning for 12 years
Author's collection

Holocaust Memorial, Miami Beach.
Grete's grandfather Liber's name is engraved on the wall.
Author's collection

Entrance to the Theresienstadt Concentration Camp, where Grete's grandparents were incarcerated from July 1942 to October 1944
(*Source: Public domain*)

The Babi Yar Ravine outside of Kiev, Ukraine, where 33,000 Jews were murdered by a German Einsatzkommando unit
(*Source: Yad Vashem*)

Chapter 73

The Impact of the Florida Phenomenon

Ponce de Leon and the other early Florida explorers erroneously thought they had discovered an island, not a peninsula. Figuratively, however, they were correct. Florida is insular.

The greed and acquisitiveness that marked these first European forays into Florida set the tone for the next half-millennium and likely beyond. Much of what afflicts Florida today is the result of these two paramount human motivations.

This was something Grete encountered frequently. When she filled a new eyeglass prescription, Medicare was billed three times for the same pair of glasses. I notified the U.S. Department of Health and Human Services (HHS) about the scam and, in return, received what amounted to a shoulder shrug, HHS's explanation being that this was a minor offense compared to the more egregious Medicare fraud rampant in Miami-Dade. Grete was outraged by the government's tepid response.

Grete and Ernest were constantly barraged by fast-talking con men huckstering all sorts of items to senior citizens. One of the more ubiquitous scams is the appliance service contract. Aunt Rose bought one of these for each of her appliances. This scam only scratches the surface of Florida cons.

Age and Youth

Miami and Florida represent both ends of the age spectrum. Florida's senior citizen population is over 25 percent, the highest in the nation. At the same time, Florida epitomizes America's youth culture, demonstrated by the surging influx of young people from Latin America and the Caribbean, not to mention South Beach where youth is worshipped like no other place this side of Hollywood.

The presence of young people was important to Grete who, although she resided in Miami Beach from ages 73 to 88, always said she felt her psychological age to be around 24. The energy field that South Florida youth exuded energized her as well.

Grete and Ernest were only peripherally affected by the criminality and drug-related violence that ravaged South Florida in the 1980s. They learned to be careful where they went . . . and when. They deplored the constant barrage of stories in the Miami *Herald* about corrupt politicians, random murders, car jackings, etc., but fortunately were never victims. One reason might be that, as they entered their ninth decade, driving became an issue. Grete wisely gave up driving when she turned 78 in 1983 before declining reflexes and judgment would have forced her to do so. Ernest only reluctantly gave up driving at age 81 in 1986 after suffering a few minor accidents. Subsequently, they traveled around town by bus and cab.

They loved visiting Everglades National Park and taking in its luxuriant collection of thousands of plant and animal species, some found nowhere else. They often walked the Anhinga Trail, marveling at nature's diversity and fecundity.

Another region they frequented, especially early in their Florida tenure, was the third leg of the state's watery triad (the first two being the oceans and Lake Okeechobee), the spectacular natural springs that dot the center of the state north of Lake Okeechobee. There are more than 600 of them and they are a source of fascination for the few tourists who discover their existence. Many of them maintain a consistent water temperature of 73 degrees year-round. Blue Springs is the winter home of more than 300 manatees. Juniper Springs is so crystal clear that its bottom topography almost 50 feet down is as crisply visible as the bottom of a bathroom sink. Rainbow Springs and Silver Springs, both heavily commercialized in the 1950s, offer glass-bottom boats enabling tourists to view the unusual flora and fauna the springs support. Grete and Ernest visited them all.

Chapter 74
Gloom over Miami

As the years mounted up, Grete and Ernest's health problems did too. Grete suffered two life-threatening health crises. In 1987, age 82, she was diagnosed with Stage 4 colon cancer, in which the cancerous tumor spread into the outer walls of her colon and was suspected of involving her lymph nodes. Major surgery removed the tumor and the affected lymph nodes in addition to several feet of colon, and Grete remained cancer-free for the remaining two decades of her life.

While in recovery, I was convinced that she was going to die and did not want to leave her side. Ernest, however, insisted on keeping a lunch appointment at Hilda's where his cousin Herbert and wife Zelda were visiting from New York. This was not the first time Ernest dismissed a serious health matter in order to attend a social event involving cousins. For a man of sound judgment about life's important matters, he was naïve when it came to the frivolous.

As Ernest no longer drove, I had to leave my mother's bedside and ferry him to the lunch. Herbert was a bitter curmudgeon who never forgave fate for interrupting his medical education in Vienna (he was a medical technician in America). He kept his spouse on a short leash. Despite Herbert and Zelda's awareness of Grete's surgery, they never asked about her. After Herbert died, Zelda came out of her domestic prison and began writing poetry and mingling with other human beings.

Grete's second major health crisis was, ironically given her adulation of Dr. Ignaz Semmelweis (see above), a battle with sepsis, a blood infection responsible for more than a quarter million deaths every year. She was 86 years old, which exacerbated the threat. When I arrived at the hospital, I was shocked at her weakness and appearance and, once again, believed this was the end. Once again, she somehow survived.

At the same time, Ernest's health began failing. The first indication was a loss of taste buds that carry the sweetness message to the brain. He began pouring sugar into his tea as if the Florida sugar industry was depending on him. This odd conduct alerted us to observe him more carefully, which revealed other behaviors indicative of cognitive problems that evolved into dementia.

I was flying down to South Florida four or more times a year, whenever there was a health or other emergency. It got to the point that it became necessary to seek an alternative to Grete and Ernest living alone.

Part Six
Arlington, 1994 - 2007

"What we have done for ourselves alone dies with us; what we have done for others and the world remains and is immortal."

Albert Pike

"Every man must define his identity against his mother. If he does not, he just falls back into her and is swallowed up."

Camille Paglia

Chapter 75
The Final Relocation

In 1994, my parents moved into our Arlington, Virginia home where we could look after them. It did not take much persuasion for them to agree to the move. Grete saw the logic of it right away (by this time, Ernest's dementia was sufficiently advanced that Grete had to assume the role of sole decision-maker), but fretted that they would be a burden. At the time, we had a 16- and 13-year old in the house, plus Baskerville, our West Highland White Terrier.

We added an addition to the house so that Grete and Ernest would have a comfortable, private "in-law" suite with a handicapped-accessible bathroom on the first floor. When they moved in, they were aged 88 and 89, respectively.

Their transition went well. Grete was the most vigorous 88-year old imaginable.

My mother's solution to overburdening us was simple. She appointed herself Ernest's primary caregiver. She did virtually everything for him, generally without complaint. Occasionally, however, his antics and behavior got the best of this otherwise most patient person. I cannot blame her for that because living with a person suffering from dementia is never easy. Despite intellectualizing it and reminding yourself that the sufferer cannot help himself, it still gets to you. While our experience with Ernest's dementia was relatively brief (two years), we experienced it again some years later when Anne's mother moved in with us for nearly five years of progressively worsening dementia.

Grete periodically lost her temper with my dad. My children were terrific with him, and Anne became his great defender and champion, demonstrating almost inhuman patience.

We quickly fell into a three-generation family routine. The best thing about it was that most of the time we were all able to be together at dinner despite our busy schedules. We all benefited from the cross-generational repartee and information exchange.

Our children derived a lot out of living with their grandmother. Moreover, they were far more eager to tell her about their daily activities than they ever were to report to us. We reaped the collateral benefits of eavesdropping. It added much to the tapestry of our lives that Grete was an incessant cross-examiner, avidly interested in her grandchildren's doings.

That was the plus side of mealtimes. Less uplifting was watching Ernest deteriorate from a once-vibrant personality who dominated dinner-table conservation, but who now could not follow and whose eating habits increasingly became more bizarre. His principal contribution consisted of questions such as: "Are you my wife? Are you my son? Is Hedy my sister? Where are we?" It was painful to observe.

Grete insisted on helping with meal preparation. Other than desserts and the occasional boiled beef (boiling was her preferred cooking mode, with frying a close second) and red cabbage, Grete never cared much about cooking. She was OK with potatoes, deriving from the multiple times in her life when they were the staple of every meal.

When not ministering to Ernest, Grete spent her days reading, talking on the phone to her sister, Rose, and various friends (by the time Grete died, only Rose was left), and maintaining an extensive correspondence. Television, even when her hearing was still good and her eyesight passable, was never that interesting to her, with certain exceptions, such as the OJ Simpson trial. She watched it every day, then exchanged impressions about every nuance with both Aunt Hilda and sister Rose each night.

Grete did not want to make any new friends her age, so even after Ernest died and her time was completely her own, she opted out of joining anything, visiting a Senior Citizens Center, or responding to invitations from other senior citizens. Our friend, Irene Wittig, had her half-Jewish Viennese mother here, but it was even impossible to persuade Grete to forge a friendship with her despite the many things they might have had in common.

Instead, many of our friends became her friends, too. When she was at home dying, several friends paid her a respectful final visit. That touched us greatly.

A high point of her weekly routine was our Saturday morning library visit, where she would stock up on books and "people-watch." She had always been a great library fan from her earliest years, but that was much more difficult in Europe than in the United States. In Vienna, libraries were few, had limited collections, and charged patrons for taking out books. During tough economic times, she could not even afford their modest rental fees.

When Grete arrived in the United States and visited a branch of the New York Public Library system for the first time, she thought she was in heaven. She was amazed that she was not restricted to taking out one book per visit and did not have to pay for the privilege. She became a regular library user for the next 68 years.

We rarely missed a Saturday library visit, even after her macular degeneration rendered her unable to read. She still insisted on going and waited patiently while I found my own books, as well as ones in which I thought she would be interested, whereupon Anne and I would read them to her.

Chapter 76
Dad Departs

Ernest became prone to falling and hurting himself, including falling out of bed at night, bed rails notwithstanding. Fortunately, his injuries were usually cuts and bruises and not broken bones. We eventually prevailed upon his primary care physician to halve the doses of several of his medications (by this time he was downing prescription meds like a drug addict) and his falling virtually ceased.

Ernest declined rapidly after his 50th wedding anniversary in March 1995. By summer 1996, it was apparent that the end was near. In late July, Grete agreed that we could invoke hospice-at-home assistance and equipment, so we obtained a hospital bed and visiting nursing care. Ernest's nighttime issues escalated and we were compelled to engage the services of overnight caregivers.

In the third week of August, Ernest's condition became grave and by the 22nd, it was clear that death was imminent. The next day was wrenching. Anne left that morning with the kids for David's freshman orientation at Cornell. They said their goodbyes to him, knowing it would be for the last time.

Ernest passed away in his sleep that night. To our regret, neither Grete nor I was with him at the time. Although we had instructed the night companion to call us if he showed any distress signs, she fell asleep and was unaware that he had died.

Ernest asked to be cremated and to dispense with any kind of memorial service. Although I agreed to respect his wishes, I felt that I could only do so regarding the cremation. Several months after he died, we held a memorial service at the temple in Geneva, New York where we had been members when I was growing up. Grete was not pleased, but she did not protest too much. The turnout was quite large. Ernest had made a lot of friends in Canandaigua.

Grete lived another ten-and-a-half years after Ernest's death. The first eight, her quality of life ranged from good to acceptable. She was able to walk, see enough to read, and hear okay.

She was so concerned about burdening us that she frequently said nothing when she should have said something. That included health matters that, once we found out about them, required hospitalization.

Chapter 77
Decline

Immediately following my dad's passing, Grete became depressed for the first time in her life and announced that she intended to starve herself to death. When this continued for several days, I became sufficiently concerned that I asked my cousin Jim (my *de facto* brother) to come from New York to see if he could cheer her up. She was always delighted by his visits. That succeeded as a temporary distraction, but shortly after Jim and his wife, Joan, left, Grete reverted. What finally turned the tide was our argument that it would be unfair to David, who was away at school, to do something so draconian without giving him a chance to see her one last time and say goodbye. Fortunately, she agreed. By the time David came home for the holidays several weeks later, Grete had forgotten about her desire to self-destruct. However, as she aged, the more appealing death appeared to her.

Grete inevitably experienced additional and more quickly recurring health crises. At age 99, she got a pacemaker after a severe bout with shortness of breath resulting from congestive heart failure and a long-time valve deficiency. Both the anesthesiologist and the surgeon reported to me that they had never encountered a patient like her . . . at any age. Entering the operating room, she lectured them on the history of anesthesia and regaled them with anecdotes of Vienna Medical School.

In September 2003, we were besieged by Hurricane Isabel. Not only were we without power for eight days, but we also had both moms with us as well as a dying dog, our beloved

Baskerville. Grete weathered the ordeal better than any of us, never complaining.

The inevitable decline accompanying very old age became noticeable over the next two years. Her hearing, vision, and mobility all deteriorated dramatically. We tried to stave off the inevitable through doctor visits, experimenting with various compensatory vision and hearing devices, and spending more time reading to and talking with her. Her mental acuity never suffered.

September 24, 2005 marked Grete's 100th birthday. We celebrated with a gala birthday party attended by a hundred guests from all over the country and Europe. We hid the fact of the party from her until three days before the event, knowing that both her objections and anxiety would be monumental. My future son-in-law, West, helped with the preparations. Despite our trepidations, she brought off her role in the affair famously and was literally the center of attention. It was a magic evening.

In mid-December, 2006, Grete had to be hospitalized for a variety of reasons having to do with being 101 years old. By the end of the year, there was little point in Grete remaining in the hospital. She came home to a hospice engagement and a hospital bed. Friends and family came to say goodbye.

The first week of 2007 was her last week on Earth. It was a difficult one for her physically, but she was still totally alert and mentally aware, and accepting of what we all knew awaited her. No complaint or railing against fate ever escaped her lips.

Grete's granddaughter Elizabeth spent the entire day January 6, 2007 by her grandmother's bed, holding her hand as she gradually drifted away from us. Anne, Grete's grandson, David, his fiancée Jessica and I were in and out of the bedroom all day long.

This was the first and only day of her long life that she was unable to communicate. She was not in a coma, but her ability to express herself had vanished overnight.

We tend to accept that a loved one's demise is inevitable and move on. Nonetheless, I had a very hard time watching my mother die. Although I was born when she was almost 41 years old, she had been a central part of my life for six decades.

Oedipal attraction had nothing to do with it. Grete and I had a special relationship on multiple levels: intellectual; emotional; psychological.

In my life, I have met and interacted with a fairly large number of individuals who rose to positions of great prominence in politics and government, entertainment, science, art, athletics and education. Some impressed me (Bobby Kennedy, Eugene McCarthy, Frank Shorter, Romy Schneider, Vladimir Nabokov, Hannah Arendt, Vincent Scully, Saul Padover, to name a few), but none as much as Grete. Her attitudes, compassion, outlook, modesty, humility, practicality, and quickness of mind and everything else about her put her on a pedestal above any of the presidents (Bush 41 and 43), scholars, etc., whom I have encountered.

As day turned into evening, we gathered around her bed for a final goodbye. While I will always regret that I was not present at my dad's side when he died, I will always value my good fortune at being present at my mom's passing. It warms my heart that my family was there, too.

During the day, each one of us spent private moments with Grete, talking to her.

Grete died at 9:30 that evening. She faced her last hours with the same dignity with which she had lived her extraordinary life.

Grete's 100th birthday, September 24, 2005
[clockwise from top left: the author, daughter-in-law Anne,
grandson David, granddaughter Elizabeth, Grete]
Author's collection

Chapter 78
Maternal Vignettes

I don't want to leave this "bio-history" without relating a few "vignettes" about Grete that informed her life and character.

Patience

Her father, David, could erupt with very little provocation. Her mother was in danger of collapsing into a deep depression at any time, at which point her personality underwent a 180-degree transformation bordering on hysteria and suicidal ideation. Her brother Ben was a nervous man, always worried about something, especially being separated from his money. His wife, Mildred, was loud, intense and hyper, but also very caring: The day before I reported for the military draft, she sent me two unwearable tuxedo dress shirts—one bright yellow turtleneck with ruffles; the other an electric blue—accompanied by a lovely note wishing me well in the Army. She was the only relative who understood what I was about to encounter and took the time to boost my spirits. I did not dare inquire as to the mystifying meaning of her gifts.

Grete's brother Otto, a brilliant man who became an Ob-Gyn, was calm on the outside, but a volcano within. He was the most complicated of the siblings and the most interesting from a psychological standpoint. The only time I got really close to him was when he knew he was dying of stomach cancer and I visited him at his home in Florida, where we spent three days talking about family.

Grete's sister, Rose, was the living definition of "impatient." She did not countenance fools easily and viewed most of humanity as fools. She also had no use for anyone whom she perceived did her wrong and was quick to cut them out of her life. Her grudges were Sicilian.

Grete's patience manifested itself in the most beneficial way to me and my childhood interests. Thanks to her wide circle of relatives, friends and acquaintances around the world, I received a steady flow of postage stamps and began collecting and organizing them with Grete's encouragement and limitless patience. She sat with me for hours while I "processed" the stamps, elaborating on the issuing countries, their history and geography, and on the people and places depicted on them. When she could not explain something, she took me to the local library to find the answer. I learned more about the world, history, geopolitics and geography from stamp collecting and from her than I ever did in school. At lunch one day in college with *New York Times* columnist James Reston, who was a week-long guest of my residential college, I mentioned the vast store of knowledge contained in collecting stamps. He told me he had done the same thing as a child. He went on to say that my Yale education was a waste of money. All I really needed, he said, were the stamps and reading the *Times* cover-to-cover every day!

Grete also encouraged me to pursue my other interests, which included an obsession with birds. She bought me my first bird book when I was five years old (I still have it) and taught me to document my sightings. Once in a Florida state park, she and I were convinced that we had seen an Ivory-Billed Woodpecker, believed to be extinct, and duly noted the sighting in my bird book. She also encouraged my collections of maps, books, butterflies, beetles, shells, rocks and minerals. She was patient and encouraging even when I brought home live bugs that probably should not have been invited into a house. However, she was outspokenly critical of my baseball card collection.

I don't want to leave the impression that Grete was indulgent. She could punish with the best of parents and occasionally even administered corporal punishment. It took a lot of provocation to drive her to that point, and I tested the limits frequently. Ernest was much quicker with the lash, but also quick to regret it later, especially when he misinterpreted something Grete told him about my misdemeanors (which were considerable). I richly deserved most of what I received.

Playing the Ponies

Canandaigua was home to one of New York State's four thoroughbred race tracks. While light years from the high standards and relative honesty of Aqueduct, Belmont and Saratoga, Grete was delighted by the proximity of a place where she could go and place the occasional bet. She would return home in high spirits even if she only won five dollars. When her father lived with us, the two of them often dropped everything and headed for the race track.

Years later when she moved in with us, she had me place bets on the annual Triple Crown races. That was easy when the news store in my office building maintained an illegal bookmaking operation in the back of the store. However, the proprietor sold the business to devout Koreans who abhorred horse betting. I was briefly able to rely on a cook/amateur bookie who worked at a restaurant near my office. When he lost his job, I had to scramble. I found another bookmaking shop located over a Vietnamese dry cleaning operation in neighboring Falls Church, Virginia. That relationship lasted only two years before a police raid shut it down. I then resorted to online betting.

As the Kentucky Derby approached each year, I bought the *Daily Racing Form* and Grete and I would spend hours poring over the assessments of that year's four-legged athletic talent. Grete was anything but a sophisticated horse player. Instead, she selected her betting choices based on either the steed's name or its stirring biography. Horses with humble histories like Derby winners Funny Cide and Smarty Jones captured her heart every time. If one of "her" horses won the first two legs of the Triple Crown, Belmont day was overflowing with excitement and anticipation for her. Her disappointment when Silver Charm, Real Quiet, Charismatic, War Emblem, Funny Cide and Smarty Jones lost the Belmont was palpable.

Toward the end of her life, her methodology paid off consistently. From age 96 to 100 (2002 – 2006), she picked five successive Kentucky Derby winners in a row and realized a nice financial haul. Her best Triple Crown run in those years was 2002-2004, when War Emblem, Funny Cide and Smarty Jones all went to the post in the Belmont Stakes having previously won both the Kentucky Derby and the Preakness Stakes. All three failed in the Belmont, Smarty Jones by a mere length at the wire, and Grete's hopes were dashed.

She was never in it for the money, but rather for the thrill. During the races, she became more excited than I ever saw her in any other context. I was always bemused by my mother's avid interest in horse racing. As far as I could tell, it was her only vice.

The Diagnostician

Grete's greatest diagnostic achievement was identifying her grandfather Liber's stomach cancer when his regular physicians believed his problem was mere indigestion. It was also her greatest regret, as documented earlier in this book.

She was always spot on when it came to the more mundane ills that cropped up in the family. Armed with her dog-eared *Merck Manual*, she would retire to her bedroom and pore over its pages after performing a visual and tactile examination of the sufferer (usually one of the children). Her analyses invariably led to the implementation of her recommended therapies. Unlike Ernest, however, she wisely kept her medical "practice" within the family.

Grete did not limit her diagnostic activities to physical health. Being from Vienna and having received her medical education at Sigmund Freud's medical school, she (and every other Viennese physician I ever met) considered herself at least a competent amateur psychoanalyst. She had done a psychiatry rotation in medical school, but opted out of pursuing it as a career specialty. That was because, with the possible exception of Freud's daughter Anna and his great friend Marie Bonaparte, few women were accepted into this closed fraternity. In addition, she remained a lifelong skeptic about Freudianism and psychiatry.

Without knowing it, she was a practitioner of *metoposcopy*, roughly translated as reading the human face. Although definitely not a Eugenicist, she fancied herself an expert on the shape of the nose, the height of the forehead, age lines, and chin variations. She constantly remarked on what someone's face and physical affect told her about a person.

While pride was not one of Grete's vices, she derived a great deal of satisfaction when one of her diagnoses proved correct. She was able to perform this special talent throughout her nineties.

"Jauses"

The simplest translation of *jause* (pronounced YOW-zeh) is a mid-afternoon snack. Revered in Vienna and by every ex-pat Viennese, a jause is much more than a mere snack. For them it is a holy ritual akin to British high tea. My parents were uncompromising jause devotees and never missed the opportunity to indulge.

Their typical jause consisted of tea or coffee and a sweet. It was also a time for setting work aside and indulging in relaxed conversation. More serious topics were reserved for the dinner table.

The jause's origins derive from an old Viennese custom that Vienna's Jewish community adopted with avid enthusiasm. Go to Vienna today and you will immediately discover that the jause is still alive and thriving.

Not Exactly the Iron Chef

Grete said that, when she got married, she could not boil water. She was not a remarkable cook by any assessment. She had a basic repertoire and stuck to it like a bulldog.

Fortunately Ernest was undemanding when it came to food. He ate anything Grete put in front of him and generally praised her efforts. It also helped that, due to his lifelong stomach issues—he suffered his first ulcer as a teenager and stomach pain was sometimes a daily occurrence, occasionally landing him in the hospital—Grete felt that he had to maintain a bland diet. Spices were non-existent in our household. Until I got married, I never heard of Cumin, Cardamom, Coriander or Cilantro . . . and that is only the "C's." Vegetables were overcooked to the point where they begged for mercy. I did not know that green beans were not naturally limp and mushy until my first meal in a Chinese restaurant. I knew my mother admired Salvador Dali's drafting skills, but this degree of droopiness was ridiculous. Chicken was boiled to the point of surrender and was generally tasteless.

The consequence of growing up in Vienna and experiencing great deprivation was that we ate potatoes almost every day for supper, usually, but not always, as a side dish. Variety was not within Grete's wheelhouse. Her association with the potato was generally one of boiled blandness. It complemented the boiled chicken perfectly.

We also ate soup almost every day. Homemade chicken soup—generally a broth, although in her nineties she began to throw in any reckless leftover that was not tied down or well concealed in the refrigerator—or Campbell's Cream of Mushroom, which even Grete could not render tasteless.

Grete was a big fan of matzo ball soup, the mother's milk of the soup universe if not perhaps its greatest achievement. Her matzo balls would not have passed inspection by the Jewish Matzo Ball Police. They were weaponized. Get hit with one and she would have had to consult her *Merck Manual* to minister to the concussed. When confronted with matzo balls outside our house, I was amazed at their softness and roundness. Grete's always came with interesting and undefinable shapes, including jagged edges that could have caused graver injuries than mere blunt force trauma. Some of them looked like Clovis culture arrowheads.

Grete would not allow us to eat a soup until it had been boiled, left to sit for 1-2 days, and been skimmed of fat several times over. She was a health food fanatic without realizing it and decades before it became popular. After Ernest died, she performed a 180-degree reversal and began eating the most unhealthy foods imaginable. When one achieves a great age, she said, one is more likely to die of something else long before clogged arteries become an issue.

Another manifestation of her health food orientation was vegetable patties, lightly fried (in vegetable oil, never butter) mishmashes that served as entrées 2-3 dinners a week.

Needless to say, I was a skinny kid, with shoulder blades that should have been registered with the FBI as lethal weapons. When I went away to college, I thought I had entered food heaven and gorged myself on all of the taboo repasts I had missed as a child. When I discovered that New Haven had a McDonald's, I was in heaven. I went to college weighing 130 lbs. and came home for Thanksgiving three months later 30 lbs. heavier.

Where Grete deviated from her desultory approach to cooking was with respect to desserts. It is impossible to grow up in Vienna and not have a yen for sweets. Grete was no exception, and her sweet tooth and that of Ernest were obsessional. Fruit dumplings (apricot and plum in particular), *guglhupf*, a uniquely Viennese light cake, and her crown jewel—*apfelstrudel*, apple strudel—represented the apotheosis of her dessert achievements. She placed the strudel dough on a cutting board and attacked it for hours to stretch the dough. It almost always came out spectacular. She gave her last strudel lessons to her acolytes—my wife, daughter, soon-to-be daughter-in-law, and several friends—when she was 101.

The best dish she introduced me to was an Austrian specialty called *topfennudeln*, noodles with cottage cheese. While Italians probably want to rush to the Tyrolean border and declare a *fatwa* when they contemplate pasta without tomato sauce, for Austrians (and me), topfennudeln takes pasta to the next level. My Italian-American wife, who grew up believing that sauce was the nectar of the gods, also eats it . . . and likes it.

Grete carried with her a much-abused *Settlement Cook Book*, a well-worn antique paperback. Despite constant referral to it, she never followed a recipe verbatim.

Vacations

Every year we spent the week between Christmas and New Year's in New York City. I stayed with my cousin Jim and his family in their Brooklyn flat while my parents stayed in the only motel within five miles, the Golden Gate. The Golden Gate's usual clientele consisted of "connected" fellows and "made" men plus a steady stream of aging ladies who rented rooms by the hour. Ernest got propositioned one evening and only realized that this was a business transaction after Grete told him.

Spring break was spent in Florida with Rose and Ted. We always either drove the whole distance (1,500 miles) over dubious highways that predated Interstate 95 or left the car in Richmond, Virginia and traveled by train the rest of the way.

Driving with my dad was an adventure. He was abrupt and had a major lead foot. He was often stopped for speeding, but rarely ticketed due to his "MD" license plate.

Unfortunately, that was not the way the local constabulary in Georgia saw it. On two separate occasions, he was caught speeding while traversing two of the most notorious speed traps in America—Jesup and Ludowici, Georgia.

Both times he argued with the local cops and lost. Pointing out his "MD" license plate made the situations worse. Grete tried to shut him up, to no avail. Ernest could never understand that the magic "MD" on a New York State license plate did not carry any weight in the rural South. It also did not help that he had a German accent.

One year, we took along a recently widowed refugee from nearby Penn Yan, New York. Whenever she saw something interesting, she let loose with an ear-shattering primal scream that came close to causing Ernest to have accidents. When this happened in those pre-seat belt days, Ernest, fearing an imminent collision, flung his right arm across Grete's chest to prevent her from going through the windshield. Sore ribs were the result. Our passenger was never invited to accompany us again.

Some years, we detoured in order to explore the rest of Florida. The north-central Florida springs were a big hit, but the best venue of all was Weeki Wachee, where comely, bikini-clad "mermaids" jiggled around under water breathing every minute or so through air tubes that hung below the surface. Viewers stood inside a sealed glass structure that hung below the water surface. Ernest loved the show. Grete was not amused.

My parents' other trips were for health reasons. Ernest's violent annual hay fever attacks were disabling, making it impossible to stay in Canandaigua. He developed an annual routine of going away for approximately six weeks every year (once he could afford to close his practice for that length of time) between mid-August and the end of September, when ragweed blooms in Western New York like spring tulips in Holland. He always sought a ragweed-free environment for his trips. Over the years, Grete and Ernest traveled to Maine, Arizona, Colorado, California, Ontario, Quebec, Western Canada, the Maritime Provinces, Austria, Italy, Switzerland, France, Spain, Portugal, Greece, Sweden, Denmark and Yugoslavia. I went along on some of their early U.S. trips when

I was very young, never enamored of their itinerary, which always included Ernest's passions—classical music and visiting cemeteries, as well as stopping at every turn in the road to take multiple, redundant, and un-captioned pictures of mountains.

On a much later trip, I joined my parents and Aunt Rose in Munich, drove to Vienna, then south to Yugoslavia. On the way, we stopped in Wiener Neustadt so that Grete and I could see the former Jaul and Blum family compounds. Ernest became very emotional, so we left for *Klagenfurt*, the capital of the Austrian province of *Carinthia*, where we lost Ernest during a walk. Grete inquired as to the nearest cemetery and, of course, there he was.

Several childhood trips were memorable. To get to Colorado in 1951, we flew from Rochester to Detroit to Chicago to St. Louis to Kansas City to Omaha to Denver. It was my first flight(s) and I was thrilled. The minute we deplaned in Denver, I retched all over the tarmac. Grete insisted on cleaning up my mess.

We drove to Aspen where a music festival featuring conductor Pierre Monteux promised Grete and Ernest many evenings of pleasure. This was good, as it neutralized the hell that their 5-year old put them through at dinner every night. I disliked the hotel food and refused to eat. Grete forced me to sit at the table until I cleaned my plate and a battle of wills ensued. I discovered during one of these sit-ins that it was possible to self-induce vomiting. After that revelation, Grete gave up.

Babysitters with Attitude

These late-summer trips made me miss school every year. This affected my parents not in the least, and I spent years AWOL for the first month of every grade from first through fifth. It never affected my grades, more a comment on elementary education in the 1950s than on my abilities.

When sixth grade came around, my constant pestering to be present at the opening of the school year (and avoid embarrassment at being "different"—I was already different enough) finally struck a chord. A babysitter was engaged to stay with me.

Over the next several years, Grete put together a collection of babysitters who could have found employment in circus sideshows. Frau K was a German immigrant who had written an unpublished book—*Der Flucht* (The Flight)—about her emigration. She forced me to read and discuss it with her while caring for me.

Frau K possessed all of the traits I associated with Germans derived from World War II propaganda films and TV wrestling shows where the scripted villains were head-shaved thugs with names like Hans Schmidt (real name: Guy Larose)—a.k.a. "The Teuton Terror"—and Fritz von Erich (real name: Jack Barton Adkisson) who brutalized their hapless opponents with "claw" holds and other Nazi tortures.

Frau K's cooking made Grete's look like gourmet meals prepared by the Barefoot Contessa. She brooked no bullshit from me and, after only 24 hours, had me sufficiently terrorized that I began counting the days until she would be out of my life.

The thought of a second year of Frau K had me begging Grete for an alternative. This one turned out to be a gentle, grandmotherly soul—Mrs. I—an emotionless widow with a robotic, Stepfordian affect who let me do anything I wanted. However, she reminded me of the axe murderer in a gothic horror movie. She had the same constant, subtle smile and was inordinately quiet. Fredericka Kruger. I locked my bedroom door at night and put a chair under the doorknob. She stayed with me for two years of parental absence.

And then it happened.

The next year, my mother hired a 24-year old nurse she knew from the local hospital, a Norwegian who, if the term "hot" had not yet been invented to describe pulchritudinous females, would have been in order to label her. She was tall, blonde, apple-complexioned, and equipped with a centerfold body. When she walked in the door to meet me the day before my parents left, I was speechless, an early teen whose hormones were running riot.

The first evening, when I came home from school, the goddess was at the stove cooking dinner. She had on an apron, a bra and panties. Period. I thought I had died and gone to Valhalla. She ate dinner that way, but I had no appetite. I could not fathom her deal. I assumed her mode of dress (undress?) was a cultural thing, something to do with being Scandinavian.

I spent the next six weeks in a state of constant *agita*, which did nothing for my academic performance. Watching her jiggle around the house in her underwear was torture. By the time my folks returned home, I was actually glad to see her go.

By the next year, I was allowed to stay home alone, and found that I could discipline myself quite well. I ate topfennudeln every night.

Many years later, when Grete was in her high 90s and sitting in our living room, she suddenly burst out: *"What was I thinking?!"* She explained to Anne—who already knew the story—that it had just occurred to her that it was probably a bad idea to have left her adolescent son in the agonizing throes of puberty in the care of a major babe.

Possessions

Grete hated owning things. Possessions, she believed, were an albatross that constrained her freedom. She was obsessed with ridding herself of "stuff." By the time she died, she owned almost no personal property.

Her determination to divest herself of material objects also led to an antipathy toward accepting gifts regardless of the occasion or giver. She grudgingly accepted books because her enthusiasm for reading neutralized her gift aversion. For her hundredth birthday party, we went to considerable lengths to prevail upon invitees to forego gifts.

The converse to her gift-aversion was a compulsion to give things away. Family heirlooms and meaningful and occasionally valuable objects went flying out of our house.

Practical Life Lessons

Grete was Elmer Gantry when it came to teaching life lessons to me and her grandchildren, and sometimes others as well. Preaching is not the best way to get a teachable moment across, but she never understood that. The exception was when she relied on her own version of the "Brandeis Brief" (future Supreme Court Justice Louis Brandeis won landmark cases before the Court by overwhelming the justices with socio-economic data), barraging the object of her advocacy with facts.

The example I remember best had to do with shaving cream. When I began shaving, she persuaded me that soap worked just as well and was much cheaper. It was a pet peeve of hers that Ernest overindulged in shaving cream. Every morning, he slathered his face until he looked like Santa Claus. Failing with her husband, she turned her attention to me, barraging me with the results of her analysis of the composition of shaving cream vs. soap. She discovered that shaving cream was really soap plus additives that gave it a foamy composition and white color. Since then, I have relied only on soap. Anytime Grete could find a way to save money was a triumph.

Bartering

Grete believed that there was no such thing as a fixed price for any retail sales object. Consequently, she insisted on negotiating, even in national retail outlets. Two examples:

- She walked into a Pier One seeking a rug. When she found one she liked, she bartered with the shocked sales associate until he gave up out of exhaustion and sold it to her for half its listed price.

- I took her to Macy's to buy tops that were already on sale. In less than ten minutes, she convinced the sales lady to sell them to her for 60 percent of the sales price.

My reaction to her insistence on bartering was a combination of embarrassment and admiration. The more I saw her in action, the more impressed I became.

Chapter 79
Eulogy

I gave my mother's eulogy at her memorial service from a few cryptic notes. What follows is an elaboration of those notes:

The only thing I have in common with Hugh Hefner is that we have both spent a lifetime surrounded by amazing women.

Most of you here knew my mom very well, some of you for decades, others for the past 12-plus years that we were blessed to have her living with us. So you know how amazing she was.

One of the things that warmed our hearts was that *our* friends became *her* friends.

Since you know much about her 101 years of life, I am only going to update you on some of the more memorable incidents of her last two weeks.

She took ill on Saturday before Christmas. Anne and I took her to the hospital emergency room. When we went in for her to be examined, the nurse said:

"Hi sweetie, what seems to be the problem?"

Mom's response quickly disabused the ER staff of their customary and off-putting condescension toward very old people: She responded: "I have fluid in my right hydrothorax. I have a history of congestive heart failure. I have a mitral valve prolapse that probably is leaking more than before, all of which makes me short of breath."

After that, condescension was off the table.

She remained in the hospital for ten days, during which I was with her much of the time. It was a good time despite the circumstances. We talked about important things and frivolous ones, too. From time-to-time, she deftly turned the conversation to weightier matters. Once, out of the blue, she asked me:

"When does Jack Kevorkian ["Dr. Death"] get out of jail?"

"In a few months," I responded. "Why?"

"That's a shame," she exclaimed. "I was hoping we could visit him and he could hook me up to his euthanasia machine."

She was not finished with this line of questioning.

"A few months is too long. How about if you and I fly to Oregon? Don't they have an assisted suicide law there?"

"I'm pretty sure you have to be an Oregon resident, mom."

She still was not finished.

"Holland, maybe? They euthanize. We could ask Phil about it."

Philomeen is our friends' Mary and Gerry Stoopman's cousin who lives in the Netherlands. She became a friend of my mom's during her visits to her cousins and often sent Grete glossy Dutch picture magazines of Holland's royal family.

I read a book to her, *Victoria's Daughters*, that she found fascinating. Her eyes were so bad by this time, due to an advanced case of macular degeneration, that she could no longer read herself, losing one of her life's greatest pleasures. I did not have a book mark with me, so every time I put the book down I tried to make it a point to remember the page where I left off. I never did. No matter. Mom was always able to tell me exactly where I had stopped reading.

The other diversion we did regularly was the daily *Washington Post* crossword puzzle. I would read her the clue and the number of letters and she would attempt to provide the proper word or phrase. She did this without seeing the crossword.

She left us a wonderful legacy and memories:

- Anne, a daughter-in-law who was closer to her than most daughters could be.
- David, a grandson who was always her champion, constantly berating me for not taking good enough care of her.

- Elizabeth, a granddaughter who has so many of her qualities (patience aside).
- Brooklyn, our daughter's pit bull who spends a lot of time with us and loved to jump up on the sofa next to mom and lay her head in her lap for some serious nuzzling.
- Our weekly Saturday morning trips to the library just across the parking lot from where we are now, where she loved to browse for books and watch the children run about.
- Her stories of growing up before World War I, going to medical school almost for free, working the tuberculosis ward as a resident, getting her piano instructor's degree.
- Listening to her tell her grandchildren how abysmal a musician I was.
- Standing on the tarmac at the Rochester airport in a snowstorm watching me go off to Fort Dix for boot camp.
- Quietly seething when my dad flipped the TV around from the living room to the dining room so we could watch John Cameron Swayze deliver the NBC nightly news while we ate dinner.
- Thanksgivings with multiple members of the Canandaigua clergy from all denominations at the table.
- Her deep sadness when we went on the Internet and discovered just two years ago that an aunt and two cousins who had disappeared during World War II had been murdered at Auschwitz.
- Her delight in the triumphs of her *de jure* grandchildren—David and Elizabeth—and her *de facto* grandchildren, David, Thomas and Devin Shomaker, Aaron and Josh Shapiro, Genevieve James and Michelle Peacock.

- Strudel baking classes for friends. The Saturday after mom died, the women of the family—Anne, Elizabeth, and Jessica—got together to bake strudel in her honor.

She was my role model, one I cannot possibly ever live up to. The best I could do was marry a woman who shares all of her remarkable qualities: compassion; devotion to family and community; responsibility; patience; modesty; self-effacement.

As a kid, we packed care packages for impoverished relatives in England and Austria.

She and my dad would hear about a refugee family somewhere in Western or Central New York and off we would go on Sunday, loaded down with groceries and sundries and tracking them down. The result: the most interesting, diverse and character-laden circle of friends imaginable . . . and all in tiny, remote Canandaigua, New York.

Her philosophy of life was simple:

- Suck it up

- Don't whine

- Don't complain

I want to close with an excerpt from one of her favorite poems: Ulysses by Alfred Lord Tennyson:

> *Tho' much is taken, much abides; and tho'*
> *We are not now that strength which in old days*
> *Moved earth and heaven, that which we are, we are,--*
> *One equal temper of heroic hearts,*
> *Made weak by time and fate, but strong in will*
> *To strive, to seek, to find, and not to yield.*

Epilogue

Grete and Ernest were two of the most grounded individuals I have ever known. Ernest's decision-making was coldly rational, as if he had conducted a cost-benefit analysis before deciding what to do. This was true whether it entailed buying a new car or electing to undergo high-risk, experimental brain surgery when more than 50 percent of the patients died on the operating table. Another example of his decisiveness and good judgment occurred when he attended a medical conference in Mexico City in the 1950s and emplaned on an *Aeronaves de Mexico* flight back to the United States. The plane did not move from the gate and, after two hours of sweltering in his seat, Ernest went forward into the cockpit. The pilot and co-pilot had disassembled the control panel and were debating passionately with one another about how to put the pieces back together again. Ernest left the plane and took the next train to Dallas.

Nevertheless, despite his excellent judgment, Ernest was an amateur numerologist fixated on the number "7" to the point where he obsessed about it at every turn. When his grandson was born at 7:27 AM on January 27, 1978, he announced that the sevens were so properly aligned that the baby was blessed and would have a wonderful, long life.

Grete, secular and non-religious to a fault, was nevertheless one of the more superstitious people I ever encountered. In her 20s, she consulted a medium who read her palm and told her she would marry late, have only one child—a son—and die of a stomach ailment. When the first two predictions came to pass, she accepted the inevitability of the third and spoke of it from time-to-time. Although no autopsy was necessary when she died at home at 101, her stomach did not appear to be involved.

I miss my mother very much. I think about her every day and, along with the emptiness caused by missing her presence, I feel incredibly fortunate that I was able to have her as a loving and forgiving parent for such a long time.

If anyone ever had a better mother, counselor, role model and all around exemplary human being in their life, then they are, to paraphrase Lou Gehrig, the luckiest person alive. She was a great lady in every respect.

Albert Einstein was probably the most famous Jew of the 20th century. In his 1934 book, *The World As I See It*, he explained his gradual, lifelong movement toward viewing himself as a Jew (culturally but not religiously) because of the following traits he identified as Jewish: "The pursuit of knowledge for its own sake, an almost fanatical love of justice, and the desire for personal independence." Einstein's definition is a nice summation of Grete.

What comforts me when I think about her life and her absence now from mine is the old Jewish legend of the *lamed vavniks*, the 36 just (or righteous) men (presumably, this status is not limited only to men) of each generation whose good works are the last best hope of mankind and the bulwark against the ruin of civilization. They do their work without acknowledgement by society and derive nothing of material value for what they do. I cannot imagine that my mother, Grete Sobel Hermann, was not a member of this pantheon.

Finally, Anais Nin once said that writing about our life allows us to experience *"tasting life twice; in the moment and in retrospection."* I was blessed to be able to live much of my mother's life with her and through her, and then to be able to commit it to paper so that future generations of my family and beyond might know about this marvelous human being.

Bibliography

Books

Abzug, Robert H. *America Views the Holocaust 1933-1945.* Boston: Bedford/St. Martin's, 1999.

Arbatov, Georgi. *The System: An Insider's Life in Soviet Politics.* New York and Toronto: Random House, 1992.

Ashdown, Dulcie M. *Royal Murders.* Thrupp, UK: Sutton Publishing, 1998.

Baker, Nicholson. *Human Smoke: The Beginnings of World War II, the End of Civilization.* New York: Simon & Schuster, 2008.

Baldwin, Neil. *Henry Ford and the Jews: The Mass Production of Hate.* New York: Public Affairs, 2001, 2003.

Bard, Mitchell G. *48 Hours of Kristallnacht: Night of Destruction/Dawn of the Holocaust – An Oral History.* Guilford, CT: The Lyons Press, 2008.

Bard, Mitchell C., Ed. *The Holocaust.* San Diego: Greenhaven Press, Inc., 2001.

Behn, Noel. *Lindbergh: The Crime.* New York: The Atlantic Monthly Press, 1994.

Bellak, Leopold, M.D. *Confrontation in Vienna.* Larchmont, NY: C.P.S., Inc., 1993.

Beller, Steven. *A Concise History of Austria.* Cambridge, UK: Cambridge University Press, 2006.

Benz, Wolfgang. *The Holocaust: A German Historian Examines the Genocide.* New York: Columbia University Press, 1999.

Berkley, George E. *Vienna and Its Jews: The Tragedy of Success, 1880s – 1980s.* Cambridge, MA: Abt Books and Lanham, MD: Madison Books, 1988.

Best, Nicholas. *The Greatest Day in History: How, on the Eleventh Hour of the Eleventh Day of the Eleventh Month, the First World War Finally Came to an End.* New York: Public Affairs, 2008.

Borkin, Joseph. *The Crime and Punishment of I.G. Farben.* New York: The Free Press (a Division of Macmillan Publishing Co.), Inc., 1978.

Borowski, Tadeus. *This Way for the Gas, Ladies and Gentlemen.* New York: Penguin Books, 1967.

Canetti, Elias. *Auto-da-Fe.* C.V. Wedgewood, Translator. New York: Stein and Day, Publishers, 1946.

Cantor, Norman. *In the Wake of the Plague: The Black Death and the World It Made.* New York: Simon & Schuster, 2001.

Caro, Robert A. *The Passage of Power: The Years of Lyndon Johnson.* New York: Alfred A. Knopf, 2012.

Cesarini, David. *Becoming Eichmann: Rethinking the Life, Crimes, and Trial of a "Desk Murderer."* Boston: Da Capo Press, 2004.

Chesnoff, Richard Z. *Pack of Thieves: How Hitler and Europe Plundered the Jews and Committed the Greatest Theft in History.* New York: Anchor Books, 1999.

Clare, George. *Last Waltz in Vienna: The Destruction of a Family, 1842-1942.* London: Pan MacMillan, 2002.

Cohen, Beth B. *Case Closed: Holocaust Survivors in Postwar America.* Piscataway, NJ: Rutgers University Press, 2007.

Cohen, David. *The Escape of Sigmund Freud: Freud's Final Years in Vienna and His Flight from the Nazi Rise.* New York: The Overlook Press, Peter Mayer Publishers, Inc., 2009. 2012.

Daniel, Clifton, Editor in Chief. *20th Century Day by Day.* London: Dorling Kindersley Limited, 2000.

Daniels, Roger. *Coming to America, 2d Ed.: A History of Immigration and Ethnicity in American Life.* New York: Perennial, an imprint of Harper Collins Publishers, 1991.

Dawidowicz, Lucy S. *The War Against the Jews, 1933 – 1945.* New York: Holt, Rinehart and Winston, 1975.

——————————. *From That Place and Time: A Memoir, 1938-1947.* New York: W.W. Norton, 1989.

Davis, Nuel Pharr. *Lawrence and Oppenheimer.* New York: Simon & Schuster, 1968.

DeJonge, Alex. *The Life and Times of Grigorii Rasputin.* New York: Dorset Press, 1982.

De Lange, Nicholas. *Atlas of the Jewish World.* New York: Facts on File Publications, 1984.

Dickson, Paul. *Sputnik.* New York: Walker Publishing Co., Inc., 2001.

Einstein, Albert. *The World as I See It.* Gloucester, UK: Stellar Classics, 2014.

Epstein, Helen. *Children of the Holocaust: Conversations with Sons and Daughters of Survivors.* New York: Bantam Books, 1979.

Fay, Sidney Bradshaw. *After Sarajevo: The Origins of the World War, Volume II.* New York: The Free Press, 1966.

Ferguson, Niall. *The Ascent of Money: A Financial History of the World.* New York: The Penguin Press, 2008.

——————————. *The Pity of War: Explaining World War I.* London: Basic Books, 1998.

Fernandez-Armesto, Felipe. *1492: The Year the World Began.* New York: HarperCollins, 2009.

Florence, Ronald. *Emissary of the Doomed: Bargaining for Lives in the Holocaust.* New York: Penguin Group, 2010.

Frankl, Viktor. *Man's Search for Meaning: An Introduction to Logotherapy.* Boston: Beacon Press, 1992.

Freud, Sigmund. *The Interpretation of Dreams.* Huntington, WV: Empire Books, 2011.

Friedlander, Saul. *Nazi Germany and the Jews, Vol 1—The Years of Persecution, 1933-1939.* New York: Harper Collins Publishers, 1997.

_____. *The Years of Extermination: Nazi Germany and the Jews, 1939-1945*. New York: Harper Collins Publishers, 2007.

Friedman, Saul. *No Haven for the Oppressed: United States Policy Toward Jewish Refugees, 1938 – 1945*. Detroit: Wayne State University Press, 1973.

Fussell, Paul. *The Great War and Modern Memory*. Oxford: Oxford University Press, 1975.

Gannon, Michael, Ed. *The New History of Florida*. Gainesville, Tallahassee, Tampa, Boca Raton, Pensacola, Orlando, Miami, Jacksonville: University Press of Florida, 1996.

Gardiner, Muriel. *Code Name "Mary": Memoirs of an American Woman in the Austrian Underground*. New Haven and London: Yale University Press, 1983.

Gelski, Sophie. *Teaching the Holocaust, Revised Edition*. Sydney, Australia: Sydney Jewish Museum, 2012.

Gilbert, Martin. *First World War Atlas*. New York: The Macmillan Company, 1970, 1971.

_____. *Kristallnacht: Prelude to Destruction*. New York: Harper Perennial, 2007.

_____. *The Somme: Heroism and Horror in the First World War*. New York: Henry Holt and Company, 2006.

Gilbert, Martin, Ed. *Churchill: The Power of Words*. Boston: Da Capo Press, 2012.

Golabek, Mona and Lee Cohen. *The Children of Willesden Lane: Beyond the Kindertransport – A Memoir of Music, Love, and Survival*. New York: Warner Books, 2002.

Goldner, Franz. *Austrian Emigration 1938 to 1945*. New York: Frederick Ungar Publishing Co., 1979.

Greene, Graham. *The Third Man*. New York: Viking Press, 1950.

Greene, Joshua M. *Justice at Dachau: The Trials of an American Prosecutor*. New York: Broadway Books, 2003.

Guttman, Israel, Ed. In Chief. *Encyclopedia of the Holocaust, Volumes 1 – 4*. New York: Macmillan Publishing Company; London: Collier Macmillan Publishers, 1990.

Hamerow, Theodore S.. *Why We Watched: Europe, America, and the Holocaust*. New York & London: W.W. Norton & Company, 2008.

Hardach, Gerd. *The First World War 1914 – 1918*. Berkeley and Los Angeles: University of California Press, 1977.

Hayes, Peter. *Why? Explaining the Holocaust*. New York & London: W.W. Norton & Company, 2017.

Heller, Celia S. *On the Edge of Destruction: Jews of Poland Between the Two World Wars*. Detroit: Wayne State University Press, 1977, 1994.

Hermann, Richard. *Practicing Law in Small-Town America*. Chicago: ABA Publications, 2012.

_____ and Margarete Sobel Hermann. *The Grandma Tapes*. Arlington, VA, 2005.

Charles Higham. *Trading With the Enemy: The Nazi-American Money Plot 1933 – 1949*. New York: Barnes & Noble Books, 1983.

Hitler, Adolf. *Mein Kampf*. Translated by Ralph Manheim. New York: Houghton Mifflin Company, 1943.

Himmelfarb, Gertrude. *The People of the Book: Philosemitism in England from Cromwell to Churchill*. New York, London: Encounter Books, 2011.

Hobsbawm, Eric. *The Age of Extremes: A History of the World, 1914 – 1991*. New York: Vintage Books, 1994.

Hofmann, Paul. *The Spell of the Vienna Woods: Inspiration and Influence from Beethoven to Kafka*. New York: Henry Holt and Company, 1994.

Holmes, Judith. *Olympiad 1936: Blaze of Glory for Hitler's Reich*. New York: Ballantine Books, Inc., 1971.

Jackson, Maggie. Distracted: *The Erosion of Attention and the Coming Dark Age*. Amherst, NY: Prometheus Books, 2008.

Jacobsen, Annie. *Area 51: An Uncensored History of America's Top Secret Military Base*. New York: Little Brown and Company, 2011.

Jevtic, Borijove. *The Murder of Archduke Franz Ferdinand at Sarajevo, 28 June 1914*. E-bookbrowse.com, 2010.

Johnson, Paul. Art: *A New History*. New York: Harper Collins, 2003.

Johnston, William M. *The Austrian Mind: An Intellectual and Social History, 1848 – 1938*. Berkeley, Los Angeles & London: University of California Press, 1972.

Judt, Tony. *Ill Fares the Land*. New York: The Penguin Press, 2010.

Kann, Robert A. *A History of the Habsburg Empire, 1526 – 1918*. Berkeley: University of California Press, 1974.

Kanner, Melvin. *The Jewish Body*. New York: Schoken Books, 2009.

Keegan, John. *The First World War*. New York: Alfred A. Knopf, 1999.

Kennedy, Paul. *Engineers of Victory: The Problem Solvers Who Turned the Tide in the Second World War*. New York: Random House, 2013.

Kershaw, Ian. *The End: The Defiance and Destruction of Hitler's Germany, 1944 – 1945*. New York: The Penguin (USA) Group, Inc., 2011.

Kranzler, David. *Japanese, Nazis & Jews: The Jewish Refugee Community of Shanghai, 1938-1945*. New York: Yeshiva University Press, 1976.

Kurlansky, Mark. *A Chosen Few: The Resurrection of European Jewry*. New York: Ballantine Books, 1995.

Lafore, Laurence. *The Long Fuse*. Philadelphia: J.B. Lippincott Company, 1965, 1971.

Large, David Clay. *Between Two Fires: Europe's Path in the 1930s*. New York & London: W.W. Norton & Company, 1990.

Laqueur, Walter, Ed., and Judith Tybor Baumel, Assoc. Ed. *The Holocaust Encyclopedia.* New Haven and London: Yale University Press, 2001.

Leighton, Isabel, Editor. *The Aspirin Age: 1919 – 1941.* New York: Simon and Schuster, 1949.

Levin, Ira. *The Boys from Brazil.* New York: Random House, 1976.

Levin, Nora. *The Holocaust.* New York: Schocken Books, 1973.

Levy, Primo. *Survival in Auschwitz.* Translated by Giulio Einaudi. New York: Touchstone, an imprint of Simon & Schuster, 1958.

Lewis, Jon E., Ed. *The Permanent Book of the 20th Century: Eye-Witness Accounts of the Moments That Shaped Our Century.* New York: Carroll & Graf Publishers, Inc., 1994

Lustig, Arnost. *The House of Returned Echoes.* Translated from the Czech by Josef Lustig. Evanston, IL: Northwestern University Press, 2001.

MacDonogh, Giles. *1938: Hitler's Gamble.* New York: Basic Books, 2009.

Mann, Thomas. *The Magic Mountain.* New York: Alfred A. Knopf, Inc., 1927.

Marek, George R. *The Eagles Die: Franz Joseph, Elizabeth, and Their Austria.* New York: Harper & Row, Publishers, 1974.

Morgan, Janet. *Edwina Mountbatten: A Life of Her Own.* London: Harper Collins Publishers, 1991.

Morse, Arthur D. *While Six Million Died: A Chronicle of American Apathy.* Oxford: Hart Publishing Co., 1968.

Morton, Frederic. *Thunder at Twilight: Vienna 1913/1914.* Cambridge, MA: Da Capo Press, 1989, 2001.

Mosley, Leonard. *On Borrowed Time: How World War II Began.* New York: Random House, 1969.

Musil, Robert. *The Man Without Qualities.* New York: Alfred A. Knopf, Inc., 1995.

_____. *Selected Writings.* Burton Pike, Ed. New York: The Continuum International Publishing Group, 2004.

Nagorski, Andrew. *Hitlerland: The American Eyewitnesses to the Nazi Rise to Power*. New York: Simon & Schuster, 2012.

Newman, Karl J. *European Democracy Between the Wars*. Notre Dame, Indiana: University of Notre Dame Press, 1970.

Nilus, Sergius, Ed. *The Protocols of the Learned Elders of Zion*. Translated by Victor E. Marsden. Tsarkoye Selo, Russia, 1905.

Noakes, Jeremy, and Geoffrey Pridham. *Documents on Nazism 1919-1945*. New York: Viking Press, 1974.

O'Connor, Anne-Marie. *The Lady in Gold*. New York: Alfred A. Knopf, 2013.

O'Kelly, Helen Watanabe, Ed. *The Cambridge History of German Literature*. Cambridge, New York, Melbourne, Madrid, Cape Town, Singapore, Sao Paolo: Cambridge University Press, 1997.

Ortner, Helmut. Translated by Ross Benjamin. *The Lone Assassin: The Epic True Story of the Man Who Almost Killed Hitler*. New York: Skyhorse Publishing, 1993, 2012.

Ostrer, Harry. *Legacy: A Genetic History of the Jewish People*. Oxford, UK: Oxford University Press, 2012.

Padfield, Peter. *Himmler*. New York: MJF Books, 1990.

Page, Bruce, David Leitch and Phillip Knightley. *The Philby Conspiracy*. Garden City, NY: Doubleday & Company, Inc., 1968.

Paldiel, Mordecai. *Saving the Jews*. Schreiber Publishing: Rockville, MD, 2000.

Peters, Joan. *From Time Immemorial: The Origins of the Arab-Jewish Conflict over Palestine*. New York: Harper & Row Publishers, Inc., 1984.

Pick, Robert. *Empress Maria Theresa*. New York: Harper & Row, 1966.

Read, Anthony. *The Devil's Disciples: Hitler's Inner Circle*. New York: W.W. Norton & Company, 2003.

Rees, Laurence. *Auschwitz*. New York: Public Affairs, 2005.

Remarque, Erich Maria. *All Quiet on the Western Front.* New York: Little Brown & Company, 1929, 1930.

Remnick, David. *The Last Days of the Soviet Empire.* New York: Random House, 1993.

Renshaw, Patrick. *The Wobblies: The Story of Syndicalism in the United States.* Garden City, NY: Doubleday & Company, Inc., 1967.

Roberts, J.M. *Europe 1880 – 1945.* New York: Holt, Rinehart and Winston, Inc., 1967.

Roth, Joseph. *The Radetzky March.* London: Granta Books, 2003.

Rottenberg, Dan. *Finding Our Fathers: A Guidebook to Jewish Genealogy.* New York: Random House, 1977.

Ryan, Frank, M.D. *The Forgotten Plague: How the Battle Against Tuberculosis was Won – and Lost.* Boston: Little Brown & Company, 1993.

Salisbury, Harrison E. *Black Night, White Snow.* Garden City, NY: Doubleday & Company, Inc., 1978.

Schnitzler, Arthur. *Night Games and Other Stories and Novellas.* Chicago: Ivan R. Dee, Inc., 2002.

Shirer, William. *The Rise and Fall of the Third Reich.* New York: Simon and Schuster, 1960.

Smith, Dennis Mack. *Mussolini.* New York: Vintage Books, 1982.

Smith, Duncan J.D. *Only in Vienna: A Guide to Unique Locations, Hidden Corners and Unusual Objects.* Vienna: Christian Brandstätter Verlag, 2005.

Stafford, David. *Endgame, 1945: The Missing Final Chapter of World War II.* New York: Little, Brown and Company, 2007.

Stepanov, Philip. *The Protocols of the Learned Elders of Zion.* Translated by Victor Marsden. Moscow: Serge Nilus, 1901.

Stephenson, Michael. *The Last Full Measure: How Soldiers Die in Battle.* New York: Crown Publishers, 2012.

Strobin, Deborah and Ilie Wacs with S.J. Hodges. *An Uncommon Journey: From Vienna to Shanghai to America. A Brother and Sister Escape to Freedom During World War II*. Fort Lee, New Jersey: Barricade Books Inc., 2011.

Tallis, Frank. *A Death in Vienna*. London: Century, 2005.

_____. *Vienna Blood*. New York: Random House, Inc., 2007.

_____. *Vienna Secrets*. New York: Random House, Inc., 2009.

_____. *Vienna Twilight*. New York: Random House, Inc., 2011.

Taylor, A.J.P. *The Origins of the Second World War*. New York: Simon & Schuster, 1961.

Terrance, Mark. *Concentration Camps: A Traveler's Guide to World War II Sites*. London: Universal Publishers, 1999.

Timayenis, Telemachus Thomas. *The Original Mr. Jacobs: A Startling Exposé*. New York: The Minerva Publishing Co., 1888.

Toland, John. *Adolf Hitler*. New York: Doubleday, 1976.

_____. *Hitler: The Pictorial Documentary of His Life*. Garden City, NY: Doubleday & Company, Inc., 1976, 1978.

Tuchman, Barbara W.. *The Proud Tower*. New York: Bantam Books, 1966.

Wangerman, Ernst. *The Austrian Achievement 1700 – 1800*. London: Thames and Hudson Ltd., 1973.

Waugh, Alexander. *The House of Wittgenstein*. Doubleday: New York & London, 2008.

Weinberg, Gerhard L. *A World At Arms: A Global History of World War II*. Cambridge: Cambridge University Press, 1994.

Weintraub, Stanley. *The Last Great Victory: The end of World War II, July/August 1945*. New York: Truman Talley Boosk/Plume, 1995.

Weiss, David W. *Reluctant Return: A Survivor's Journey to an Austrian Town.* Bloomington & Indianapolis: Indiana University Press, 1999.

Wiesenthal, Simon. *Every Day Remembrance Day: A Chronicle of Jewish Martyrdom.* New York: Henry Holt & Co., 1987.

Wistrich, Robert S. *A Lethal Obsession: Anti-Semitism from Antiquity to the Global Jihad.* New York: Random House, 2010.

Wolff, Robert Lee. *The Balkans in Our Time.* New York: W.W. Norton & Company, Inc., 1956, 1967.

Wyman, David S. *The Abandonment of the Jews: America and the Holocaust, 1941 – 1945.* New York: Pantheon Books, 1984.

Yergin, Daniel. *The Prize: The Epic Quest for Oil, Money & Power.* New York: Simon & Schuster, 1991.

Zeigler, Philip. *Mountbatten.* New York: Harper & Row, Publishers, 1985.

Zweig, Stefan. *The World of Yesterday.* Lincoln, NE: University of Nebraska Press, 1964.

Encyclopedias

Deffontaines, Pierre, Ed. *Larousse Encyclopedia of World Geography.* Adapted from Geographie Universelle Larousse. New York: Odyssey Press, 1964,1965.

Laqueur, Walter. *The Holocaust Encyclopedia.* New Haven: Yale University Press, 2001.

Atlases

Gilbert, Martin. *The Routledge Atlas of the Holocaust, Third Edition.* London: Routledge, 2002.

National Georgraphic Atlas of the World, 8th Ed. Washington, DC: National Geographic, 2005.

Articles

600 Years of Medicine in Vienna: A History of the Vienna School of Medicine. Alfred Vogl. Vol. 43 *Bulletin of the New York Academy of Medicine,* pp. 282-299 (1967)

The Chemistry of Auschwitz (Version 1.8). Richard J. Green. *www.holocaust-history.org,* 1998.

Tracking the Reaper. Cathy Shufro. *Yale Alumni Magazine,* July-August 2007, pp. 32 – 39.

Plays

Hochhuth, Rolf. *The Deputy: A Christian Tragedy.* Translated by Richard and Clara Winston. New York: Grove Press, 1964.

Weiss, Peter. *The Investigation.* Translated by Jon Swan and Ula Grosbard. New York: H. Wolff, 1966.

About the Author

Richard L. Hermann is the author of 11 books, including the award-winning *Managing Your Legal Career* and most recently, *Encounters: Ten Appointments with History*. He is an attorney, a former law professor and the founder and president of Federal Reports, Inc. (sold to Thomson Reuters in 2007). He writes a weekly op-ed column and a legal blog (legalcareerview.com). Hermann is a graduate of Yale University, the New School University, Cornell Law School and the U.S. Army Judge Advocate General's School. He also served with the U.S. Army Atomic Demolition Munitions Team in Germany. He lives with his wife, Anne, in Arlington, Virginia and Canandaigua, New York.

www.ingramcontent.com/pod-product-compliance
Lightning Source LLC
Chambersburg PA
CBHW070521010526
44118CB00012B/1046